RUTH PADEL

The Poem and the Journey

And Sixty Poems to Read Along the Way

VINTAGE BOOKS

London

Published by Vintage 2008

2 4 6 8 10 9 7 5 3 1

Copyright © Ruth Padel 2007

Ruth Padel has asserted her right under the Copyright, Designs
and Patents Act 1988 to be identified as the author of this work

First published in Great Britain in 2007 by Chatto & Windus

Vintage
Random House, 20 Vauxhall Bridge Road,
London SW1V 2SA

www.vintage-books.co.uk

Addresses for companies within The Random House Group Limited
can be found at: www.randomhouse.co.uk/offices.htm

The Random House Group Limited Reg. No. 954009

A CIP catalogue record for this book
is available from the British Library

ISBN 9780099492948

The Random House Group Limited makes every effort to ensure that
the papers used in its books are made from trees that have been
legally sourced from well-managed and credibly certified forests. Our
paper procurement policy can be found at:
www.randomhouse.co.uk/paper.htm

Mixed Sources
Product group from well-managed
forests and other controlled sources
www.fsc.org Cert no. TT-COC-2139
© 1996 Forest Stewardship Council
FSC

Printed in the UK by CPI Bookmarque, Croydon, CR0 4TD

THE POEM AND THE JOURNEY

Ruth Padel's poetry is widely praised for 'dazzling linguistic mastery' and far-ranging focus. Her non-fiction, including *Tigers in Red Weather* (about her journeys through the jungles of Asia), is also highly acclaimed. As Chair of the UK Poetry Society (2004–6) she presided over radical change.

All I know is what the words know.

Samuel Beckett, *Molloy*

'Would travel.' I daresay. Who wouldn't?

Agatha Christie, *A Murder Is Announced*

Each word is a step on the road. Each line has its own journey.

Patsy Rodenburg, *Speaking Shakespeare*

Contents

Acknowledgements

Warm thanks for criticism and comment to Myles Burnyeat, Elaine Feinstein, Pedro Ferreira, Fiona Sampson and members of Kindlings; to Henry Fajemirokun, for robust argument that pushed me to define things; Raficq Abdulla for introducing me to Attar and for guidance about the *haj*; Garry Kenard for mountaineering references; to Myles Burnyeat for help with *theoria*; and to Gwen for 'Two Lighthouses', Keats's sonnet about sonnets, and her criticism, encouragement and support.

Many thanks to the Francis Head Bequest for a grant administered by the Society of Authors which enabled me to finish the book.

Thanks also to people who invited me to give talks which forced me to formulate ideas. To Martin Golding, for inviting me to talk at Peterhouse. To the Poetry Association of Scotland, for inviting me to give the 2005 Hugh MacDiarmid Lecture at the Edinburgh Poetry Library, and to Michael Schmidt for publishing the result of that in *PN Review* (vol. 31, no. 5, May 2005). To Magdalene College Cambridge for inviting me to give the keynote lecture at a conference, 'Metre and Versification – the State of Play', as part of its 2006 Year in Literature Festival, and to Fiona Sampson for publishing some of it in *Poetry Review* (vol. 96, no. 2, Summer 2006).

Finally to Rebecca Carter, who works much too hard but (as all her lucky authors know) to fantastic effect, in deep gratitude for her friendship as well as her sensitive, generous and insightful editing.

Note

Apart from the numbered poems, discussed in Part Two, and the epigraphs (which I couldn't keep out because, as I say in Part One, poems do become a guide – a guide to thought, a hand along the road) all poetry quotations are in italics while those in prose are in quotation marks.

Preface

Poetry's effects are inward and personal. It is still what it has always been, a necessary art, enriching what goes on privately inside us through our lives. It fortifies our inwardness. And so it is the ideal thing to hang on to, in our very externally driven world of image and screen, surface and soundbite. Yet it is not much valued publicly today.

Some people say it is fading. This is a very old complaint, which poetry has always got on fine by ignoring. Sir Philip Sidney's remarkable work *An Apology for Poetrie* was published in 1595. (A second different publisher printed it as *The Defence of Poesie*.) Sidney called this work 'A pittifull defence of poore Poetrie, which from almost the highest estimation of learning is falne to be the laughing stocke of children'.

That was four hundred years ago, before Shakespeare wrote *Twelfth Night*, *Hamlet* or *King Lear*. Milton's parents had not even met.

Many of the people who currently say 'poor poetry' is fallen, or at any rate is dwindling, work in parts of the media which are so quick-paced, so fame-and-news focused, that they have no time to know the good poems being written, in all their wonderful variety; nor to see how poetry is loved and read by people at grass-roots level all over the country.

You cannot, unfortunately for publishers, use book sales to measure how much people value poetry. It is a living art. It depends on intimate relationships between each reader and the words of each poem. The reader may not feel the need to own the book those words appear in. Poems address universal issues and communicate important things, but the way they work is, in a way, the opposite of any media.

'Media', like mediation, involves being 'between'. Between us and the news, us and the world. But poetry comes out of a private self and, when it matters to someone, goes straight into another self. No other medium can or should get in between.

Hundreds of thousands of people love poetry today. They go to a growing number of poetry festivals throughout Britain. They read, write and argue about poetry passionately. But of all the arts it has least money given to it, and the least public attention. There are three major poetry prizes in Britain but chain booksellers do not highlight or stock copies of the shortlists as they do with fiction prizes.

Partly as a result of this lack of attention, many people have lost confidence in approaching poems. They feel disfranchised from their own poetry; poetry written in their time, for them. They sense there is something there they may need but do not know how to go about getting it.

This is a waste, not only of the brilliant poetry around today but also of the minds and hearts for whom poems have always been written – and still are.

This book is a quiet bid to redress that. It is about reading poems, about journeying through them and with them; about valuing their place in your own life.

Ruth Padel
London, September 2006

Part One

Journeys

Reading is complicity in the creative process.

Marina Tsvetaeva

We learn what poetry is – if we ever learn – from reading it.

T. S. Eliot

1   *The Journey of a Poem and the Journey of Reading It*

There is no one secret to reading a poem, but the nearest I know is to think of it as a journey. Where are the thought, the sound and the feeling coming from, and where do they land up? 'Each word is a step on the road,' the National Theatre's voice coach Patsy Rodenburg tells student actors learning to speak Shakespeare. To give words to an audience, she says, you have to feel the 'journey of thought' in them, the shape they make. 'Try walking', she tells the actor, 'the journey of the poem.'[1]

In life, too, poems and journeys go together. Both move. Both take a bit of time and effort. Both let you reflect on other things as you go. Both can upset and surprise you. There may be boring moments; or moments that seem boring at the time though afterwards you realise they were crucial. Both give you new windows on the world, take you out of yourself but let you more deeply into yourself at the same time. They get you to new places.

So what is the journey of reading a poem?

There are as many ways of travelling as there are travellers. Virginia Woolf has a vivid image of reading a poem in her novel *To the Lighthouse*. Mrs Ramsay is sitting opposite her husband, absorbed in a poetry anthology. They have not had an easy day. He is a philosopher and wonders if she understands what she's reading. Probably not: he likes to believe she is 'not clever, not book-learned at all'. We see him watch her read, then hear what reading feels like to her: swooshing up through a flower jungle ('anthology', from Greek *anthos*, 'flower', literally means 'collection of flowers'). She is

> climbing backwards, upwards, shoving her way up under petals that curved over so that she only knew, this is white, this is red . . . Swinging herself, zigzagging this way and that, from one line to another as from one branch to another, from one red and white flower to another . . . climbing up branches this way and that, laying hands on one flower and then another.

She settles on a Shakespeare sonnet.

> *Nor praise the deep vermilion in the rose*, she read, and so reading she was ascending, she felt, to the summit. How satisfying! How restful! All the odds and ends of the day stuck to this magnet; her mind felt

3

swept, felt clean. And then there it was, suddenly entire shaped in her hands, beautiful and reasonable, clear and complete, the essence sucked out of life and held rounded here – the sonnet.[2]

Afterwards, as husband and wife talk, her mind is still 'going up and down, up and down with the poetry'.

Who decides what understanding is? Is a philosopher the only judge? What matters more in reading a poem, heart or head, instinct or analysis? Is there only one kind of understanding?

Mrs Ramsay is lucky. With the confidence of her class (upper middle, highly cultured) and her time (1920s), she can walk into a poem, feel welcomed and enriched by it, and rest in its beauty without worrying what it means. That is luxury travel. If you are used to poems, you can read without worrying about meaning, as a toddler used to dogs will pat a bouncy labrador unafraid. But some children shrink from the friendliest spaniel, not realising that all it wants is contact, and some people shrink from poems because they are not used to them, and don't realise that what poems want is connection.

Connection is part of what a poem is for. It needs to matter to you personally, instinctually, sensually, before there's any question of meaning. I once heard John Burnside say, 'When I read a poem that turns me on, it isn't accessible at once. There's a mystery to it. What draws you in is the music.'

'What's the music?' someone asked.

'How the words hang together and grab you, how they speak to you even when you don't yet know what they are saying.'

When you are 'grabbed' like that, and the poem suddenly matters, it becomes yours to enjoy just as Mrs Ramsay enjoys the sonnet. No worries about understanding: she goes with the music.

Getting grabbed, making a relationship to a poem instinctively, is as involuntary as falling in love. It is the primal act on which poetry depends, the relationship all poems hope to make with readers as they go out into the world. One poem, mattering suddenly to one reader. 'The right reader of a good poem', said Robert Frost, 'can tell the moment it strikes him that he has taken a mortal wound. That he will never get over it.' 'Insight comes as a lightning-bolt,' said the philosopher Walter Benjamin. 'The text is the thunder-peal rolling long behind.'[3]

Falling in love may begin as a bolt from the blue but if love lasts you start to explore the reasons for attraction. The same is true of a poem. Having been grabbed, you start to ask why. Enter analysis and interpretation.

Coleridge divided readers into four types. He said the best reader was a 'Moghul diamond', someone who 'profits by what they read and enables others to profit by it too'. After that come the 'Sand-glasses' who remember nothing of what they read and just go through a book to get through the time. Thirdly, the 'Strain-bags' remember 'merely the dregs of what they read'. Worst of all are 'Sponges', who 'absorb all they read and return it nearly in the same state only a little dirtier'.[4]

There is no reason why we cannot all be Moghul diamonds. We all grow as readers, all the time. You can step into a poem as on to an escalator and simply be carried along, like Mrs Ramsay, but you can also enjoy working out what it's up to. If it's a good poem, the more you put into working it out, the more the process of reading gives you. And because you've developed your reading muscles, the more you get from other poems too. Working it out is part of the pleasure the poem wants to give.

T. S. Eliot says there are different stages of becoming a good reader. You begin intuitively, enjoying some poems, binning others. After a while you start organising your experience of reading. You find you're reading each poem in the light of others and under-standing them all more precisely, even ones you've read already. You see more in them and enjoy more.[5]

Every Greek schoolchild today learns 'Ithaca', the poem by the early-twentieth-century Greek poet Cavafy which uses Homer's *Odyssey* as a blueprint for our journey through life, and gives unexpectedly wise advice about our attitude to that journey.

Odysseus (whom the Romans called Ulysses) has spent ten years away at war. He keeps trying to get back home to his small rocky island, Ithaca, but is constantly blocked. Cavafy's poem says, in words which could be about reading a poem as well as the journey of life, that you shouldn't be in a hurry to reach your destination. Part of the point of having a goal is to enjoy adventures on the way to it:

> *Ithaca gave you your lovely journey.*
> *Without it, you would never have set out.*

In reading a poem one goal is, let's say, understanding. But you should enjoy getting there, and everything you hear, feel or think as you go. Every reading of a poem, every reader's journey, is different. How we enjoy poems, said W. H. Auden, is related to how we enjoy everything else. 'It is our pleasure, not someone else's.'[6] We all approach every poem with our own baggage.

Keats, like all great poets, was a passionate reader. He never knew Greek: he did not have an élite education like Tennyson. He had heard how wonderful Homer was and when he read him (in the Elizabethan translation by George Chapman) he was overwhelmed and wrote the poem that made his name, 'On First Looking into Chapman's Homer'. In it he describes reading Homer for the first time as discovering a new world. *Much have I travell'd in the realms of gold*, he says (meaning he has read a lot of other poetry) but now, like Cortez on a thrilling journey to discover South America, he is awestruck to see, from a *peak*, this new landscape glittering beneath him.[7]

If we are lucky, we develop through our lives as readers just as we do in other ways. In the gym, everyone starts with specific talents of balance, strength and instinct. You practise skills, develop muscles, learn from experience, stretch your capacity to do new things. It is the same with reading poems. We start with our instincts and sense of what-we-respond-to. This will be the basis of our individual taste. But our taste will develop. T. S. Eliot said no one was born with infallible discrimination. 'Genuine' taste, he said, 'is founded on genuine feeling'. Your taste in poetry is related to all your other loves. 'It affects them, is affected by them, and will be limited as oneself is limited.'

Developing your taste in poetry is part of the overall development of you – your personality, your character. Wordsworth said that 'accurate' taste in poetry was an 'acquired talent' which developed from experience of 'the best models'. 'Inexperienced' readers had to judge for themselves but he warned them not to judge too quickly. If you haven't given much time to poetry, instinctive judgement may let you down, he says, and you'll miss things. Be patient, be open. Listen.[8]

As in living, so in reading. We learn by doing it. Developing our taste in poetry, or food, clothes, even people, is part of how we come to be more ourselves.

2 The Two-Thousand-Year-Old Complaint

People sometimes tell me they find modern poems difficult. They also say the age we live in is radically different from a golden past when everyone understood all poems. But some poets have always been accused of obscurity. We know this because the Athenian comic dramatist Aristophanes made jokes about it in the late fifth century BC.

Aristophanes knew what he was talking about. He was a brilliant poet himself (*The Muses were looking for a shrine*, says a poem by the philosopher Plato, *and found it in the soul of Aristophanes*), and his funny, wildly imaginative comedies include highly technical literary jokes. At ancient Athens, comedies were staged after the audience had sat through many tragedies, so of course the comic poets made jokes about tragedy. Aristophanes' comedy *The Birds* pokes fun at tragedy's complex choral odes.

His audience knew the ins and outs of choral odes intimately: choral song was one of the great art forms of ancient Greece. (Aristophanes too wrote intricately beautiful examples.) They were highly wrought poems with elaborate metaphors, in a different dialect of Greek and more complex rhythms than the verse dialogue of a play. Aristophanes rudely suggests that people found them boring. *Look at our wings*, sings his bird chorus to the audience. If you had wings, you could get away from those awful tragic odes:

> *Just imagine having wings at the theatre!*
> *You'd never need to stay for the tragic chorus*
> *But fly off when it got boring and come back*
> *After lunch for the comedy.*[9]

Another of his comedies, *The Frogs*, contains the West's first sustained bit of literary criticism. This time, long lyrics are not called boring but obscure.

This play, set just after the popular, real-life tragic poet Euripides has died, shows Dionysus, god of tragedy, going down to Hades to fetch Euripides back. But Dionysus winds up judging an underworld duel between Euripides and an older tragic poet: Aeschylus, famous for complex words and ambiguous imagery. The winner will be led back to life by Dionysus.[10]

The poets debate their art. Aristophanes makes Euripides say that the tragedy he inherited (from Aeschylus) was bloated with words:

I had to diet tragedy! I distilled all that verbiage, the legacy of Aeschylus. Aeschylus threw into his lyrics *enormous wild-bull words with bristling crests and shaggy eyebrows, incomprehensible to the audience. Not a single word was clear.*

Aeschylus *is* difficult, even today. Wonderful, but ambiguous. (I once had a pupil whose father's ghost appeared to him on the London Underground and forbade him to read Aeschylus.) There are choral passages whose meaning scholars and translators still argue about. Apparently they foxed contemporary listeners too. Dionysus says he liked the shaggy ambiguities himself but yes, he did have sleepless nights trying to work out what exactly they meant.

I never used haphazard words, says Euripides. *And I always plunged straight into a play./My opening speeches explained the situation. I was democratic.*

Another argument you hear today. Easy to understand means popular, popular means democratic; therefore better.

The Chorus defends Aeschylus in terms that also find echoes in modern comments about poetry. *Aren't you afraid today's audiences are ignorant/and don't know how to understand any more?*

This duel goes on for pages. Aeschylus takes Euripides's prologues, which Euripides boasts are so nice, clear and democratic, and shows how unoriginal they are: they all open with exactly the same syntactical structure. The whole thing is brilliant: very funny, highly literary but also clearly very popular. Aristophanes is dishing it out on both sides, laughing at tricks of the trade used by both his colleagues.

Scholars have argued for centuries about what Aristophanes really believed, but in the end he makes Dionysus pronounce Aeschylus the winner. Maybe he did think Euripides had dumbed Athens down and corrupted public taste.

Since then, many great poets and poems have been labelled obscure. Tennyson, for instance, always felt wounded and misunderstood by reviews. When (in 1832, aged twenty-three) he published his first proper collection, some critics called it 'unwholesome' and 'metrically faulty'. He felt so mauled he said he would 'never be dragged before the public again'. He didn't publish for ten years and even after he became Poet Laureate (1850) the criticism didn't stop. Critics called 'Maud, or the Madness', title poem of his 1855 collection, which he thought one of the best things he'd written, 'obscurity taken for profundity'.

'Maud' is a long poem narrated by a mad speaker who kills the brother of the girl he is obsessed with. Tennyson thought he'd made it obvious that the speaker is mad. The poem begins, he expostulated to a friend, 'with a false comparison: *blood-red heath*'. But 'there is no such thing in nature. He sees the heather tinged like blood because his mind has been disordered. All along, he was intended to have a vein of insanity.' The now-famous words *Come into the garden, Maud* were intended 'to have a taint of madness'.

But his readers identified the poet with the speaker, objected to praise of the Crimean War and accused Tennyson of warmongering. And what happened to Maud, people asked? (The poem did not spell out that she died.) Today, unreliable narrators are two a penny. But no one wanted them in 1855, especially not in poems.[11] The basic complaint was one you can hear today about poems in general (and something like the complaint which Aristophanes' Euripides hurls at Aeschylus): I don't like this poem because it's not instantly clear.

But every art has to move forward. Tennyson was a genius and an innovator. His poems may seem easy, now, but he was not interested in the easy. (He was not always proud of his popular Laureate poems.) He certainly did not seem easy to contemporary readers. He was moving the goalposts. And when goalposts get moved, audiences often find the new obscure. With something genuinely new, we may have to take its authenticity on trust. The writer and critic George Steiner distinguishes between inventing and creating. You can understand at once, he argues, something that is merely invented, but what is created 'opens new ground'.[12]

In the early twentieth century, sixty years after critics attacked 'Maud' for obscurity, the 'new ground' opened was Modernism.

The contemporary poets whose work appears in this book were and are writing out of the whole tradition. They have live, deep connections with poetry going back to Chaucer. But they are also standing on the shoulders of Modernism and some continue to be seen as Modernist, or 'late Modernist'.[13]

There are divisions within today's poetry community around all this. Some Modernists would call other poets in this book 'mainstream' and this name would be derogatory. They would call poets published by commercial presses 'commercial'. But all today's genuine poems, whether Modernist or mainstream, go back to Eliot and Pound, who spearheaded Modernism in Britain and provoked an important battle between what was popular and what was authentically original.

This battle has points of similarity with Aristophanes' poets' duel but is still going on in Britain today. One thing at stake in it is the most vital thing of all, fresh language. Another is poetry's relation to its audience.

Popular poetry draws, says the poet Eavan Boland, on the 'old joys of memory, sentiment and song'. These are important; but you can overdo them. By 1909, genuine poets felt poetry had become cosy and empty (Eliot afterwards called it 'stagnant') and simply gave the public the versifying it wanted. Which, said Pound, was 'sonority . . . like a goose'.[14] The popular poets were those whose minds (says the critic C. K. Stead) 'ran at the level of public expectation'. The audience was breathing over the poets' shoulders, 'demanding flattery rather than truth.'[15]

After the First World War, Eliot and Pound recharged English poetry. Flinging away banal outworn ideas of what was 'poetic', they chucked out archaic inversions of natural word order, empty effects ('above all,' said Pound, reviewing Eliot in 1917, 'no rhetoric') and padding – words only put in for metre and rhyme. They brought into poetry the language that lives in our mouths, words you hear around you.[16]

At the same time Robert Frost was working out his own theories in America. In 1913 he wrote to a friend that the music of his poems came from 'what I call the sound of sense'. He meant the rise and fall of pitch, patterns of stress in how people actually talked. The sound of sense was 'the abstract vitality of our speech'. Poets need an 'ear and an appetite for these sounds of sense'. They must 'learn to get cadences by skilfully breaking the sounds of sense, with all their irregularity, across the regular beat of the metre'. Today's good poets are heirs to these ideas. Fifty years after Frost, Robert Lowell said what he was after in his own collection *Life Studies* was 'poems pliant as conversation'.[17]

Modernism let all this happen. It shattered conventions which said that only specific language and subjects were 'poetic'. But it also shot into poetry many of the things Picasso introduced to painting: collage, mixed textures, refraction, fragmentation. As in painting and music, Modernism reached out to alien or ancient cultures that seemed repellently barbaric to conventional eyes. T. S. Eliot's poem *The Waste Land* drew on the Arthurian Grail legend, relating it to modern life. He put erudite notes at the back, which many people resented. Pound also used ancient Chinese, Latin and Provençal poetry, and a wild range of modern arcana (including high finance). Both reeled into their poems quotations from other languages. They were mixing material from everywhere, ancient and modern, familiar and alien, demanding a whole reseeing and rehearing, challenging facile dependence on conventional tools.

To some readers, this was offensively obscure. Reactions were similar to the art world's reactions against Cubism, which demolished the idea of a readable narrative picture. The *Morning Post* called Pound and Eliot 'literary bolsheviks'. One reviewer of Eliot's 'The Love Song of J. Alfred Prufrock' (1916) called the poet a rebellious boy out to shock and puzzle 'at all costs'. In 'trying to describe modern life', this 'boy' had forgotten that what matters in poetry is beauty: 'However much you may have observed the world around you it is impossible to translate your observation into poetry without the spirit of beauty controlling the vision.'

He wagged a patronising finger. Pound and Eliot, he said, were 'drunken helots'. Another reviewer in 1923 said he 'gave up' *The Waste Land*. 'A grunt would have served as well.' What a pity that 'a man who can write as well as Mr Eliot does in this poem should be so bored with existence that he doesn't mind what comes next or who understands it'.[18]

Criticism of Modernism still continues.[19] Modernism battled on behalf of everyday speech but today, ironically, it seems to some people élitist, since Eliot and Pound draw on special knowledge (about the Grail legend, for instance, or foreign poetry). And since the First World War (even more so after the Second World War when education diversified) some areas of knowledge have increasingly come, in Britain, to seem the preserve of an academic few.

Modernism lost poetry a lot of its popular audience. It made people uncertain about trusting their instinctive judgement. Eavan Boland says Modernism asked its readers 'to give up a vast, sun-splashed hinterland where troubadours had sung'.[20] 'Modernism spoilt everything for us,' said James Fenton (ex-Professor of Poetry at Oxford) in the *Guardian* in 2005. 'It slammed the door on the past, took the glass of art out of our hands and smashed it.' Fenton was talking about painting but his words sum up what some readers feel today about Eliot, Pound and all their heirs, Modernist or mainstream: that these obscure words are nothing to do with them and if they read a poem they want instant satisfaction. Why put up with obscurity? Why should any poem be 'difficult'?

Normally, the relationship between poem and reader rests on an unspoken agreement.[21] The reader has to trust there will be something to understand and agrees to work at it a bit if necessary. The poem promises that you can understand if you try, there is meaning to be found. George Steiner calls this a 'contract of intelligibility'. He suggests that there are four main types of difficulty in this relationship.[22]

The first type come from limitations in me, the reader. A poem mentions something I don't know about. Pound's *Cantos*, for instance, allude to financial dealings between steel and armaments industries and use obsolete words from Shakespeare. I have to look things up. Difficulties like this, says Steiner, are external. They are 'burrs on the fabric of the text'. You have to 'do your homework'. Then they are gone.

The second type of difficulty is also in the reader. I may find a poem emotionally inaccessible and recoil against something in its tone or subject. It does not fit my sense of poetry. I just can't sympathise with it. Steiner is mostly talking, here, about poems from the past. His answer is, first, more homework. Learn the poem's social context, the ideas of the day. When I know more about where the poem is coming from, maybe I can open up to it more generously.

But maybe I can't. An open mind – keeping personal taste at bay as long as possible – is one of the most important things you need to read well. But you can't keep it at bay for ever. There are good poems you really won't like. You can't leave your taste at the door, like muddy boots. I may do my best to see the poem from its own perspective but still not be able to feel and like it. I am still me. V. S. Naipaul once asked an old lady in a tropical garden about a flower's scent. He knew the smell from his childhood but had never known its name. 'We call it jasmine,' she said. Jasmine. Of course he knew it, but to him it was only 'a word in a book' and had nothing to do with that smell, that flower. 'The word and flower had been separate in my mind for too long. They did not come together.'[23] You can learn a meaning but cannot force yourself to feel what someone else feels about a word; or a poem.

Steiner's last two types of difficulty, however, lie in the poems themselves. His third covers poems whose style, language and thought are difficult to work out, at least at first.

T. S. Eliot says a poem 'exists somewhere between the writer and the reader'. If a responsible poet deliberately adopts an off-putting style or subject, which is likely to 'restrict' his or her number of readers, 'this is a special situation, demanding explanation.'[24]

What sort of explanation for 'restricting readers' might we find today? The reason may simply be personal: a poet shielding other people (lovers, children, parents) and his or her private life. Or there may be political reasons. In a repressive regime, poets wrap their meaning in obscurity, which protects poet and readers from arrest, torture, exile, death. Or they use 'allegory', which originally means 'speaking otherwise'. When I was doing poetry workshops in Burma in 2002, Aung San Suu Kyi told me the Burmese censors constantly suspect allegory in poems. 'They black out phrases like "a flower falls to earth",' she said, 'in case it means a student killed by the police.'

Cassandra, the novel by the East German writer Christa Wolf, is ostensibly about an ancient prophetess but is really a coded comment on the surveillance-driven world of Communist East Germany. Her heroine Cassandra describes a 'language war' happening at Troy before the Greeks attacked, while the city mentally prepared for a real war it knew it would lose. Ordinary words changed their meaning. 'We were not allowed to call it "war",' says Cassandra. And so her prophecies of disaster were, like political poetry, obscure. 'We have no name for what spoke out of me.'[25]

But there have also, always, been poets of real power working from this kind of impulse who were not personally or politically motivated. Poets like Aeschylus, or the seventeenth-century metaphysical poets who wanted, Steiner suggests, to slow down the way readers understood a poem. Their difficulties deepen the way I make contact with the poem. They wake up meanings and energies in words; meanings I would not otherwise notice. And so they provoke me into seeing and hearing newly. Metaphysical poems, like Modernist poems, yield up what they are saying gradually, almost as if you are working them out in another language. This is how Eliot too must have come across to new readers. When Housman hit out against the Thirties vogue for the metaphysical poets he was implicitly attacking Modernism.

Explanations of this type of 'difficult' style lie in the poet's particular feelings about language. There have always been poets who meant to be difficult because they wanted to shake language up. To speak 'otherwise' in a newly creative way, recharge words by shock tactics from within the language, scotch the shopworn words, banality and rhetoric used by everyone else. They wanted to distort, melt or displace ordinary language, in order to revitalise the poem and poetry.

The American Modernist John Ashbery (see Poem 29) developed his 'difficult' voice while living in Paris in the Fifties. He had published one collection in an earlier style. Now he felt something was lacking and was searching for another 'tone of voice'. He began copying scraps out of popular magazines, collaging them into poems, experimenting. Some of the results, he said later, were 'so fragmentary as to defeat most readers'. He did not think of publishing them, then: he saw them as 'stages on the way to something else'. Like T. S. Eliot earlier, he was bringing into his poetry the outside world, its new languages, obsessions, messages. Post-war America was an uneasy and confusing thing to haul into poetry, very complex under all the apparent simplifications; and the simplifications themselves were unacknowledgedly violent. Through addressing these, Ashbery could express the fragmentation he experienced, though his base material was that same world's arch-communicator and arch-simplifier, the popular magazine. Though people call his work difficult, he himself respects a 'bond between communication and language'. He feels that in poetry 'something is transferred from somebody to somebody else'.[26]

But Steiner's fourth type of difficulty breaks the 'contract of intelligibility' between poet and reader. Steiner calls it a 'move towards darkness'. He thinks it peculiarly modern.

What is involved here is linguistic violence which may come out of the poet's violent sense of betrayal. In a recent collection, Geoffrey Hill (see Poem 13 below) expressed a passionate sense that today's culture has betrayed the English language and its riches. He did it through 120 poems numbered for the days of Sodom.[27] Hill is steeped in the history of the English language; these poems use the language of the Internet, of advertisement, to expose the empti-ness of today's public speech. They emanate a sense of language betrayed. This is language fighting against its own corruption.

But the betrayal may go the other way: the poet feels betrayed by language. Steiner's great example of the fourth difficulty is Paul Celan, who was born in Romania in 1920 but spoke German at home. German was the language in which he first read and wrote poetry. In 1942 his parents died in the camps: German was his

14

medium, his language of poetry, but also the language of the holocaust that had killed his parents and millions like them.

What do you do if you can never trust your language again and the holocaust is what you have to 'say'? 'There's nothing in the world for which a poet will give up writing,' Celan said. 'Not even when he is a Jew and the language of his poems is German.' So he developed a German of his own, forging strange metaphorical compounds to create a dense, extraordinary language. He was rebelling against the language from within. At some moments, says Steiner, 'we are not meant to understand at all'. Interpretation is intrusion. Celan felt violated by people swarming round his poems trying to interpret them.[28]

So there are genuine (what Steiner calls 'honest') reasons for writing impenetrably. The later poems of J. H. Prynne (see Poem 37) seem to many readers to refuse to communicate; to intend not to be understood. Prynne clearly believes passionately in language, but his poems suggest that words are never enough. It is as if the language the poet loves can never communicate everything and he wants, one critic says, to 'keep open the wound of not being able to bring the fragments together'.[29] To me, his poems emanate a love (of language) which is steeped in despair, as if language is our only hope of relationship but will always let us down.

There is a paradox about truly impenetrable poems. Why try and communicate the uncommunicable? Why put the poem out there if it is impossible to understand? Who for?

Steiner believes this paradox goes back to the German philosopher Heidegger, who said 'The Language itself speaks' (*Die Sprache sprecht*). The poet does not decide to be unintelligible: it is the language that decides. Language is in charge, not the poet. Some poets will love this idea. 'In a poet's involvement in language there is an element of helplessness,' writes Geoffrey Hill. You are 'at the mercy of accidents, the prey of one's own presumptuous energy'. John Donne, he says, felt that in writing you are, in some sense, passive in relation to language: language is mysterious, you are helpless before it.[30]

Other poets will hate the idea that language speaks through you and you can do nothing about it. They will feel it is a cop-out: poems need to communicate to the reader-neighbour in your head. If you tear up the contract of intelligibility and surround your words with electric fencing or barbed wire, is it really a poem you are writing?

But sculptors make art out of barbed wire itself. And even with this fourth difficulty, what seems 'difficult' to one generation may not always seem difficult to the next. Blake and John Clare seemed difficult and alien at first to readers. So did Shelley, who said he wrote for an 'ideal' audience. Early audiences could not cope with Beethoven's late quartets. He was accused of 'abrupt modulations, anything but beautiful'. Now they are the summit of the quartet repertoire. Today *The Waste Land* does not seem out to shock: but is the beginning of a new age.

All good poets are wary of the language they struggle with. They cannot let it ride them. Even a poet who feels swept away by language has to take responsibility. You are accountable. You must shape your own syntax, grammar, vocabulary, the fabric of your text, even though language, like an avalanche or glacier, has hard dangerous things in it, and these sweep down at you from its flow through history. You struggle between feeling something is coming at you from outside and the need to be active, to shape and pare.

But there is another way of thinking about 'difficulty'. Prynne himself suggested it – in 1961, when he was working (like Ashbery a decade before) towards his own late Modernist voice. Maybe, he said, difficulty is not 'in' either the reader or poem. The poem is not difficult, I am not difficult: difficulty is what I encounter when I enter the poem. Just as I meet difficulty when I enter and try to understand that larger thing which poetry addresses and reflects: life, the world. Both poem and world have a quality Prynne calls 'resistance'.[31] The words of a poem, and the way they co-operate with each other, resist me. As I try to understand, this resistance shows itself as difficulty.

Coleridge called the words of a poem 'hooked atoms'. Each one meshes and cross-meshes with all the other words. They branch across, twine round each other. They 'resist', in Prynne's word, because they are a closely woven net of relationships, a springy web of meaning, image and sound, just as a film is the complex result of a complex process: not just shooting scenes but cutting and splicing.

The tool we need to tackle a poem or the world, says Prynne, is imagination. The push has to come from us, the readers, as well as the writer. Our imagination has to meet the writer's halfway, push us through the hooking atoms into the words, enjoying their springiness, how they resist as well as how they communicate. That tension, between the words' resisting and communicating, plus our response to it, makes the spring of the poem. It also lets us enjoy it. Keats said we all hate poetry 'that has a palpable design upon us – and if we do not agree seems to put its hand in its breeches' pocket'.[32]

Telling us what to feel (as packaged toys pre-empt imagination by creating the fantasy rather than letting children fantasise for themselves) is for the tabloids; not for poems. The poet and author Mark Haddon (who wrote *The Curious Incident of the Dog in the Night-time*) says if you can pinpoint what you admire in a poem, 'you're looking for something shallow. I like poetry when I don't quite understand why I like it. Poetry isn't just a question of wrapping something up and giving it to someone else to unwrap. It doesn't work like that.'[33]

Wallace Stevens said a poem should 'resist the intelligence, almost successfully'. Good poems are not over-explicit. They want you to discover what you feel for yourself. Nor do they simplify. Geoffrey Hill says that intelligence doesn't like simplification and the Palestinian poet Mourid Barghouti identifies why. Simplifying, he says, 'takes the accessible and the easy from the human condition and so blurs that condition instead of defining it'. If you simplify, you 'misrepresent what is human at the moment of pretending to celebrate it'. We and our lives are much more difficult than most poems. Difficult to ourselves, difficult to each other. On any ordinary day, says Hill, 'we meet far more real difficulty than in most poems'.[34]

Why shouldn't poetry be a bit chewy? Unobvious at first, like clever TV ads, comedy or films? We, and our world, are complicated. Shouldn't our poetry be up to that? As Hill says, why should poems be 'less than we are'?

4   What's Wrong with Cliché? And Why Shouldn't 'Most Popular' Mean 'Best'?

But if a poem is going to resist you, how do you know it is worth your while?

Being difficult to understand does not make a poem good. But nor does being easy. Very often, what is easy to understand is simply flattering the reader, confirming what he or she thinks.

If people resent poetry they think is 'difficult', they become vulnerable to what is instantly easy, what makes them feel safe. T. S.

Eliot points out that liking a bad poem, and thinking it is good, 'is very different from enjoying a good poem'. Someone who has not read many poems 'is always liable to be taken in by fakes' and may 'prefer the sham' because fakes and kitsch are 'more easy to assimilate than the genuine article'.[35]

But what's wrong with poems flattering me, confirming my beliefs, consoling my sorrows? What's wrong, for example, with Patience Strong? Her real name was Winifred Emma May and she was born in 1907. She started publishing verse in the *Daily Mirror* in 1935. For forty years she published weekly verses in *Woman's Own*. Their selling point, according to one obituary, was 'simple homely words that touched the heart'. She admitted, said the *Telegraph*, that 'there might not be much literary merit' in her verse. But what do we think about its appeal?

A poem by U. A. Fanthorpe tackles this problem. It begins very loftily:

> *Everyone knows her name. Trite calendars*
> *Of rose-nooked cottages or winding ways*
> *Display her sentiments in homespun verse*
> *Disguised as prose.*

It patronises and despises.

> *No doubt such rubbish sells.*
> *She must be feathering her inglenook.*
> *Genuine poets seldom coin the stuff . . .*
> *Their message is oblique . . . nor does it pay.*[36]

Then it reveals where it is set – a hospital – and introduces an epileptic patient. The very word 'patient' gestures to both parts of Strong's pen-name: to people who need strength and patience. This man couldn't join the Ambulance Brigade because of his epilepsy. *But I'd have liked*, he says, *to help*. He needs help himself, that's why he's there. He opens a little book wrapped tenderly in cellophane. Here is Patience Strong. (*Cosy musing in the usual vein*, jibes Fanthorpe's poem.) He points to a page. *See*, he says. *This is what keeps me going.*

Fanthorpe has swiped the ground from under her poem's and her reader's patronising feet. At your peril do you despise what people hang on to in pain. No one who has not been in a position in which they have to depend on Patience Strong has the right to knock her. If you want to call her verse sham you have to have good arguments.

So what are they?

The Times once set up, like Aristophanes, a poets' duel. 'What happens when two top protagonists square up?' the headline asked. Simon Armitage (see Poem 53) and a businessman (a poetry patron who writes verse) were asked to evaluate each other's poems.

The businessman said he used sestinas, villanelles, metre and rhyme. 'All true poets', he said, 'once wrote like that! Readers enjoy traditional forms. Modernist poetry' (he meant contemporary) 'has lost its way.' He said he had 'this dreadful idea poetry should be entertaining' and so he 'played to the gallery'. Here is some of his work.

> *When I was but a boy*
> *The dark was full of dread,*
> *I trembled then as monsters filed*
> *To loom beside my bed.*
>
> *Ogres on the stairs*
> *Must blush at what they built*
> *Or wet themselves on angry chairs*
> *By mirrors filled with guilt.*

He looked at Armitage's poems and said he liked how one 'bounced along' but 'didn't feel moved by it'. He didn't understand another 'after five read-throughs!' He thought a third had two great punch-lines, but 'I was dying to get hold of it and turn it into a villanelle! I will, if Simon turns one of mine into free verse. (Now there's a challenge!) I was itching to structure it. A great many more people might enjoy it.'[37]

This is the market approach to poetry, the Instant Appeal school. The more people like a poem, the better it is. Popularity proves value. You can start attacking this with an analogy from cookery. If you add monosodium glutamate to a dish, the flavours come out artificially sharply. Because the taste is more obvious, more people enjoy it. (Even in Bangladesh, which has a wonderful cuisine, a restaurateur told me people order him to add monosodium glutamate.) But it has little appeal for people whose palates are developed, who care about cooking or (since MSG is a carcinogen) health. The fact that more people like dishes with monosodium glutamate does not make these dishes 'better'. And anyone starving would like them too, just as the man who needed help treasured Patience Strong.

For poetry, the monosodium glutamate is cliché. Clichés appeal instantly and make people feel safe. They help society hang together. Queuing in snow for a bus, you might swap clichés with other freezing passengers. Worn words about silver linings, darkness before dawn and pots that never boil can make you feel you are in this together. The words mean little; what is sustaining is the temporary contact.

There are two basic reasons why clichés have no place in a poem. First, a cliché is not your own thought. (If you think you have minted it you're kidding yourself.) A cliché is not thought but a substitute for thought. It avoids genuine communication.

Second, the words are not fresh and original either. They are second-hand. It is different if the poem is twisting or playing with a cliché. That can wake words up and release new energies in them. Pound, reviewing Eliot in 1917, talked of Eliot's 'constant aliveness; his mingling of a very subtle observation with the unexpectedness of a backhanded cliché'. But the words of an unquestioned, unplayed-with cliché mean practically nothing, and words that mean nothing have no place in a poem.

In a poem every word has got to play an interesting, lively part, just as every brick takes stress in an arch and every husky pulls its weight in a team. Poems are no place for lazy words. Words that do not mean are cellulite. They get in the way, deaden and disfigure the poem: wasted space, wasted time, inert meaning, pointless sound.

Simon Armitage agreed the businessman's verses 'worked for a lot of people' but said they showed a 'wilful, almost bloody-minded, ignorance of contemporary writing' and didn't 'bear critical scrutiny'. His most fundamental criticism was that they did not use the speech patterns of today. '*When I was but a boy* sounds like someone remembering how poetry used to be. When Housman used phrases like that, his diction had a relationship to the way people talked then. This doesn't. It sounds like poetry from a bygone age.'

Language is constantly changing. Its lifeblood is how people use it outside poetry, all round us: what you hear (as Robert Frost urged) in the street. Frozen poeticisms from the past, words which nobody would actually say, have no business in today's poems except in comedy or historical pastiche. As Eliot says in 'Little

Gidding', *Last year's words belong to last year's language.* Would you take a contemporary film seriously if it used phrases like 'but a boy' in its dialogue? It is imitation coinage; language from the heritage shop.

Armitage also pointed out that archaic language like this leads 'to old-fashioned sentiments'. Cliché does not only avoid genuine communication and thought, but also genuine feeling. Poems are made of words but the feeling has to be fresh and real too. 'Human maturity', says Mourid Barghouti, 'is the foundation for artistic maturity. The heart of it is detailed knowledge of life. What is important is the insight, the sensitivity with which we receive experience. These are features no work of art can do without, whatever the lived experience.'[38] Even under conditions of extreme suffering like living under occupation, poets must feel freshly what they are writing about, not fall back on the cliché of it. Only if you feel it new can you say it new, and only if you say it new will it be a genuine poem. In every tradition, poets who want to speak genuinely must 'escape from used language, to language that speaks itself for the first time'.[39]

In 1798, Wordsworth prefaced his groundbreaking *Lyrical Ballads* with a warning that, though those who understood poetic tradition would realise what he was up to, some readers might feel he had 'descended' by imitating real-life rural speech. He thought they might 'struggle with feelings of strangeness and awkwardness' and 'look round for what they thought of as poetry'. He said that poetry had a 'very disputed meaning' and asked them not to let 'pre-established codes' stop them enjoying the poems. If, he said, you find the language 'too low, too familiar, not dignified enough for what you think poetry should be', ask yourself if you see real human feelings and characters in it as well. Do human incidents come across in a 'natural' way?[40]

Four years later, in 1802, he added a Preface to explain why his poems were different from what readers expected of poetry. He said he wanted them to address ordinary life imaginatively: in an 'unusual way' and 'language really used by men'. He felt his 'low and rustic' characters showed 'primary laws' of human nature and passion, communicating feeling more forcibly, simply and accurately, and in 'a plainer, more emphatic language', than conventional poetry of the day. He utterly rejected current 'poetic' diction, with its empty personifying of abstracts and tired figures of speech: old devices by which bad poets tried artificially to 'raise poetry above

21

prose'. The words might be beautiful but had been degraded by being 'foolishly repeated by bad Poets'. He wanted for poetry, in fact, what good poets want today: language people speak, not out-of-date poeticisms.

Some Instant Appeal adherents today, however, write angrily to the Poetry Society saying they themselves 'stand for tradition', because poems they write 'keep traditional forms'. They accuse the Poetry Society (which runs a competition sometimes won by poems with no end-rhymes) of 'betraying tradition'. But what really betrays tradition is fake-archaic language and empty adherence to past formulas. Both betray poetry's tradition of renewing language.

Tradition is an explosive thing to stand for. It means Aeschylus, the metaphysical poets, Clare, Shelley and Tennyson's 'Maud'; Coleridge with his exacting standards of good reading, Aristophanes with his astute laughs at writing. That's a long list of electric, demanding, searching sensibilities: of poets whose own work rejected instant appeal. *Traditio* means 'handing on'. But what poems hand on is not simply a question of external forms, and form does not depend only on rhyming the line-ends. Anyone who thinks 'structuring' means a rhyming pattern is taking tradition's old mac for the thing itself. Poets delight in pattern. They look back to and often steal from older poems. 'Foraging in the tradition', as Heaney puts it.[41] But they don't do this to copy. They do it to renew. Live tradition is the opposite of copying.

The paradox is that breaking from tradition is a way of developing it. Breaking away is itself traditional. Good new poetry traditionally keeps up a live conversation with two things at once: the real world now, and other poems, past poems. This is what Wordsworth was up to, and Pound and Eliot. And the real-life Euripides, who took tragedy further for new audiences. 'The music of today could not have been created, and therefore cannot exist, without the music of the past,' says the conductor Daniel Barenboim.[42]

Poetic tradition works like a relay torch race. You never know who's going to run with the fire. In different languages and generations, the flames leap between genre, voice, tone and ideas. Tradition is the miracle that happened when the Roman poets Catullus and Virgil engaged with Greek poets, the European Renaissance tangled with Greek and Latin poems, the nineteenth and twentieth centuries turned to the Elizabethans – and, again, to the Greeks.

Tennyson, for instance, played with the words, images and

emotional contexts of the Greek and Latin poems he grew up with. One of his lifelong experiments (and achievements) was the psychologising narrative poem he called an idyll. He began creating it from 1830 onwards, using and taking forward the Alexandrian idyll, a stylised genre invented in the third century BC. Through its artificially confected, mainly rural characters, the ultra urban Alexandrian idyll laughed at Realism in a highly sophisticated, literary way. Before Tennyson there was no idyll in English. When Browning's *Dramatic Idylls* came out in 1879, Tennyson murmured (you may think of him now as a bearded old monument but he was as easily hurt as any poet), 'I wish he had not taken my word "Idyll".'

If Tennyson had just copied the Alexandrian model, his poems would have died in their tracks. But all his life, from his twenties to his eighties, he wanted to 'make something modern'.[43] So did Ezra Pound, when he turned to Provençal troubadours and ancient Chinese poetry. Even Modernism's revolution was traditional. Eliot recognised that Tennyson had been, in his day, a trailblazer, and drew on 'Maud' for *The Waste Land*.

Tradition too is a journey. It is still going on, but along many different routes. That's why the poems in this book are so various. Poetry today has room for many voices, popular and oblique, mainstream and avant garde; but only if they are fresh and real. Not stale and not a fake.

Plato, in his *Republic*, imagines human beings as prisoners in a cave. All they can see is shadows on a screen, which they take for reality. Then someone gets out of the cave, sees real things, comes back and says reality is out there; what they have seen all their lives is only imitation. (They laugh at him. Eventually, because he wants them to see the 'real' for themselves, they destroy him.)[44] Fanthorpe's point is important. Of course everyone is free to value any poem. The man in her poem really does treasure Patience Strong and I have no right to laugh at that. But I do wish I could offer him the real thing. Some people prefer instant coffee to real: I believe valuing the real thing, in poetry if not coffee, matters. I think it is better.

Some cars are better than others, some poems are better than others. The differences lie in how they are made and what they are made of. You want good technology and design, makers who know what they are doing and no second-hand parts. Are you going to trust to the worn-out chassis of cliché, the recycled tyres of archaic poeticisms? Will they get you where you want? As with cars, the way to know poems are good is by understanding a bit about how they work and trying out different examples: experiencing and examining the best.

Modernist and avant garde, or mainstream and popular, real poems all have one vital thing in common. As you read more of them you increasingly find clichés a turn-off. You want fresh thought and feeling, interesting music, worked words, new insight. You want, in fact, the most traditional thing of all: subtlety.

Despite what the *Times* businessman may think, Armitage is a master of subtle structure and rhyme. Subtlety is what Instant Appeal is really against. But yesterday, tomorrow, 2000 years ago or today, subtlety is essential to good poetry. What is truly traditional in poems is not particular patterns but subtlety in patterning. And in the end, that subtlety depends on a poem's smallest particle.

5 'The Syllable, that Fine Creature', and One of Its Favourite Relationships: Rhyme

Ezra Pound called making a poem 'the dance of the intellect among the words'. But words are made of smaller units still, and the American poet Charles Olson said the real dance was 'among the syllables'. The syllable, he said was 'the minim and source of speech', the 'king and pin' of poetry. What poets should worry about, what makes the harmony, is 'the syllable, that fine creature'.[45]

The word 'syllable' comes from the Greek verb *sullambano* (from *sun*, 'with' and *lambano*, 'I grab hold'), which can mean a variety of things: 'collect', 'combine', 'lay hands on', but also 'say several things in one word, grasp a meaning, understand'. *Syllabe*, the noun, can mean something active ('mental grasp', 'realisation') or passive (a thing that is 'held together'). This is why Greek grammarians used it to mean 'several letters taken together in one sound'. A 'syllable'. For syllables in poems, we should honour the active as well as the passive sense of the verb. A syllable is 'held together' by letters, but it also makes active relationships with other syllables to form words. And in a poem it reaches out to and echoes syllables in other words to suggest connections and meanings.

That is what a poem depends on: these actively hooking atoms, the syllables whose relationships 'hold' a poem 'together'.

'Listening for the syllables is everything,' said Olson. 'Syllables rule and hold the line.'

You might compare this with music, whose expression comes from the relationships of individual notes. Daniel Barenboim says that musical expression 'comes from linkage – Italian *legato*, "bound". When we play five notes that are "bound", each is in relation to the preceding note and the note that comes after.'[46]

All good poems harmonise through syllables. Syllables make the words that contain them feel right together so they produce – well, Olson called it beauty. (Syllables let words 'juxtapose in beauty'.) But we might just as well say 'meaning'. Or 'music'. The syllables, by relating to each other, create all three. Their music is the meaning. The meaning is the music. That's the beauty.

Ancient Greek poetry did not count the number of syllables in a line, as in some poetic traditions (see Poem 4). It organised the line by its number of metrical units. These units came to be called 'feet'; an image we still use today.

There were strict rules for the number of long and short syllables in each 'foot'. (A spondee, for instance, was two long syllables, as in the word 'mainstream'; a dactyl was a long syllable followed by two shorts, as in 'follower'.) In some feet you could substitute some syllable patterns for others, but only in specific places in the line. This was complex enough, but these rules only applied to verse in which you repeated the same kind of line (as in, say, Shakespearean blank verse). Things were even more complex in those choral lyrics laughed at by Aristophanes.

Choral odes mainly worked in paired stanzas (though some lyrics, especially for solo voice, were stanza-free, almost like jazz cadenzas). There might be several pairs and each pair had a different rhythmic pattern. Greek grammarians called the first stanza of each pair of stanzas the *strophe*, 'turn', and the second the *antistrophe*, 'turn back'. The line lengths kept changing. But the miracle of this art was that in each pair of stanzas, whatever the line was like, every syllable of the *antistrophe* exactly mirrored, long or short, the corresponding one in the *strophe*. Philologists call this technique 'responsion', because in each line the syllables of the second stanza respond to those of the first. The chorus danced while they sang; the syllables mirrored their physical gestures and steps. The chorus, surrounded by a circular audience, sang the *strophe* while 'turned' (say) to the right of the dancing floor. Then, having 'turned back' to the left, they copied those gestures and steps the other way round for the *antistrophe*. Gesture for gesture, syllable for syllable, the symmetry was both physical and musical, and the poet organised it all: composed the music, trained the chorus, wrote the words. His relationship to those words and syllables was semantic and emotional but also physical and choreographic.

English is very different. We react not to the length of a syllable but to its stress. (Stressed syllables did not matter in ancient Greek. The accents on Greek words denoted tone.) In a line of English poetry we listen, consciously or unconsciously, for the number of stresses, or beats. But it is still the syllables that make words feel right together. We don't normally do anything as intricate as responsion, but syllables have to echo over the stanzas and lines so they can create relationships between the words they are in; relationships which colour and generate new meanings for the whole poem as you go.

The poet's job is to get syllables to belong to each other so ear and mind are satisfied; so that readers, even if they don't understand at once, can trust the words, feel they belong together musically and emotionally, and believe that meaning will flower from their relationships.

Syllables do this in many ways. By repeating rhythmic patterns, for instance. Or by harmonising vowel sounds. When you sing, you sing vowels: you cannot sing a consonant. Consonants break words up. You can pattern and play with them, use their relationships to create atmosphere, but it is vowels that make the music. One of the syllables' favourite ways of creating these all-important relationships is rhyme, and it is vowels that generate most types of rhyme.

Rhyme satisfies the ear (our own ear – ancient Greeks would have none of it). It satisfies our understanding because it is a way of getting words to greet each other. Poets are conscious of it all the time. Half-rhyme, consonant rhyme, vowel-rhyme; vowels echoing from inside one line and across to another and even across stanzas. And then, of course, there is end-rhyme – which, as you can see in this book, many of today's poets use; always in combination with other sorts of rhyme.

But some people (mainly ones who don't read much contemporary poetry) feel that end-rhyme is the only rhyme. End-rhyme is a perennial rallying cry for Instant Appeal supporters, whose other name is the It's Gotta Rhyme school. They take end-rhyme as the defining characteristic of 'tradition'. By his words 'using rhyme', the businessman in *The Times* meant 'putting rhymes in particular patterns at the ends of lines'. He thought pre-established regular rhyming pattern was poetry, was tradition.

But you have to consider (again) tradition's complexity. Half the greatest poetry in English is not end-rhymed (Milton, Wordsworth, Shakespeare, Tennyson). English argument about rhyme is itself an old and bitter tradition.

The great rhyming wars broke out in England 400 years ago. Blank verse began in English around 1540, following Italy's *versi sciolti da rima*, 'verses freed from rhyme'. By 1600, blank verse was blazing triumphantly out of the language and was becoming one of the great achievements of the Elizabethan age. In 1602 the poet and songwriter Thomas Campion (1567–1620) wrote a blistering attack on 'the unaptnesse of Rime in Poesie'. Bad poets, he says, 'rime a man to death'. The 'popularitie of Rime creates as many Poets as a hot summer flies'. Rhyme should be used 'sparingly, lest it should offend the eare with tedious affectation'.

The poet Samuel Daniel wrote furiously back, 'proving', he said, 'that Rhyme is the fittest harmonie of words that comportes with our Language'. By calling 'our measures grosse, vulgare, barbarous' Campion was a traitor to rhyme. If it be so, Daniel snarled sarcastically, 'we have lost much labour to no purpose'.[47]

Ben Jonson weighed in with a satirical rhyming poem, 'A Fit of Rime against Rime'. *As soon as lazy thou*, Jonson says to 'rime', *wert known / All good poetry hence was flown*. His poem accused rhyme of *Wresting words from their true calling, / Propping verse for fear of falling*. Rhyme, in fact, wrecked everything: *Jointing syllables, drowning letters, / Fastening vowels as with fetters*.

The nub of Campion's protest was laziness and banality, and that is still the problem today. It is fatally easy to rhyme badly and stalely. If you rhyme, it had better be fresh, better be good. Otherwise it doesn't just spoil your poem, it betrays rhyme itself.

Milton too was against rhyme. He said rhyme acted on poets as 'a constraint to express many things otherwise, and for the most part worse, than else they would have exprest them'. *Paradise Lost* does not end-rhyme. Nor do Shakespeare's plays, or much Tennyson and Wordsworth. The argument went on. Poets always have furiously divergent views about writing poems. (Look on the Internet: Campion and Daniel would have had a high old time in the chat rooms.) A poem is a very small thing: this is a tiny crucible of an art. You work very hard, on your own, to make something portable, compact but full of subtlety, which you feel condenses the

27

whole world in a little space. Then it is totally overlooked by that same world. Of course there are bitter arguments. Practitioners feel intensely, work very hard and know the world barely cares.

But the general dust of this debate did settle into a nervous equilibrium. It was agreed that rhyme was not essential to English-language poetry but not superfluous either. It was an important quarrel. T. S. Eliot saw it as 'part of the struggle between native and foreign elements' in English-language poetry. It was as a result of that controversy, he argued, that some of 'our greatest poetry was created'.[48]

Today, many poets end-rhyme in some poems (several in this book, for instance) but not in others. Good poets who consistently end-rhyme tend to be either very subtle or satirical (or both). Good end-rhymes do not work alone. They operate within a web of syllable relationships through the poem.

Instant Appeal and Gotta Rhyme fans feel that end-rhyme creates the form and that's that. But the structure of a poem does not depend on end-rhyme; and no end-rhymes does not mean no structure. Even in 'free' verse, the beat is not regular but (as in jazz) that doesn't mean there is no pattern or structure. 'All poetry has formal properties,' says the American poet Stephen Dunn. A good free-verse poem creates, he says, 'not only the shapes within the container but the container itself'. The sounds of the first lines set up, he says, 'a series of promises and expectations' (about sound, rhythm, syllable and sense) which govern the rest of the poem. 'The manner in which we keep our promises is one way form comes about.'[49]

Structure is created, above all, by the poem's movement. Movement of thought through syllables, and also musical movement through these syllables' relationships; which creates further relationships, emotional, imaginative and associative, between specific words.

You could say the syllables are molecules of movement, and that structure is the pattern in which they move.

6   Poetry Is Movement

'The song of a nomad', said the Russian poet Josef Brodsky, 'predates the scribbling of a settler.'[50] Not surprising, then, that one of the earliest metaphors associated with poetry should be Homer's *paths of song* which the Muses 'teach' or 'implant' in a poet.

Especially since the poets Homer describes are mainly wandering bards, settling at one court for a while and then (like bluesmen in the 1920s) moving on.[51]

Later Greek poets developed Homer's image. Pindar (who seems to have invented the idea of the Muses' 'chariot') was commissioned to write odes commemorating victories in fifth-century BC sports contests, often chariot races. His poems breathe a sense of the poem itself as a track. *Even early poets found the highway of song*, he says. *Friends*, he says teasingly, *I've been whirled about at the crossroads where the paths diverge, though I was treading the right path before.*[52]

The first recorded use of 'foot' for the unit of a poetic line comes from the end of that same century, in Aristophanes' poetic duel in *The Frogs*. Aeschylus, outraged at a line of Euripides, attacks the liberties Euripides took with tragic metre. *See this foot?* he asks. *And* – at which point commentators assume Aristophanes organised comic stage business involving boots – *this one?*[53]

So there it is, by 405 BC. The 'foot' entered all Western languages, reminding us that a poem moves (and its reader moves with it) one step after the other. Poetry is movement. And since a poem, whether in Greek or English, moves through its syllables, the American Black Mountain poet Charles Olson called the syllables' relationships 'kinetic'.[54]

'Stanza' means 'room' (maybe Brodsky's scribbling settlers thought that one up), but even in a stanzaic poem you move on through the house of the poem and its different 'rooms'. It is still a journey.

So we are back where we started, with the journey. But there are many types of journey and reasons for journeying. And few interesting journeys go straight, as a crow might fly. They wind about. *On a huge hill*, says Donne in *Satires* 3,

> *Cragged and steep, Truth stands, and he that will*
> *Reach her, about must, and about must go.*[55]

That *about and about* is crucial. *Versus* comes from Latin *verso*, 'I turn' or 'twist'. ('Turn about, often violently', says the Latin dictionary.) *Versus* originally meant a 'furrow' (from the 'turn' of the plough), then 'line' or 'row'; then 'line of verse'. A poem moves from one line to the next, turn and turn about. 'Verse' is a 'turning'. No wonder a voice coach urges actors to 'walk the journey' of a poem and 'turn' when they reach a new thought.[56] And this 'turning' idea crops up in many words for poetry's joints and parts – the *strophe* and *antistrophe* of Greek odes, the *volta* ('turn' of direction) in a sonnet.

The sonnet, that 'little song', came from Italy. In the thirteenth-century Sicilian court a *sonetto* was recited or sung to lute or mandolin, possibly inspired by the Provençal troubadours' *sonnette* (supposedly named after sheep bells echoing through Provençal hills), but also by Arabic poems and the great Islamic poets. The form took shape in that multicultural Sicilian court, and when it migrated to the Italian mainland, Petrarch (1304–74) put his brilliant stamp on it. The template was established as fourteen lines in a gently unequal proportion: an octave or octet (eight lines) and a sestet (six lines). The convention was that the octet built a lyric argument or picture and the sestet 'turned' the attention or tone to reflect on the octet's statement and vision. It opened the idea out, universalising it. Or made it personal, 'turning' it inward.

The 'Italian' sonnet (often called 'Petrarchan', after its most famous practitioner) had only four rhymes. The octave was *abba abba*, the sestet *cdc dcd*. In the early sixteenth century Thomas Wyatt brought the sonnet into English. He translated Petrarch's Italian and Ronsard's French sonnets, and Elizabethan poets after him developed an English form, often called the Shakespearean sonnet (after *its* most famous practitioner). They were adapting the pattern for a language which had fewer natural rhymes than Italian and evolved a blueprint of seven rhymes, *abab cdcd efe fgg*. (Spenser, twelve years older than Shakespeare, invented another variant: five interlinked rhymes, a middle way between the Italian and English forms: *abab bcbc cdc dee*.)[57]

But it has long been the case that not all sonnets rhyme. Even by Keats's day, poets were challenging the traditional patterns. His sonnet 'On the Sonnet' complains about predictable rhymes and wants to make something new. Keats shuffles the rhymes around:

> *If by dull rhymes our English must be chained*
> *And like Andromeda, the sonnet sweet*
> *Fettered, in spite of painèd loveliness;*
> *Let us find out, if we must be constrained,*
> *Sandals more interwoven and complete*
> *To fit the naked foot of poesy.*

He says poets must be *misers of sound and syllable*, must tear away *dead leaves* (meaning, among other things, words only there for a rhyme) *in the bay-wreath crown*. Eventually, the solution to the sixteenth-century rhyme wars came to apply to sonnets too: that rhyme is not essential, but not superfluous either.

Nor do all sonnets have fourteen lines.[58] Milton wrote sonnets with extra lines called 'tails' ('caudate' or 'tailed' sonnets). So did Gerard Manley Hopkins (who also wrote 'curtailed' sonnets, with fewer than fourteen lines). Meredith wrote sixteen-line sonnets. Yeats wrote a thirteen-line sonnet called 'The Fascination of What's Difficult'.

George Herbert's poem 'The Wreath' (1633) is a curtailed sonnet.

> *A wreathed garland of deservèd praise,*
> *Of praise deservèd, unto Thee I give,*
> *I give to Thee, who knowest all my ways,*
> *My crooked winding ways, wherein I live –*
> *Wherein I die, not live; for life is straight,*
> *Straight as a line, and ever tends to Thee,*
> *To Thee, who art more far above deceit,*
> *Than deceit seems above simplicity.*
> *Give me simplicity, that I may live,*
> *So live and like, that I may know Thy ways,*
> *Know them and practise them: then shall I give*
> *For this poor wreath, give Thee a crown of praise.*

The title describes the poem's own movement and shape. Herbert wreathes each line into the next line with a key word (*praise/praise*, *give/give*, etc.). The fifth line breaks that pattern. The thought 'turns', the poet corrects himself. No, he does not live in *crooked winding ways* (*crooked* because they are the path of a sinner, but also because they are the ways of art, of poetry, of this wreathing bending poem), but rather 'dies' in that crookedness. True life, leading to God, is a *straight* line, not *crooked*.

After that break in the pattern, in the fifth line, we go on with the wreathing linkage of line to line via a repeated word. In these four central lines, the sequence of end words seems almost blasphemous: the line runs from *God* to *deceit*. But the repeated word *simplicity* brings us back to faith, turning apparent blasphemy into *devoted praise* and ushering in the last four lines whose end words (*live*, *ways, give, praise*) are a mirror image of the first four. Via 'ring' composition (a technique in which the last line brings back a word, theme or image from the first), this *wreath* of a poem, with its windings, turns *simplicity* into a *crown of praise*.

In another of his poems, Herbert points out that plain truth is a contrast to the *winding* ways of art. *Is there in truth no beauty?* he asks. *Is all good structure in a winding stair?*[59]

'The Wreath' is itself an answer. The point of intricate design is not showing off but (as with the fan vaulting, stone tracery and tangled carvings of Gothic cathedrals) praising God. Pattern is movement and meaning.

Good pattern is also hard work. The effort that goes into it is tribute. Michael Donaghy called this poem 'no mere puzzle box but a labour of intense devotion'.[60] By the end, readers have undergone a little journey of faith through which they may understand better the place from which they started. Most good poems are adventures: journeys that do not follow a straight line or go where you expect. *Perhaps / The truth depends on a walk around a lake,* said Wallace Stevens.[61] There are deviations. And when you reach your goal, the journey has changed how you see that goal.

Poems by the French Symbolist poet Mallarmé (1842–98) are often taken as the supreme example of 'pure' poetry. He loved metaphorical obliquity and 'turnings', not forward linear momentum. He thought poetry had gone wrong (i.e. too straight) ever since Homer. Poetry's primal magic, he said, was circular, lyrical and mythic. Real poetry was pre-Homeric Orpheus descending into death via the spiralling staircase of his song.

The journey of good poems contains many such spirals; interlocking journeys of thoughts, feelings, associations, images. Also of particular sounds, consonants, vowels, rhythms and parts of speech: verbs, interrogatives, pronouns, adjectives. As the poem moves forward (which, *pace* Mallarmé, every poem also has to do), all these journeys interact like migrating birds flying across the moon, or dolphins moving together up a river.

One way of entering Poem 37 by J. H. Prynne, for instance, is to trace in it three interlinking journeys. The journey of the verbs; of what happens in the poem to physicality, to bodies; and also of what happens to and around the word *we*. Different journeys circle and jostle each other through a poem like clubbers on a dance floor – and that, in fact, is one way of seeing their interaction: as the other sort of movement to which turning and re-turning are vital, dance.

Euripides, training his chorus in the Athenian sun, must have felt the poem as a dance very physically. As I said, Pound called making a poem 'the intellect's dance among the words', and Charles Olson rephrased that as a dance among the syllables. Eliot's poem 'Little Gidding' says that a poem's words support each other in a dance. Each takes *its place to support the others*. A poem is *The complete consort dancing together*.

We are patterning animals – pattern-hungry, pattern-seeing. We believe (and hope) that pattern gives meaning. Once people had seen pattern in the stars, they could sail by them, plant grain by them, use them as models in geometry. In poems, the pattern does not have to depend on rhyme, be regular, or be a pattern another poem has used before. ('As for technological apparatus,' the American poet Frank O'Hara once said, 'that's just common sense: if you're going to buy a pair of pants you want them to be tight enough so everyone will want to go to bed with you. There's nothing metaphysical about it.') Your pattern must simply make words and sounds form relationships with each other through their tactile being and through their meanings.

Hence the bag of tricks we call technique. Alliteration, rhyming, metaphor. Cunning play with tone, register of voice, etymology, puns, latent meanings of words. Hence prosody (which means 'the tune added to the ode, the song') – the study of metre, rhyme, stanza, form. The spiralling dance and winding stair are poetry's road to truth. Not necessarily plain truth. *Poets tell many lies*, said Solon, the Athenian lawgiver-poet. *We know how to say many false things as if they were true*, the Muses sing to the Greek poet Hesiod. (*We also know*, they add, *how to say true things – when we want*.)[62] Picasso said art was 'a lie that makes us realise truth' and the artist must 'convince others of the truthfulness of his lies'. A poem's 'lies' *are* true, though, to what the poet sees, feels and imagines. Otherwise they are worth nothing. 'You have to be true to your own sensibility,' says Heaney. 'The faking of feelings is a sin against the imagination.'[63]

Since feeling and imagining are multiple, and often self-conflicting, the truths of a poem may contradict each other. 'There is never any such thing as one truth to be found in dramatic art,' says Harold Pinter; and the same goes for poetry. 'There are many.'[64] 'Do you have no contradictions?' asks the Czech author Vladimir Holan. 'Then you have no possibilities.'

That, perhaps, is what good poems offer in the end: possibilities of seeing new truths. *I dwell in Possibility*, says Emily Dickinson:

> *A fairer House than Prose –*
> *More numerous of Windows –*
> *Superior – for Doors –*

It is through pattern that a poem can open those doors. Experience is complex; the truths which pattern reveals or suggests are likely to be complex so the pattern must be, too. That's the paradox. Pattern gives meaning but is also artifice. To reveal the world newly, and also truly according to the poet's imagination and sense of the world, it shows the world other than it is.

That's why at the heart of poetry is a movement which presents things other than as they are: metaphor.

7 Making Strange: The Leap of Metaphor

> I hate to be tied down to say this means that, because the thought within the image is much more than any one interpretation.
>
> Tennyson

Greek roads used to be full of little three-wheeled vans with METAPHORS written, in Greek, on their front. I once asked the driver of one what his job was. 'Taking something', he said, 'from one place to another.' That is also the classic definition, Aristotle's definition, of metaphor.

Writing any poem is a process of discovery. An attempt to reach a truth, says Kathleen Jamie. Discovery and awakening, says Jorie Graham. 'I couldn't look myself in the eye', said Donaghy, 'unless I used verse as a means of discovery, rather than a method of persuading my audience of what I thought I already knew.'[65]

Poems discover best when, as a poem of Seamus Heaney's called 'Making Strange' puts it, they *go beyond what's reliable*. You must describe what is in front of you, says this poem. For example, a bush of *sweetbriar after rain*. But not only as it is. Describe it also as 'like' something else, something it is not, remote in time or space. Say, *the cornfield of Boas*, which Ruth in the Bible gleans as a stranger. Keats's 'Ode to a Nightingale' calls that same field *alien corn*. The cornfield was foreign to Ruth and she was foreign to it.[66] In Heaney's poem, this cornfield is alien to the poet's local plant, the *sweetbriar*. What connects them is comparison – that mysterious word 'like'; and imagination, the '*imago*-making' that reaches out and finds comparison. (You can't, said Wallace Stevens, get beyond the images.) The philosopher Heidegger said the true image 'lets the invisible be seen. And so imagines the invisible as something alien to it.'[67]

As a boy, Heaney used to hide in a hollow tree where he felt 'at the heart of a different life', and looked at the 'familiar yard' with different eyes, 'as if it were suddenly behind a pane of strangeness'. His poems run on that relationship between familiar and strange. Creativity, he says, combines 'the security of what is known' with 'the challenges and entrancements of what is beyond'.[68] That's metaphor. It 'makes' something 'strange', takes you beyond what's ordinary, to see with new eyes. Dr Johnson said it was made of two ideas; Lorca called it 'the equestrian leap that unites two worlds'. People tend to describe metaphor by metaphor – the metaphor of physical movement which joins two different things or two places, as if mapping the world anew.[69] Metaphor is the most extreme movement powering a poem's journey. Aristotle says metaphor 'carries a foreign word [*allotrios*, "alien", "strange"] across to a "home" [*oikeion*, which also means the "proper", "normal" way a word is used: its "original" sense]'.[70]

Various related concepts come from Latin equivalents of *metaphora*. The Latin for the Greek word *meta* is *trans*: 'over, across, beyond'. So 'translation' and 'transference' both originally mark the same 'carrying across' movement as *metaphora*. In psychoanalysis, patients 'transfer' feelings about their parents on to the therapist. In translation, meaning is carried over from one language to another.[71]

'Transport' (from *portare*, another Latin verb for 'carry') describes the same movement. It's what the little Greek vans do; but passion, love and music also cause 'transports of delight'. Metaphor and its related concepts are at the heart of communication between people. Whether mercantile, emotional or linguistic, something is 'carried' to a new place or person.

To create a metaphor is to take a word with a specific freight of associations in its 'home' use on a voyage to the unknown: into a 'foreign' context. Aristotle's examples come from a seafaring and agricultural economy. *The ship ploughed the sea* transfers a whole network of feelings about furrows and fertility from the earth to ocean. The 'foreign' word, *plough*, makes a difference: we feel differently about the sea once we hear 'ploughing' connected to it. Take a ship that *wings over the sea*, or sun *scattering its rays* to sow *god-created light*. In its 'home' use, *wings* belong to birds. Applied to a ship, this 'foreign' word colours the new context with associations of flight, vulnerability, life, emotion, intention. *Scatters* injects associations of sowers, seeds, fertilising, nourishment and growth into how we think about sunlight and the way it touches earth.[72]

It is an odd thing to do, to make an 'image' comparing home to foreign. But it is an enormous step forward in dealing with the world. In his novel *The Inheritors*, William Golding describes Neanderthal man faced with *homo sapiens*, his threatening supplanter, discovering how useful metaphor is in making sense of a new piece of the world.

> Lok discovered 'Like'. He had used likeness all his life without being aware of it. Fungi on a tree were ears . . . In a convulsion of understanding Lok found himself using likeness as a tool as surely as ever he had used a stone to hack at sticks or meat. Likeness could grasp the white-faced hunters with a hand, could put them into the world where they were thinkable and not a random and unrelated irruption.

We are driven, somehow, to understand 'here' in terms of 'elsewhere'; to, in Beckett's words, 'speak of things that don't exist, or only exist elsewhere, if you like, if you must, if you can call it existing. Unfortunately it is not a matter of elsewhere but of here.' Through metaphor we can go, says Beckett, 'where the voice belongs'. Through voice, through language, we summon strangeness to help us know the familiar and vice versa. Metaphor allows us to 'get out of here and go elsewhere, go where time passes and atoms assemble an instant, go where the voice belongs perhaps, where it sometimes says it must have belonged, to be able to speak of such figments'.[73]

But in saying something is 'like' something else, you are also saying it is not that thing. Metaphor separates as well as joining its two things, two worlds. The *cornfield of Boas* both is and is not the *sweetbriar after rain*. Metaphor, in fact, is what Prynne describes as *a view*:

> *a window*
> *on the real data, not a separate copy*
> *of that data.*[74]

George Eliot suggests it might be a pity that we depend so much on metaphor, 'seldom declare what a thing is, except by saying it is something else':[75] that we live, think and see ourselves through and as what we are not.

But poems love it. *From this the poem springs*, says Wallace Stevens,

> *that we live in a place*
> *That is not our own and, much more, not ourselves.*[76]

8 Metaphor We Live By: The Journey of Life

We are travelling animals. We love myths of wanderers. Don Quixote, the Flying Dutchman, Wandering Jew. We love them in music, from Schubert's *Wanderer Fantasy* and *Winterreise* ('Winter Journey'), to folk songs like 'Gypsy Rover' and pop songs claiming 'Wherever I hang my hat, that's my home'. We love them in sayings ('Have gun, will travel') and literature, like Kerouac's *On the Road* and endless travel books.

We enjoy seeing ourselves as nomads, as seekers hoping for new revelations round the corner. *We knew the islands were beautiful*, say the wistful voices of Odysseus' sailors in the thirties poem *Mythistorema* by the Greek poet Seferis:

> *somewhere here, near where we were searching:*
> *the slightest distance.*[77]

Tourism feeds all that. From the Grand Tour to Jane Austen's heroines marvelling at the Peak District, 'touring' has been popular since the eighteenth century. We long to see, learn, experience (if only vicariously) worlds and lives outside our own. *Pray that your way be long*, says Cavafy's 'Ithaca':

> *Pray to enter with delight, on many*
> *summer mornings, harbours you have never seen before.*

We use this travelling to describe our living, too. 'I love talking to the old,' says Socrates at the beginning of Plato's *Republic*. 'We can ask them, as we ask people who have travelled a road we too must take, what the path is like. Rough and difficult, or easy and smooth?' *In the long journey out of the self*, says the American poet Theodore Roethke,

> *There are many detours, washed-out interrupted raw places*
> *Where the shale slides dangerously*
> *And the back wheels hang almost over the edge*
> *At the sudden veering, the moment of turning.*
> *Better to hug close, wary of rubble and falling stones.*[78]

Most people find journeys change them. The Roman poet Horace, whose poems were characteristically grounded in his own land, said, *People who run across the sea only change their sky, not their mind.* (*Coelum non animum mutant qui trans mare currunt*). But it depends who's doing the running. Growing 'up' is moving 'on'; journeys are bound up with knowledge. Even a 'learning curve', a vertical arc on a graph, suggests a winding road – an adventure, a quest for knowledge, a journey into what you don't yet know.

The first person in the West to describe knowledge as a road was the poet-philosopher Parmenides (born about 515 BC) who wrote a long poem on the nature of Being. In his introduction (the *Proem*), he is riding in a chariot pulled by *wise mares* on the Way of Truth: *a road far from the paths of men*. These mares set him *on the resounding road to the gates of Night and Day*, then '*Maidens of the Sun*' steer him *straight on to the highway*. His poem is a journey into knowledge.

The Greek word *theoria* originally referred to physical travel. It derived from a verb to 'watch', *theorein* (whose related alternative was *theasthai*, from which we get 'theatre'). *Theoria* was the process of 'travelling to observe' a religious or athletic spectacle. Then you came back and described it to those who hadn't seen it. In the fourth century BC, Plato took over the noun *theoria* (with its associations of witnessing to what you have seen), and turned it into a journey of thought. He waved his Platonic wand – and a journey to learn about the world became *the* metaphor for travel in the mind, for the adventure into understanding: 'theorising'. Adventure, says Salman Rushdie, 'may have much to do with the pushing back of frontiers, but few topographical boundaries can rival the frontiers of the mind.'[79]

Aristotle used the same image. Wisdom, he said, is a long hard walk. We move forward to truth on a journey of arduous enquiry.[80] And this image also found its way to the heart of Christianity. 'I am the Way, the Truth, the Life,' says Jesus.

Via (Latin for way) and *viator* (wayfarer), along with *peregrinus* (wanderer) and *peregrinatio* (sacred wandering) are vital concepts in early Christian thought. *I am a stranger and a pilgrim, as all my fathers were*, sings the Psalmist. 'Dearly beloved, I beseech you as strangers and pilgrims' begins the First Epistle of St Peter. We are all 'pilgrims, strangers on the earth', Paul writes to the Hebrews. We must keep our eyes fixed on our heavenly goal. Pope Gregory said the 'just man' saw earthly comfort only as a traveller sees a bed at the inn: he rests in it bodily, but mentally he is already elsewhere.

The early Church Fathers, when they read Homer, interpreted Odysseus as the human soul yearning for God. Tied to the mast (so he can hear the Sirens but not be lured by them to death on the rocks), he is every Christian going forward in the ship of the Church: lashed to the Cross, aware of the world's alluring songs but not deflected by them from the right path.[81]

Tennyson's Odysseus, in his poem 'Ulysses' is *always roaming with a hungry heart*. James Joyce's is a Dublin Everyman. We are all Odysseus: *homo viator*, humanity en route to God, trying to reach a sense of our identity; stumbling, veering off-course, but learning new things. *The soul is a wanderer and fugitive ever, driven by the decrees and laws of gods*, said Plutarch, quoting the pre-Socratic philosopher Empedocles.[82] Many people today might respond to the idea that our whole lives are a journey into the unknown: that it is our fate never to reach our goal, to be always seeking. It resonates to Milton's line about Adam and Eve after the Fall: *The world was all before them*. Tennyson imagined Odysseus putting Ithaca back together then longing to set out again. *It is not too late to seek a newer world*:

> all experience is an arch wherethro'
> Gleams that untravell'd world, whose margin fades
> For ever and for ever when I move.[83]

Even old men should be explorers, says T. S. Eliot in 'East Coker'. *We must be still and still moving / Into another intensity.*

The image of life as a journey is important far beyond the Western religious tradition. You find it, as the Guide to the Museum of Pilgrimage at Santiago de Compostela explains, 'in all religions that have expanded beyond a single territory'. For Buddhists, life is a journey towards enlightenment, the Tao is the Way. To the Hindu holy man on the path to knowledge (see Poem 21) human life is pilgrimage: a simultaneously physical and spiritual journey.

That apparently small-scale adventure of thought and sound called a poem is particularly suited to reflect our own lives as a journey. That, I think, is why in many cultures the most vivid expressions of life as a journey are great poems.

9 Adventure, Quest, Pilgrimage and Homecoming; Treasure-Seeking, Asylum-Seeking, Exile

Not for nothing does Homer call poetry *the paths of song*. Most great ancient journeys are poems. Even before Homer's *Odyssey*, Virgil's *Aeneid* or Dante's *Inferno*, there is the ancient Sumerian epic *Gilgamesh*, the first long poem to be written down.

Gilgamesh travels with his friend Enkidu to the Cedar Forest. Enkidu dies and suddenly Gilgamesh becomes afraid of death. To find the secret of immortality, he journeys through wilderness, mountains and the waters of death to someone who explains about a plant that makes you immortal and tells Gilgamesh the story of the Flood. Gilgamesh finds the plant, loses it, returns to his kingdom and writes his story (plus the story of the Flood) on stone. This, the end of his journey, is described at the poem's beginning:

> *he saw everything and experienced all emotions*
> *from exaltation to despair, was granted a vision*
> *into the great mystery, the secret places,*
> *and the days before the Flood. He journeyed*
> *to the edge of the world and made his way back, exhausted*
> *but whole. He carved his trials on stone tablets.*[84]

Skip to the twelfth century and the mystic epic *Conference of the Birds*, by the Persian poet Farid Ud-Din Attar. That journey represents the soul's quest for the divine. The Hoopoe leads other birds on a journey through seven valleys to 'the king'. But Attar's readers are also reading their own psychological and spiritual story.

The birds' ordeal is their ordeal too. Those 'valleys' represent stages of spiritual experience such as love and understanding but also detachment, unity, bewilderment, deprivation, death. As in *The Wizard of Oz*, when they reach their goal, 'the king' is not what they expect. In the Buddhist underworld the soul has to look into a mirror and the mirror is judge of your past life. So in this Sufi vision, 'the king' turns out to be a mirror in which the pilgrim birds see their journey. They see all their struggles, including the shameful moments.

The *Conference of Birds* was reworked by the fourteenth-century poet Geoffrey Chaucer as *The Parliament of Fowles* and it was also Chaucer who wrote the first long journey poem in English. *The Canterbury Tales* is about pilgrims on the way to a shrine; but it is really about stories. Each character, and each tale, is a stage on the reader's journey. Instead of different islands and societies (like those encountered by Odysseus), the reader meets different stories. Pope Gregory warned the pilgrim against taking pleasure in digression and adventure along the way before you reach your goal:

Sometimes on his travels through life, the just man will seek out discomfort, and refuse to dwell in the pleasantness of transitory surroundings, in case delight in the journey delays his arrival. By attaching his heart to peregrination he might lose his reward when the heavenly *patria* comes in sight.[85]

But in a poem the *winding ways* (to quote George Herbert) are part of the pleasure. They make the adventure of both poem and journey.

Another great English journey (not a poem, this one) is Bunyan's *Pilgrim's Progress from This World to That Which is to Come* (1678). Again physical dangers represent spiritual dangers: the Hill of Difficulty, Valley of Humiliation, Valley of the Shadow of Death, Doubting Castle's dungeons, Giant Despair. The journey has got to be hazardous. Danger, effort and suffering are the point; they define the adventure and the adventurer. *She loved me for the dangers I had passed*, says Othello, explaining why Desdemona fell in love with him. It is not the glittering harbours we've been to that leave their mark on us but the hardship, the dangers. Bunyan's Mr Valiant-for-Faith carries 'marks and scars' proudly to the end. They are 'a witness that I have fought'.

Gilgamesh, Odysseus, Attar's birds and questing Arthurian

knights encounter dark trackless forest, stormy moors and raging seas; meet offended demons, wicked enchantresses, man-eating giants. *Don't be afraid*, says Cavafy's poem 'Ithaca', of man-eating giants. *You won't meet them unless you carry them with you in your soul*. But we do carry them in our soul. We are doubting fearful animals as well as danger-meeting ones, and the inner counterparts to external dangers are an important part of the journey: our disorientation, grief, moments of near-giving-up, all the mental, emotional and spiritual 'valleys' which Attar's birds go through. When Odysseus is so near Ithaca he sees shepherds tending their fires, his foolish crew open the bag of winds. They are blown away again and even Odysseus thinks of leaping *out of the boat and dying in the sea*.

Loss and grief are part of the journey too. Attar's poem is driven by tragedy and loss. Thousands of birds die on the way.[86] So do Odysseus's sailors, Aeneas's helmsman, Gilgamesh's friend Enkidu.

And the end?

It may be a homecoming. (Every voyage, said Hegel, is towards the source of our homecoming.)[87] The *Odyssey* belonged to a cycle of Greek epics called the *Nostoi*, 'Returns Home'. (The others only survive in fragments: after sacking Troy, all Greek heroes had a hard time getting back to Greece.) Odysseus would be outraged at Cavafy's prayer for a long journey. We first see him weeping, marooned on an island; he comes home disguised as a beggar, recognised only by a dying dog. His one goal is return to his right place and true identity.

The 'homecoming' may be understanding – either of God or of yourself. Don Quixote sees he was ridiculous: 'For there are no birds this year in last year's nests. I was mad, but I am sane now.' It may be the realisation that truth lies in you or your 'own back yard', as at the end of *The Wizard of Oz*. In Edward Bond's play *Narrow Road to the Deep North*, the poet Basho returns from pilgrimage having found the enlightenment he sought: 'I saw there was nothing to learn in the north. You get enlightenment where you are.' This is both right and wrong, says Rushdie. By journeying to a 'deep north', the traveller can 'gain knowledge that is not available elsewhere and then, by living to tell the tale, offer it to us'.[88]

But whatever the end is, it means you also have to leave the world of the journey, say goodbye to the adventure, the world travelled through. In *Pilgrim's Progress*, the summons to 'cross the river' comes for Mr Standfast in a message that his 'wheel is broken at the cistern'. For Mr Valiant-for-Faith, the message is a 'pitcher broken at the fountain'. He leaves his sword 'to him that shall succeed me in my pilgrimage', and goes down to the river saying, 'Death, where is thy sting?'[89]

There is another sort of journey, though, and another sort of home. Virgil's *Aeneid* is the epic of the refugee. This journey too begins with Troy. The hero has lost his Trojan identity and home. He has to forge a new one by founding Rome. The *Aeneid* often echoes the *Odyssey*, but Aeneas was on the losing side. He rescues his son and father from the sack of Troy but loses his wife. Like Odysseus, he has no choice. The journey is thrust upon him: gods say he must go to Italy. In Africa, blown off course, he explains, *Italiam semper fugientem sequor*, 'I am following Italy constantly fleeing before me.'

The fall of Troy is the West's first great metaphor for the destruction which lies behind exile and creates the refugee seeking a new home. It is the metaphor that ushers in a history of civilisation as not only the building of new cities but the loss of old ones; history of diasporas, multiple exiles from poverty, famine, occupation, war; and of holocaust survivors. Fragmented, unhoused identities from which new identities have painfully been built while seeking 'asylum', the 'unplunderable place'.

There are other reasons than exile and immigration for going to new worlds. Treasure, for instance. The Argonauts sailed off to steal the Golden Fleece. Their story was written up in the third century BC by Apollonius of Rhodes; their European equivalents were Raleigh and co., raiding Africa (see Poem 31), Asia, the Americas.

But as well as pillage there is pilgrimage, whose treasure is inward and sacred. Pilgrimage needs three things: a sacred place, a sacred journey and a sacred goal. In most faiths it has five stages. You leave ordinary life behind, make the journey, reach the place, visit the shrine, return. You can go to Mecca by train, plane or car: many people in Egypt paint their mode of transport on their houses, and the notion of the journey is vital in Islamic spirituality. In India, criss-crossed with routes of pilgrimage, the journey is a vital part of worship. The Museum of Pilgrimage at Santiago de Compostela explains that the pilgrim's goal is 'personal transformation' which happens gradually over the journey and is complete at the moment of arrival at the shrine.

All these story patterns – adventure, quest, homecoming, pilgrimage and exile – blend into each other. Together they colour how we think of life's 'journey'. In Christian thought pilgrimage collides with exile. Our journey begins with flight from the Garden of Eden and aims at the Celestial City. It is a painful path through an alien world forced upon us because we are sinners. The first words of *Paradise Lost* are *Of man's first disobedience*. The last are *solitarie way*. The twelve books between show how *disobedience* leads to *wandring steps* away from Eden. Exile became the Christian's spiritual quest to get back to God. There is a physical journey from a Garden to a City, but the way out is the way back; and both are God. The devout man is both a stranger to the world outside the Garden (a world God did not originally intend for him) and a pilgrim en route to God.

This is why Eliot, in 'Little Gidding', blends pilgrimage into a return which is a new way of seeing where we began:

> We shall not cease from exploration
> And the end of all our exploring
> Will be to arrive where we started
> And know the place for the first time.

10   The Path Within: Journey to the Underworld

My last journey pattern is one that marks most lives at some point: the journey into yourself.

Modern 'inner journeys' take many forms. Many novels by the early-twentieth-century writer Herman Hesse (who was always after 'the path within' – he underwent psychoanalysis with Josef Lang) are shaped by the hero's journey into finding his true self. *Siddhartha* (1922) blends psychoanalysis with the Eastern idea that everyone's path is mapped by karma. The hero grows up on one side of a forest river. He crosses it, experiences the world, crosses back and stays by the river. Retreat to the forest is into the 'unity of all things'; by the river he becomes truly himself.

Forests are classic places to lose and find yourself, but often the knowledge or self-knowledge for which the inner journey quests is found only in deeper darkness: the underworld.

Death itself is often seen as a journey. In the fifth century BC, Greek Orphic religion inscribed guidance for the dying on small gold wafers like the one now in the Paul Getty Museum, found in Thessaly in north Greece, incised around 400 BC:

You will reach the well-built house of Hades. On your right, you will see a spring near a beautiful cypress tree, where the souls of the dead drink. Do not drink from it! Further on you will find fresh water from the lake of Mnemosyne [Memory].

But some mythic heroes entered the underworld alive. This was the most dangerous quest of all – the *katabasis*, 'descent', a journey so powerful that it influenced all sorts of later quests. Plato's *Republic*, for instance, is a ten-book-long quest for moral knowledge but its first word is 'I went down': *katebēn*, the verb from which *katabasis* derives.

Like pilgrimage, *katabasis* was a quest. Maybe to bring something or someone back from the dark. As Aladdin had to enter the cave to find his lamp, so Heracles had to steal Cerberus the watchdog and Orpheus to bring back his beloved to life. (Aristophanes sends this up in *Frogs*, when Dionysus goes to Hades to fetch Euripides.) But sometimes the quest is to hear advice from a dead parent or seer.

This is a vital idea for poems: the quest for words you can only learn in the dark and from the dead. (Writers learn all the time, says Margaret Atwood, from the dead.)[90] Odysseus does not actually enter Hades – he gets shades to come to him by offering them blood to drink. He does it to hear how to get back to Ithaca from a seer; he also learns what's going on at home from his dead mother.

In the *Aeneid*, Virgil echoes not only Homer's *Odyssey* but other Greek poems (now lost) which described Orpheus, Heracles and Theseus going down to Hades and what they saw. Aeneas has a dream in which his dead father tells him he will reach Italy and found Rome but first must go to the underworld with the Sibyl, *to seek a meeting with me* and learn his future properly. So when he lands in Italy (at Cumae, just below Naples, close to *the gate of the underworld*), Aeneas asks the Sibyl to show him the way to Avernus, the underworld. She warns him: *Facilis descensus Averno. Easy to go down to hell / the doors stand open night and day*. Coming back is harder: *hic labor, opus hoc est*. These words have resounded, in Virgil's heartbreaking economy and unmatchable musical-psychological power, throughout Western imagination. Heaney translates them by, *To retrace your steps and get back to upper air, / That is the real task and the real undertaking*.[91] The Sibyl helps Aeneas find a gold bough to offer the Queen of the Dead. Then he *enters his journey*: such a dangerous one that the poet too must make an offering before he describes it. Virgil prays to the gods who rule the spirits, to Chaos, to silent shades of the dead and *dark silent wastes* they inhabit. He asks their blessing so he may describe their realm:

> Let it be right for me to tell what I've been told
> and reveal what lies hidden, deep in mists beneath the earth.

Carrying the gold bough, Aeneas walks through the dark with the Sibyl, *shadows all about them*. They travel *the road that leads to Acheron's rolling waters*, are ferried over the Styx, put Cerberus to sleep with honey cakes, find Aeneas's father and hear Rome's future.[92]

Dante echoes all this in the *Inferno*. His poem, reporting both his own inward journey and the path of human salvation, is driven by personal self-loss and anguish, but Aeneas is the blueprint. Dante's journey begins with being lost, midway on the *path of his life*. Coming to himself in a *dark wood*, he realises he has fallen into sin and ignorance. He tries to get out by climbing a hill touched by morning sun, but three wild beasts drive him back and down. A rescuer appears: the shade of Virgil. Just as Aeneas's dead father advised Aeneas, so Virgil tells Dante he must take another road, and go on by going down – to and through hell. Dante follows Virgil. *Necessity brings him here*, Virgil explains to the ferryman, *not pleasure*.[93]

As an image for the journey of life, *katabasis* has huge spiritual, emotional and psychological potential. You can see it as a dip into the unconscious, an inner journey into the past, memory, your deepest self, maybe into breakdown and out of it, in order to find yourself more fully. Whatever your Sibyl says, it is possible (the great *katabasis* poems show us) to go to hell and come back.

Most great writers tackle *katabasis* at some point. 'If you're a poet you're called upon', says Heaney (a great poet of memory), 'to honour the dimensions of the art.' And the deepest of those dimensions is, of course, the underworld.

In his *Sonnets to Orpheus*, Rilke says you can't be a poet unless you go down to the dead. (*You have to have been among the shades / and tuned your lyre there . . . you have to sit down and eat with the dead.*) You belong to both this world and the underworld; you bring back for readers knowledge gained in inner dark. Maybe all writing, says Margaret Atwood, 'is motivated, deep down, by a fear of and fascination with mortality – by a desire to make the risky trip to the Underworld and to bring something or someone back from the dead'. You may find this odd, she adds: 'It is a little peculiar. Writing itself is a little peculiar.'[94] She once proposed to writer colleagues that Gilgamesh was the original first writer. He journeyed, returned and wrote up what he learned. Writer colleagues agreed with her:

'You go, you get the story, you're whacked, you come back and write it down on stone. Or it feels like stone by the sixth draft,' they added. 'Go where?' I asked. 'To where the story is,' they said.

What the writer finds, on the inner journey, is the story. 'The story is in the dark,' says Atwood. 'You can't see your way ahead. Poets travel the dark roads. Inspiration is a hole that leads downwards.' She quotes Adrienne Rich's poem 'Diving into the Wreck' (which I discuss later, see Poem 6):

> There is a ladder.
> The ladder is always there . . .
>
> I go down . . .
>
> I came to explore the wreck.
> The words are purposes.
> The words are maps.
> I came to see the damage that was done
> and the treasures that prevail.[95]

11 'To Be Your Guide': The Words, The Book, The Poem

At some point on most mythic journeys the goal is words. A poem's journey is made of words, and the act of writing, according to Margaret Atwood, is 'a process that leaves a trail . . . There's a path.'[96] Ever since Dante followed Virgil into hell, poets have included other poets, dead ones, in their *katabasis* – 'masters' who give advice about their future path in life or poetry.

Eliot's 'Little Gidding' is a *katabasis* driven by personal experience of a special sort of hell (fire-fighting in the London blitz) as well as his knowledge of the *katabasis* tradition. (*What the dead had no speech for, when living*, he says, *They can tell you, being dead*.) In *the uncertain hour before the morning* (and after an air raid), the poet meets a shadowy figure who looks like *some dead master* and talks about poetry (*our concern was speech, and speech impelled us / To purify the dialect of the tribe*).

In Heaney's 'Station Island', the pilgrim poet confronts figures from his personal and literary past who help him understand what has gone into the making of himself as poet and man, and where he should go now. He has a series of meetings and conversations with the dead. This is *a road you travel on your own*, he is told. The last encounter tells him to cast away all advice, and just write:

> *Let go, let fly, forget.*
> *You've listened long enough. Now strike your note.*[97]

All Heaney's work suggests that the past is not something which the present replaces but what our own minds, now, are made of. We take past images and words with us into the future journey; we read, write and see new life with them.

Coming back from *katabasis*, in the last poem of 'Station Island', the pilgrim feels *like a convalescent*. He takes the hand of a composite figure. Like the *master* in 'Little Gidding', this is a *compound ghost*: a special Heaney mix of Irish writers, Homer, Virgil, Dante and Eliot himself.

> *I took the hand*
> *stretched down from the jetty, sensed again*
> *an alien comfort as I stepped on ground*
>
> *to find the helping hand still gripping mine,*
> *fish-cold and bony, but whether to guide*
> *or to be guided I could not be certain*
>
> *for the tall man in step at my side*
> *seemed blind, though he walked straight as a rush*
> *upon his ash plant, his eyes fixed straight ahead.*[98]

If no knowledgeable guide is available to show the path, a traveller's mind may call one up. Many mountaineers have met an imaginary guide at difficult moments. In 1933 the British climber Frank Smythe, alone at 8300 metres on the north side of Mount Everest, felt accompanied. It was a 'feeling so strong that it eliminated all loneliness'. When he slipped, this 'companion' held him by a rope. He stopped to eat mint cake, turned round to share it and was shocked to find no one to give it to. Only when he saw camp did he suddenly feel a link was snapped, that he really was alone. In 1988 Stephen Venables climbed the Kangshung face of Everest and was nearly at the summit when an old man appeared who accompanied him for the rest of the day. On the way down, he spent the night on a ridge with the old man. At dawn he looked down to the South Col and saw tents and real colleagues. He turned his head: the old man was gone.[99]

In reading, says the inspirational teacher to his pupil in Alan Bennett's play *The History Boys*, the 'best moments' happen

> when you come across something – a thought, a feeling, a way of looking at things – which you thought special and particular to you. Now here it is, set down by someone else, a person you have never met, someone even who is long dead. And it is as if a hand had come out and taken yours.

A book is the perfect guide. But of all books a good poem, with memorable resonant words, is one of the best. It is portable, compact, and there is always more to find in it. For Dante, it was Virgil. Charles Darwin took Milton's poems on his five-year voyage in the *Beagle*. In the anonymous medieval morality play *Everyman*, the eponymous hero has to go on a long difficult journey (to the grave, in fact). Most of his friends desert him, even Fellowship. Good Deeds stays loyal but is too weak to be any use. Only Knowledge says she will come along to help:

> *Everyman I will go with thee and be thy guide,*
> *In thy most need to go by thy side.*

In 1905 the London publisher Joseph Dent was planning a series of world classics in cheap editions he hoped would appeal 'to every kind of reader'. He appointed Ernest Rhys as series editor. They discussed many possible titles for the series and despaired. One day, walking through Garrick Street to the office in Bedford Street, Rhys suddenly remembered those lines from *Everyman*. He rushed into the office quoting them. Dent stared incredulously. Then, 'Everyman's Library!' he repeated. 'You've got it!' That title worked because the journey of life is a universal image and because a book – words that can be read, reread and thought about on the road – is so portable and shareable. Heaney's final guide strides along beside him, but only for a while; words stay with you. Literature: the guide that stays by your side. Every aspect of the ancient cluster of associations about the journey of life leads back, eventually, to words: to 'knowledge' and poetry.

The most famous *katabasis* of all is that of the archetypal poet. After Orpheus fails to bring back his dead love Eurydice from Hades, he can still sing. He sings the universal witnessing to loss (see Poem 60). The maenads (maddened female followers of Dionysus) tear him to pieces, possibly because he insists on singing of Eurydice rather than attending to them. (The world is often jealous of the poet's attention.) They toss his head into a river. But even as it floats downstream to the sea, it goes on singing. Like the voice of murdered Orpheus, poems survive when their maker has died. One thing they do is witness to the singer's journey: its wonders, beauty, love and suffering.

The suffering to which poems sometimes testify may be caused by external things – politics, cruelty, wickedness or civil violence as in Poem 22 by Ciaran Carson, set in the Northern Irish Troubles of the Seventies. Throughout the twentieth century Russian and East European poets testified to brutal repression which created, said Czeslaw Milosz, a special perspective on poetry: 'We tend to view poetry as a witness and participant in one of mankind's major transformations.' In horror, you need language you can rely on. 'The poetic act changes with the amount of background reality embraced by the poet's consciousness.'

People who live through cruelty and suffering on this scale, who live 'the fragility of those things we call civilization', know that what surrounds us is not guaranteed, as Milosz says 'It could just as well not exist – and so man constructs poetry out of the remnants found in ruins.'[100] But even in today's shopping-padded Western life, we all come up against fragility and discover the truth of his phrase – that 'what surrounds us is not guaranteed'. Lives are shattered in a moment. Cancer happens. To you, to someone you love. The car crash, terrorist attack, teenage child on heroin.

In the West, many people like to think we live in a Sunday supplement world in which everything works perfectly. This is a default position, a dream world. The reality (which writers, and particularly poets, tend to see sharply) is a precarious confused provisionality – *a makeshift hut*, says Rilke in the first of his *Sonnets to Orpheus*:

> *a shelter nailed up out of darkest longing,*
> *with an entryway that shudders in the wind.*

This makeshift precariousness, says Rilke, is poetry's home: where it sets up its *temple*.[101] I suspect poetry is a universal human need, that everyone has a poetry-shaped hole in them. And though today many people fill this hole with other artefacts like pop music, they often turn to the real thing when the precariousness makes itself intensely felt: in moments of national disaster (hundreds of people turned up to a poetry reading in New York after 9/11) or personal grief and joy at funerals and weddings.

One reason people love reading biographies and memoirs is seeing the road someone else took. You are not alone, says the memoir. I was where you are now: in misery, fear, happiness, love; in watching and wondering about the world. Poems specialise in that revelation. Well-turned and tuned words can distil or reflect your own situation, show where others have been, how someone else survived. As the last line of Poem 9 says, *We were once here*. Joseph Conrad saw human life as a walk over a crust of barely cooled lava through which we might drop at any minute. To live is to keep surviving the dangers and excitement of the journey; to write or read poems is to share the dangers, joys and reflections on that journey.

I recently put this into practice by accident. When frightened – facing the dentist, injections, operations – I've always said poems to myself. Journeying through Asian jungles in search of tigers, I found myself in different fear. In Laos I had to go 300 miles through trackless jungle by kayak and was terrified. I had never kayaked in my life and the river was full of rapids. Before getting into that kayak, I learned this Emily Dickinson poem and to steady myself, said it over and over as I went:

> *Civilization – spurns – the Leopard!*
> *Was the Leopard – bold?*
> *Deserts – never rebuked her Satin –*
> *Ethiop – her Gold –*
> *Tawny – her Customs –*
> *She was Conscious –*
> *Spotted – her Dun Gown –*
> *This was the Leopard's Nature – Signor –*
> *Need – a keeper – frown?*

> Pity – the Pard – that left her Asia –
> Memories – of Palm –
> Cannot be stifled – with Narcotic –
> Nor suppressed – with Balm

Saying this poem through the splashes helped close my mind to rocks. Right paddle down – *Civilization* – next rock – *spurns the leopard* – left paddle, bump down chute – *was the leopard* – spin, crunch on shallow basin, jerk forward, hoosh sideways down waterfall – *bold*? As we went, I asked myself what it was about.

One, isolation: *civilization spurns* her. Two: her own *nature – tawny*, wild, *spotted*; not like others. When she's alone that doesn't matter, *deserts* don't *rebuke* her. Should a man – a *Signor, keeper*, some male guardian of convention – complain about her nature? No – this maculate *dun gown* is what she really is, she won't pretend to be otherwise. Three: loss – this *pard* has *lost her Asia*, some experience she treasures. Four: her memories of it will not to be *stifled* or *suppressed*, even if they hurt. As I and my guide emptied the kayak of water onto a slimy bank I thought, 'It is about being who she is.' Isolated – and never mind what people think. No blocking memories just because they hurt. It was all, I saw (or thought I saw), about bravery.

A year later, walking down a Sumatran mountainside in thick jungle that was home to tigers, three species of cobras (two of them spitting kinds), kraits and pit vipers, and having lost the path just before sundown, I found myself saying that poem to myself over and over again. I felt I now understood physically why Dickinson put dashes in her poems. Each phrase was just enough for a breath, enough to say before the next search for a snake-free handhold. The dashes helped me find the next firm root, get my toe out from a liana, unhook a sleeve from a thorn, slide ten feet on bending bushes, dig a hand into leaves hoping no vipers were among them.

My real guide was out of sight, but Dickinson's mysterious dashes were everything – my momentum, my rhythm. The pauses made sure my foot would not meet wobbly rocks. For hours I clung to that poem mentally and moved to it physically. Unlike Mrs Ramsay swishing upwards through her flower forest, I was going downwards. That poem was my guiding hand, my keeping going. I felt, 'This is what all good poems do: press on, physically and spiritually, through risky tangle.'

Sullambano again. Everything about how a poem moves and

coheres is about that verb's two meanings – 'holding together' and 'understanding'. That's what keeps the poem, the reader, the traveller, going.

Good poems can light a dark moment, give you something to hang on to, let you reflect on what you see and where you are in a new way. They light a way out. When her husband died, the writer Joan Didion said there were days when all she hung on to was a poem. 'For a day or two, I relied on Matthew Arnold's "The Forsaken Merman".'[102]

Poems can make you see with new eyes the happy moments too. Just as you are not the only one to lose lover, parent, child, homeland, so you are not the only one to fall in love, have a child, be entranced by beauty and strangeness.

Even when they explore imaginary situations, good poems are still about real experience. Milosz called poetry 'the passionate pursuit of the real'. Heaney says the 'order' a good poem makes is true 'to the impact of external reality' (the impact, rather than the thing in itself) as well as 'to inner laws of the poet's being'.

Some bond, Heaney suggests, between inside (the poet's own reality) and outside (shared reality) is crucial. A good poem satisfies your intelligence and appeals to your feelings, makes a 'fluid relationship' between the innermost part of your mind and what you think about on the surface. Somehow, mysteriously, this 'restores you to yourself'; it helps you 'grow up to' whatever you have stored in yourself during your life.[103] Which is why every reader receives the poem differently.

Even when they are not overtly about the big things, good poems still resonate with our vulnerability. Vulnerability is poetry's strength. It is knowledge of that vulnerability that makes enjoying the world – our children, ourselves, each other, the weird stuff out there – such a miracle.

Poems run on imagination, on saying things otherwise than they are. They are, said Marianne Moore, 'imaginary gardens with real toads in them'.[104] An artificial made thing, a container and a frame, in which you find true things. Good poets know that if they are not emotionally and imaginatively honest while writing a poem, true to their own sense of what it is to be human, the poem will not work.

Good poems make new sense of the human condition, your condition – happy, baffled, wounded, tragic, estranged, entertained, alert or hurt. They give new perspectives on real life as you live it. Poems from all eras and cultures can do that, of course, but today's poems do it in today's terms, and in a world whose fabric and landscapes we recognise. That's one reason we keep needing good contemporary poems. They help us make new strange sense of our journey and re-see the world we live in, now and here.

12   So . . .

I have organised the poems in this book around different stages on the journey of life. They begin as children begin, with wondering. Wondering about our origins and what we are doing here; about nature and the environment; about childhood itself, and ways we reach out to where we are: religion, prayer, history. They carry on wondering, through love, marriage, parenthood, divorce and war and into ageing, illness, loss, grief; and on through surviving all this.

These are contemporary poems, using the furniture and language of life we share. But they reflect ancient questions which any traveller might ask at each stage of a journey. 'What is this place?' 'Who am I?' 'Who are you in relationship to me?' Questions everybody asks in some way, at some point. In the final group of poems, the end of the journey, the emphasis is not so much on ageing and grief but on how you survive them: 'How can I live without you?'

After each poem I discuss its journey and how a reader might share it. On one hand, these readings are as objective as I could make them. I am a working poet, trained as a classical scholar. As a child I learned poems by heart, read them, listened to them. My father was a psychoanalyst, a former classics teacher and an incurable educator. He taught me Greek, and sat me down to read Aeschylus and Virgil with him. I became very used (rebelliously, often) to attending minutely to words, hearing how they work in a line of poetry, listening for a whole spectrum of what they might mean. To sifting, rejecting, extending implications. By this accident of life I bring with me, for better or worse, a lot of interpreting.

But everyone reads with who they are, and brings to poems their own blind spots and hobby-horses. I've mixed objective comment with my subjective responses.

No one can help doing that. This is poetry, not maths. (And even in maths, after a certain stage, some of that mixing must go on.) But I hope I've flagged any moment when I interpret beyond what is provably 'there'. I'm not the 'correct' reader, only *a* reader; I'm not sharing right answers but offering a process: how I or you can bring all of ourselves to a poem so it stays with us, enlightening, enriching. There's no limit to the associations different readers can bring to a good poem. Part of a poem's life is the personal connections each reader brings to it.

The world of every poem is unique. You go into it as into a new room. At first glance, you take in many things consciously and many more subconsciously. At your second and third glance you notice more details, understand how these work on you, how they create a tone and feel, and why you are reacting as you are. In a room, you might notice a red cushion echoed by an off-red rug. The soft texture of a chair answered by a bunch of flowers. You might not even realise you notice it, but the matching and answering affects you all the same. In a poem, sounds which half-echo each other (a repeated pronoun, or the tonal register of different words) are all clues: to the speaker, the poem's voice, the movement of its thought.

I can't imagine anyone liking all these poems equally, but I am suggesting ways of reading them all as openly and fairly as you can before you decide about liking.

People who know the poetry world may raise eyebrows at putting some of these very different poets together, but if you make no prior assumptions about different camps of poetry why should you care? Part of the strength and fun of poetry today is its extraordinary variety. It is a mansion with many rooms. There has always been domestic violence in poetry's house. Inhabitants of some rooms want to knock others down and evict their tenants. These quarrels keep going on. When they have principles behind them (as in the seventeenth-century 'rhyme wars') rather than jealousy, these quarrels are important. They keep poets frisking and testing their ideas and their language.

But what matters most, what matters to contemporary readers, to people in their own lives, is attending generously to good poems wherever they come from.

And also reading clearly. If a thing is worth explaining, it is worth explaining clearly. There are many subtleties in these poems but no empty floweriness or rhetoric; nor any, I hope, in the ways I try to follow them.

I am very much not saying, 'Take my word for it, this poem means what I say.' Instead, I want to open doors and suggest a clear, trustable process by which you can follow the poem's journey yourself, bringing with you your own associations.

These poems are not always representative of their poet. I've included some information about the writers because readers may like to know where poems come from and seek out a particular poet's work. But it is the poem and words that matter.

The journey a poem makes may seem small-scale and private compared to the sweep of a novel or a film watched by millions all over the world. But that is part of its power. Poems are portable altars. Their journey can take in the world and outer space, and still be bounded in a nutshell. You can carry one in your head or your pocket and still find new things in it.

Good poems stand up for the effort of attention that we all need to keep making, today more than ever, to what it is like to be human.

Part Two

Poems

Poetry is like shot-silk with many glancing colours. Every reader must find his own interpretation.

Alfred, Lord Tennyson

There is never any such thing as one truth to be found in dramatic art. There are many. These truths challenge each other, recoil from each other, reflect each other, ignore each other, tease each other, are blind to each other. Sometimes you have the truth of a moment in your hand, then it slips through your fingers and is lost.

Harold Pinter

Prologue

Beginning the Journey

How can you decide on the *way* of setting out, if you do not first know where you are going, or at least with what purpose you are going there? Sometimes I took my autocycle, sometimes the train, sometimes the motor-coach, just as sometimes too I left on foot, or on my bicycle, silently, in the night.

Samuel Beckett, *Molloy*

The traveller is about to set out.

Important journeys often begin from a strong feeling or a dream. Dante's *Inferno* begins with the speaker in mid-life crisis having 'come to' himself in a dark wood. Bunyan's *Pilgrim's Progress* begins with a dream. 'As I walked through the wilderness of this world, I laid me down to sleep.' In Shambhala Buddhism, the beginning of the journey is the broken heart.

Dark woods, dreams and broken hearts are fine reasons to start a journey. That rush of feeling is your ticket to ride. But what are you riding *on*? How are you going? You must have something, even if it's just a pair of boots. Dante and Bunyan's pilgrim go on foot. Don Quixote's mare Rosinante may not look glamorous but does have four legs. Odysseus makes a raft, Aeneas builds a fleet to get away from Troy.

The journey itself may dictate the transport. For a poem, you need a trustable musical shape which will move you on but keep you on track. Symbols and images are useful too. Something to carry or wear which becomes part of your journey. A badge, to remind you what spirit you are going in; an emblem, to believe in on the way. In Shambhala Buddhism, that journey beginning with a broken heart is symbolised by the Himalayan tiger. Hindu pilgrims to the god Ayappa's shrine, in Kerala, wear black clothes and a necklace. Tibetan pilgrims carry a prayer wheel. When villagers in Santiago de Compostela started selling empty shells to pilgrims to use as spoons (at least that's the story) the badge of Christian pilgrimage became the scallop shell.

> *Give me my scallop-shell of quiet,*
> *My staff of faith to walk upon,*

wrote Walter Raleigh, the night before he was due to be beheaded. *And thus I'll take my pilgrimage.*

In this introductory poem the image is double: a bicycle and a pavane, a piece of music which is also a dance. The vehicle and music are the poem's own transport. As in a famous song by the early blues singer Robert Johnson, this transport is also image for the song, or poem, itself:

> *The train it left the station with two lights on behind*
> *Well the blue light was my blues and the red light was my mind.*

61

1 Michael Donaghy

Machines

Dearest, note how these two are alike:
This harpsichord pavane by Purcell
And the racer's twelve-speed bike.

The machinery of grace is always simple.
This chrome trapezoid, one wheel connected
To another of concentric gears,
Which Ptolemy dreamt of and Schwinn perfected,
Is gone. The cyclist, not the cycle, steers.
And in the playing, Purcell's chords are played away.

So this talk, or touch if I were there,
Should work its effortless gadgetry of love,
Like Dante's heaven, and melt into the air.

If it doesn't, of course, I've fallen. So much is chance,
So much agility, desire, and feverish care,
As bicyclists and harpsichordists prove

Who only by moving can balance,
Only by balancing move.

Michael Donaghy (1954–2004) was born into the Irish-American community in the Bronx. In 1985 he moved from America to London, where he taught poetry and worked as an Irish musician. His innovative, metaphysical, wise and playful poems were deeply felt and perfectly crafted. He won the Whitbread and Forward Prizes, and for twenty years was an important presence to many younger poets in the UK as teacher, encourager and inspirer.

If a poem is a journey, if we have to follow its movement and pattern, where do we start?

This first journey is longer than most that follow, because it introduces important aspects of reading and form.

I'm going to start with the layout. At first glance, simply counting lines in stanzas, we feel this poem as both symmetrical and asymmetrical. Stanzas of three and six lines are followed by stanzas of three and five. It looks balanced but it isn't, quite. Eventually, we will find that the way it plays with symmetry formally reflects the ideas it explores, especially the risk of trying to balance. At every level, this poem will relate two different elements, equally and unequally at the same time.

Its first image, and first rhyme, is a *bike*. It ends, in the last two lines, by repeating two ideas: *balance* and movement. Throughout, in its own form and the way it moves, it is concerned with keeping *balance* while being aware you might lose it at any moment.

It is also concerned with connecting: connecting images, lovers and words. Its first word (*Dearest*) connects the speaker to the addressee. *Connected* rhymes with *perfected*. Whether you are bicycling, playing pavanes or loving someone, you come to *grace* through connection.

Yet you may be disconnected at the same time. Whether in love, or in writing a poem, you may be absent (see the tenth line, *if I were there*) while seeming to be present. Or vice versa.

Balance and fall, presence and absence: this poem deals with opposites. (Two wheels of the bike, perhaps.) The first two words also set up a tension between two different registers of voice. *Dearest* suggests a love poem, an idea picked up by *touch* in the tenth line, *desire* in the centre of the fourteenth line, and *love* in the third stanza. *Love* engenders the rhymes *move* and *prove*, the rhymes for *love* in one of the great sixteenth-century love poems, 'Come Live with Me and Be My Love' by Christopher Marlowe. But instead of the loving beseeching of Marlowe's words, *Come live with me and be my love*, the imperative (*note*) suggests a very different voice: scholarly, didactic. A register and tone backed up by references to classics and classical music (*Purcell, Ptolemy, Dante*) and *prove*, the final rhyme to *love* (and not a full rhyme); as if the speaker has been concerned to make a point, *prove* a theorem.

Only two words, and already we have two kinds of possible emotional relation to the poem, and several ways of reacting to the speaker.

Formally, the poem seems to be in two halves. The first has two stanzas (one of three lines, one of six), the second (introduced by *So*) has two stanzas of three lines plus an extra couplet. The first 'half' has nine lines, the second eight.

So the ninth line, *And in the playing, Purcell's chords are played away*, seems to be what makes the poem asymmetrical. But seen from another viewpoint (forgetting stanza breaks, just counting the overall number of lines) it is the central spine of a different symmetry: the dividing line between what you gradually realise are two octaves ('eight lines') of a sonnet. But each represents a different type of sonnet.

The first stanza throws you off any sonnet scent. You don't expect sonnet stuff because, in traditional sonnets, you only get a set of three lines at the end in the sestet. In fact, these first three lines disguise the four-line principle of the rhyming scheme of the first eight lines (*abab cdcd*): the octave of a Shakespearean sonnet.

But after the *away* line, instead of the sestet we expect, we get another octave. Its interlinked scheme (*aba cab cb*) recalls the sestet of an Italian sonnet, which only has four rhymes, like a Petrarchan sonnet. On the page, you don't see it as an octave. It begins with a three-line stanza, and the second could be another three with an extra two at the end.

That central ninth line, therefore, changes everything. Oh! you think. This is a sonnet and not-a-sonnet. Anything can happen now, to the rhyme scheme, lovers, cyclist, harpsichordist. The musician may stumble, cyclist fall (see *fallen*).

After *away* we get a sonnet-like 'turn' (*So*). The cyclist has 'turned' a corner. We veer into another direction and realise that *away* referred to more than the playing of *Purcell's chords*. The speaker is not with the beloved at all (*If I were there*). He himself is *away*.

So that central word *away*, the only end-word with no partner, is more telling than we realised. It subverts the partnership feel of the first two words. *Dearest*, *note* suggested the partners were together. The speaker seemed to show her (if it is her) something. Now we learn they are apart. There may even be a pun, a joke about infidelity, in *played away*. This speaker is even more unreliable than we thought.

So far, the poem has stressed a connection between *perfected* and *connected*, suggesting that being *connected* by love leads to *grace*, that the lovers are in harmony, symbolised by *chords* and likeness (*Dearest . . . these two are alike*). It attached to their relationship the homing image of *concentric gears*. Now we learn all this was uttered *away* (maybe even playing *away*) from the loved one. How can a distant beloved *note* a pavane – or anything about this pavane – which she can't even hear? The poem's relation to the beloved is as complex as its relation to its own voice and the sonnet form.

After the revelation of *away*, in the new scenario of the second half, *talk* (which also suggests the poem itself) makes up for *touch*. Both depend on technique (*gadgetry*); on a sense of being *alike* which moves into *this talk* and on up to the *heaven* which *Dante* describes in the third part of the *Divine Comedy*, when his beloved Beatrice leads him into the heavenly spheres of Paradise. (The Greek astronomer Ptolemy said the planets moved in 'epicycles'. Following Ptolemy, Dante describes sun, moon and planets revolving round a stationary earth at different speeds, each creating its own sphere, or heaven.)

If, however, creates a second turn. While reminding us that technique and *gadgetry* can falter and cyclists fall (*if it doesn't, of course, I've fallen*), the line disturbs another rhyme scheme. If the first turn was a cyclist's wobble in one direction, this is a wobble in another.

So far in this second half we have had *there*, *love*, *air*: a pattern of *aba*. We expect another *b*, to rhyme with *love*. But no, *love*'s partners, its rhymes, are postponed. Instead we get a new sound, *chance* (which prepares, though we don't know it yet, for the resolution, *balance*) and a new pattern emerges, *aba cab*.

At every level, then, this poem is juggling two opposing things: two wheels, two registers of voice, two forms of sonnet-rhyme, two voltas, two basic images (a classical *pavane*, a modern *bike: twelve-speed*, just as some modern music is twelve-tone). Also two people, two halves of a poem, two ways of seeing its symmetry.

This sense of two worlds is resolved at the end by chiasmus. Chiasmus (called after the Greek letter *chi*, a long X with dangling legs) takes two elements or words and reverses them. You could draw a *chi* through the last two lines, which 'connect' (a key word and idea throughout the poem) *moving* to *move*, and *balance* to *balancing*.

These lines state the poem's culminating insight that love (and, implicitly, a poem) can only go forward by risking a fall.

Whether you are loving, cycling, playing pavanes or writing poems, you only get *balance* if you *move*. By balancing two words (*balance*, *move*) as it moves through the lines, the chiasmus also exemplifies the very idea it is stating.

Again Donaghy echoes an earlier poet. If the rhymes *love*, *prove* and *move* have recalled Marlowe's famous love poem, Yeats is also a presence. The earlier line *the cyclist, not the cycle, steers* gestured to a famous line by Yeats, *How can we know the dancer from the dance?*. Now, in this final chiasmus, Donaghy reflects another famous poem, 'An Irish Airman foresees his Death', in which Yeats uses the word *balance* as one of two balanced elements in a statement about needing balance:

> I balanced all, brought all to mind,
> The years to come seemed waste of breath,
> A waste of breath the years behind
> In balance with this life, this death.

Musically, we can track the procession of conceits through the poem by following the journey of two related sounds, the swishing sound of S and SH, starting with the title's central consonant.

We move from *Dearest* through *harpsichord, Purcell, racer's, speed, machinery, grace,* to *simple*. But the soft S is broken by a pattern of hard Ks: *alike, harpsichord, bike, chrome, connected, concentric* (which like *cyclist, cycle* and *harpsichordists* combines soft S and hard K).

Already softness is back with *Schwinn*. Then we get *cyclist* and *cycle* (with the unheard S of that Yeats line behind, *dancer from the dance*) and *Purcell*.

The second half begins with S, moving from *So* to *should* through *effortless,* to end in the lover's, poet's or mathematician's dream of melting; *air*. Then, after the warning that let-down may come at any time, we get *course, so, chance, so, feverish, bicyclists, harpsichordists, balance, balancing*.

The journey of this sound suggests the soft hiss of tyres, swish of spokes and buzz of harpsichord strings but also the *ssh* of intimacy (see *talk, touch*) in the relationship between poet and beloved, poem and reader. A relationship which proceeds by *balancing,* and which is always on the (last word) *move*.

Move is what planets do; hence the earlier reference to *Ptolemy* and *Dante's heaven*. *Planetai,* 'planets', comes from the Greek for 'wander'; Ptolemy suggested what pattern their wandering followed. The image of stationary earth and 'wandering' star, and the idea that errant wandering is actually part of a hidden pattern, colours the relation of beloved and poet. *Played away* may imply a momentary lapse, an interrupted personal rhyme scheme, but the poem's *I* is still centrally *connected / to another*. The planets move unevenly through *heaven* but keep revolving (in what Dante calls their 'spheres' – the word is not in the poem but its rhymes, *gears* and *steers,* are) around earth.

The last act of *The Merchant of Venice* opens with two lovers looking at the night sky. The man, in a didactic vein somewhat similar to the opening of this poem, tells his love to sit and look. He explains that the *motion* of the heavenly bodies is also their music:

> *There's not the smallest orb which thou behold'st*
> *But in his motion like an angel sings.*

He tells her *such harmony is in immortal souls*, then commands attendant musicians to

> *With sweetest touches pierce your mistress' ear*
> *And draw her home with music.*

If this poet has *played away* and *fallen*, he too, this love poem suggests, will be drawn home with its own music.

I hope I've not made this poem seem complicated. It is not 'difficult' in any of Steiner's senses. Yes, Schwinn needs to be looked up, at least I had to: he was a nineteenth-century German bicycle designer who went to America in 1891, designed a brilliant bike, and founded a Bicycle Company. We may or may not know about Ptolemy or Dante's heaven but the poem gives us enough to go on: to realise that both Ptolemy and Schwinn were involved in concentric movement and *gears*. And it is (among other things) the mechanisms of poetry that this poem is talking about. It points teasingly to the concentric mechanics (*gears*) which let a poem move forward.

Carrying us somewhere new (like the 'transport' of love), it does what every good poem must do (as the last word reminds us): it moves. And as it does, it can also 'move' readers emotionally. I've seen this poem move audiences who were unaware in their conscious minds of the crafting that went into it. Yet it was the craft they were responding to. In Shakespeare's words, the poem drew them with music.

Once you have shared its intricacies you enjoy it that much more. The words themselves are not particularly 'resistant'. What is intricate is their relationship. Thanks to the *gadgetry of love*, meanings and implications mesh and move through the syllables in a *machinery of grace*. Like the pavane, the words are danced movement between two people. The lovers. Or poet and reader. This is a love poem whose image is both a bicycle, transport for the journey, and a musical dance. And its title, 'Machines', is Donaghy's very conscious metaphor for all well-made poems.

I

Where Am I? What Is All This?

What country, friends, is this?

William Shakespeare, *Twelfth Night*

The traveller looks round.

Like Viola, washed up on an unknown coast at the beginning of Shakespeare's *Twelfth Night*, we all have moments when we wonder what we're doing here, what 'here' really is. *Going through life is not the same as walking across a field*, says Pasternak's poem 'Hamlet'. In a poem called 'Into the Day', J. H. Prynne sees us as *dark scouts* walking *blankly in the universe*. Poems in this section ask where we are. They wonder about the world we walk through. What it holds, what it means.

Some places, where we feel truest, seem to anchor us. They are our home ground: where we 'find ourselves', 'come to ourselves'. But do we really know them? What forces lie beneath? *This land is not the sweet home that it looks*, says Auden's poem 'In Praise of Limestone', suggesting that what lies beneath forms us in ways of which we are unaware. What we *see* is *a limestone landscape*. But underneath, what we *hear*, is *the murmur / Of underground streams*. In this section, when the speaker of Heaney's poem enters *galleried earth, elsewhere, underneath, an engine powered / Rumbled, quickened*.

And what about other inhabitants? Dangerous animals or divinities may reveal themselves unexpectedly. Christopher Middleton's tarantula, John Burnside's old gods and (for the colonists in Elizabeth Bishop's poem) *big symbolic birds* and *sooty dragons*.

Everyone's home ground and old gods are different. Many of the places in poems I have chosen for this first section are rural. Maybe my own old gods were at work, prodding me to pick these poems, rather than others. But the wondering they explore applies as much to city streets, the office, and your own house. In ancient Greece the home crackled with divinity just as wildly as the countryside. Gods who jealously demanded respect inhabited the threshold, door-hinge and roof, like the electricity that threads invisibly through our own walls. Wherever you live has power in its shadows.

We all live in another landscape too. At birth, we are catapulted into a particular language; some people into several. (There are five bilingual poets and one trilingual in this book.) Our language is also a 'place' we lead our life in. We need it to be *a real place*, says W. S. Graham, because we *have to put up with it / Anyhow*. It is in language that we reflect on our experience, worry about the world and ourselves. Like physical places, language has unexpected forces at work that sometimes leap up out from under the familiar surface.

Poems bring those forces out. They make us aware of what lies beneath our words as well as our feet.

This is where the journey starts. With poems that wonder what we are doing here, what is under the skin of the world we have been given to live in.

2   Gwyneth Lewis

The Flaggy Shore
(*for Nora Nolan*)

Even before I've left, I long
for this place. For hay brought in before the rain,
its stooks like stanzas, for glossy cormorants
that make metal eyes and dive like hooks,
fastening the bodices of the folding tide
which unravels in gardens of carraigín.
I walk with the ladies who throw stones at the surge
and their problems, don't answer the phone
in the ringing kiosk. Look. In the clouds
hang pewter promontories, long bays
whose wind-indented silent coasts
make me homesick for where I've not been.
Quicksilver headlands shoot into the night
till distance and the dying of day
dull steel and vermilion to simple lead
blown downward to the dark, then out of sight.

Lewis, born in Cardiff in 1959, was appointed Wales's first National
Poet in 2005. She writes in both Welsh and English but Welsh was
her first language. She has worked as a journalist in New York, a
documentary producer at BBC Wales, and has published six books
of poetry. Several have won prizes; a TV documentary was made
from her poem inspired by an astronaut cousin's voyage to repair
the Hubble Space Telescope. She has also written two prose books,
Sunbathing in the Rain: A Cheerful Book about Depression, and a
memoir of a voyage on a small boat from Cardiff to Africa.

Her language is lyrical, precise, imaginative, often surreal, deeply
rooted in landscape and place. This poem questions the concept
of place while describing an archetypally Celtic landscape, the
Flaggy shore in Co. Clare, part of the Burren's fissured limestone, a
coast of boulders looping into Galway Bay with hills, loughs,

underground caves, megalithic tombs, ruined abbeys and Celtic crosses beyond. Heaney describes the Flaggy shore in a poem called 'Postscript':

> *The ocean on one side wild*
> *With foam and glitter, and inland among stones*
> *The surface of a slate-grey lake is lit*
> *By the earthed lightning of a flock of swans.*

And, he adds, *you are neither here nor there.*

Lewis's poem too feels neither here not there. It is about being in *this place* and elsewhere at once, paradoxically *homesick for* where you have never *been* while longing for where you actually are.

The one Celtic word *carraigín* (meaning edible seaweed – you can even have it in ice cream) is embedded in a tide of English. This speaker, talking about feeling both here and not-here, is using English and not-English words. She is between languages as well as places and the poem moves between contradictory activities too. Between making, ordering or containing (*brought in, stanzas, fastening, folding, gardens*) and unmaking, not solving, moving away: *unravels, problems, clouds, shoot, distance, blown*). Between connecting (*eyes . . . hooks, with the ladies, look, the ringing kiosk*) and refusing connection (*don't answer the phone*).

It begins with longing and a vision of careful order (*before rain*), but ends by 'shooting' *into the night, into the dark, out of sight.*

It also moves, at a very local level, between alternative meanings. In the central section it is clear who throws *stones at the surge* (those ladies). But what about *and their problems?* Do they throw stones at their *problems* as well as at the *surge?* Or is the speaker walking *with* the ladies' *problems?* And who is not answering the *phone*, the *ladies* or the speaker? English can get away with these syntactical ambiguities, where a more inflected language like Latin could not. But ambiguity is an important part of how this English poem, set in a Celtic landscape, works.

At *Look*, the poem lifts us away from human things and their ambiguities to another world – the sky, which mirrors the shore where we began with its *promonotories, bays* and *coasts.* All this is *in the clouds.* The speaker who 'longed' (without having *left* it) for *this place* of *hay*, seabirds and *tide*, is now *homesick* for a *silent* other world.

This is where colour begins: in *clouds.* In the first chunk we have metaphor (*like*; *like*; *bodices of the tide*), texture (*glossy*, *metal*) and sound (*ringing*). But *in the clouds*, the metals have colour. First *pewter*, then (in the last four lines which carry us away *into the night*) *quicksilver*, *steel*, *lead*. And a gash of *vermilion* in the middle.

But there is ambiguity in this world too. Where do the *headlands* of these last four lines belong: the real world, the Flaggy shore of the title, or the cloud world which pulls the speaker away? This ambiguity is reflected in a moment of linguistic ambiguity too. At first, in the second-last line, you feel that *dull* could be an adjective (as if *dull steel* balances *simple lead* leaving *vermilion* to shine on its own at the line's centre). In fact it is a verb, whose subject is *distance and dying of day*. These two things *dull* the sunset's *steel and vermilion*.

The form underlines this feeling of veering between alternative worlds and meanings. It is a block poem of sixteen lines. (Like Heaney's, as it happens.) Two chunks of six lines (end-stopped at *carraigín* and *been*), then a smaller one of four, tied by the rhyme of *night* and *sight*. Appropriate to a poem at the edge of the sea (whose end-words are full of shifting liquid, from *rain* to *tide*, *surge*, *clouds*, *bays*, *coast*), the blank verse lines mostly have three or four beats. Some stretch to five, most importantly the last, which puts into action the 'longing' of the first line, by moving further *out of sight*. So the form both is, and is not, a sonnet.

It moves like a sonnet. It starts with description, then turns to *clouds* which 'reflect' the *place* where the poem began. It is smoothly punctuated, like Shakespearean blank verse, by stops for breath and sense. In the first chunk, we breathe at the full stop after *place*, after the first beat of the second line, then at the end of six lines, at *carraigín*, and in the second chunk come to an abrupt stop, a big breath, at the poem's centre (*Look*), then run on again in that other world, as if the tide has reached a far point and turned, as far as the twelfth line where we breathe again (after *been*), then flow on to end *out of sight*. A classic sonnet has eight lines of four plus four followed by six but this is twelve lines of six and six, followed by four. So here is another 'between'. This poem is between a sonnet and not-a-sonnet.

At many levels, then, the poem is a tug of war between two meanings, languages, forms and worlds. It questions what belongs where, who belongs to what. Welsh is an ancient Celtic tongue in the modern world – with, Lewis has written, 'half a million speakers and numbers in decline'. To speak it, she says, is 'to know the sound of a long, unbearable farewell'.[1]

As with many formative twentieth-century writers (Beckett, between French and English, Nabokov and Brodsky between English and Russian) her sensibility belongs to two languages at once.[2] Her poem is set on an edge. A tidal poem, to-ing and fro-ing between land and sea, looking two ways. It even sees the *shore* two ways. We are not so much between land and sea as between land plus sea on the one hand (the earth, in other words), and sky on the other.

So this poem, titled for a particular place, is about being in two places at once. The archetypal experience of Celts in the English world; and more widely of all migrants in the multicultures of today.

3 John Burnside

The Old Gods

Now they are condemned
to live in cracks
in bubbles of plaster and rust
and spiders' webs
behind the furniture:

speaking a derelict language
to empty space,
sealed with the vapour
in bottles, closed in the blown
robins' eggs
in some abandoned loft.

Each has its given power.
Each has its heart, its secret,
its local name,
and each has its way of learning
the skill of return,
the science of bleeding through, when anger or fear
is fuzzing the surface,
making us dizzy and whole.

Burnside, a Scottish poet born in 1955, has won the Whitbread
Prize and published nine collections of poetry plus novels, short
stories and a painful, insightful memoir of his father. He worked as
factory hand, labourer, gardener and for ten years a computer
systems designer, then returned to Scotland in 1995 and now
teaches Creative Writing, Literature and Ecology in Fife. His
intensely lyrical, delicately tangling poems call on dream, myth,
memory and religious questioning for reflections on the meaning of
life in a semi-suburban landscape, and he has a keen eye for the
domestic detail that sums up an emotional or spiritual life.
'The lyrical impulse', he says, 'begins at the point of self-

forgetting.'[3] His poems are full of glimpsed presences, ghosts, angels, ancestors, our own unlived lives. His language is always on some edge between the concrete and the abstract. Normally abstractions are the great enemy of vivid writing. You can't make a reader see 'anger', but you can convey it through an image, or what an angry person says or does. But Burnside brings abstracts alive; and divinity (an abstract concept which can have urgent physical manifestations) is an important element in his work.

This poem pictures multiple pagan gods under the surface of the suburban life and mind. It comes from Scotland, so *old gods* may imply old Celtic gods who have dwindled to linger on as folk memory: will o' the wisps, the good folk. But they also suggest ancient Greek gods who were simultaneously abstract and personal, and lived in the human world in physical things and activities like fire, hunting, sex, market place, river, hearth.

One way of seeing this poem's journey is from concrete to abstract, and ultimately towards the mind reflecting on abstractions. It flags this journey through the end-words. In the first stanza, lines end in concrete nouns. The first three are monosyllables (*cracks*, *rust*, *webs*), the fourth a three-syllable generic noun which is already getting less specific, *furniture*. Some of the next stanza's end-words are concrete (*eggs*, *loft*), others are more nebulous though you can still sort of hear and see them: *language*, *space*, *vapour*. The last stanza's lines end in fully abstract nouns, *power*, *secret*, *name*, *learning*, *return*, *fear*.

Shifted by that word *return*, the poem itself apparently 'returns' to the concrete in *surface*: a key word, for the poem is all about looking under surfaces to find remnants of *old gods*.

But this *surface* is really an abstract in disguise. It is a metaphor, the *surface* of a mind 'fuzzed' by emotion. The poem's concrete-to-abstract journey may begin with chinks in the floorboards but it ends up in the psyche.

You can track this journey by the musical changes that accompany it. Most lines have two or three beats and the music swings between long O and EE plus ER. The long O of *old* in the title occupies the central stanza (*closed*, *blown*) like an empty moan at the centre of each word (and of the poem), emerges again in *local* and finishes in *whole*. EE begins with the first active participle (*speaking*), continues in *sealed*, *each*, *each*, *each* and mutates into *fear* at the end of the longest line: the line which spells out what the *old* gods get up to, where they survive. You can hear EAR as a shift from EE to

ER, the syllable which begins and ends the first word that slips away from the concrete, *furniture*, is picked up as the last syllable in *vapour*, moves into *power*, gets buried (like the *old gods*) in *learning* and *return*, 'surfaces' in *anger* and goes to earth in *surface*.

The poem starts with old gods *now condemned*, imprisoned like criminals in what is hidden, in-between, *behind* (*cracks, vapour in bottles*), enclosed in decay: *bubbles of plaster and rust, blown robins' eggs, spiders' webs*. Adjectives for where they *live* appear in the second stanza, and suggest the gods themselves are *derelict, empty, sealed, closed, blown, abandoned*. Following the poem's first verb, *condemned*, these adjectives makes it sound as if the old gods are dead and gone.

But the abstract-filled last stanza tells us they still possess *given power*. The double repetition of *each has* suggests how many and how individual they are still, how active in both the physical world and the psyche.

Greek gods reflected their culture's insight into human nature. We are psychically multiple, subject to many different impulses and loyalties. Their different local names reflected an early civilisation of localities isolated from each other by mountain or sea. This poem's *old gods* may reflect memories of a Celtic culture of isolated human centres: villages, but also individual people. They have individual 'powers', 'secrets' and *local* names. To make their presence felt *each* 'learns' something new: *a skill of return, a science of bleeding through*.

This unexpected image lengthens into the longest line, the only pentameter, as though an extra thought were *bleeding* urgently *through* the poem's form. The image could come from colour printing, but even in printing 'bleed' is a metaphor. Colour seeps through like blood through a bandage. We have had dry dead things, *plaster, rust*. Now blood, hot, wet, colourful, comes *through* in ourselves as we realise what the poem is truly about: how the old gods' behaviour and resurfacing affects *us*.

'We' appear suddenly (as an acted-upon object not an active subject) in the last line. The poem begins with *they* (as if the gods are nothing to do with anything) but ends with *us*. We, in the end, are what *old gods* are about and where they *live*. We are the ones who have *given* them their *power*.

The last stanza moves towards redemption. The *gods* started out, in the first line, *condemned*. In the last, they make *us whole*. The poem has moved not simply from concrete to abstract, but towards resurfacing whatever feels *empty*, *closed*, *abandoned* or *derelict* in ourselves. As we read, we realise the retreat of these *old gods* was a lessening within us. The *cracks* and *empty* spaces were concrete, but were also images for disused and cobwebby parts of ourselves.

Gods 'bleeding through' to make us aware of them confuse *us*. *Dizzy* (suggesting blood loss) picks up the *zz* of *fuzzing*. How we feel (*dizzy*) is intimately connected to the way gods penetrate our *surface*. But though upsetting, this process also heals and completes us (*whole*). This *return* reconnects us to what we have forgotten: things that were once important, the *eggs* in the attic, *language* we once knew.

The poem began with a passive past participle (*condemned*) and the passive past continues through the second stanza (*sealed*, *closed*). But it is present active participles (which begin with *speaking* in the second stanza) that dominate the last (*learning*, *bleeding*, *fuzzing*, *making*). Whatever these gods did and stood for, in the world and in our souls, is not passive and past. It is active within us. The music carries the message, the syllables' relationships realise the poem's target idea. As EE and long O (of *sealed* and *closed*) are revisited in *dizzy* and *whole*, so something old, forgotten but important, even sacred, 'surfaces'. Hidden things resurface not only in the world but in *us*.

Disturbing the Tarantula

The door a maze
of shadow, peach leaves
veining its wood colour,

and cobwebs broken
breathing ah ah
as it is pushed open –

two hands
at a ladder shook
free the tarantula, it slid

black and fizzing to a rung
above eye-level,
knees jack knives,

a high-jumper's, bat mouth
slit grinning
into the fur belly –

helpful: peaches
out there, they keep growing
rounder and rounder

on branches wheeled low
by their weight over
roasted grass blades; sun

and moon, also, evolve
round this mountain
terrace, wrinkling now

with deadly green
emotion: All things
are here, monstrous convulsed

rose (don't anyone
dare come), sounding through
our caves, I hear them.

Middleton was born in Cornwall in 1926. In 1966 he moved to
Austin, Texas, to teach German literature. He has published many
collections as well as translations from German. He has always
experimented. His poems mix romantic realism and surrealism.
They glint with metaphor, precise observation, metaphysical wit
and sometimes grim humour.

This one takes off from a vision of horror coming into the open,
a *monstrous convulsed rose* which leads to a new vision of the universe
around it. The *door* is a real door, *wood colour* checkered with *leaves*,
but also a door into a *maze of shadow* (invoking the Cretan labyrinth
which contained the Minotaur). Traces of the monster in this
shadow are there for all to read (*cobwebs*). The door to it is almost
animate itself (*breathing ah ah / as it is pushed open*).

What *hands* and *ladder* have *broken* is some seal between daylight
and nightmare now *grinning* in the open. It threatens the *hands*
and *eye* of the observers, but in the second half (beginning in the
sixth stanza) the poem starts responding to the spider as *helpful*.
The journey is clear now: a movement towards realising that *all
things / are here*. As the whole world is *wrinkling* in response to the
tarantula, the speaker can 'hear' something *sounding through our
caves*, some truth emerging from caverns of the unconscious.

In most English-language poems, the principle of organisation of
words is by the beat you register as you listen or read. But here the
organising principle is the number of syllables. This is syllabic verse.
Each stanza has fifteen syllables.

Many poetic traditions (especially Welsh and Japanese) have
forms which depend on the number of syllables, not beats. The
best-known form of syllabic verse today is Japanese haiku, which has
seventeen syllables in three lines of five, seven and five syllables and
became popular worldwide in the twentieth century. Borges and the
Mexican poet Octavio Paz wrote Spanish haiku; George Seferis
tried it out in Greek. Early twentieth-century English poets
experimented with other forms of syllabic verse (Robert Bridges
wrote nearly five thousand lines of it). So did Marianne Moore and
Dylan Thomas. Middleton's poem was written in the early Sixties,
when the American Beat poets were writing in syllabics.

People have argued about whether the ear can actually hear the lines of syllable-counted poetry at all, since they are not organised by metre, nor are they free verse which depends on the word's natural rhythm. But this poem is given cohesive music by the vowel sounds, which make each stanza hang together and link them as it goes. The AY of *maze* links to *veining*, the OH of *broken* to *open*, the UH of *wood* to *pushed*. *Ah ah* is picked up by the key word *tarantula*. *Caves* in the last line picks up *maze* in the first, so the music as well as the sense underlines the labyrinth motif of the opening and closing lines.

The poem is about something *disturbing*, yet the form is anything but disturbed. The equal-syllable stanzas contain and belie the vision of violence which the images of *jack knives* and *slit*, plus the energetic adjectives (*fizzing*, *monstrous*, *convulsed*) provide. Alarm is the least important thing. The urgent warning, *don't anyone dare come*, is in brackets. It is not important, at least not in the poem.

What matters to the poem is not danger but the journey from *door* to *tarantula* and on to the perception (*I hear them*) that something frightening and powerful really is there all the time, in the world, our imagination and in ourselves, though it is normally unspoken and unseen. The point is not terror but epiphany.

The opening is descriptive, simple, full of nouns and present-tense verbs (*breathing*, *is pushed*). Then comes past narrative and past-tense verbs (*shook*, *slid*) and a subjective adjective (*grinning*). Then comes comment and reflection in *helpful*, prefacing more emotional subjective adjectives (*deadly*, *monstrous*). Finally we return to the present tense: *keep growing, evolve, wrinkling, are, dare move, sounding, I hear*. We come up to date with consciousness and the now. There has been a revelation. We understand something more about the world.

Just as *bat mouth* looks forward to *caves* in the final line, so *helpful* turns us away from the spider itself to attend to the whole context: what is *out there*. The spider vision has been *helpful* to a mind reacting to everything *round* (picking up *rounder and rounder*) the *mountain terrace*: helping it to reach a vision of the whole universe from heavenly bodies to *caves*.

The journey from physical adjectives (*black*, *fizzing*, *fur*) to emotional interpretative ones (*helpful*, *deadly*, *monstrous*) marks the overall journey of a poem that starts with a *door* and moves towards perception, explanation and finally revelation of violence and beauty (*convulsed rose*): what these tarantulas, and disturbing them, might mean to 'me': the persona which manifests itself at the end as suddenly as the spider does at the beginning: the speaker, *I*.

This poem, invoking the monster in the Cretan labyrinth which Freud used as image for the subconscious, was written in the Sixties when Freudian ideas were exploding into literary studies. It is about a spider but also about the self – about confronting what you knew was there inside (even if you refused to read the signs, the *cobwebs*): *deadly green emotion* and *grinning bat mouth*. Confronting what dwells in the *caves* inside you is (says Freudian doctrine) *helpful*. It also makes you see and *hear* the world *out there*, listen objectively to the whole world's *sounding caves* as well as those of the subjective imagination.

5 Penelope Shuttle

Taxing the Rain

When I wake the rain's falling
and I think, as always, it's for the best.

I remember how much I love rain,
the weakest and strongest of us all;

as I listen to its yesses and no's,
I think how many men and women

would, if they could,
against all sense and nature,

tax the rain for its privileges;

make it pay for soaking our earth
and splashing all over our leaves;

pay for muddying our grass
and amusing itself with our roots.

Let rain be taxed, they say,
for riding on our rivers
and drenching our sleeves;

for loitering in our lakes
and reservoirs. Make rain pay its way.

Make it pay for lying full length
in the long straight sedate green waters

of our city canals,
and for working its way through processes

of dreamy complexity
until this too-long untaxed rain comes indoors

and touches our lips,
bringing assuagement – for rain comes

to slake all our thirsts, spurting
brusque and thrilling in hot needles,

showering on to anyone naked;
or balming our skins in the shape of scented baths.

Yes, there are many who'd like to tax the rain;
even now, they whisper, it can be done, it must be done.

Shuttle, born in Middlesex in 1947, has lived in Cornwall since
1970, published many collections, several novels, and two works of
non-fiction with her husband, the poet Peter Redgrove with whom
she shared a remarkable artistic union. Her most recent collection is
driven by his death. Shuttle's poetry puts a high value on image,
sensuality, nature and the body. 'The body is the great poem,' said
Wallace Stevens (an important influence on her work) and Shuttle's
poems remind you that the poem itself is a body. They also blend
elemental forces like water, earth or lightning with the visionary.
They talk of the domestic (motherhood, depression, a daughter
becoming a woman) but do it through myth and dream.

This poem moves by developing the image of the title and its
stressed syllables, AX and AY. The first is repeated in *tax*, *taxed*,
untaxed, *tax*; the AY of *rain* is repeated (according to my count),
in twenty-seven later words. The poem opens with *I*, but ends with
they and develops an opposition between them. *I* values rain and
what it stands for – *for the best, I love rain. They* are *many men and
women* (underlined by *many* in the last couplet) who are *against
sense and nature*. The journey is an adventure into the imagined
mindset of this *many*, developing the fantasy that *they* want to *tax
the rain*.

'For me,' says Shuttle, 'the way the poem breathes gives it form.'
This poem moves from the actions of *I* (*wake, think, remember,
listen*) to the imagined direct speech of *they* in three big breaths (at
the end of each long sentence), plus one more for the final couplet.
Through these breaths, the poem wriggles deeper and deeper into
the voice of the enemy. *They* become bossier and bossier. In their
final *whisper*, after the last breath, *they* shift from *can be done* to *must
be done*. But *I*, imagining all this, undercuts 'their' bossiness.

Their undercutting happens through increasingly seductive
images of what *they* supposedly want to *tax* and punish rain for.
Lying full length, dreamy complexity, touches lips, assuagement, slake,

thrilling, showering, balming, scented baths. With its *yesses* and *no's*, its *splashing, muddying* and *amusing itself*, rain behaves charmingly, naturally, sensually, like a child or animal. It enriches, disturbs, soothes. It is unpredictable, paradoxical and basic (*roots*), lengthens lines, revels in the languor of nature outside (*long straight sedate green waters*), then can charge *indoors* and act (in short lines) directly on *our lips.* Its contradictions (*yesses and no's*) include *brusque hot needles* but also *balming assuagement.*

The poem builds up rain's power through the hissing of S repeated after a short vowel (as in *tax*, but also *best, weakest, strongest, yesses, processes, complexity, yes* and *must*), and also in *sense, soaking, splashing, grass, sleeves, lakes, straight sedate, city, processes, assuagement, slake, thirsts, brusque* and *whisper.* In the fifth line (*listen to its yesses*), the *rain*'s is the voice the *I* first hears before imagining the punitive voice of *they.* At the end the S hiss invades the voice of the opposition. It is *they* who *whisper.* Through rain's imaginary persecutors and their speech, in fact, the poem brings out all the attractive sensuality of *rain*, showing up as absurd (as in the whole title image, *taxing rain*) 'their' possessive attitude to nature.

On the journey of this poem, the music and imagery are part of each other. The musical journey takes the sound of the title image into the heart of the enemy, the voice of that *they.* The image-journey develops the absurd idea of *taxing rain.* By developing activities for which the materialist voices supposedly want to tax and punish rain – all the wayward generous things rain stands for in our lives and world – the poem makes clear the absurdity is on the other side. Would-be controllers who think they own the earth and see it in financial terms are the ones who are really absurd.

Midnight Salvage: Poem 6

Past the curve where the old craftsman was run down
there's a yard called Midnight Salvage
He was walking in the road which was always safe
The young driver did not know that road
its curves or that people walked there
or that you could speed yet hold the curve
watching for those who walked there
such skills he did not have being in life unpracticed

but I have driven that road in madness and driving rain
thirty years in love and pleasure and grief-blind
on ice I have driven it and in the vague haze of summer
between clumps of daisies and sting of fresh cowflop odors
lucky I am I hit nobody old or young
killed nobody left no trace
practiced in life as I am

Rich, born in 1929, is one of America's best-known poets, has published nearly twenty volumes of poetry and criticism, and received many prizes. Her passionately political, personal, resonant work explores myth, her Jewish heritage, love, sexual politics and much more. It stands up for compassion, with ferocious focus but the freest possible forms. Reading her, you feel forcibly how the way words work on the page, if they are the right words, itself expresses integrity, generosity and freedom. She was a vital voice in the mid-Sixties (and was attacked as a 'radical lesbian feminist') in feminist and anti-war movements.

She received the National Book Award for her 1973 collection *Diving into the Wreck*, which speaks of rescuing something from heartbreak by diving into the centre of the pain. A shipwreck is a perfect image of past disaster. George Seferis's masterpiece 'Thrush', written in 1946 after the German occupation of Greece, reflects on the horrors of the occupation and war, and is titled for a ship sunk in that war; Rich's wreck is an equally layered image. Her exploration of it expresses many things at once. The sunk hulk is the past: the poet's, but also that of all women in a culture and a history controlled by men. Her 'dive' explores the crusted myths of war between the sexes. The poet-explorer has a knife to cut her way in (and cut apart the structures), a camera to record the finds and a 'book of myths'. The poem is a quest for truths inside the myths, of which the poet herself is part. She is after *the wreck and not the story of the wreck / the thing itself and not the myth*.

Twenty years after *Diving into the Wreck*, her sequence *Midnight Salvage* took further this image of rescue. Rich often works without punctuation and in this poem that absence has particular point. The car that veered off the road killing a man also ignored punctuation: rules of driving, above all of stopping; the 'craft' of the road. In *life*, there are no stop signs. In this poem, all we have to depend on is words. Their rhythm, their *speed*.

Leaving unpunctuated that most classical of forms, the sonnet, and lengthening the traditional fourteen lines by adding one more, Rich crafts a poem whose paradoxes of form match what it is talking about: control and its failure, destruction of trusted craft, potentially disastrous moments of recklessness versus the luck of survival.

The first chunk is an octet in very simple language. Though it is about death on a *curve*, the first three words take us, the readers, safely *past* danger. This part of the poem is about being *safe*, about a *road which was always safe* (bringing out the safety in the title image, *salvage*). After the key word *salvage* and the next end-word, *safe*, there is no full stop. Yet a capital letter comes at the beginning of the following sentence. This poem is about observing but not obeying the rules of the poem's own road.

The lethal *curve* appears again, first in the plural at the beginning of a line, then at the end of the next, as if the driver is skidding from one end of the line to the other, seeing *curves* suddenly on the opposite side of the *road*. At the end of the fifth line, *curve* is balanced by *walked there*, two emphatic long syllables (like *run down* and *that road*), which are repeated in the same place in the seventh line. These *people* have always *walked there*, in the same place on *that road* which *the young driver did not know*. Young drivers do not know that much, yet, about *people* and their not knowing can destroy *old* craft.

The octet's last line explains why: lack of *skills*. The poem does not blame the driver. Instead it turns from simple language to a new register: language you might use in a legal document, a ceremonious, painstaking form of explanation. The participle *being* is like the present participles in police reports. The inversion of normal word order (*he did not have such skills, I am lucky, I am practiced in life*) stresses the words *skills, life,* and the unusual negative *unpracticed* (rather than, say, 'inexperienced'). Just before the turn of the sonnet, before the sestet, the poet summons a more archaic formal tone to sum up the cause of the tragedy.

The second chunk is a traditional sestet plus one more explanatory line, *practiced in life as I am.* The octet was about tragedy that came from being *unpracticed.* This second part is wilder. Longer lines, more compound words, more imagery. It is about taking *that road* and its *curve* in all sorts of danger, both outside (*ice, haze,* and *rain, driving* against a *driven* car) and inside: *madness,* 'blinding' passions of *love* and *grief,* distractions of *pleasure* and the senses (*vague haze of summer, daisies, sting of fresh cowflop odors*). It is about luck that gets you through safely, acquiring *skills* of holding *the curve* at *speed,* becoming *practiced in life.*

The extra last line is, as it were, the lucky line. The sonnet proper ends on a half-rhyme with the octet's talismanic word *safe: trace.* Then we get the extra, the reason for the poet's good luck, *practiced in life as I am,* answering *unpracticed.* No blame, just a contrast of good and bad luck.

This poem on the death of a *craftsman* is about speed, movement, and *skills,* so its own movement, skills, craft and rhythm are crucial. The first three lines start out in dactylic metre.

A dactyl is a long syllable followed by two shorts. It comes from the Greek for 'finger', *daktulos,* a word which is itself a long syllable followed by two shorts. Poets often use it together with its opposite, two short syllables followed by a long: an anapaest. (A word which also illustrates the rhythm it refers to.) Poets have always used both dactyls and anapaests for quick-flowing rhythm and a story. The *Iliad, Odyssey* and *Aeneid,* epic poems that flow on through long adventurous narratives, all open and continue with dactyls. So we are starting at speed, in words that talk of speed and movement, and instantly introduce the lethal *curve.*

But the first line bumps down into two spondees. A spondee is two long syllables, the metrical unit that slows a line most: *craftsman, was run.* The line ends in a single long (*down*). The second line has only one anapaest (*there's a yard*) before the same dragging effect begins. More spondees: *called Mid*, *night Salv*. The dragging rhythm and long final syllable of both lines give sound to what the words describe: a car slowing when it runs into a man, a walk that ends in death.

The third line is another pentameter. Again it begins dactylic (*he was walk-*), but ends in a different rhythm dominated suddenly by the iamb (short long): *-ing in / the road*. There is one more dactyl (*which was al-*) but we end up iambic (*-ways safe*).

We began with a six-beat line, went on with a three- or four-beat line, and now settle into pentameter, the default metre of English-language poetry and Shakespearean blank verse: the mainly iambic line of five beats. The feet are felt as iambs, though for any of them poets can use a spondee, dactyl, anapaest, trochee (long syllable followed by a short) or tribrach (three shorts) instead of an iamb. This is the metre into which, since the sixteenth century, English verse has 'naturally' fallen. The safest metre, for a *road that was always safe*.

But the next change of rhythm gets across at once how unsafe any *safe* really is. The next four lines focus on *The young driver*, and as soon as he comes in we hear natural speech rhythms, and a stress on *young*, *driv-*, *know* and *road*. The octet ends in a line as long as the opening but changing the tone, which gives the cause of the accident. Lack of *skills*, lack of practice *in life*.

The second part, the part of the sonnet that normally opens out the idea or turns it round, begins with *but*. The speaker signals the contrast of her own experience of *that road* with *the young driver*'s. It begins with an iamb (*but I*), and rings changes from six-beat to three-beat lines as if the voice is driving *curves*. Slowing, speeding, it continues what the octet began, repeating combinations of words (*that road*, lines four and nine; *walked there*, lines five and seven; *I have driven*, lines nine and eleven; *nobody*, lines thirteen and fourteen; *I am*, lines thirteen and fifteen); suggesting a route *driven* over and over again past and through the same words, landmarks and *curves*.

The poem moves through swerves of attention to different people. First the *old craftsman*, then *the young driver*, then *I*. Also from present-tense description (*there's a yard*) to past-tense continuous narrative (*he was walking*), on to past-historic narrative (*did not know*, *did not have*), to the perfect tense (*I have driven*), and back to the present in a personal way. (*I am*, rather than the impersonal *there's a yard*.) By this journey, the poem performs a similar rescue to Rich's earlier collection *Diving into the Wreck*. Something is 'salvaged' from disaster. The word has undertones of 'salvation' and 'safety'. The irony, in this poem, is that it is done in the dark, and *the yard called Midnight Salvage* is *past* the place *where the old craftsman was run down*.

As *the young driver* lacked *skills*, so the poem lacks the most basic writing tool, punctuation. But it does have all the ancient tricks by which words, their rhythm, pace and tone, hang together to make a beautiful, deeply felt artefact. In honour of an *old craftsman*'s death, what it 'salvages' is craft.

7   W. N. Herbert

Breakfrost

The frost is touching everything before the sun:
each blade has a pencil nudity that makes
the yolk-like orange seem already old,
each flatness reached, brick-like,
as though all cold was urban.
Sheep crunch its windscreen splinters,
horses' heads are glued to it down the blue
flanks of shade. Each leaf is a sucrose flake.
Its intimacy is more exhausting than light.

Morning's sepia, like medieval photographs,
has to fight its way through every scattered grain.
And hollows will persist, like patches left
by the Dark Age bulks of giant sleeping saints,
since Christianity was like a glacier.

Each shadow stuck to it like a tongue
is long and brittle. Everything is biscuit,
feather, spit, viscous, barbed, as though
the land was bait for light, hooking it
and holding it close, gutting the photons
for their kernels of warmth.

Herbert, born in 1961 in Dundee, lectures at Newcastle University
and writes both in English and Scottish. He has been called a cross
between MacDiarmid, Dostoevsky and Desperate Dan; his imagina-
tive poems, visually sharp, filigreed and illuminated, full of puns and
wordplay, are always fresh and surprising, at a teasing angle both to
the Scottish tradition and to its relationship with English poetry.

The Laurelude, title of the book from which this poem comes, is
a pun on Wordsworth's *Prelude* with a nod to the relations between
what Herbert calls the 'Laurel and Hardy of nations': Scotland and
England. Its subjects range from Czech cartoons to Burt Lancaster,

Robbie Burns, William Burroughs, and a 'sensitive male publisher' who realises, when his wife has a baby, it is over nine months since he made love to her.

The title of this poem is another pun. This is a winter 'breakfast' when *frost* 'breaks' up in morning sunshine. The journey is from *frost* to *warmth*. The first stanza moves from *frost* to *light*, the second from *Morning's sepia* to *glacier* (echoing *sepia*), the third from *shadow* to *warmth*. It is a counterpoint of dark (see *Dark Age*) and *cold*, *light* and *warmth*, a white pastoral which does not mention white (the nearest it gets is *sucrose*) but rather *orange*, *blue* and *sepia*; a world of *light* (lines nine and eighteen) punctuated by *hollows*, *Dark Age*, *shadow*, ending with *photons* (which picks up *photograph*), all dominated by the noun that begins it, *frost*. In the second stanza, *morning's sepia* has to *fight its way through* this *frost*. In the third, *shadow* is *stuck to it*.

The poem gives a detailed picture, like a medieval manuscript, of what *frost* touches. It is as particular in its attention as the *frost* itself. Between the *everything* of the first and sixteenth lines, we get *each* four times (for *blade*, *flatness*, *leaf* and *shadow*). It is a poem without people except the sensibility of the poet-observer: a Disney's *Fantasia* vision of elemental competition between cold and warmth, light and dark. And yet it is all impression. The unspoken observer (through *like* and *as though*) records how this world comes across subjectively, suggesting this has an emotional effect (*its intimacy is more exhausting*) on the observer (or some imagined observer). This 'seeming' is recorded in apparently objective statements: *each blade has*, *each leaf is*, *each shadow is*, *everything is*.

From the second line, among the physical details we get analytical abstract nouns, as if an art historian were commenting on a manuscript: *pencil nudity*, *flatness*, *intimacy*. This commenting voice moves on via *medieval* (and the surprise of coupling that word, in playful anachronism, to *photographs*) to make historical comparisons (*like*, *like*), revealing the landscape not only as a work of art (as in the first stanza) but as an emotional geology, affected by the weight and movement of religion (*giant saints*, *Christianity like a glacier*).

In the last stanza, this comment voice sums up what *everything* looks like in five nouns and adjectives that take us further into the poem's final images of the *land* as a fish-hook aimed at catching *light*, and of individual *photons* like caught trout *gutted* for *warmth*.

The sound conjures the crunchiness of cracking ice. The title's key consonants ricochet all through, climaxing in the final stanza.

94

T in *frost, nudity, flatness, splinters, to it, its intimacy, exhausting, light, fight its, scattered, persist, patches left, saints, Christianity, stuck to it, tongue, brittle, biscuit, spit, bait, light, it, it, gutting.* The K of *makes, yolk-like, brick-like, cold, crunch, windscreen, flanks, sucrose flake; like, scattered, Dark, bulks, Christianity, like;* and *stuck, biscuit, viscous, hooking, close, kernels.*

Musically, vowels hold together this cracking, breaking world. The O of the key feeling, *cold*, is prepared for by *old* and *yolk*, underlined by *as though, hollows* (in the central line of the central stanza, the lowest point of the picture), *shadow*, and *as though*, and reappears paradoxically in *holding close*. The winter landscape is still *cold*, even in the *light*. The short U of *sun* is prepared for by *touching*, echoed in *urban* and *crunch*, opened out in *grain*, comes back properly in *tongue* and *long*, and lingers on in *photons*. The EE of *each* runs on through *seem, each, sheep, windscreen, each leaf, sepia, medieval, sleeping, each.*

But each stanza also has a soundworld of its own, as the poem moves from straight description through historical fancy into the metaphorical close. In the first, the long U of *nudity* is picked up in *glue, blue,* and *sucrose*. The third has that violent word *fight*, whose long I (as in the unspoken word *ice*), is repeated in *like* and *like*, moving us further into metaphor. The last is dominated by the short I of *brittle*: *it, is, is biscuit, spit, viscous, it, it.*

The poem journeys towards an *as though*, a metaphorical way of seeing this land. In keeping with this journey, the structure too looks 'like' normal stanzas which are not, when you look close, equal. It starts with a nine-line stanza whose line-ends hold it together (*sun/urban, makes/flake, brick-like/light*) but not in a hearable pattern. Then we have a five-line stanza, held together by ends to the inner lines, *grain* and *saints*. Then a six-line stanza, bonded by *tongue/photons, biscuit/hooking it*. The appearance is contradicted by the details.

Through its structure, as well as its images and counter-intuitive or anachronistic ideas (*as though all cold were urban; medieval photographs, Christianity like a glacier, bait for light*), the poem reveals a winter landscape touched both by *frost* and *sun*. A landscape which is 'like' what we know but different. Full, when we look close, of waywardness and surprise. But does this surprising-ness belong to the land, or to the imagination and impressions of the observer? By interweaving subjective and objective, *is* and *like*, the poem has bound the two so close we cannot tell.

Granny Scarecrow

Tears flowed at the chapel funeral,
more beside the grave on the hill. Nevertheless,
    after the last autumn ploughing,
they crucified her old flowered print housedress
        live, on a pole.

Marjorie and Emily, shortcutting to school,
used to pass and wave; mostly Gran would wave back.
    Two white Sunday gloves
flapped good luck from the crossbar; her head's plastic sack
        would nod, as a rule.

But when winter arrived, her ghost thinned.
The dress began to look starved in its field of snowcorn.
    One glove blew off and was lost.
The other hung blotchy with mould from the hedgerow, torn
        by the wind.

Emily and Marjorie noticed this.
Without saying why, they started to avoid the country way
    through the cornfield. Instead they walked
from the farm up the road to the stop where they
        caught the bus.

And it caught them. So in time they married.
Marjorie, divorced, rose high in the catering profession.
    Emily had children and grandchildren, though,
with the farm sold, none found a cross to fit their clothes when
        Emily and Marjorie died.

Born in England to American parents in 1933, Stevenson grew up
in Michigan where her father was a philosophy professor, came back
to England in the Fifties and now lives in the north-east. She has
published fifteen poetry collections, criticism and biography

(focusing particularly on other American poets, Plath and Bishop).

Stevenson originally wanted to be a musician and feels, like Walter Pater, that 'All art aspires to the condition of music'. Her clear, cadenced poems have subtle, unshowy grace and radiate a sense of being on the edge. She writes, as she has lived, between puritan New England and England itself. Time and history are important themes. The America she grew up in, she says, 'no longer really exists'. Her breakthrough book *Correspondences* (1974) focused on a nineteenth- and twentieth-century archive of letters of an American family over several generations. 'Granny Scarecrow', first published in 2002, is set in England and driven by a vision of change to land and people over five generations (from *Gran* to Emily's *grandchildren*). At its heart is loss. Its journey is from *tears* to *died*. The tone is elegy, beginning with *Gran*, opening out to a whole lost way of life. The passage of time is marked at the beginning of stanzas one (*Tears flowed*), three (*but when*) and five: *it caught them. So in time* . . .

The first stanza opens in a closed, rural, ritualised world (*chapel; last autumn ploughing*). The rustic ceremonial tone prepares us (a little) for the oddly violent metaphor *crucified*. The next stanza introduces the next generation, already making changes (*short-cutting*) but still keeping the affection implied in *tears* (*wave, wave back*), and using the frequentative, imperfect tense for actions done over and over again (*used to pass, would wave, would nod*). The third stanza opens with *but*, introduces change (*began to look*), uses the past historic tense (*arrived, thinned, blew, was lost*) and describes a falling off (*thinned, starved*) – a dimming, loss, and spoiling (*lost, blotchy, torn*).

Things are moving fast. The girls react. Changes spark change in them (*started to avoid*). The fourth stanza continues the past historic (*noticed, walked, caught*) which moves away from the archaic ceremonies with which the poem began. The girls *started to avoid the country way*. The rural is passing: the line sums up what the poem is about, the abandonment of 'country ways'. The girls take to *the road, the stop, the bus*. In the last stanza, they cannot change anything.

It is the bus that *caught them*, but the way it is put, at the opening of the stanza, makes it sound as if the new world has also *caught them* and absorbed them into urban life. They were part of the world's change, but can do nothing about it now. The *farm* has been *sold*, their lives are different from *Gran*'s in her *housedress*. One is *divorced*, and *high in the catering profession*.

The scarecrow's two lost gloves parallel the two girls. One *blew off and was lost* (or *divorced*). The other *hung in the hedge*. Lives still come and go in the countryside. Some women have *children and grandchildren*, others are on their own and rising *high*. But the old custom of finding a cross *to fit the clothes* of the dead has (the poem's last word) *died*.

Stevenson always experiments with form and music. In this poem she has centred the lines to give a visual echo of the main image: Granny's clothes (standing for the *old* world, the old *print*) *crucified* as a scarecrow, arms spread *on a pole*. Each line is a *crossbar* or (in the last stanza) a *cross*, slung on the poem's centred axis.

The rhyme scheme is also centred. The two outside lines rhyme (a consonant rhyme: *funeral/pole*; *this/bus, married/died, school/ rule*). So do the inner lines, the second and second-last (*never-theless/housedress, profession/when*). But the central line stands free.

'End-rhymes are not enough,' Stevenson has said. 'Every word-sound in a poem should find an echo in another, neighbouring word's sound.' Elegy likes long vowel-soundss, and the sound which blows through this poem which begins in *tears* is the O of *old*; of lament. It returns in the middle stanza in *ghost, snowcorn, hedgerow* and *mould* (that sign of age and neglect which rhymes with *old*). It returns again in the last stanza with *So, rose, though, sold, clothes*. En route through the poem, the long O is supported by the related OO of *school, rule* and *blew*. While in the long I of *beside, crucified, live, white, arrived, why, time, high*, the poem prepares for the last word, *died*.

The word *crucified* suggests a violent side to this loss. From the start, the poem has an uneasy relation to what it mourns. It begins with straightforward *tears*, but *nevertheless, they crucified* (that unnamed *they* echoing the Gospels). Crucified what? *Her old housedress – live*. That startling word *live* prepares us for its opposite. Granny Scarecrow is dead; but has an afterlife as a *ghost*. At first a benign waving presence (*mostly, as a rule*) in a *field, it* encourages the girls on their own *way* to *school* and a new world.

The *but* begins in the central stanza, with *winter*. The field has *snowcorn* in it, the *ghost* has *thinned* (as the long I of *arrived* thins to *thinned* and *wind*). S*nowcorn* (which might be winter wheat or a metaphor for frost) sounds beautiful but un-nourishing. The older generation fades into the barren picturesque while the younger catches the bus *from the farm*, moving away *from* the old.

Yet there was cruelty as well as warmth in the old *way*. See *crucified* and *live* at the beginning. No one now looks out *a cross to fit clothes* when people die, but who wants a *cross* in their life? The poem elegises the old *country way* and the *cornfield*, but admits there was pain in it. Granny's *housedress* on its *pole* hung *high* for a while (though one glove ended hanging in a hedge). Marjorie *rose high in her profession*. Not all changes are loss.

Salopian

All day, the drone of a saw,
and resin across the pines
of dark Mortimer Forest.
With each completed sever
it fell by a whining octave.

By dusk, in the clearing they'd made,
all that remained was their dust,
the dottle from someone's pipe
and ranks of seasoning limbs
weeping congealing amber.

*

The heat, the fragrance of hay,
the incontrovertible end
of summer, the country halt,
boarding the single-track train,
weeds prising the platform oblique
where they waved and waved and waved.

*

Dewed cowslips, roses, the grave
under a yew in the garden
of lichened Pipe Aston church,
a dusty Visitors' Book. . . .

We were once there: 17th
of June 1975.

Born in 1946 in Liverpool, Reading is a deeply original dis-
enchanted romantic, fiercely erudite, savage, comic, with a wild
range of forms. Over many collections, his poems are driven by fury
at pain, ugliness, brutality, and the need to make poetry matter so

much it jolts you into seeing newly. He often brings classical Greek and Roman metres to bear on modern squalor (he's been called the 'laureate of grot'). He plays with and messes up poetic form to parallel the way contemporary life toys with and messes up the world.

His poems can look as rebarbative as a litter-strewn street. He hauls tabloid atrocities, graffiti and naïve, ill-spelt letters into poems as fossil evidence (he often uses imagery from geology and pathology) for what our barbaric species gets up to. He also throws in typographic strangeness: lacunae, square brackets, crossings out. He replaces words with symbols, breaks syntax into fragments, piles words on top of each other like dangerous bricks, and plays with different voices (like his cleaner's) and uses 'found' material: statements from newspapers, things overheard on the street. One poem, following the court report of youths who mugged an elderly couple, ends by satirising in tabloid headlines not only the poem but its poet trying to witness to pain, in a fist shake at poetry's weakness to do anything about a tragedy: *Trite impotent iambic journalese,/ Reading Raps Raiders/Poet Pete Protests.*

He maintains poetry's dignity and importance paradoxically, therefore, by making it tackle the grubbiest things. His poems point out he *doesn't make it up you know.* Glossing over ghastliness would mean admitting poetry has no human point any more, is not up to modern life. His poems (especially his powerful book *C*, a hundred poems on cancer) insist poetry must address the pity of things but not prettify. *Muse, sing the grotty. Scant alternative.*

This poem is gentler and more conventional than most: almost tongue-in-cheek conventional. It is pastoral, set in a country churchyard like Thomas Gray's famous 1751 poem 'Elegy Written in a Country Churchyard'.

The title is an archaic word meaning 'from Shropshire' (as in Shrewsbury's Salopian Brewing Company or Salopia Coaches). Reading lives in Shropshire, which after the Norman conquest was called Salopshire and then Salop. The title gestures to Shropshire's famous public school Shrewsbury (whose old boys are Salopians) and the male pastoral of Housman's *A Shropshire Lad*. (A poem in the same collection, evoking an inmate in Shrewsbury Prison, is called 'Shropshire Lads'.) So the title warns us to keep an eye out for death and boys; maybe the death of boys. Maybe, you wonder on a first read, that *grave* belongs to a *Salopian*, an old boy from Shrewsbury.

The first stanza suggests the poem is about time (*all day*) and change (*completed, fell*). By the second (following the first with an asterisk, as if to suggest time passing), time has moved to *dusk*. Not much 'remains' now. Chopped stumps are *weeping*. The third stanza has no main verb and feels like a lopped heap (as in the *clearing* after the *saw*) of perceptions and memories (*heat, fragrance*, some *incontrovertible end*; a *halt*; a repeated *waving* on a *platform*).

The fourth stanza reaches *the grave*, the churchyard, a *Visitors' Book*, and ends in a row of dots. The last two lines are not separated from the last stanza by an asterisk like the others. They seem to be not part of the poem's structure but a comment on it, such as *visitors* write in a *book*, signing up to the place, the moment.

The death images that lead up to *grave* begin with *sever* and *fell. Dusk*, in this context (a poem implying the ancient image of life as a day), might hint at the evening of life, picked up by *dust* (a traditional image for the dead), *all that remained, dottle from someone's pipe, limbs, weeping* and *congealing*. By the end of the second stanza, the build-up of images makes it feel as if the *drone* and *whining* of the *saw* have been the noise of battle, the felled trees were *ranks* of felled soldiers, and *all that* 'remains' is the soldiers' *dust* and *limbs*, blood and wounds (rather than *resin*) *congealing*; and *weeping. Seasoning* suggests not only chopped trunks becoming timber but young soldiers becoming 'seasoned' veterans (or dead heroes).

Reading is drawing on one of poetry's oldest images for human mortality, which runs through Homer, Virgil, Milton, and later English classics. Men die like leaves, soldiers fall on the field like a pine falling on the mountain or poppies in harvested corn.

Gerard Manley Hopkins uses the same image in three poems which all, I guess, stand behind this one.[4] He describes poplar trees as *fresh and following folded ranks* being *felled*; tells a young girl *grieving*, when *autumn* leaves fall *like the things of man*, that she is really grieving for herself, her own mortality; and in talking of our blindness to that mortality says we all *wave with the meadow* and forget the *sour scythe* of death is approaching. The same image, of course, lay behind Pete Seeger's Sixties song 'Where have all the flowers gone?'. The young men in that song have all *gone to graveyards.*

Another young man's fall is in here too: another light going out. Phaethon, whose name means 'Shining', son of the Greek sun god, drove his father's chariot too near the sun and fell. (See *fell* in the first stanza.) His sisters wept so much that they turned into black poplars weeping amber tears. (See *weeping, congealing, amber*.)

So when we get to the third and longest stanza's *country halt* and *single-track train*, the *weeds* suggest mourners' weeds as well as a countryside empty of young men (who might normally pull up destructive *weeds*). The images shout World War One: women waving and waving from the *platform*, Housmanesque lads surrounded by *fragrance of hay* boarding a *single-track train* never to return in September 1914 (much more *end of summer* than the poem's month *June*); and also the *incontrovertible end* of an era. This 'waving' line, the poem's longest, lengthens the stanza as if the emotional farewell steals a line from the stanza to follow.

There are four stanzas, like the spring, summer, autumn and winter of a life. The journey, from *forest* to *garden*, rests on the organic image of human life with its seasons and days, sap, wither and fall. The fourth stanza, the shortest, has more plants. But instead of the first stanza's *pines* in a *dark forest*, we get *yew*, a *garden*, *lichen* round a church. There's *dust*, as in the second stanza, but now on a *Visitors' Book*. The war is over, *clearing* has been *made*, the waving and *weeping* done. Even the *book* is *dusty*. There is nothing for us observers and aftercomers to do except record our visit.

This poem which plunders classical literature also has a classical metre. The first line of each stanza starts with a spondee: *all day, by dusk, dewed cow-*. So does the extra couplet (*we were*). But mainly this is anapaestic trimeter, a three-beat line based on the anapaest (like *seventeenth*). Anapaests are commonest in limericks but also turn up in mournful poems like Matthew Arnold's 'Rugby Chapel'.

Musically, 'Salopian' is held together by long vowels. Above all the AY of *grave*, prepared for by *day, octave, made, remained, fragrance, hay, train, waved, waved, waved*, which finds a disguised half-echo in the IVE of the last syllable, *1975*. Also the OR of the opening word (which signals the theme's universality) *all*, and the EE of *each, completed, seasoning, weeping, congealing, heat, oblique, we*, and the last syllable of *17th*.

The poem also balances echo-words in and across lines within a stanza: a balancing trick perfected by Roman poets. In the first stanza, *pines* at the end of a line balances *whining* in the middle. In the second, *dusk* at a beginning see-saws against *dust* at the end. In the third, *heat* at the beginning of a line balances *oblique* at the end of another. In the fourth, *garden* at the end balances *Aston* in the middle.

It is all even and complete, but fades away in dots. This *end* is not entirely *incontrovertible*. The last stanza lacks something. Not only has its fifth line been taken by the previous stanza: it also lacks witnesses and the personal voice. And so we get the extra, unintegrated couplet; and this poem, which began in *all* and *each*, journeys finally to *we*. The time and place recorded at the end stand for all places, dates, private memories and attachments lost as *each completed sever* of the *saw* falls across our own lives.

The poem's journey is towards *the grave*. We are not told whose. The very specific time and place, the *once* of *we were once there*, suggests it could be a particular grave; but at another level it seems to be everyone's. We are all, in a sense, *visitors* at a *country halt*, and all of our *single-track* to our journey's *end* will fade away in dots. You can even read the line with *grave* in it as spanning the whole arc of life itself, from *dewed cowslips* (life's morning and spring) through *roses* (life's prime and summer) to *the grave*. So though 'Salopian' seems to move from universal to personal, *each* to *we*, it also moves from the particular (this particular *saw*, *clearing*, *country halt*, church *garden*) to the universal. *We* are all implicated in this journey, in mortality.

Brazil, January 1, 1502

> . . . embroidered nature . . . tapestried landscape.
> *Landscape Into Art*, by Sir Kenneth Clark

Januaries, Nature greets our eyes
exactly as she must have greeted theirs:
every square inch filling in with foliage –
big leaves, little leaves, and giant leaves,
blue, blue-green, and olive,
with occasional lighter veins and edges,
or a satin underleaf turned over;
monster ferns
in silver-gray relief,
and flowers, too, like giant water lilies
up in the air – up, rather, in the leaves –
purple, yellow, two yellows, pink,
rust red and greenish white;
solid but airy; fresh as if just finished
and taken off the frame.

A blue-white sky, a simple web,
backing for feathery detail:
brief arcs, a pale-green broken wheel,
a few palms, swarthy, squat, but delicate;
and perching there in profile, beaks agape,
the big symbolic birds keep quiet,
each showing only half his puffed and padded,
pure-coloured or spotted breast.
Still in the foreground there is Sin:
five sooty dragons near some massy rocks.
The rocks are worked with lichens, gray moonbursts
splattered and overlapping,
threatened from underneath by moss
in lovely hell-green flames,

attacked above
by scaling-ladder vines, oblique and neat,
'one leaf yes and one leaf no' (in Portuguese).

The lizards scarcely breathe; all eyes
are on the smaller, female one, back-to,
her wicked tail straight up and over,
red as a red-hot wire.

Just so the Christians, hard as nails,
tiny as nails, and glinting,
in creaking armor, came and found it all,
not unfamiliar:
no lovers' walks, no bowers,
no cherries to be picked, no lute music,
but corresponding, nevertheless,
to an old dream of wealth and luxury
already out of style when they left home –
wealth, plus a brand-new pleasure.
Directly after Mass, humming perhaps
L'Homme armé or some such tune,
they ripped away into the hanging fabric,
each out to catch an Indian for himself –
those maddening little women who kept calling,
calling to each other (or had the birds waked up?)
and retreating, always retreating, behind it.

Bishop (1911–79) is one of the twentieth century's best and most loved poets. She won nearly every poetry prize in America when alive; today her standing increases by the hour. Twenty years ago, many British students had never heard of her. Now she is on first-year 'Introduction to Poetry' courses. Even people who read no other poet love Bishop's work. She is a constantly growing influence, at the basis of any modern canon.

She was born in Massachusetts. When she was eight months old her builder father died; when she was five, her mother disappeared into a mental home. She grew up with grandparents. At Vassar she met Marianne Moore, a lifelong friend. Her first collection appeared in 1946; then she met Robert Lowell, another lifelong friend. For sixteen years through the Fifties and Sixties she lived in Brazil with the architect Lota de Macedo Soares. Twelve of their years together were the happiest Bishop ever knew. But Lota, battling mental illness and arteriosclerosis, started fighting with all her friends. In 1967 she committed suicide. In 1970 Bishop began teaching at Harvard. She too battled depression, alcoholism, asthma and psoriasis. Her generation of American writers was the first to grow up after the Modernist revolution. They matured during the Depression and the Second World War and (coincidence or not) many were scarred by alcoholism, family break-ups, mental problems and suicide.

Bishop is an intensely personal poet and readers have very personal reactions to her. But she was not 'confessional'. She was a wonderful correspondent (*One Art*, her selected letters, is on the shelf of anyone seriously interested in contemporary poetry) and some of her letters are very frank and open.[5] But the poems are not after self-expression. There are landscapes, seascapes, historical, biological and philosophical explorations. She was a passionate admirer of Darwin's writings. Ideas, and a constantly foraging musical craft, shape the poems.

So does her painter's eye. She was a gifted primitive painter herself.[6] The personal emotion collects in her visual detail, giving the descriptions an extraordinary intensity. One of her first memories was of a swan boat ride with her mother (still in mourning for her father) in Boston. A swan bit her mother's finger. She always remembered *The hole in the black glove and a drop of blood on it*. Her poem 'The Sandpiper' describes a bird running along a shore (*Poor bird, he is obsessed*). She explained that 'All my life I have lived and behaved very like a sandpiper, just running along the edges of different countries and continents, looking for something'.

Early critics, tuned to confessional poetry, missed this intensity. They called her poetry cool and distanced. Few would say that now.

This poem from her Brazil years describes jungle round Rio not only through her own painter's eye but also as it *must have* seemed when the first Christian colonisers came. It is about going into (and how you see) a new world; about people seeing *Nature* as a man-made thing, a tapestry; about the fact that how people see nature determines what they do to it.

Its journey is from apparently objective seeing, a could-be innocent eye on virgin jungle, to subjective seeing which applies to this jungle its own alien moralising values – which (by the end) are openly hypocritical. Seeing jungle in Christian terms, the colonisers damage it, importing the *Sin* they think they find there. The journey ends with them acting on *Sin* (*a brand-new pleasure*). Seeing Nature as art, they 'rip into' what they see as *hanging fabric*. The loss of Eden, Fall of Man, colonial rape and exploitation all shadow this poem's journey; but very subtly.

The title controls how we react as we read. *January 1, 1502* says this is about beginnings. *January* derives from *ianua*, Latin for door. (Two-headed Janus is god of the door.) *Januaries*, the first word, picks up *January* of the title, but the plural shows they are repeated. The poem pitches us into two worlds: the modern world where *our eyes* see, but also the beginning of a particular year at the beginning of the sixteenth century. The speaker (in *we*) experiences *January* and *Nature* here over and over, but the second line takes us from the speaker's world to the new sixteenth century, to see not only through *our eyes* but *theirs*. *Must have* takes us back five hundred years, to the first colonists in (as we know from the title) *Brazil*. Who were (as the last line of the second section reminds us) *Portuguese*. From the second line, the whole poem is an imaginative leap into their response to *Nature's* greeting.

The first section sets going a voice of art criticism appropriate to the art critic Kenneth Clark cited in the epigraph. A way of seeing which does to Brazilian jungle what the title of his book describes, turns *Nature* into art. Two arts, in fact: painting and words. This art-crit voice is knowledgeable, points things out (*every square inch filling in with foliage*, as if on a Rousseau canvas), and uses technical words (*relief*) precisely, almost pedantically (*occasional lighter veins and edges*).

But another voice comes in, more individual and impressionistic. *Big*, *little*, *giant* (twice) and *monster* sound childlike. An innocent eye (to counteract the knowledgeable one) on an innocent landscape. Child-seeing; the infancy of seeing, like Adam in Paradise. *Monster* could be a joke, a smile. Or it could be the beginning of something more sinister, and if so is the beginning of emotional evaluation, rather than simply objective description. *Too* after *flowers*, and *rather* after *up*, move us further into the personal. This is not a critic's considered account but a confiding voice sharing immediate responses, letting us in to the retina, as the brain receives information of colours and flowers. This is a fresh seeing of *fresh* landscape, Edenic seeing for Edenic Nature.

A hundred and fifty years after those colonists came to Brazil, the seventeenth-century religious poet Thomas Traherne described with a brighter-than-bright glow his child perceptions (*those pure and virgin apprehensions I had in my infancy*) of growing up in Herefordshire, in his prose reflections, *Centuries of Meditations*:

> Certainly Adam in Paradise had not more sweet and curious apprehension of the world than I. All appeared new and strange at first, inexpressible rare and delightful and beautiful . . . I was a stranger, which at my entrance into the world was saluted and surrounded with innumerable joys . . . All things were spotless and pure and glorious. I knew not that there were sins or complaints or laws. I was entertained like an angel with the works of God; I saw all in the peace of Eden.[7]

His poems speak to the same kind of child-seeing, innocence in Eden, backlit by religion. Take 'Wonder':

> *Rare splendours, yellow, blue, red, white and green,*
> *Mine eyes did everywhere behold.*

Or 'Eden':

> *I knew not that there was a serpent's sting*
> *Whose poison shed*
> *On men did overspread*
> *The world.*

Or 'Innocence' itself:

> *My ravisht sense*
> *Was entertained in Paradise, and had a sight of Innocence,*
> *Which was beyond all bound and price.*

We hear all this in Bishop too. But at the end of her first section, *as if just finished* gestures back to the epigraph, with its freight of knowingness and art. These *eyes* are looking at the jungle as art, not *Nature*. There may be Eden here. Maybe God has *just finished* making it. But *taken off the frame* suggests the art is human, not divine; it suggests tapestry (as in the epigraph) and casts a retrospective eye back to *satin* (line seven), the first texture word in all this colour, size and shape. From here on, we will think of this jungle in terms of artefact, of woven softness.

The second section's first four lines bring back the art critic tone (*backing, detail, brief arcs*). More evaluative adjectives come in (*simple, delicate*); some (*monster*) might be symbolic too (*broken, swarthy*). When the poem turns from inanimate nature to animate, it pronounces the very word *symbolic*.

Symbolic changes everything. Nothing is *symbolic* in a vacuum. *Symbolic* means human beings, and we are looking not through *our* eyes but *theirs*. This is someone else's symbolism, and symbols mean seeing one thing in terms of a particular set of others. What these people see in this *fresh* tapestry is a product of their culture and thought.

But *symbolic* is also part of art criticism. The art critic voice describes the *birds* technically (*in profile*), cataloguing colours and pattern as it did leaves and flowers, presenting them as stiffly heraldic and male, withholding (from any *eyes*) half of what they are (*each showing only half his puffed breast*). What *eyes* see is not all the story.

Now we realise that everything *eyes* have registered so far was anyway only background. This section has sixteen lines. The eighth introduces the second half and the *foreground*. Its climax is *Sin*.

The poem's first two words had capital letters. Giving *Nature* a capital speaks to a human value system. We have seen not *nature* but *Nature* seen by specific *eyes*, as art; as something that *greets* us, something in relation to ourselves (whoever we are). *Sin*'s capital S follows suit. In twenty-four lines we have journeyed from *Nature* to *Sin*.

Sin appears at first as *sooty dragons*, part of the child voice but belonging also to the snowballing religious symbolism. Behind *symbolic birds, puffed and padded* (suggesting medieval knights) and *dragons* looms St George and the battle of Christian faith versus a Christian idea of *Sin*.

We do not yet know what these *dragons* (and *Sin*) look like. Instead the poem shifts to their *massy rocks*, described at first (like the *leaves* and *birds*) in art-speak. *Worked with lichens* (evoking tapestry). *Gray moonbursts* (like the *silver-gray relief*). Then the impressionistic voice bursts in. *Splattered* is not art-speak but violent, subjective. *Overlapping* echoes it, pushing the pace forward, giving us three short As in quick succession (*massy, splattered, overlapping*) followed swiftly by *attacked*. The vowels, like the colours, are *overlapping*. This impressionistic voice sees colours, too, in terms of drama, violence, subjectivity. The *moonbursts* (or *lichens*) are *threatened from underneath, attacked from above*. The moss is *lovely hell-green flames*.

We had green in the *foliage* (*blue-green, olive*). But that sounded objective. *Hell-green* is the opposite. Green is the traditional colour of dangerous magic, of Green Knights and serpent temptresses. The flame-ball which draws the princess in Disney's *Sleeping Beauty* to touch the spinning wheel is green. *Hell-green* picks up the religious harmonics (*symbolic, dragons, Sin*). And *lovely*? It enjoys the colour but also the violence (both of the visual effect, and of the associations), making clear how far we have moved from the objective tone we seemed to start with.

In two sections, the poem has moved from apparently objective to openly subjective, evaluative, *symbolic*. The *scaling-ladder vines* (evoking a town under siege), with their *Portuguese* pet name, show that the colonists named what they saw (like Adam in Eden) while projecting their values (and activities) upon it. The poem's journey so far has followed the imagined reactions of the colonists from a *fresh* gaze and apparently objective voice, to a subjective gaze that sees *hell* and *Sin* in Eden – and maybe enjoys it.

The small third section describes this *Sin*, these *dragons*. They are only *lizards*. But the drama begun with the *lichens* is continued with them. There is a female on heat, apparently. The moralism of the imagined Portuguese colonists moves instantly into sexuality. What is *wicked* is her tail, *red as a red-hot wire* (evoking other colours associated with hell: scarlet women, *hot* sex). *All eyes are on her*.

Eyes, and what they *are on*, focus for what the poem is about. *All eyes* leads straight to the *Christians*, the colonists themselves, whose eyes the poem has so far looked through. But *Just so* changes the perspective. The poem is no longer imagining this world through *their* eyes, but seeing them in this new world, acting upon it, making it their own – as art does.

They are *hard as nails* (picking up *red-hot wire* rhythmically as well as metallically). So far, most textures have been soft (*satin, leaves, veins*). Even *rocks* were *worked with lichens*. Threat and attack came from *moss* and *vines*. But the hard K of *Christians* introduces hard things: *armor, hard, glinting, creaking*.

Nature is now related entirely to them (*they found it all*). It is *not unfamiliar*. They came from sixteenth-century Europe; tokens of civilisation they know are absent (*bowers, lute music*) but they can see something *corresponding to* it. Not just an *old dream of luxury* (which all colonists exploiting another world's wealth enjoy, and often is *already out of style* back home) but *lovers' walks, cherries to be picked*.

Cherries follows the lizards' lead into sex and *brand-new pleasure*. This really is the Fall of Man. Only hardcore hypocrisy can blame the lizards for *Sin* now.

Brand's short A echoes the As of the attacking imagery in the second section. *Brand-new* also echoes the child-tone of *giant* and *monster*. These newcomers are 'branding' the world they have taken, setting their mark on it. The afterthought (*wealth, plus*) recalls the afterthought in the first section, when the poem refined its looking with a dash followed by *up, rather, in the leaves*. This introduces the shock of the ending, which begins at *Directly after Mass*.

Religion has been established. The colonists have imposed their own culture and with it their own *Sin*. *L'Homme armé* reflects the *padded* birds but also their own *armor* and hardness. *Ripped away into the hanging fabric* reflects the rape of the land, the femaleness of *Nature* (*she*, line two), the *worked* softness of the jungle (and tapestry, normally woven by women rather than men), and the femaleness of the *lizard* whose *tail* is *wicked* and *red-hot*, enticing males, asking for it, asking *all eyes* to be *on* her.

Each out to catch an Indian for himself, from an American poet, holds undertones of 'Red Indians', and the destruction of their culture too. These two lines sum up all colonial enterprise as rape and greed (*for himself*). The irony of the *Christian* ideology which sees Nature not just as art but as *Sin*, or *moss* as *lovely hell-green*, comes out in the timing of their rape: *directly after Mass*.

Maddening shows how deeply this poem has worked its way into the colonists' mindset. The Indian women are *maddening*. They are also *always retreating* behind the *hanging fabric* of *Nature*: however strongly the *hard* colonists rip through Nature's soft fabric, they will never see or know it all.

You could say much more about the journey of this poem's music. Bishop had an exacting ear. The poem sounds as if written in one sitting, with free cadences (many in groups of seven-line phrases) like improvised jazz, and lines based on the pentameter but breathed by shorter lines, sometimes only two beats.

But the intertwining journeys of echoing syllables, vowel sounds, consonants (*inch/foliage, edges/finished*, for instance) weave an aural tapestry of significant relationships through the poem which matches the visual and emotional tapestry of the whole. It sounds

112

free and fluid. (The American poet Richard Wilbur said Bishop's poems sound 'inexhaustibly fresh'.) But that comes from their subtle, intricate music and that in turn came from long crafting. Bishop's poem 'The Moose', which also sounds so natural, took sixteen years to write. Bishop worked slowly. *Do / you still hang your words in the air, ten years / unfinished*, asked Robert Lowell:

> *glued to your notice board, with gaps*
> *or empties for the unimaginable phrase –*
> *unerring Muse who makes the casual perfect?*[8]

11 W. S. Graham

Second Poem from *What Is the Language Using Us For?*

1

What is the language using us for?
It uses us all and in its dark
Of dark actions selections differ.

I am not making a fool of myself
For you. What I am making is
A place for language in my life

Which I want to be a real place
Seeing I have to put up with it
Anyhow. What are Communication's

Mistakes in the magic medium doing
To us? It matters only in
So far as we want to be telling

Each other alive about each other
Alive. I want to be able to speak
And sing and make my soul occur

In front of the best and be respected
For that and even be understood
By the ones I like who are dead.

I would like to speak in front
Of myself with all my ears alive
And find out what it is I want.

2

What is the language using us for?
What shape of words shall put its arms
Round us for more than pleasure?

I met a man in Cartsburn Street
Thrown out of the Cartsburn Vaults.
He shouted Willie and I crossed the street

And met him at the mouth of the Close.
And this was double-breasted Sam,
A far relation on my mother's

West-Irish side. Hello Sam how
Was it you knew me and says he
I heard your voice on The Sweet Brown Knowe.

O was I now I said and Sam said
Maggie would have liked to see you.
I'll see you again I said and said

Sam I'll not keep you and turned
Away over the shortcut across
The midnight railway sidings.

What is the language using us for?
From the prevailing weather or words
Each object hides in a metaphor.

This is the morning. I am out
On a kind of Vlaminck blue-rutted
Road. Willie Wagtail is about.

In from the West a fine smirr
Of rain drifts across the hedge.
I am only out here to walk or

Make this poem up. The hill is
A shining blue macadam top.
I lean my back to the telegraph pole

And the messages hum through my spine.
The beaded wires with their birds
Above me are contacting London.

What is the language using us for?
It uses us all and in its dark
Of dark actions selections differ.

Graham (1918–86) may be little read by the public but was one of
the most important and original voices of the twentieth century.
Poets revere him. 'He used language as if he were discovering it as
he went along,' said Dennis O'Driscoll. 'I found his language

magical,' said Harold Pinter. 'What happens when you read a poem that sends a shiver is a mysterious thing. He could sing like nobody's business and had enormous skill. He's dealing with such delicate potentials – silence and the other side of language.'

Graham's mother was a shopkeeper from the West of Ireland, his father a Scottish engineer. He was born in Clydeside, left school at fourteen, trained as an engineer, studied philosophy and literature in college for a year, and in the Second World War worked in munitions in Glasgow. He brought out a collection of poems in 1942, became a friend of Dylan Thomas (his early work was very close to Thomas), and in 1943 decamped to a caravan in Cornwall. Where he stayed, on the move as copywriter, fisherman or coastguard, concentrating on poetry, becoming friends with St Ives artists. In 1955 his first major collection *The Nightfishing* appeared. He settled permanently in Cornwall, in classic poet's poverty. 'We have no telephone or car; an outside toilet with jug of flowering currant,' he told a journalist. 'When something comes up like fixing the front door we have little, but I am able to put the capitals at the beginning of my lines and cook a good steak and kidney pie.'

Like Dylan Thomas, he got drunk. His wife and friendships were crucial to his life and work. The poet-persona of his poems, however, is an isolated traveller (his 1944 collection was *The Seven Journeys*), following language through tiny balances, echoes and shifts of syllable or stress into an unknown horizon: *This is no other place / Than where I am, between / This word and the next.*

Language was increasingly an important subject in his work. 'A poem is made of words,' he wrote early on, 'not of the expanding heart.' (He also said he found that 'difficult to remember'.) In his *New Collected Poems* you see his language (which began opaque, curdled, coiled) becoming increasingly barer. Easier to read, but keeping its mystery.

This two-part poem, published in 1977, is the second poem in a sequence of three. Its Part 1 lays out the stall: the poem is about an *I*, a *you*, and the *magic medium* of language in which their *Communication* (with a capital C) takes place.

So what does the poet *want* to *make* in this *magic medium*? (*Making* is a key word in Part 2, reminding us that the Greek word for poet, *poietes*, comes from the verb *poiein* 'to make' and means simply 'maker'). Not *a fool of myself*, but *a place for language in my life*. The *magic* of this *medium* is in communicating *across* (a word

116

important in Part 2, which shows these statements in action and is full of crossings; *crossed the street, across the sidings, across the hedge*): *across* all barriers between one self and another, even the barrier of death. Poets reach out to earlier poets. They want to *be understood* by poets they love, even *dead* ones.

But language has a sinister side, a *dark* which is allied to the title's question. Language is bigger than *us*: it may be a master, rather than a servant. The question has a sinister ring. It opens the poem and recurs at the beginning of Part 2, halfway through Part 2 and at the end. As the question surrounds the poem, so language surrounds us. At the beginning of Part 2, the surrounding word *Round*, in the same part of the line as *shape*, seems to answer the question *what shape*? When it *puts its arms round us*, is this comfort (underlined by *pleasure*) or constraint like a straitjacket?

Robert Graves's poem 'The Cool Web' said that language dims things, gets in the way of us experiencing the world.[9] It webs and *winds us in*, *chills* anger, *dulls* scent. In Graham's poem, language is bigger than us but is about *Communication* between people. It can be *real* – if we try.

Language can also make *mistakes* (which maybe are exemplified in Part 2). S*elections differ*, like the choices, acts and words of *Willie* and *Sam*. We make different choices in language as in life. Word choices (*selections*) are also *actions*, with consequences and weight in our lives – as in a poem, which is also a 'selection' of words.

Language, says Part 1's first stanza, has a *dark*. Part 2 shows Part 1's ideas in action. First in *dark action*: obscure actions and words happening at *midnight*. Then in *morning* on *a blue-rutted* and *shining blue* road. First between two people, then between a self surrounded by the media of *Communication*: a *road*, a *telegraph* wire full of *messages, contacting London*.

Part 1 is full of making and wanting. *I am not making, I am making, I want, I want to be able, I would like to.* Part 2 tries to fulfil the wants by staging an encounter between two people: communication in action (however inconsequential). And then a lone *morning* walk (which might perhaps *help to find out what it is I want*). After repeating the big question it switches from abstract questioning to the human and physical by picturing language putting *its arms / Round us*.

Part 1 says what *matters* is *telling each other about each other*: this is language that speaks of doubles to reflect the mirroring of one self in another, *I* in *you*. (*Each other alive, each other / Alive.*) In Part 2 the meeting, the *Communication* (such as it is), is also full of doubles. Repetitions surround the encounter with *double-breasted Sam* (on *Cartsburn Street* out of *Cartsburn Vaults*). As soon as he shouts, an *I* comes to meet a *you*, provoking a string of mirrorings and repeats. *Street* is repeated; *how* at the end of the fourth stanza is picked up in *Knowe* and *now*. The fifth stanza, the meeting's climax, is full of repeats. (*I said and Sam said*; *To see you.* / *I'll see you*; *I said and Sam said*.)

But there are *mistakes*, too, as Part 1 forecast. What is said does not match. The people and the words miss and leave each other. *How* did *Sam* know who I was? (More you and I: *you knew me*.) By *voice*, apparently. The speaker has, after all, said he wants t*o speak and sing*.

But *Sam* says he *heard* his *voice* on a hill which exists only in an Irish song, 'Maid of the Sweet Brown Knowe', whose girl (who lives on a hill, *knowe*) refuses to marry a boy who parties at an inn. (*You rap and you call and you pay for all, and go home by the break of day*.) The boy decides to *leave you where I found you, at the foot of the Sweet Brown Knowe*. The song stages a communication that does not work. Sam (*thrown out of* those *vaults* – drunk, maybe, like the boy in the song) plunges us into strangeness. Are we in a song, or a poem, or real life?

Willie doubles the strangeness, replying *O was I now*, which answers *Knowe* musically but is no straight answer to what Sam said.

Sam tries again, *Maggie would like to see you*. He gets back, *I'll see you again, I'll not keep you*.

Sam is already *a far relation*. Now *Willie* turns *away*: farther than *far*. He crosses *sidings* (sidelining his *far relation*) of the *railway*, that ancient image of distance and parting. Part 2 has twelve stanzas and here, exactly halfway, the title question comes back again. So do abstract ideas. But now they seem to be shadowing the human relationships. As *I* turns *away* from *Sam*, and replies only enigmatically to his language, we hear that *Each object hides in a metaphor*. We get another repeat, of *Willie*, but the entry of the critical word *metaphor* has changed things and the *Willie* in this second half of Part 2 is *Willie Wagtail*. And instead of *the West-Irish side* of the poet's family we get the *West*, which is where this *smirr of rain* comes from.

This Scots (not in fact *Irish*) word (for *light drizzle*) *drifts across* the English poem (as in 'catch my drift' perhaps) just as rain *drifts across the hedgerow*. Again (as with the song) the poem makes us ask, are we in art or life? The *blue-rutted road* is a *Vlaminck road*: Vlaminck, one of the Fauve artists, stressed the primacy of pure colour. The *hill* is *a shining blue macadam top*. Is this an *object* 'hiding' *in a metaphor*? Is this a hill from the song (*the Sweet Brown Knowe*) or a *Vlaminck* painting? Or is it real (whatever that is by now)? Is the poet *out here to walk* or to *make this poem up*? Or both? In which case, is living the same thing as writing *a poem*, using language which is simultaneously *using us*?

The whole poem (like the sequence it comes from) is a question. Part 2 illustrates the question asked in Part 1, but does not answer it. It is itself a pretty *dark* (as in the sense of mysterious and ambiguous) act of selection (as in *selections differ*) and *Communication*.

The verbs of Part 2 are acts (as in the first stanza's word *actions*) of *communication*, and eventually of refusing communication: *shouted, met, knew, heard, said, see, see, turned away*. The first half of Part 2 moves from *mouth* to direct speech, dialogue and *voice*. But it ends in *midnight* and *sidings*. The meeting is sidestepped. The second half has more evasive verbs: *hides, drifts, walk, make up, lean, hum through*.

But from Part 2's halfway point, where the two men part, and after the *railway* (which, ever since railways began, has always been *a metaphor* not only of communication and uniting people but also keeping them apart, whirling them *away* from *each other*), the poem increasingly focuses on nouns that are images of communication: *railway, road, telegraph, wires, messages*. These (and that *hedge*) are *objects* which both join and divide people, as *metaphor* both joins and separates two words and things.

This idea of 'hiding' *in a metaphor* puts metaphor in an ambiguous light, following on from the suspect title idea of what language gets up to. Language has *its dark*. Metaphor, that leap by which language can say what is not, may be a leap into darkness, into hiding.

Since *objects hide in a metaphor*, as well as being revealed by it, we get more coded metaphors for *communication*. The semaphor of the *wagtail*, with its flicking tail and poet's name. Other birds, *on beaded wires*. A metaphor that is doubly condensed: the birds are *beads* because they are *like beads* on a wire.

What about the music: the *selections* (that *differ*) of syllable, sound and stress?

From a rhythm point of view, the *prevailing weather* is four beats

119

and nine syllables to a line. There are a few variations. Some lines have fewer beats; some stretch into five beats (ten syllables, classic iambic pentameter) especially when 'reaching out' is an issue, as in the penultimate line of Part I's last stanza: the hopeful line, which states the poet's ideal way of being, *all my ears alive*. Or the third line of Part 2's second stanza, where human contact is finally made.

As for rhyme: the line-ends of the first and third line of each stanza mostly (but not always) rhyme. Approximately, as the poem's human communication is approximate and makes (as you could say the rhymes do) *mistakes*: *for/differ*; *myself/life*; *other/occur*, *respected/dead*; and in Part 2, *for/pleasure*; *how/Knowe*, *for/metaphor*, *smirr/or*, *spine/London*.

But one vowel sound grows in importance through the poem: OW (as in *how*) begins in Part 1 with *anyhow*. The poet says he is stuck with language so might as well use it as 'really' as he can. It reappears in *find out* (the hope which ends Part 1) and snowballs through Part 2 as the poem does find *out* how *Communication* works in human relationships: *out*, *shouted*, *mouth*, *how*, *Brown Knowe*, *now*, *out*, *about*, *out*.

The poem is (and asks) a question it never answers. But though it does not answer why or what, Part 2 does go some way to answering Part 1's questions and wants. It shows *how*. How *Communication* makes *mistakes*, but also *how* (given *us*, the readers who join the poet's *I* in feeling the effect of *language* upon *us*) something can, in the end, *be understood*. Not just through *telegraph wires* and *messages* but through a poem.

District and Circle

Tunes from a tin whistle underground
Curled up a corridor I'd be walking down
To where I knew I was always going to find
My watcher on the tiles, cap by his side,
His fingers perked, his two eyes eyeing me
In an unaccusing look I'd not avoid,
Or not just yet, since both were out to see
For ourselves.
                As the music larked and capered
I'd trigger and untrigger a hot coin
Held at the ready, but now my gaze was lowered
For was our traffic not in recognition?
Accorded passage, I would re-pocket and nod,
And he, still eyeing me, would also nod.

                        ~

Posted, eyes front, along the dreamy ramparts
Of escalators ascending and descending
To a monotonous slight rocking in the works,
We were moved along, upstanding.
Elsewhere, underneath, an engine powered,
Rumbled, quickened, evened, quieted.
The white tiles gleamed. In passages that flowed
With draughts from cooler tunnels, I missed the light
Of all-overing, long since mysterious day,
Parks at lunchtime where the sunners lay
On body-heated mown grass regardless,
A resurrection scene minutes before
The resurrection, habitués
Of their garden of delights, of staggered summer.

                        ~

Another level down, the platform thronged.
I re-entered the safety of numbers,
A crowd half straggle-ravelled and half strung
Like a human chain, the pushy newcomers
Jostling and purling underneath the vault,
On their marks to be first through the doors,
Street-loud, then succumbing to herd-quiet . . .
Had I betrayed or not, myself or him?
Always new to me, always familiar,
This unrepentant, now repentant turn
As I stood waiting, glad of a first tremor,
Then caught up in the now-or-never whelm
Of one and all the full length of the train.

~

Stepping on to it across the gap,
On to the carriage metal, I reached to grab
The stubby black roof-wort and take my stand.
From planted ball of heel to heel of hand
A sweet traction and heavy down-slump stayed me.
I was on my way, well girded, yet on edge,
Spot-rooted, buoyed, aloof,
Listening to the dwindling noises off,
My back to the unclosed door, the platform empty;
And wished it could have lasted,
That long between-times pause before the budge
And glaze-over, when any forwardness
Was unwelcome and bodies readjusted,
Blind-sided to themselves and other bodies.

~

So deeper into it, crowd-swept, strap-hanging,
My lofted arm a-swivel like a flail,
My father's glazed face in my own waning
And craning. . . .
                    Again the growl
Of shutting doors, the jolt and one-off treble
Of iron on iron, then a long centrifugal
Haulage of speed through every dragging socket.

122

And so by night and day to be transported
Through galleried earth with them, the only relict
Of all that I belonged to, hurtled forward,
Reflecting in a window mirror-backed
By blasted weeping rock-walls.
                              Flicker-lit.

Born 1939 in Co. Derry, Northern Ireland, Heaney grew up on his father's farm and at boarding school, read English at Queen's Belfast, taught there until 1972 and moved to the Irish Republic. His first collection *Death of a Naturalist* came out in 1966. By the 1970s people were echoing Lowell's phrase about him: 'best Irish poet since Yeats'. From 1982 (keeping his home in Ireland), he taught part-time in America (from 1984 at Harvard), was Oxford Professor of Poetry 1989–94, has won the Whitbread Prize twice and the Nobel in 1995.

Inside that arc is a thinking life of immense humanity and care for poetry and its power for good. He is what Blake said a poet should be, a custodian of 'the holiness of minute particulars', subtle movements of syllable, cadence and echo that make meaning and make music. He has also published vital translations and criticism. His essays are a touchstone for all poets thinking responsibly about their art.

He trusts the tradition: not just English poetry, everything from Anglo-Saxon to ancient Irish, Dante, European poets, Seferis, Cavafy, Virgil. His alertness to it parallels his poetry's intense feel for loam and what grows in it, what it contains. His first book opened with the now-famous poem 'Digging'; his imaginative ground is so much *both* the whole poetic tradition *and* the physical land he grew up in, that the one becomes the image of the other in his poems.

The title of this one (title poem of his twelfth collection, published in 2006) is taken from the London Underground but embodies the way in which (I have suggested) good poems are forward movement but also 'turns'. It recalls the spiral staircase down which Mallarmé saw Orpheus descending and Dante's 'circles' in hell.[10] Many of its echoes are also specific to Heaney's work. Published forty years after his first collection, it is a 'making strange' of London's Underground; a book of circlings-back, of returns.

Returns, above all, to darkness. His first book closed with the

123

credo he has kept to: *I rhyme / To see myself, to set the darkness echoing.* The second was *Door into the Dark.* Also to Virgil and the whole tradition of *katabasis*, descent to the underworld, especially those explored by Virgil and Dante. Heaney translated some of Virgil's *Aeneid* 6, the book in which Aeneas goes down to Hades and meets his dead father, in 'The Golden Bough', the first poem of *Seeing Things* (1991), driven by longing to see his own dead father. His book *Station Island* (1984) was both a pilgrimage and a Dantean descent through circles of the dead.[11]

He is also returning to the physical intensity of 'district'. On the cover of *Field Work* (1979) was a magnified map of a district he lived in and still works in. Here, he adds this theme to *katabasis*: the 'district' is Hades. Finally, he returns to Tollund Man, the ancient murdered figure through whom he addressed the violence of Northern Ireland in *North* (1975).

This poem is made of five sonnets, the first and last of which he wrote first, intending to write an 'underground' journey in a spirit of strangeness, ending with a vision of his father (as 'The Golden Bough' requested) reflected in his own face, but taking with him his old tutelary spirit from earlier poems, Tollund Man, who reappears as an Irish busker. 'One of my own nation', said Heaney, reading this poem for the first time in London.

After suicide bombers attacked the London Underground in July 2005, he added three inner sonnets backlit by the menace of bombs. When this book came out, he said on a BBC interview that when he heard about 9/11 he immediately thought, 'This is about the Palestinians,' explaining that Catholics in Northern Ireland used to identify with the Palestinians.[12] He had written through decades of bombings and deaths. (*What blazed ahead of you?* he says to a murdered cousin, in 'The Strand at Lough Beg'. *A fake road block? The red lamp swung, the sudden brakes and stalling / Engine, voices, heads hooded and the cold-nosed gun?*) Now, as this poem became shadowed by 9/11 and its ramifications, he brought fear alive in a tunnel where bombs might explode at any moment. What began as a personal underworld journey became suffused with awareness of a new violent rift in the upper world where *sunners* lie *on body-heated mown grass regardless.*

'For me the sonnet is about containment,' he says. In this poem the outer sonnets, written before the bombs, can afford to relax, to break: the first in the eighth line, a classic *volta*; the last in the fourth line (after mentioning his father) and after the eighth. A well-behaved, eight-and-six sonnet with a sestet starting classically *And so*.

But in the three inner sonnets the only break comes at the exact centre of the whole poem, between the seventh and eighth lines of the third sonnet: where crowds go down, *succumbing to herd-quiet* with a row of dots in which you try not to think of cattle trucks, of people 'herded' to a dark they won't return from.

Here is where the question rises, *Had I betrayed or not, myself or him?* What about this relation to the busker, that *coin* ungiven, the *nod* of *recognition* between two Irishmen in London, poet and busker standing in for the ferryman (who takes the coin of passage) and Orpheus playing *tunes* in the underworld? What about this uncertainty over giving (*the unrepentant, now repentant turn*), which is *always new to me, always familiar*?

It is as if the central sonnets, aware of the bombs, clench together in the mysterious safety of poetic form, vulnerable but controlled, to 'contain' the unspoken fear and order the disintegrating mayhem behind the journey. Yet they also acknowledge at their core a split of hesitation and doubt. Doubt about betrayal, about self in relation to other. You can do nothing about it but go past.

A crowd flowed over London Bridge, so many, says Eliot in *The Waste Land*, quoting Dante's vision of the dead. *I did not think death had undone so many*. Heaney's poem too is heavy with awareness of so many dead, as well as our own precariousness. We are *caught up* (sonnet three). We're in the dark and can do nothing about it. We are *bodies* (sonnet four), *Blind-sided to themselves and other bodies*. There's no *safety* (sonnet three) in *numbers*.

Yet the poem ends with rhyme: itself an image of order. A rhyme to *relict*: something left, something that 'remains'. It ends also with light, even if only intermittent, in the darkness. *Flicker-lit*.

One way into the maze is to follow the journey of inwardness in the speaker.

He *knew* he *was always going to find* the other. This busker with a *tin whistle* (the Irish instrument) belongs to him (*my*) like a stalker or a minder (*watcher*); some footloose alter ego (*on the tiles*). In this foreign *corridor*, *both* are *out to see / For* themselves.

But alternatives (to act or not) are starting up for the speaker, reflecting his hesitation about going *down* (repeated in sonnet three's *another level down*). He'd *not avoid* the other's look, *Or not just yet*. He alternately fingers and lets go a *coin* in his pocket, and describes this in a language of crime (*hot*) and military violence (*trigger and untrigger, at the ready*).

These mental alternatives begin something which marks the poem throughout, which you might call a sense of twoness.

You can hear the speaker as a blend of archetypes that are constantly shifting between two roles: Tollund Man and Orpheus, son and stranger. The language too keeps doubling words back on themselves (*eyes eyeing me*, sonnet one; *half . . . and half*, sonnet three; *ball of heel to heel of hand*, sonnet four; *iron on iron*, sonnet five).

This *katabasis* (like all in the end, perhaps) is about relationship: about the self and the maybe unknowable other. But is this relationship between two selves antagonistic? Or is it a pairing, as in the pairs of active verbs (*larked and capered*, *repocket and nod*, sonnet one; *ascending and descending*, sonnet two; *jostling and purling*, sonnet three; *waning and craning*, sonnet five)? Are these two figures mutually *unaccusing*, or not? What is their *traffic*?

This twoness (and doubt about it) comes to a climax with his *father's glazed face in my own waning*. As 'The Golden Bough' desires, he visits the underworld and sees his father again, but only in his own reflection, now he is older (*waning*). This is his father and not his father, there and not there, alive and dead. The speaker ends up going *forward* (though in sonnet four, *any forwardness was unwelcome*), but as the *only relict / Of all that I belonged to*.

Another way the poem expresses this twoness is through the speaker's active and passive roles. He begins active (*I'd be walking down*) but by the end of sonnet one he is passively *accorded passage*. Sonnet two's first line continues the military undertones behind the *triggered* image, but also the passivity of *accorded*. As you go *down* you become acted on rather than active (*posted*, *moved along*). His only active verb is emotional (*I missed*) and the subjects of verbs are other things to whose atmosphere he is reacting: the *elsewhere engine*, *white tiles* and *passages*.

The sestet gives it what he misses, what he saw in the *light*: all those vulnerable bodies, behaving as if their threatened city is *their* very own *garden of delights*, title of the triptych by Hieronymus Bosch which starts off in the Garden of Eden (the world as God made it), whose central panel is packed with fleshy human beings disporting themselves surreally and disgustingly (what human beings make of the world), followed by punishment in hell (what divine punishment makes of them). Heaney, reminding us that an explosion might happen any moment, describes *A resurrection scene minutes before / the resurrection*. You could hear the adjective he applies to *summer* (*staggered*) as a transferred epithet: it refers to something different from the noun it actually applies to. (The classic example is *In going to my naked bed*: *naked* really refers to me, not the bed.) It echoes the military imagery (*triggered*, *eyes front*), suggesting the unseen terrorism at work. *Minutes* later, if bombs go off, the *sunners* may be *staggered* by what happens – and far worse staggering will happen down here.

In the third sonnet, the speaker is active again (*re-entered*) and feels safer (*safety of numbers*). The *so many* (in Eliot's phrase) are now crowds pushing *to be first through the doors*. The speaker mentally steps back as those ambiguities come up again in his feelings, again connected to the ungiven-to busker (*always new to me, always familiar, unrepentant, now repentant*). After this central drama of moral worry (marked by dots after *quiet*), standing in for physical worry about whether it is safe to get on this train, comes the *now-or-never whelm*. No going back. The *train* ends the third sonnet. In the fourth he steps *across the gap*, is *on my way*. He has acted and has to go on being active. He grabs *the black roof-wort* of a handle which summons all the plants of Hades (especially perhaps Moly in the *Odyssey*, which defends you against transformation): *I take my stand*.

More of the subtle military imagery. At some level this is a foot-soldier getting ready to be attacked. *Well-girded*, *on edge*, but still a chance of escape (*my back to the unclosed door*). The emotion we hear about surrounding this journey is now given to us directly in *wished*, rather than implied by the way it is described. *Wished* is the first emotion verb since *I missed*. After not wanting the doors to close, hoping not to go forward, to stay in the *pause before the budge*, comes the jolt. And the fourth sonnet ends with *bodies* – summoning, in the subliminal story told by the imagery, the possibility of bodies that are no longer alive, as these ones luckily are.

The poem ends in movement, with no closure for the dark journey we are all on. The whole fifth sonnet is a hurtling forwards, which brings back the past (father's glazed face) only to remind you that you are on your own (*only relict*). *Deeper* picks up *down* in the second line of sonnet one and first of sonnet two, but it also suggests that we are going deeper into the *katabasis* tradition, with archaic language like translation from Homer (*lofted*, *aswivel*) and archaic objects (*flail*), as if seeking for security in old remembered poems and quotations, depth of mind and welcoming humanity they rest upon.

The inner life of emotion (which, as in Heaney's Northern Ireland poems, includes profound compassion as well as horror) is transferred at the end from the speaker into epithets for the rock-walls. *Blasted* and *weeping* describe the way the tunnels were made and their dampness, but also mourn what happened here and might happen here again any minute.

I have no room to go into Heaney's signature music, syllables and echoes, vowels and consonants: how the UN of the all-frightening unspoken word 'under' (from the first line's *underground*) gathers associations in the second sonnet (*underneath, rumbled, tunnels*) is paradoxically underlined by words for things of the light (*summer, sunners*) and continues in *throng, numbers, strung, newcomers, underneath*; or how, as the fear quickens, the voice replays falsely reassuring little clichés in the third sonnet (*on their marks, now-or-never, one and all*). The journey and the fear will have to speak for themselves.

II

Who Am I and Where Did I Come From?

– I come from my childhood, as from a homeland.

Antoine de Saint-Exupéry, *Flight to Arras*

ROSENCRANTZ: We were sent for.
GUILDENSTERN: Yes.
ROSENCRANTZ: That's why we're here. (*He looks round, seems doubtful, then the explanation.*) Travelling.
GUILDENSTERN: Yes.

Tom Stoppard, *Rosencrantz and Guildenstern Are Dead*

The traveller looks back, trying to connect this present self with what lies behind. How did I get here? Why did *that* road lead to *this* self?

The poems in this section explore identity: origins, memory, nationhood and childhood. How did growing up in that particular place and time (rural Jamaica in the Fifties for Jean 'Binta' Breeze, rural Worcestershire during the Second World War for Geoffrey Hill, Pune in the Seventies for Sujatta Bhatt), and the way you dealt with it – the self you discovered yourself to be, or made yourself into, as a child – make who you are now?

Mark Doty's children identify with the hidden self, a tortoise in its shell. His poem suggests each child wants and finds a shaping spirit within themselves by which they will deal with the world. Children in other poems wonder where they came from (Jacob Polley), learn to swim (Katherine Pierpoint), learn to judge people as father does and then stand up to him (Hugo Williams). The disabled child in Carole Satyamurti's poem learns to make metaphors for, even make bitter jokes about, her own limitations. In Louise Glück's poem, memories from childhood work in the adult when normal life collapses, giving strength to go on.

Growing up is realising you are on a journey with a long way to go and dangers to face. You are shaped by national origins as well as personal ones and may have to learn to identify yourself against other people. Ciaran Carson's poem set in Sixties Belfast reveals a child learning the dangers of belonging to the tribe. Or maybe the child faces emigration over the sea, as in Jean 'Binta' Breeze's poem. For Sujatta Bhatt, who was born in Hyderabad and now lives in Germany, the journey to be faced includes religious pilgrimage and the struggle to become a poet.

13   Geoffrey Hill

Mercian Hymns VI

The princes of Mercia were badger and raven. Thrall
    to their freedom, I dug and hoarded. Orchards
    fruited above clefts. I drank from honeycombs of
    chill sandstone.

'A boy at odds in the house, lonely among brothers.'
    But I, who had none, fostered a strangeness; gave
    myself to unattainable toys.

Candles of gnarled resin, apple-branches, the tacky
    mistletoe. 'Look,' they said and again 'look'. But
    I ran slowly; the landscape flowed away, back to
    its source.

In the schoolyard, in the cloakrooms, the children
    boasted their scars of dried snot; wrists and
    knees garnished with impetigo.

Born in 1932 in Bromsgrove, Worcestershire, Hill is one of the most important poets now writing in English. His poems divide readers. Many see his work (with many collections, prizes and honours) as one of the most important achievements of the last hundred years. Others find him difficult.

His poetry is often (but not always) dense, layered, full of paradox and allusion. Complex, visionary, erudite, it can be swashbucklingly disdainful of easy thinking and is formally very skilful, in many wildly different ways, it flashes with jewelled images and phrases, but rests on a granite sense of the sacredness of words and architecture. He has been an important influence on many very different contemporary poets.

Hill addresses the big passionate subjects: history, Christianity, guilt, atonement, suffering, myth, war, love, reparation, genocide; the erosion of modern language, our debt to the dead; landscape, art, music, geography and history (especially English). He is always reinventing himself, experimenting with both form and theme. His images are felt and thought to the full, richly sensuous, powerfully intellectual, with extraordinary intensity.

He grew up in the West Midland village of Fairfield. His father was a village policeman, his mother often ill. He lived much of the time with his grandmother who carried on the traditional cottage industry of nail-making. He is proud, he says, 'to have been born into the English working class'. Aged eight, he saw Coventry burning at night on the horizon, set alight by German bombs. He sang in the village church choir till he was eighteen, went to the County High School in Bromsgrove (which the poet David Jones also attended), read English at Oxford and went into academe. He taught English first at Leeds, then Cambridge. He moved to Boston in 1988 and now lives in Brookline, Massachusetts. In addition to many poetry collections he has published important essays.

This poem is from *Mercian Hymns* (which won the 1971 Whitbread Prize): an astonishing series of prose poems about growing up in Worcestershire for which he used the figure of the historical and mythical King Offa (as in Offa's Dyke); who reigned over most of England south of the Humber between AD 757 and 796. Hill calls Offa the 'presiding genius' of Mercia (the West Midlands). The sequence plaits Hill's own wartime childhood into Offa's. The *he* is both the early English prince who'll be a king, and the twentieth-century boy who'll be a poet.

This poem describes the boy growing up *at odds with* peers who boast about temporary surface things (*scars*) while he identifies with deep permanent things ruled by creatures who traditionally symbolise not only the depths and heights of English countryside (digging into earth, commanding crags) but also its wisdom: *badger and raven*. To conjure the ancient magic he found in this landscape, Hill uses nouns from the sacred medieval space of an English carol (*princes, thrall, resin, candles, mistletoe*). The verbs, archaic (*fruited*) or unexpected (*garnished*), add to the heraldic, church-glass glow around mucky things like *snot* and *impetigo*.

The poem is about choosing the ancient, deep and strange; choosing alienation. Like Wordsworth's *Prelude*, it is about the making of a poet. The *source* is geological, as if the whole landscape were both a river flowing *back to its source*, and the welling *source* of poetry. Honey and flow are early Greek metaphors for poetic inspiration. What he *drank* from is a Worcestershire version of the Pierian spring in ancient Greece, guarded by the Muses, created when their winged horse Pegasus (symbol of inspiration) knocked the ground with his hoof. Hill will make his poems from this *chill sandstone*, but also from the *honeycombs* of the English poetic tradition.

From the words *hoarded, fruited, clefts, gave myself, toys, candles* to *mistletoe* (which oversees kissing), a sexual undercurrent also runs through the boyish exploration of natural and human landscape, and underlies his rejection of what is around him (*tacky*) and his separateness. The poem ends with physical 'garnish' (*impetigo* on *wrists and knees*). It is a covertly sexualised vision of discovering not only your own poetic depths but also all the bodies to which the growing boy is *in thrall*: your own, those of other people and the body of the landscape.

At first, the startling power of this poem seems to come from its rich vocabulary. The voice flings linguistic treasures down as if language itself were the gnarled mysterious landscape it describes – under which flows a sacred spring from which words, like buckets, haul up new meanings as the poem's journey tracks the boy's maturing need for isolation.

The poem presents a boy *lonely among brothers*, but this Merlin-like boy who refuses the surface of his world also refuses the label *lonely*. *But I fostered*, he says. *But* is his word (*but I ran slowly*). He was not, in fact, *lonely among brothers*; he *had none*. Instead of a brother (or foster-brother) he *fostered a strangeness*. He did not want to *look* at easy Christmas magic, evocative as the *candles* and *mistletoe* are. He calls them *tacky*.

Among the *unattainable toys* to which he *gave* himself was, perhaps, exactly what this poem is: a vision of something packed and sensuous, both archaic and innovative, both backward- and forward-looking.

Hill has said that the 'proof of a poet's craft' is bringing together 'local vividness' and 'overall shape', and making them one. This, he says, is the 'truth-telling' a poet does. So what about this poem's 'overall shape'?

Like the growing boy (poet or king), the form refuses convention and creates its own world. On the one hand this is a prose-like poem, bunching words like grapes in each stanza, hanging them (as do the rest of the poems in this sequence) from the single stem of the first protuberant line. Yet it is also a sonnet, with fourteen lines and a 'turn' of thought after the *landscape* flows *back to its source*, the point where attention switches from lone *I* to *the children*.

But though it looks shaped by the layout it draws shape more deeply from the rhythms and vowel echoes which bind it together. We start with dactyls in a strong, archaic-sounding narrative sentence, ending in that word *raven* whose rhythm and vowels will echo on in *freedom* and *sandstone*, and return in *resin* and *children*. The opening sentence of four beats could be the first line of a conventional poem, but each stanza opens with a different rhythm (the last one starts in the *O my darling* rhythm of 'Clementine', making almost explicit the child-sexuality underlying *schoolyard*, *cloakrooms*, *wrists and knees*).

This poem is not going to play by normal poem rules. It will make its own shape, will not be *in thrall* to convention. Those words *in thrall*, after the opening sentence, disturb any idea of a conventional poetic line. *Thrall* (in a poem that begins with *princes*) sets up musical echoes (*hoarded*, *orchards*) and intellectual ones. There are modern undertones: 'enthralled' (by watching *badgers*); a child *in thrall to* adult rules. But at the historical level, here is a young medieval king surrounded by dangerous competitors. His servitude is a contrast to the *freedom* of wild animals and also to those who have power over him (for now); those who rule what will be his kingdom: the *princes of Mercia*.

In this poem's soundworld, the two-syllable word is king. In the first stanza, *Princes*, *Mercia*, *badger*, *raven*, *freedom*, *orchards*, *fruited*, *sandstone*. In the second, *lonely*, *brothers*, *fostered*, *strangeness*. In the third, *candles*, *resin*, *apple*, *tacky*, *slowly*, *landscape*. In the last, *schoolyard*, *cloakrooms*, *children*, *boasted*, *garnished*.

Within that, we hear variations on O and A. The OR of *thrall*, *hoarded*, *orchards* mutates to AR (*gnarled*, *branches*, *schoolyard*, *scars*, *garnished*); the AY of *raven* is echoed in *strangeness*, *gave*, *unattainable*, *again*, *away*; the short A of *badger* in *apple*, *tacky*, *back* plus the nasal AN of *candles*, *ran*, *landscape*.

While making a new form, this poem sees everything as new and ancient at the same time. It describes the process of growing towards your own way of being in the world, becoming the discoverer of *strangeness* in yourself and outside, while illustrating this strangeness in the form it lies on the page. Above all it turns on that other long vowel, I, which appears on its own in the first three stanzas (*I dug and hoarded*; *I drank*; *But I*; *But I*) and in the last in that startling final word *impetigo*.

The form is an experiment in *freedom*, in choosing new rules and shape. Like the boy, it ignores people saying *look*. It listens to the *landscape*, as it flows *back to its source*. It is prose poetry which has chosen *freedom* from the past, but which is still *in thrall* to poetry's deepest tradition: that words make clear a poem's sense and shape by relating to and echoing each other.

Smoke

My father kept a stove
with dog's legs
on a pink hearthstone.

One morning he climbed down the icy stairs
and spread his palms
on the blood-warm metal flanks.

He cranked open the iron doors,
like a black bank safe's,
but found no heat and ash heaped in its place.

He cracked grey whittled coals,
released brief blue flames,
and knocked downy soot through the bars of the grate.

The ash-pan, softly loaded
and almost as wide as a doorway,
he carried like dynamite through the dark house,

his bright face blown with smuts.
At the back door
he slid the ash into a tin dustbin,

then snapped sticks,
crumpled newspaper,
struck a match

and dipped it between the kindling.
Smoke unrolled, flames spread,
the rush of the stove eating air started up,

and my father would shake on rocks
from an old coal hod
and swing the doors shut.

But this time
he took a book, broke its spine
and slung that on instead:

his diaries,
year by year,
purred as their pages burned,

their leather boards shifted, popped
and fell apart.
Soon I would arrive,

pulled from under my mother's heart,
and grow to watch my father
break the charred crossbeam of a bird from the flue,

wondering if I too
had hung in darkness and smoke,
looking up at the light let down her throat
whenever my mother sang or spoke.

Polley, born in 1975 in Carlisle, published his first collection (from which this comes) in his early twenties. His poems are subtle, musical, imaginative. The journey here is from that first end-word *stove* to a child wondering if he had hung in *smoke* inside his mother like the dead *bird* in the *flue* of that stove. It gets there via images of living and dying creatures, starting with *kept* (as if the *stove* were a pet), travelling on to *dogs' legs*, *pink*, *blood-warm*, *flanks*, *downy*, *eating air*). It gestures to killing (*broke its spine*) and describes books 'purring'. Finally it reaches the live child, *charred* dead *bird*, and the child's *wondering* about life and death.

The ancient images it draws on sleep in all Western psyches. The hearth as mother's womb has been around in Greek lyric poetry since the sixth century BC, nourished by the image of Hestia, Greek goddess of the hearth. The fire of sexual love is even older. But this poem wakes them up. It is called *Smoke*, and there is none of that without fire. There has to be fire in the grate before the child can be born. The child somehow seems the product of all this effort around the *stove*, which the father gave his life to (*his diaries*, his life to date): of the father's nurturing and caring before the child was born *from under* mother's *heart*.

The central section describes how the *father* tended this *stove* as

139

if the child was watching. The verbs seem (at first) to describe his activities on *one morning*. He *carried, slid the ash, snapped sticks, crumpled newspaper, struck, dipped*. Then *smoke unrolled; flames spread*.

But at *would shake*, we realise these were repeated actions, something the father did every morning. Later, in the twelfth verse, we find the child had not even been alive on that particular *morning*.

The poem tells us this (*soon, I would arrive*) by repeating *would* from *father would shake*, using *would* as part of a future verb (*would arrive*), not a past repeated act (*would shake*). This suggests we should connect the two. The child who will arrive in verse twelve will, in the future, also watch all these repeated acts of care. The last five verses (from *The ash-pan*) must refer to repeated acts that the father did every morning, which the child (once born and sentient) would watch.

So *But this time*, beginning the tenth verse, swings back to *found no heat and ash* in the third. This what made that *one morning* different. He did not, in fact, do any of the things described in verses five to nine. *Instead*, he burnt *his diaries*. For warmth, because there was no coal; but (the poem implies) he was also giving up his own past, his separateness, for the new family as his partner became a *mother*.

The poem does not explain. It just shows a series of actions, the father's repeated acts (tending the *stove*), and his two single acts, burning the diaries, breaking the brittle *charred bird*. It also shows the child making images for its own pre-birth existence from his father's acts, his mother's inwardness.

It gets across a feeling of being at the centre of the house and its warmth. Of *looking up*, even before he was born, *at the light*. Of feeling that the selves and words of both parents went into making him, and preparing for him. The lost words of the father's *diaries* were given up for him. Light came to him *down* the mother's *throat* when *she sang or spoke*.

The music is as connective as the images. The O of that all-important *stove* blows through the poem like the *smoke* in which it keeps reappearing: in *hearthstone, open, no, coals, loaded, blown, smoke unrolled, stove, old coal, broke*. And then, after a pause, in *grow, smoke, throat, spoke*.

The short E of *kept* in the first line is repeated in *legs* in the next line, and *spread* in the next verse. The IME of *climbed* widens to *palms* and *warm* in the second verse; the ANK of *flanks* is picked up in the next verse by *cranked* and *bank*; the AY of *safe's* followed by *place* and (the next verse) *grey*, *flames*, *grate*, then *doorway* and *face*, to reappear in *shake*. The EE of *brief* echoes *released* and picks up *heat* and *heaped*; *cracked* picks up *black*, and is echoed in *match* and *snapped*; *dustbin* picks up *smuts* and its short U carries on in *rush*, *up* and (in the ninth verse where the poem pauses) *shut*.

Then come the two burning stanzas. Their *instead* echoes *spread* in the eighth stanza. The run of twinned vowels perhaps suggests flickering flames and marks these two stanzas out as the decisive event: *time/spine*, *took/book*, *his/diaries*, *year/year*, *purred/burned*.

The child will come after the books fall *apart*; the running-stitch connections over stanzas begin again. *Heart* picks up *apart*, *too* picks up *flue* and the final four-line stanza brings back the long O of *stove*. The poem discloses preparations for creating a tightly bonded family. Everything hangs together: vowel sounds tie each stanza together and make relationships across stanzas; one image blends into another, future acts blend with past acts to make a warm poem of tight inner connections about connectedness.

No

The children have brought their wood turtle
into the dining hall
because they want us to feel

the power they have
when they hold a house
in their own hands, want us to feel

alien lacquer and the little thrill
that he might, like God, show his face.
He's the colour of ruined wallpaper,

of cognac, and he's closed,
pulled in as though he'll never come out;
nothing shows but the plummy leather

of the legs, his claws resembling clusters
of diminutive raspberries.
They know he makes night

anytime he wants, so perhaps
he feels at the centre of everything,
as they do. His age,

greater than that of anyone
around the table, is a room
from which they are excluded,

though they don't mind,
since they can carry this perfect
building anywhere. They love

that he might poke out
his old, old face, but doesn't.
I think the children smell unopened,

like unlit candles, as they heft him
around the table, praise his secrecy,
holding to each adult face

his prayer,
the single word of the shell,
which is no.

Doty, born in 1953 in Tennessee, spent much of his childhood
moving around America. His father was a civilian member of the
Army Corps of Engineers, shifting to one job after another. Doty
has published seven collections (and three books of autobio-
graphical prose), received many American awards, and lives in New
York and Houston, Texas, where he teaches. He emerged in the
Nineties as a leading gay poet in American letters, especially in *My
Alexandria*, about his lover dying of AIDS, which won the UK's
1995 T. S. Eliot Prize.

His work specialises in lyric glitter, focusing on sheen and surface:
the scuffed skin of a crackhead in a New York subway crumbling like
moth-wing dust. The shimmer Doty sees in the world mirrors the
opalescent language in which he describes it. *Every sequin*, he says
defiantly in one book, is *an act of praise*.

This poem sums up that enterprise of looking for the inner in the
surface. Its central image is the accessible interior under the *alien
lacquer* and *plummy leather* of a tortoise's shell. (American says
'turtle' for English 'tortoise'.) The self, or meaning, hides behind a
surface *the colour of ruined wallpaper, of cognac*. This meaning or
self is like the *face* of God. It *might poke out, but doesn't*. It is *a room*
from which the children are *excluded* (as they are from other things
in grown-up life) but which they can *carry anywhere*. It is a *perfect
building*, a *house* they can *hold* in their *own hands* even though the
room is *closed* against them, refusing to be known (*the single word of
the shell is no*). But the fact that they know it is alive in there delights
them.

Because, the poem suggests, it is like them. They too *smell
unopened*. They want the adults *to feel the power they have* over the
tortoise. They also identify with the tortoise's power *to make night
anytime he wants* and keep his inner life, face and self secret (*praise
his secrecy*), while able to *poke out* any time. And also with how the
tortoise may feel *at the centre of everything*.

The key repeated words are *feel*, *want* and *face*. The relations of the ideas those noises stand for make the drama of the poem.

The central verse begins *anytime he wants*, and the central line of the whole thing is (appropriately) *he feels at the centre of everything*. The first two times *want* appears, the *children* do the wanting. By the central verse, it is the tortoise that (supposedly) *wants*.

In the first verses it is *we*, the grown-ups, whom the children want to *feel* something. At the centre, the tortoise *feels at the centre*. But with *face*, it is the other way round. The first *face* is the tortoise's. The *children* do not see it, just as we never see the face of God. When *face* reappears (as a word in the poem but not a real face in the scene) it is *an old old face* (the one thing about the tortoise with which the *children* cannot identify). Finally it is the *face* of each adult, as the *children* hold the creature's unseen face up to each in turn. For the tortoise is at the centre not only of the *children*'s feelings, but of how they relate to the adults: what they *want* the adults *to feel*, what they *show* and hold *out* to them.

Normally, a *face* is an outside surface which shows the inside, the feeling. But the tortoise can hide its whole face. *Nothing shows*. The children's complex delight in this is a bunch of feelings that feel visible to the poet (*they want, perhaps he feels as they do, they don't mind, they love that*). They *praise his secrecy*, love having *power* over a creature that can do what they cannot: withhold himself, deny communication.

The poem turns what the *children* feel about the tortoise into an image for all human understanding. We search for meaning in the world as ancient alchemists searched for the 'buried god', *deus absconditus*: the secret divinity or meaning in all created things. (The tortoise's face is unseen, *like God*. What *the children* hold to the adults is *his prayer*.) We search for meaning but may find it most in how the world refuses it to us.

The dominant sound in the first stanzas, up to *never come out*, is the EL/EEL ending reiterated in *feel* (*turtle, hall, feel, feel, little thrill, pulled, he'll; feel, table, smell, candles, table*), leading up to *single shell*. After *never come out*, other sounds emerge as important. *Wallpaper* begins an end-syllable, -ER, which gathers momentum through *leather, clusters, centre* (central word of the central line), *greater*, into *prayer*.

The vowel of the all-important title word which stages the final refusal, the withholding which the children are paradoxically *holding out*, is prepared for by *hold, own, show, closed, though, shows*, *know, so, though, don't, poke, old old, unopened, holding.*

Doty's characteristic blend of surface description and abstract insight begins with the *children* in relation to *adults*. They delight in something that can say with its whole body and being a word which is a vital item of currency between *children* and *adults*. The tortoise-package of outer surface and inner self is an image for the *children* who are *unlit candles* and *smell unopened*, in love with the power to *hold out*, to make grown-ups *feel* things while being able, themselves, to say *No*.

Baptism

Brighteye, Faith and me
we get baptise same day
in de Holy Spirit
in de Holy sea
crass fram where de church stan
like a mountain on de plain
crass fram de Police Station
where de sinners held in chains
we was likkle children
grown in Sunday School
dressed in white
legs crossed tight
nat to let the devil een
Dat bright bright Sunday mawning
de sea lie dung so calm
Pastor tek we han in turn
and lead we to de lamb
but wen Brighteye turn come
jus as de choir raise a hymn
a wave lif up so big, Oh Gawd
Pastor an Brighteye cyan swim

Born in Jamaica in 1956, Breeze was brought up by her grandparents in rural Jamaica, studied at the Jamaican School of Drama and came to Britain with the leading dub poet Linton Kwesi Johnson, whose fusion of reggae rhythms, spoken word and politics inspired the radicalised black community of Britain in the Seventies and Eighties. In Britain, Breeze became the first woman performer in this traditionally male-dominated field. She has published four collections, and divides her time between the UK and Jamaica.

In one poem she says she wants to *make words / music / move beyond / language / into sound*; in performance she often sings or chants. Her dramas and characters speak to her experience as actress, choreographer and theatre director. She draws on Jamaican and Trinidadian speech rhythms and storytelling, moving between Jamaican, Standard English, and the language of an earlier Jamaican generation. Her work ranges from childhood memories of Kingston to contemporary life in inner-city London, exploring inner aspects of black women's experience through personal stories and historical narrative.

The book in which this poem appears charts life between two places. A remembered childhood in Jamaican hills, dominated by Church, schoolroom and the *bush* (an image, with its *undergrowth of herbs*, for pervasive sensuality) and shared with two other girls. Brighteye and Faith follow the same mischievous female path towards sexuality as the speaker, the *me*. All this is backlit by the now of urban Britain.

The book is a mosaic of immigrant voices. It is a book about beginnings, that links the beginnings of English literature (Chaucer, the King James Bible) with Caribbean lives remade in a new land. A Jamaican widow in Brixton Market is Chaucer's Wife of Bath arguing with St Paul about sex, insisting there's nothing wrong with polygamy. (She's had five husbands since she was twelve and *shall welcome de sixt one / wenever im choose to arrive*.) In a steamy rehearsal room an actress playing the Messiah dreams *of tropical thunderstorms* instead of this *cool, measured* British vision of the Bible. Where *only Burger King is open*, she wants to *lift the roof / and open us to rain*, wants *something to break the clouds / bring chaos* – as, in this poem, a *big wave* clobbers the orderly baptism.

This kaleidoscope of songs, poems and prose pieces is a parable of immigration. Some don't survive: 'Mamma is nat the same, is like she living here but her spirit gawn back to Jamaica.' Family dispersal is the norm: 'All de time ah crying to go wid mamma, an Daddy, ah call im dat but im wasn't mi fadda, my fadda did go do farm work in America an never come back, an Daddy married my mother wen she come to Englan.' Yet overall the energy of Jamaica, summed up in the *bright* of *Brighteye*, survives transplanting to the chip shops round Trafalgar Square; and flourishes.

This poem comes early in the book, after a prose piece ('Learning') about *de fus likkle bwoy ever put im han eena mi panty*. These are songs of innocence, experience and initiation. Sexual comes before religious (as Brighteye before Faith). The *legs crossed tight* in this poem (*nat to let the devil een*) have been opened in the previous poem when *Patrick's han jus slide mi panty to one side an start play music*. Sex and religion belong together as a *bright* anarchic source of richness and *music*.

The different aspects of life the girls learn is all one whole. The poem says so formally: it is a single block held together by rhyme. Inside that, two quatrains lead to a central movement of five lines (*we was likkle children . . . let the devil een*) which is followed, symmetrically, by two more quatrains.

Rhymes and half-rhymes of alternating lines hold each quatrain together: *me/sea; stan/station, plain/chains; calm/turn/lamb; come/hymn/swim*, and the central section is ringed by *children . . . een*. But its two central lines rhyme close together, illustrating exactly what they are about: holding the centre *tight*. Inner rhymes and vowel echoes across lines (*Brighteye/baptise, dressed/crossed, Sunday/dung*) strengthen the cohesive effect of the end-rhymes in a landscape that seems (as described by this confident child-voice) so sure of its givens: *holy spirit, church, mountain* and *plain*, but also *police station* with *sinners in chains*.

This image of punishment and prison leads into the longer central section, the speaker's own self-image. What they were, then: their smallness, *white* innocence, attempts at self-protection. Into this comes *Pastor*. The *sea*, like a trusting child, lies down *so calm*. He takes their hands, to *lead we to the lamb*: an image of initiation, a man leading a girl into the sea. The *choir* raises a *hymn*, the *wave* lifts too, and *Oh Gawd* becomes an image of disaster, not praise. Baptism is engulfment, seduction, growing up.

And not only into sexuality. This sea, *calm* till the *big wave*, is the sea of life facing *likkle children*. It is not just a *Holy sea*, but in the context of this book the *sea* which all these mothers, grannies and children will cross as emigrants. The title poem of this collection, 'The Arrival of Brighteye', is a mix of prose and song evoking diaspora, immigration, and the joy of remeeting family and friends in England after years apart. And its refrain runs, *Brighteye, Brighteye, / going crass de sea / Brighteye, Brighteye, / yuh gwine remember me?*

17 Katherine Pierpoint

Swim Right Up To Me

I first learnt to swim at home in my father's study
On the piano-stool, planted on the middle of the rug.
Stomach down, head up, arms and legs rowing hard;
I swam bravely, ploughing up the small room,
Pinned on a crushed stuckness of stomach to tapestry,
The twin handles hard on my elbows on the back-stroke.
A view down through four braced wooden legs
To the same thin spot in the rug.
My mother faced me, calling rhythmic encouragement,
Almost stepping back to let me swim up to her,
Reminding me to breathe;
And wiping my hair and eyes with her hand
As I swam and swam on the furniture against a running tide,
Pig-cheeked, concentrating on pushing and pushing away,
Planning to learn to fly next, easy,
Higher than the kitchen table, even. The garden wall.

Pierpoint was born in 1961 and her first book (1995) won her the title of Sunday Times Young Writer of the Year. Her poems see familiar things enticingly clearly and newly. They often luxuriate in the physical strangeness of domestic places but this one is about a process: learning, growing up. It begins where music begins (*piano-stool*) and ends by swooping away over *The garden wall*.

The sixteen lines are equally divided between two parents. They begin in *father's study*, where the speaker is described with passive participles (*planted*, *pinned*), as well as active verbs (*learnt*) often qualified by a rather grown-up retrospective adverb, as if the speaker is remembering her child self with a rueful adult smile (*rowing hard*, *swam bravely*). In the second half, *mother* has all the action for the first four lines (*faced*, *calling*, *stepping*, *reminding*, *wiping*), till the learning is cemented and the child's active participles swarm back suggesting further things that can now be learnt (*concentrating, pushing, planning*) till the final impossible verb, *fly*.

One principle of learning (and swimming) is repetition, and the words that characterise effort are repeated too (*hard, hard, up, up, stomach, stomach, legs, legs, rug, rug*). This repetition culminates with the child finally getting it, putting the repeated words next to each other: *swam and swam, pushing and pushing.*

I, the sound and the identity which begin the poem (and which the poem is about), echoes through the first half (*my, I, my*, widening out in *braced*) and gathers strength in the second, as the child learns to swim and imagines growing up (*my, reminding, wiping, my, eyes, I, tide*). It tilts into *away* and triumphs in the dream of the last two lines: *fly, higher*.

In the first half, short U runs from *study* to *rug, stomach, up, up, crushed stuckness, stomach*, and back to *rug*, and repeated S (accompanied by the occasional hard K or G) accompanies each initially difficult task: *first, swim, father's study, stool, stomach, arms, legs, swam, small, crushed stuckness, stomach, tapestry, handles, elbows, back-stroke, braced, legs, same spot, faced, rhythmic encouragement, stepping, swim, rug*.

But at *reminding me to breathe*, the poem begins to stress the second rather than first letter in the all-important word *swim*. This is the turning point, the poem's shortest line. The child has learnt to *swim* and must concentrate on the *next* thing. Flying, getting *away*. In the great achievement, *swam and swam*, we hear the W of *rowing, twin, down, wiping*, which now continues into the getaway words *away* and (the last word) *wall*.

In the *father* half, the child is fixed and static. She *swam bravely, arms and legs rowing hard*, but *planted* and *pinned*. Her *view* is *down*. Wooden *legs* (not hers) are *braced*. She cannot get away from a *spot in the rug*. Nothing moves on. Always *the same thin spot*. Then mother calls her into rhythm, and *almost* steps *back*, as if the static child really can 'swim right up to' her, as in the title.

At this, poem and child flicker into fluid action which culminates in the longest line, ending in *running tide*.

Every word can shift the tone. This poem gives us a double perspective, balancing the physical experience and perspective of the child with the retrospective glance of an adult. The final *fly next, easy*, and *higher than the kitchen table, even* give the child's words and fantasy – with, again, that adult smile. *Easy* and *even* suggest the child's perspective, the low-to-the-ground-eye view (*down through four braced wooden legs*) and hemmed-in body (*crushed stuckness*). But the adverbs and adjectives speak of the adult looking back, leading to the adult joke of *pig-cheeked* followed (since pigs flying is an image of the impossible) by *learn to fly*.

One problem readers of poetry have now, as opposed to classical or Victorian times, is the range of possible reference and experiences available to the poet, which we may not share. Everyone listens to different music. You cannot tell from this poem if Pierpoint listens to Kate Bush, for instance, or not. But the textures and sense-impressions of her work strongly remind me (at least) of Bush's album *The Sensual World*, and the poem seems close to Bush's song 'The Fog', which ends 'swim to me' and compares learning to swim, with a father's help, to learning grown-up love.

Whether or not Pierpoint knows Kate Bush's work, her poem offers indirectly the same experience that Bush's song addresses. Remembering being taught to swim becomes a way of reseeing your home life, with your parents, as a preparation for sexuality: for learning *to fly*, to grow away from your child-body's *crushed stuckness*, out of that *small room* called *home*, *higher than* your first known *kitchen table*.

Vita Nova

You saved me, you should remember me.

The spring of the year; young men buying tickets for the
    ferryboats.
Laughter, because the air is full of apple blossoms.

When I woke up, I realised I was capable of the same feeling.

I remember sounds like that from my childhood,
laughter for no cause, simply because the world is beautiful,
something like that.

Lugano. Tables under the apple trees.
Deckhands raising and lowering the colored flags.
And by the lake's edge, a young man throws his hat into the
    water;
perhaps his sweetheart has accepted him.

Crucial
sounds or gestures like
a track laid down before the larger themes

and then unused, buried.

Islands in the distance. My mother
holding out a plate of little cakes –
as far as I can remember, changed
in no detail, the moment
vivid, intact, having never been
exposed to light, so that I woke elated, at my age
hungry for life, utterly confident –

By the tables, patches of new grass, the pale green
pieced into the dark existing ground.

Surely spring has been returned to me, this time
not as a lover but a messenger of death, yet
it is still spring, it is still meant tenderly.

Glück, born in New York in 1943, grew up on Long Island, has published many books, received many honours, including the 1993 Pulitzer Prize for her collection *The Wild Iris*, and was American Poet Laureate 2003–4.

Her delicate, scrupulous poems explore sex, death, memory and transformation, blending ancient myth with modern sensibility. The poetry is softly austere, a recollection not so much of experience but of reactions to experience. She writes many book-length sequences: this is the title poem from one of those, which says goodbye to a long partnership. Its touchstone is Dante's *La Vita Nuova*, a landmark in the literature of courtly love which celebrates his love for the woman he worshipped from afar till her death in 1290 (though he married two years later). Glück's sequence braids grief into intimations of 'new life': fresh spiritual growth after love is lost.

This poem has several strands with different inner voices kept at first carefully separate. The single lines come from the deepest place and follow their own journey. This inner voice starts by addressing a lost *you* (the lover still in her head), telling him *you should remember me*. When we hear it again, it is further on towards recovery. *I woke up* has double potential – waking from real sleep, and waking *up* metaphorically or emotionally to new possibilities (*realised I was capable of the same feeling*, i.e. of *laughter* or anything else which *apple blossoms* might suggest).

In its third entry, however, this voice finishes the thought (that *sounds or gestures* expressing joy in new life are preparation for something *larger*) by suggesting these promises of hope may not work out. They may stay *unused*, *buried*.

At that point the poem changes. To see how, we need to listen to the other voices.

The three-line stanzas seem to come from a different place in the psyche: a commenting, analytical voice, one that says *like*, that compares. *Sounds like that from my childhood*; *something like that*; *sounds or gestures like a track laid down*.

This second inner voice compares present (*throws*) and past (*laid down before*). It explains (*simply because*) and evaluates (*crucial*). In the last stanza, the third three-liner, it begins *surely*: explaining, concluding, drawing together the future (*messenger of death*), present (*is spring*) and past (*has been returned*; *this time not as a lover*) to decide what it *is meant*.

The third inner voice records sense impressions. These begin in

153

the present and go back to the past, to *childhood*. This voice has few main verbs. It just registers *sounds* and *gestures* on which the analytical voice will comment. It opens in a lake landscape full of human joy in *spring* (a key word, which nearly begins and nearly ends the poem). It records impressions – which are also images of looking forward to something more (*buying tickets* for a voyage; *apple blossoms* that come before the fruit).

After this the other two voices come in again: the lonely deep voice, then the comment voice. Then this impressionistic descriptive voice resumes with observations that are also images for what might be round the corner. *Tables under apple trees* are more preparation, for sitting, talking, laughing, company. There are *deckhands raising and lowering colored flags* in communication; colour, display, celebration. A *young man*, conjured from *young men* in the second line, throws *his hat* in the lake.

Throws is the only main verb this voice offers: an act of entering or celebrating life (like throwing your hat in the ring perhaps) which the poem connects to love (*sweetheart accepted him*).

Here the analytical voice comes back, says *crucial*, analyses the descriptive voice's physical observations in abstract terms (*sounds or gestures*) and compares all this to making a record (*track laid down before larger themes*).

Then the lonely voice comes in with its single line, suggesting promise never comes, the *track* will be *unused*, images of hope and new life get *buried*.

But this word *buried* acts as cue for the descriptive voice to return. What is *buried* can be unearthed by memory or dream. What was stored in you long ago can suddenly come alive. This voice turns its power of recording sense impressions on to the past: to two visual images, *buried* since *childhood* (picking up *I remember . . . childhood* from the analytical voice's first stanza). First, *Islands in the distance*, another image for something which you (as a child) expect to reach one day. Something waiting for you, something you will find. In terms of the poem's earlier images, these islands belong with the ferryboat *tickets*, as if this is where the *young men* and any *sweetheart* will be going. Second, a nurturing image: a suddenly recovered *vivid* memory (*having never been/exposed to light*) of *mother holding out* the *little cakes*; of life held *out* to you by *mother*, life on a *plate*. Just as (in the poem) this 'new life' by the lake is *holding out* its own little images of hope and *spring*.

At this point the analytical voice (which first said *I remember*) seems to take over from the describing voice. This is where the energy and new life start up. This passage lengthens to become the longest stanza. The analytical voice comments on the cake memory (which is, *as far as I can remember, changed / in no detail*).

This is the voice that sees cause and effect. Earlier it said *because*. Now it says *so that*. And the poem moves to waking again. *I woke up* came in the fourth line. Now we hear *I woke elated*. We realise the *islands* and *cakes* were maybe a dream from which the speaker *woke* in line four.

The voices have merged now. So have the times, *childhood* and the present. So have dream and memory. It is not the speaker as a child who wakes *elated, hungry for life, utterly confident*, but the speaker now: *at my age*. That memory of cakes must have come in a dream from which the speaker *woke up* into the poem.

So far, the poem has moved from images of *spring* outside, through memories of being *capable* of *feeling*, or of her *mother*, to elation and new life. Now the descriptive voice, shouldered out of the longest stanza by the analytical voice, returns for two more lines of observation.

First, those *tables* again. By the end, we will realise the whole poem is about the return of feeling and hope, and has prepared for the actual word *returned*, in the last stanza, by little verbal and pictorial returns: *young men/young man; apple blossom; apple trees; tables/tables*.

Secondly, *patches of new grass* (more images of new feeling and life) appear in the *dark existing ground*. The ground, as it were, in which the lonely voice of the single lines has existed up to now. Their *pale green* is *pieced into* what was already there, just as the poem has *pieced* Lugano's real world of people and ferryboats *into* the pre-existing memories which were part of the speaker's psyche already.

Things are coming together. In *spring*, the different voices and different times of this poem are becoming one. Cue for the conclusion: *surely spring has been returned to me*.

The *re* of *returned* summons up the *re* of remembering which is (in the poem's own word) *crucial* to the poem. The first line, apparently addressed to the lost *you*, precedes the first *I woke up*, as if the first words, *You saved me, you should remember me*, were part of the dream from which she *woke*. But though it is *you* who *should remember*, the real remembering is done by the speaker: at *laughter* (as people queue for ferryboats, *I remember sounds like that*) and at the memory of cakes (*changed in no detail, as far as I can remember*).

After the repetitions, the *re* of return and remember, the poem says *this time*. There have been other 'times'. Not just *childhood*, but the implied time which this poem does not speak about except to say *you saved me*. But *this time*, spring does not involve, as it must have then, *a lover* (like the *young man* with an imagined *sweetheart*).

That word *lover* echoes the nurturing *mother* of memory and dream; and that figure is the one whose loss drives the whole sequence. The *lover* is absent: *this time* spring is *a messenger of death*. The poem may be gesturing to the mix of new life and death in one of Modernism's most famous poems, Eliot's opening lines in *The Waste Land*, where April is cruel, and new blossom comes from *dead ground*.

But *death* in Christian terms, Dante's terms, is also 'new life'. In Dickens' novel *Bleak House*, the dying Richard talks of 'beginning the world'. 'Not this world,' says the narrator as Richard dies, 'the one that makes this right.' There is a dying in this poem too, but also a sense of rebirth and making right.

The poem begins with what seems like reproach. *Remember me*: words which Dido sings to her departing lover before she leaps on to her funeral pyre in Purcell's opera *Dido and Aeneas*. But the rhythm of these two words is reproduced exactly in the last two words: *meant tenderly*. This is the rhythm impression the poem leaves us with.

The journey, through complex shifts, is from valediction and reproach to tenderness. The *track* of emotional and mental experience (through three different inner voices that become one) follows images of *spring*, constantly aiming at precision through uncertainty (*something like that, as far as I can remember*).

It is as if the speaker, connecting new *spring* images from the outside world with inner memories and dreams, realises she has found nurture in the whole lot together, via her remembered optimism as a child: her *mother holding out cakes*, a vision of *distant islands*. She receives the whole lot as gifts *meant tenderly*, and ends by suggesting that even this poem, which begins in apparent reproach, is *meant tenderly* too.

Broken Moon

Twelve, small as six,
strength, movement, hearing
all given in half measure,
my daughter,
child of genetic carelessness,
walks uphill, always.

I watch her morning face;
precocious patience as she hooks each sock,
creeps it up her foot,
aims her jersey like a quoit.
My fingers twitch;
her private frown deters.

Her jokes can sting:
'My life is like dressed crab –
lot of effort, rather little meat.'
Yet she delights in seedlings taking root,
finding a fossil,
a surprise dessert.

Chopin will not yield to her stiff touch;
I hear her cursing.
She paces Bach exactly,
firm rounding of perfect cadences.
Somewhere inside
she is dancing a courante.

In dreams she skims the sand,
curls toes into the ooze of pools,
leaps on to stanchions.
Awake, her cousins take her hands;
they lean into the waves,
stick-child between curved sturdiness.

She turns away from stares,
laughs at the boy who asks
if she will find a midget husband.
Ten years ago,
I showed her the slice of silver in the sky.
'Moon broken,' she said.

Born in 1939, Satyamurti grew up in Kent, lived in America,
Singapore and Uganda before settling in London where she teaches
sociology at the University of East London. She won the 1986
National Poetry Competition and has published several collections
and a *Selected*. Her poems focus on people, especially on sympathy
for the gallantry of disability and disadvantage; like a stammering
father who invents his own words. This, the title poem of her first
collection, moves towards the metaphor in which a disabled child
aged two describes the moon. A metaphor which is tragically apt for
her as well.

The poem starts with her size (*small as six*) and shape (*walks
uphill always*), to her self-dressing battles (*sock, foot, jersey*) and
black jokes at herself (*lot of effort, little meat*) or at outsiders
(*laughs*). It journeys back in time to her babyhood *ten years ago*,
reflected poignantly in her *delight*, as she grows up, not only (like
any child) in *a surprise dessert*, but in things that are growing
properly (*seedlings taking root*), whose shape endures (*fossil*).

The poem says her *hearing* is only *half measure*, but moves
towards music which depends on *measure*. She has the power to
shape music (*paces exactly, firm rounding, perfect cadences*). Despite
her limitations (*stiff touch*) and her fury at them (*cursing*), she has
inner agility. *Inside,* instead of 'pacing' Bach, she makes paces of her
own. Dances *a courante* (the 'running' dance). *Skims, curls, leaps.*
But *awake*, she is a *stick-child*. It is her cousins who curl and move
freely (*take, lean, curved*).

The last stanza moves from cousins to outsiders. Her act is to turn
away and laugh at the idea of an imaginary outsider who might
become an insider, a *husband*. Who would also be a *midget*.

This is the cue for the poem to introduce the idea of nurturing,
which was refused by the child herself in the second stanza – *my
fingers twitch, / her frown deters*. The *I* introduced in the first two
stanzas but deterred at the end of the second, comes back. But
halfway through this last stanza the daughter, even aged two, can

surprise. She brings out in that metaphor some of the richness within herself. And the poem ends on her own act – *said*.

All along, the poem has built up a picture of her determined, intelligent, creative interiority: *precocious patience*, *deters*, *jokes can sting*, *dressed crab* (the joke that follows 'dressing' herself); *aims*, *firm*. This enables her to deal with moments when the *stick-child* image comes back at her from other people's *stares*.

The poem's progressive understanding of her strength leads up to her creativity in producing the *broken moon* symbol. The mother seems the strong one: pointing at the moon through her own metaphor, *slice of silver*. But the child comes back with a savagely perfect metaphor to cap it. Mother's fingers *twitch* to help, but the poem is about the daughter's powers, not limitations. She may seem, like a waned *moon*, *broken*. But from the first line on, the poem gets stronger with the child's waxing *strength*. A tragic poem, but an admiring, proud one too.

The child is *small as six*, and there are six stanzas of six lines each. The poem is shaped like her. Just as the child *walks uphill always*, and everything is effort, so the poem proceeds with effort. It does not ease joins with an 'and' between the girl's actions (*hooks*, *creeps*, *aims*) and what she enjoys (*seedlings*, *finding*, *dessert*). She is *given* physical powers *in half measure*. The poem too has a *half measure* line of only three beats, occasionally stretching to four or five (*Yet she delights in seedlings taking root*), sometimes falling back on one (*my daughter*) or two (*her jokes can sting*; *somewhere inside*).

In the first half, the vowel sounds holding each stanza together suggest tight living in a constricted body. The short E of *twelve* is echoed in *strength*, *measure*, *genetic*. The OR of *small* in *all*, *daughter*, *walks*, *always*; picked up in *watch* and *sock* of the next stanza, then lost. The first stanza's *six* is picked up by *twitch* in the second. But this stanza has rather the AY of *face*, *patience* and *aims*. The third stanza is dominated by long *I* of *life*, *like*, *delights*, *finding*, *surprise*.

As we learn the child's powers, the poem's fibres loosen. We still get vowel links: AH (*Bach*, *dancing*, *courante*), ER (*cursing*, *perfect*, *curls*, *curved*, *turns* and the five times repeated *her*, which ends up in stressed position, at a line-end); short A (*exactly*, *sand*, *stanchions*, *hands*, and the unstressed syllable of *husband*); AY (*paces*, *awake*, *take*, *waves*, *away*). But the poem is preparing to let her speak. The last two lines move from the OH of *showing* to her own OH in *broken*; from the mother's *slice*, *sky* and *silver* to *said*. But the child has the last words. They are musically unpartnered – and, like her, unique.

Making Friends with Ties

His khaki tie was perfectly knotted in wartime.
The tail was smartly plumped.
The dent became a groove
where it entered a sturdy, rectangular knot,
never a Windsor.

This groove came out
in exactly the same place all his life,
never in the middle,
but slightly to the left.
'You have to get it right first time,'
he told me, my first term at school.
'Otherwise you go raving mad.'

I was so impressed by this
I didn't listen in class.
I made friends with people's ties, not them.
One day when I was drunk I told him,
'I don't like the groove!'
His face softened towards me for a moment,
'Don't you, dear boy? Well, I'm *delighted*.'

Williams, born in 1942 in Windsor, son of an actor and a model, went
to Eton, and the glamorous, financially precarious background of his
childhood has a strong, archetypally English presence in his poems.
He published his first book in 1965; many followed. He won the
2000 T. S. Eliot Prize, has been awarded the Queen's Gold Medal
for Poetry and writes a 'Freelance' column for the *Times Literary
Supplement* whose keynote is amused, helpless observerdom. His
work runs on wry wit and meticulously controlled informal tone:
casually elegant, deceptively simple. It is apparently artless art, like
that of Fred Astaire whom Williams sometimes quotes: 'If it doesn't
look easy you aren't working hard enough.'

Williams's voice is rueful, understated, deeply against attitude striking or learned allusion. The seventeenth-century Japanese poet Matsuo Basho said that form, and the way you join parts of a poem, should seem 'light as a shallow river flowing over its sandy bed', and Williams feels there is more intensity in plainness than decoration. 'Simple stuff operates without the safety net of the poetical.'[1]

Many of his poems draw on his theatre background. Performance, appearance, style and mirrors, masks and haircuts are all prominent. The more theatrical (*God give me strength to lead a double life*, begins a well-known poem), the more apparently candid the speaker becomes. One theme is the double-edgedness of form. We need it, poems need it, but is it, in the end, hollow? Is form all there is? In a poem about making love the speaker wonders where the line breaks will go in the poem he will write afterwards. Another theme is never entirely understanding what happens to you as you grow up, grow old, find love, lose it, worry about it. One poem, which imagines being an old man who has a tube stuck through his penis and is never told why, infuriated a bunch of public-school sixth-formers whom a friend of mine once taught. 'No one should be *allowed*', they complained, 'to write poems like that.'

This poem is about a father and son, but we get no description of either. Instead, over half the lines describe the knot in the father's tie. The all-important thing is appearance. The word 'father' never appears: it is there behind *he* (*his tie*, *his life*, *he told me*, *I told him*, *his face softened towards me*). Ruefully amused, the poem shows the father's image and beliefs shaping the son who grows up to realise his father had limits, while suggesting that his father's insistence on style affected everything in the son, down to this very poem and the wry humour with which it describes that father.

The father's voice is public-school gentlemanly in the Second World War. *You have to get it right first time* is the advice that carries the son through his *first term* (echoing *first time*). The penalties for doing the wrong thing come at the end of each of the first two stanzas. They are increasingly weird. *Never a Windsor.* (Wrong sort of knot, no explanation why.) *Otherwise you go raving mad* suggests how disproportionate is this emphasis on appearance.

The third stanza describes the effect of the father's example (*so impressed*). Extremes beget extremes (*made friends with people's ties, not them*). Halfway through the last stanza, the boy has grown up, can get *drunk*, form his own judgement of his father, *his* values, ideas, ties.

Humour and lightness are everywhere, of course, but the details that impress the small boy (*smartly plumped*, *dent*, *groove*, *rectangular knot*) increasingly suggest the poet's retrospective scepticism.

The first line, a pentameter, suggests this will be a formal English poem to match a formal English tie, so immaculately judged for every occasion, even *wartime*. But the second and third lines stop all that. Despite the stricture *get it right first time*, the poem is not going to copy father's form. It will make its own rhythm, as the speaker will form his own outlook on the world, and on 'ties', with all the resonance that word has. Filial bonds as well as clothes.

So this poem becomes a *perfectly knotted* tie of its own, cutting its own style. All the line breaks *in exactly the* right *place* for the natural cadences of conversation. Like the tie, it is *slightly* asymmetrical. The first stanza has five lines, the last two seven, like a tie with knot at the top, *plumped tail* below.

In the last stanza, son *delights* father by saying he dislikes what the father was desperate to *get right*. This is a father you only please when you stop admiring him. In the last two lines, instead of the *never* or *otherwise* (the father's warnings, what he feels you must avoid at all costs) comes the father's change in attitude to the boy. *His face softened towards me.*

But only *for a moment*. A whole childhood without that softness seems to flicker behind those words. The father calls the son *dear boy* just as the son shows independent judgement about the all-important question of style. (*I don't like.*) The smoking-jacket phrase *dear boy* suggests the son has had affectation rather than affection all along, during the growing up that the poem silently indicates from *first term at school* on. Appearance was *perfect*, at the expense of feeling. The poem journeys towards suggesting how the son distances himself from the father, but also that this distancing was one of the father's own lessons. The father used form to distance. That tie was a barrier, as well as display.

Amused, elegiac, witty, critical and (underneath) poignant, the poem reflects the father's central lesson that what matters most is form, while suggesting there may be other things that matter too – but can one ever get to them?

Swami Anand

In Kosbad during the monsoons
there are so many shades of green
your mind forgets other colours.

At that time
I am seventeen, and have just started
to wear a sari every day.
Swami Anand is eighty-nine
            and almost blind.
His thick glasses don't seem to work,
they only magnify his cloudy eyes.
Mornings he summons me
      from the kitchen
and I read to him until lunch time.

One day he tells me
'you can read your poems now'.
I read a few, he is silent.
Thinking he's asleep, I stop.
But he says, 'continue'.
I begin a long one
in which the Himalayas rise
            as a metaphor.
Suddenly I am ashamed
to have used the Himalayas like this,
ashamed to speak of my imaginary mountains
to a man who walked through
      the ice and snow of Gangotri
            barefoot
a man who lived close to Kangchenjanga
      and Everest clad only in summer cotton.
I pause to apologize
but he says 'just continue'.

Later, climbing through
           the slippery green hills of Kosbad,
Swami Anand does not need to lean
on my shoulder or his umbrella.
I prod him for suggestions,
ways to improve my poems.
He is silent a long while,
then, he says,
           'there is nothing I can tell you
                      except continue.'

Bhatt, born in Ahmedabad, East Gujarat, in 1956, grew up speaking Gujarati in Pune, went to America aged twelve and later studied writing at the University of Iowa. She has taught in America but now lives in Germany. Her first collection (1988) won a Commonwealth Poetry Prize. She has published many since.

As you'd expect, her poems explore different geographies and memories. The Gujarati language and her Indian childhood form 'the deepest layer', she says, of her identity. Her work explores her divided heritage (one poem describes her grandfather reading Tennyson while imprisoned by the British) and the idea of home. They brim with different characters, sensual detail, history, relationships. They bring together different parts of their speaker's identity: an Indian poet writing in English, but in America; a woman poet in a male tradition.

This one is from her first collection, full of poems about becoming. It begins where it ends – with *green*, in *Kosbad*, in the *monsoons* which make these *hills slippery*. It speaks of two journeys which intersect at the poem's emotional centre: the speaker's hoped-for future journey as a poet; the past pilgrimage made by the old man to Gangotri in the Himalayas, where there is a glacier and famous shrine.

The structuring principle in the loose form is a group of three lines of three beats each (*In Kósbad dúring the monsóons*). But (reflecting the repeated command *continue*) the poem meanders and spills over like many of the things it mentions: the long winding journey, the *sari* (all flow and foldings), *slippery hills* and rain in *monsoons*.

It begins in the present tense. The initial three lines set the outside scene geographically, with *Kosbad*, but also mentally too, by the universal impact the landscape has on *your* (or anyone's) *mind*. *Monsoons*. These *shades of green*.

Once the scene is set, the main body of the poem begins. Another three lines for the next item: the speaker.

Again the poem is precise, but now about *time*. We are still in the present tense but a different sort of present: a long moment in the continuous past, which the poem recreates as if it were the present (*I am seventeen*).

This chunk is eight lines, with appendages. The first three give the speaker's gender at a moment of transition (*just started / to wear a sari*). The next three introduce the protagonist, *Swami Anand*.

Here the three-beat line lengthens, for this is the subject the poem is really addressing. The first of these lines has an extra tail (*and almost blind*) and the lines begin to spill over. The one physical detail given about the Swami is his blindness. The poem began with the visual vividness of this place, but the old man cannot see it. He has *cloudy eyes*. His *thick glasses don't seem to work*.

The two characters make contact: the young speaker so visually impressed, the old man so visually dimmed. After *he summons me* comes another spill-over. The young sari-wearer emerges from the woman's traditional retreat, *the kitchen*, in a half-line hung shyly from his active verb, as if her line does not have the authority to begin a line of its own. The eighth line of this chunk, however, beginning *and I read*, does. For the girl is reading at the old man's *summons*, reading someone else's words, reacting to someone else's authority.

Now the longest chunk: fourteen lines, heart of the poem, height of the feeling. It seems to start with another three lines, as if the three-line group is still the principle of organisation. We are still in the present tense but now at a particular moment in the past (*one day*). The poem has moved from the continuous to a single event. The old man invites her to read her own *poems*. He even says *now*, as if this has been the point all along and he knew it.

But this group of three lines lengthens to four. She expects a reaction and is disconcerted. When *he is silent*, she stops, instead of reading *until lunch time*.

The next group of three lines, beginning *But*, contains the first '*continue*', and continues (obediently) with her reading *a long one*. The poem becomes explanatory about the process of poetry itself (*rise as a metaphor*), as young poet reads to old pilgrim.

The technical, self-conscious word *metaphor* breaks the long chunk into two halves of seven lines. It arrives at the end of the seventh line where she (aged seventeen) *suddenly* becomes self-conscious, *ashamed* (of her poem, of her inexperience and his experience), aware that what she is taking for decoration he has known, and suffered in, as real. Her Himalayas are *imaginary*. She has *used* these holy mountains *like this*, as *metaphor*. He knows them as they are.

The poem starts spilling over again, to conjure the long journey, *ice and snow*, holy remote places. And what he wore: not a *sari* in a *kitchen* like her; but *summer cotton* even close to *Everest*.

At *I pause to apologize*, tone and form return. This is the young poet's anxious, self-conscious mode. But why feel *ashamed*? Why *apologize*?

'A poem is an approach toward a truth,' Kathleen Jamie has said. 'We seek inner permission, because we know that when we are writing in this new place we will have to seek truths.' And, 'The place we enter when we are writing a poem is a moral place.'[2] But where's the morality in using truths you have not experienced yourself?

There are several levels to this worry. You may be using a truth that belongs more truly to other people: exploiting someone else's experience. Elizabeth Bishop reproached Robert Lowell, for example, for putting into his poems verbatim the anguished letters of the wife he had just left.[3]

The less extreme, less personal form of this problem is writing about something far away, which you have not seen yourself.

Metaphor is a leap away to something foreign. Remember Heaney's poem 'Making Strange: *speak of the sweetbriar* as it is but also as what it is not, *the cornfield of Boas*. Imagination is everything. But you have to be responsible about your leaps into the foreign. They have to be, in some way, true. This poet has not experienced the Himalayas herself but is reading to a man who has. She has come up against the big moral problem in 'using' anything in a poem: that you need humility, utter trust in what you are doing, awareness of what you are doing, for *metaphor* not to feel, or be, self-promoting and shallow.

When Heaney was looking 'for images and symbols' which would be 'adequate' ways of writing about 'our predicament' in Northern Ireland, he read about murdered Iron Age bodies preserved in peat in Jutland. He used their murders, especially the murdered figure called Tolland Man, as a metaphor for murders happening all round him. *Some day I will go to Aarhus*, he wrote, *To see his peat-brown head*. When he wrote that, he said later he suddenly felt 'a completely new sensation, of fear'. He told himself, 'You had better *mean* this' and vowed to go there exactly as his poem said.[4]

You must be truthfully behind your symbols and metaphors. You must make the poem, and your relation to it, true. Making a poem is not a light thing to do (even if the poem itself is light). This seventeen-year-old poet *suddenly* sees the problem of 'using' something to which someone else has a realer relation. She is coming up against the fact that while a good *metaphor* is not decoration – it is organic to the poem – a bad one is fake. Is she treating India's holy *Himalayas* as a fashion accessory?

When Louise Glück was fifteen, she wrote a poem about a dying deer. She said long after, 'The problem was, its declared subject was a fraud. My interest did not begin with a deer but with a metaphor. The poem as a whole was mystical to the point of absurdity. Yet something in the language was true and deep.'[5]

When you start out, you don't think about fraud and truth. You meet those questions en route; you only learn to trust what's true in your words and your imagining by doing it. That, perhaps, is what Swami Anand means by *continue*.

There are other, related issues for this young poet. For Indian poets publishing in England or America, there are problems about exoticising their culture and their country's most glamorous features – about not exploiting them, not being facile about them. *Metaphor* is one of the first things that can be facile. You have to avoid what Hugo Williams calls 'the safety-net of the poetic'.

Plus she is a young girl, Swami Anand an old man. The authority of Indian poetry (like most) is traditionally on the side of the ancient, the male. This is the poem's drama: a young female poet, on a journey towards understanding her responsibilities as poet, finds her future artistic journey is bound up with an old man's past holy journey, into real mountains and his own truth.

The fourteen-line chunk finishes at the repeated word *continue*. But this time Swami Anand puts *just* in front of it. This gives her permission to 'go on'. Just by reading to him, she has encountered the moral worry she will have to confront in her writing life. As when he walked *barefoot through ice and snow*, the only thing is going on.

The final chunk is another group of seven lines. Again a three-line group (ending in *umbrella*) begins it. She has moved out of the *kitchen*, out of other people's words, moved on from shame. They are both in *the hills* now, both doing what he did on his journey, *climbing*.

Here, in real hills, he has not only authority but physical self-reliance. So what if he cannot see properly? He *does not need to lean* on her or his *umbrella*. The person using anything like an *umbrella* is the girl (*I prod him*). She wants to get on, *improve my poems*.

On these *slippery* slopes of an Indian Parnassus, the place where this poem began, the two journeys become one: the mountain pilgrimage, the writing of poems. Her *mind* may forget any colour but *green* in these *green hills* but he, though *almost blind*, knows that what matters is direction and momentum. Go on. There will be *other colours*. And the only justification for *having used* other people's experience in poems is learning to make poems well. '*Just continue*'.

To make this point formally, the poem ends in its spilling mode. The line-fragments, and his words, *continue* away into the distance, out of the poem.

O

The teacup stain on the white damask table-cloth was
    not quite perfect. Never-
Theless, I'd set my cup exactly on it, like it was a stain-
    remover.

I sipped the rim with palatable lip. I drank the steaming
    liquor up.
My granny would then read my future from the tea-leaves'
    leavings in the cup.

I stared into enormous china O and saw its every
    centrifugal flaw,
The tiny bobbles glazed in its interior of Delphic
    oracle. I yawned

Into its incandescent blaze of vowel like the cool of
    dudes in black fedoras
At high noon; trigger-fingered, shadowless, they walked
    beneath sombreros.

They stopped me inadvertently and asked for my identity.
    I did not know
Until the mouth of a gun was pressed against my forehead,
    and I felt its O.

Carson is an Irish musician and scholar, Professor at Belfast's
Seamus Heaney Centre. A Northern Irish Catholic born in 1948,
he was educated at Queen's University Belfast and has written nine
collections, four prose works, a guide to Irish traditional music, an
award-winning translation of Dante's *Inferno*, and has won the Irish
Times Literature Prize as well as the T. S. Eliot and Forward Prizes.
  Like two other poets here, Carson spoke English as a second

language. He says the ghost of the Irish language 'hovers behind' the way he writes English. He delights in the elements and relationships of words, and has written sequences based on alphabets (including the police radio alphabet). His *Belfast Confetti* shows language used to spy and to murder: a bomb is packed not with only ironmongery but *a fount of broken type*.

Violence is a major theme. Carson grew up in Northern Ireland and his work echoes with poems by other Northern Irish poets – poets both of his own generation like Paul Muldoon and the one before, like Seamus Heaney and Derek Mahon. His second collection, *The Irish For No*, established him as a major poet before he became the first winner of the T. S. Eliot Prize, and introduced his long, reeling line, seething with anecdote, history, erudition, humour and passion.

Like Muldoon's poems, Carson's make vivid the relationship of words to things. For both, the wordplay (both philosophical and musical), the mix of wide-ranging beauty, eclectic vocabulary, comedy, violence and profundity resonate with the great freeing Irish Modernists, Joyce and Beckett.

Here, for example, he enjoys the sonority of *palatable*, a long word used in an unusual way; he is also yoking two registers, high and low – the Latinate *palatable* and the colloquially ungrammatical *like it was a stain-remover*. As in Joyce and Beckett, all this can be comic while saying something very serious about what language is capable of.

This poem comes from one of his alphabet sequences and is full of its letter, O. The first two stanzas introduce O as circumference: the circular *stain*. The inner, central stanza concentrates on its centre: *enormous china* which the boy sees as the inside of an oracle. O's journey through the poem marks the journey of the thought, from the short O of *cloth*, *not*, *on*, the OO of *remover*, OR of *liquor*, OH of *O* and many other Os, short and long, towards the O of *know*. The child who sets his *cup* over a *stain* as if it could cancel it and tries to see future and past in a *cup* comes to *know* his *identity*, and that it is always under threat.

The poem begins with *stain*; with a Catholic child aware of sin, aware that human things are *not quite perfect. Never.* The line break in *nevertheless* suggests both that nothing human is 'ever' *perfect*, and that despite the Fall (or *stain*) you do what you can: *set* your cup *exactly*, adjust to *stain* as if you could apply a *stain-remover* to sin. The *cup* on *white damask* gestures to the communion *cup* on an altar *cloth* (and Christ's prayer, 'let this cup pass from me') which does remove *stain*.

As *granny* reads his *future* in *tea-leaves* he looks in too, seeing the cup's *interior* in terms of what he is (presumably) learning about at school. More religion: the *Delphic oracle*, whose sibyl foretold the future ambiguously so you did not understand the prophecy properly until your fate had happened.

Greeks called Delphi the 'navel' (*omphalos* word of two Os) of the world. Above its prophetic temple was written 'Know Thyself'. The poem stages this command as a drama. The boy does not *know* his identity *until* a *gun* is imprinted on his own temple.

Behind this poem is also, I guess, the poem 'Spelt from Sibyl's Leaves' by Gerard Manley Hopkins, whose style and complexities often echo in Carson's lines. In Belfast, the olive leaves of ancient Greece have become *tea-leaves* and the sibyl is *granny*, reading the *future*.

In that *cup*, he sees what he watches on TV or at the cinema: people he might want to be in a fantasy *future*: cowboys in American or Mexican hats, hands on guns; cowboys with special language and names (*cool dudes*) in *shadowless* Hollywood violence.

The words *high noon* conjure the scene in *High Noon* where Gary Cooper waits alone in a shuttered town for the approaching gunmen. In the last verse this dream violence comes home. The celluloid *they* of the fourth verse becomes the *they* of his own streets. *They stopped me*.

He does not *know* his identity or his future *until* a *mouth*, not of the sibyl or granny but a gun, brands him with violence, printing O on his *forehead*. Violence, not remote, faraway, ancient or cinematic but here and now, makes you *know exactly* who you are.

He also learns his identity through verbs: by being made the object instead of subject. He was subject of most of the first verbs (*I'd set, I sipped, I stared, and saw, I yawned*). Then *they* step in and make him object of their verb (*they stopped me*). He learns (*I did not know until . . . I felt*) there are aspects of himself (*my identity, my forehead*) to which others react; he ends as an object in other people's world.

The line of roughly nine stresses is so long that each stanza looks like a quatrain, but in fact it is five rhymed couplets. It offers (aptly for a city riven by two opposed identities, Catholic and Protestant) two ways of seeing the line, two ways of seeing its form.

Each couplet makes its own soundworld and criss-crossing

echoes. Sometimes the first line rough-rhymes two words in the middle and the end, or its second half echoes the rhythm of the first like an Irish reel (*I sipped the rim with palatable lip. I drank the steaming liquor up; They stopped me inadvertently and asked for my identity*). In the first verse *quite* echoes *white*; in the second, *lip* echoes *sipped* while *up* and *cup* flicker back to them, and *leaving* echoes *steaming*. In the third, *flaw* echoes *saw*, while *oracle* echoes *centrifugal, bobble, vowel,* and *interior* echoes *china*.

The fourth verse is boyish fantasy, where violence emerges but only, at first, in dreamland, with little room for internal rhyme play. Only *noon* echoes *cool* and *dudes*. In the fifth, reverberation returns for the grown-up words *inadvertently, identity*.

The first verse plays with the consonants of the first word, *teacup*. T (*stain, white, table, not quite perfect, exactly, it, it, stain*), C (*damask, cloth, quite, perfect, cup, exactly, like*) and P (*perfect, cup*). The second carries on the P (*sipped, palatable lip, up, cup*), and echoes the long EE of *teacup*: that word from which all the others branch out, that *cup* which contains the boy's vision of past and future but does not foretell the *gun*.

After the short I of *sipped, rim, lip* (which continues in *liquor*) comes the long EE of *steaming, read, tea-leaves, leavings*.

The third verse, the poem's centre, echoes with the unspoken word 'awe' (*saw, flaw, yawned*). That long A ripples out to *stared* and *glazed*. The awe is, perhaps, for the *Delphic oracle*, the ancient centre of the earth and here this poem's centre.

Yet that central word *centrifugal* means 'fleeing the centre'. From this point on, the boy's fantasies keep leaking forward, and so do the sounds. In the fourth verse, *blaze* continues the sound of *glazed*, and the final EL of *centrifugal* and *bobbles* rolls forward into *vowel* and *cool* and on to the fifth verse, the bringing-up-short moment, *until*. The final ESS of *shadowless*, for celluloid gunmen, will return in *pressed*.

The music turns on different ways of hearing O (short and long O, OR, OW, OO). The images turn on different ways of seeing O: a *rim* or circle like the *stain, cup* or hat-brim (*fedoras, sombreros*), or space inside that *rim*. The cup's *interior*, a head inside a hat like the boy's, nearly blown apart at the end.

In Irish English, crockery is 'delft'. This pun on 'Delphi' (implied, rather than spoken) resonates with Derek Mahon's famous poem, 'Courtyards in Delft', which also addresses obliquely the Northern Ireland conflict. Just as Heaney took Tolland Man as a metaphor for the Northern Irish situation so Mahon made a Vermeer painting of Dutch backyards resonate with the Belfast he grew up in, whose violence was hidden behind domestic façades. His poem puns on the town Delft and breakable domestic 'china'.[6]

Without 'the', *Delphic* does not really refer to Delphi the place but is an adjective which means 'unknowable', 'riddlingly ambiguous'. What the boy sees in this ambiguous (and breakable) *china* are tiny *flaws* which are *centrifugal*, suggesting the way a city or a building might explode under the *centrifugal* force of a bomb.

Behind this must, I think, be the famous words of Yeats in 'The Second Coming':

> *Things fall apart: the centre cannot hold;*
> *Mere anarchy is loosed upon the world.*

Carson's poem opened with a child having tea. But the *stain* on *white damask* is not removed by teacups, and this is a city whose centre may not hold, where boys get *stopped* by armed men. In these streets tea-leaf readings are no more use to him than the riddles of ancient Greece. *Granny* cannot foretell or prevent ambush.

When he yawns, mimicking the O of the blankly oracular china, he enters an exotic removed world. The *incandescent blaze*, the O in the middle of *vowel*, the *interior* of the *white* cup-oracle, turn into an empty cowboy street. But just as Delphi echoes granny's fortune-telling, so Hollywood *dudes* in *black fedoras* prefigure Belfast streets where *trigger-fingered* violence wears black-stockinged hoods.

The final scene gestures to another Northern Irish poem with Os and guns in it. Paul Muldoon's poem 'The Sightseers' is about a family Sunday outing to inspect a roundabout: 'the first in mid-Ulster'. This roundabout is an O; an uncle describes how Protestant gunmen held *a pistol so hard against his forehead, / there was still the mark of an O when he got home*. In Muldoon, the uncle escapes the gun but carries its O *home*. In Carson, the O is the mark of the Delphic command: *know* yourself. When *asked* for your *identity*, you *know* yourself at gunpoint. The final O is realisation. Oh – this is who I am.

III

Reaching Out: Playing, Praying and Discovering

> A stranger here
> Strange things doth meet, strange glories see
> Strange treasures lodg'd in this fair world appear,
> Strange all and new to me;
> But that they mine should be, who nothing was,
> That strangest is of all, yet brought to pass.
>
> Thomas Traherne, 'The Salutation'

> What are all those
> fuzzy-looking things out there?
>
> William Carlos Williams, 'The Last Words Of My English
> Grandmother'

Listening and looking, the traveller reaches into the world to make sense of the strange things in it.

The poems in this section suggest how unknowable and odd the world is. Artefacts, for instance; things that human hands have made. Gas mantles, in Kit Wright's poem; books, lavatories and telephones in Craig Raine's. Robin Robertson's speaker about to move house (that image of a life you have made for yourself) finds the house itself moving.

There are also animals. 'Since we do float on an unknown sea I think we should examine the other floating things that come our way very carefully; who knows what might depend on it?' wrote Elizabeth Bishop to Robert Lowell once, enclosing a clipping on racoons, something he may not have realised he needed to know much about.[1]

Animals suggest ways of thinking about ourselves. *The lizard's glint, the horse's velvet blanket / will surprise you into veiled hope one day*, says John Ashbery's poem. But how knowable are they really? *What do you know of my breach?* asks Farish's unseen whale. The elephant in Mimi Khalvati's can caress your breast with his trunk, or *follow the undulations in B minor of the Iphigeneia in Tauris*.

An external creator might give meaning to all this. Wondering about implications of what you see and hear can be very close to praying. In R. S. Thomas's poem, the blackbird's song conveys God's thought to us, bridging a gulf between us and a presence *beyond the silence*.

The patron saint of such looking – a way of looking that is a kind of praying – is the Herefordshire mystic poet Thomas Traherne whose prose reflections *Centuries of Meditations* complement his poems' sense of being foreign to the world. *I was a stranger . . . The corn was orient and immortal wheat, which never should be reaped nor was ever sewn*.

But the poems in this section are not only about wondering; they are also about alienation. You can't wonder deeply about something without realising not just how odd *it* is but how odd *you* are standing in front of it, finding it odd. Is what we see our own *desperate eye looking too hard*, asks Jorie Graham's 'Prayer'. Or is it *the eye of the world looking too hard* back?

At the end of this section, we approach the part of the journey which becomes, to most people, the most important. The *unexpected latitudes* (in Pauline Stainer's phrase) of other human beings.

The journey begins to darken here. Sorry. As I said in the Introduction, poems can restore us to ourselves but do not console. Poetry is not a feel-good art and poems are not Elastoplast. They enrich but do not cure. Relationships with other people may give the traveller the most delight of anything in this world (see Part IV, Poems 33, 37–42) but also the worst pain. What we 'sight' in Stainer's poem is a ship carrying a cargo of appalling cruelty. Ian Duhig's speaker looks back at what he did to someone else, then turns to God not in wonder and metaphysical speculation (like the poems of Graham and Thomas) but obsessed confession. *Bless me, Father, I have sinned.*

23 R. S. Thomas

Blackbird

Its eye a dark pool
in which Sirius glitters
and never goes out.
Its melody husky
as though with suppressed tears.
Its bill is the gold
one quarries for amid
evening shadows. Do not despair
at the stars' distance. Listening
to blackbird music is
to bridge in a moment chasms
of space-time, is to know
that beyond the silence
which terrified Pascal
there is a presence whose language
is not our language, but who has chosen
with peculiar clarity the feathered
creatures to convey the austerity
of his thought in song.

Thomas (1913–2000), born in Cardiff, was a sailor's child. He read
Classics at Bangor, trained in Cardiff for the Anglican Ministry, was
ordained in 1936, published his first collections as a rural parish
priest during the Second World War (establishing religion, nature,
Welsh history and rural life as his hallmark themes), was awarded the
Queen's Gold Medal in 1964 and nominated for the Nobel in
1997. He learned Welsh, wrote poems in English, prose in Welsh
(including a third-person autobiography *Neb*, 'Nobody'), and was
an outspoken Welsh republican. He outraged non-Welsh-speaking
Welsh by saying you could not experience Welsh culture properly
except through its language, and outraged everyone else by saying
it was a good idea to torch English-owned holiday homes in Wales.

He loved birdwatching and lived in rural parishes all his life. 'I suppose I've been chosen to receive revelation via nature. I feel more able to worship in the countryside than I would in town.'

After his first collection (1946) he published over twenty more. The poems are profoundly religious, profoundly Welsh. There is a *Collected*, but also many uncollected poems and this small poem on a huge subject, the existence of God, appeared in a magazine in 1998.[2]

It seems so simple. All one block, but in two parts. The first is like an ancient Welsh riddle poem with ritualising repetitions, *Its, Its, Its*. The answer to the riddles, of course, would be the title word.

Halfway through the eighth line comes a pastoral command (reminding us Thomas was a priest). *Do not despair*. Then begins the second part in which, at first sight, the word *is* seems to balance the repeated *its* of the first. *Listening is to bridge*; *listening* also *is to know*.

But the third *is* is syntactically different. It depends on that verb *know*, and refers to what we know: *that there is a presence*. Then comes a fourth *is*, again dependent on what has just gone.

Language and syntax are becoming more complex as the poem goes on, with a relative clause, then a further relative dependent on that. This fourth *is* refers to the *language* of that *presence* we know. It *is not our language*.

Throughout this second part, *is* shifts its place in the line. End-word in the tenth line, penultimate beat in the twelfth, second word in the fifteenth, first word in the sixteenth.

You begin to realise that the first part lacked any *is*. (*Is* only appeared in the third 'riddle'.) That part gave us first the absence, then the presence of the key existence word. But in the poem's second part, this vital little word dodges about. *Is* becomes a shifting presence.

The poem is about whether God *is*, or not. Pascal's wager was religious insurance policy. If you believe in God and He exists, fine. If you don't and He doesn't, again fine. But what if you don't believe and He does exist? That's what *terrified Pascal*. His wager was a bet on God's existence. If you believe and He doesn't exist, never mind. If he does, you're covered.

But the poem is not cynical. It moves from the blackbird's *eye* through its *melody* and *bill* to refusing *despair*. From *listening* to knowing. It is a journey into faith in God's existence. By the way it plays with *is*, withholding it at first, letting it creep in, balancing it against the repetitions of *its*, letting it extend and depend on the growth of more complex thought, it makes you realise that *is* is the crucial word.

The poem restates the unspoken question 'Does God exist?' (which Pascal's wager is about) in terms of words, syllables, and their relationships. Does *is* exist, or need to? (Lines one and four do without.) Is there a stable place for *is* in the line? Is there a place for faith in God's existence in our lives? If so, what and where is it?

The last line gestures back to the riddling atmosphere of the first part by answering these unspoken questions with a word that rhymes with *is*. *His*, meaning God's. Appropriate for a poem whose last word is *song*, it answers its own questions musically, through the relation of *is* and *his*.

The journey starts with seeing: with the glitter of *gold* in *dark*; with *evening shadows*, which presumably include the shades of old age. (Thomas was eighty-five when this poem was published.)

From the bird's *eye*, with a star in its *dark pool*, the poem moves to the bird's melody, whose *suppressed tears* are as liquid as the eye's *pool* – and also *husky*, like the voice of Dietrich or torchsong. Religious poetry has always used erotic yearning as a vehicle for religious longing.

The blackbird is not a flocking bird. In medieval Latin it is *merula*, 'dark girl', the bird that goes alone, an image of isolation. This is music in solitary darkness, beauty and tears hidden or suppressed. A star in a pool, something you have to go deep to find. But precious, worth the effort.

The third image makes that going deep active. You must 'quarry' *for* it. The gold of the blackbird's *bill* is *the gold one quarries for* in *shadows*.

This riddle part establishes that the visual and the aural belong together. Its three images (gesturing perhaps to Wallace Stevens' poem, 'Thirteen Ways of Looking at a Blackbird') find beauty and *gold* in dusk, huskiness, darkness, *tears*.

The brightness we find there may be connected with the name of the star which *never goes out*. French prayer addresses God as 'Seigneur' and Sirius, name of the Dogstar, begins with 'Sir'.

This first part of the poem prepares for the idea of *distance* at the poem's heart and *chasms of space-time* or *presence beyond the silence* in the second part. The impersonal *one* (*one quarries for*) suggests all of us have to look hard to find brightness in the dark. So *Do not despair*. Don't think it's all dark. Treasure is there if you dig for it.

181

In the second part, the gaze is on *distance*. The first part is full of concrete nouns (*eye, pool, Sirius, bill, gold, shadows*). There is something unseen in their midst but we can identify and perceive it with our senses: *melody*. The second part, however, is full of abstract nouns we cannot see (led up to by that central word *distance*): *silence, presence, language, clarity, austerity*.

But even the abstracts lead to *melody*, or rather to *song*. Concrete and abstract come to the same thing by a different route. All roads, the poem suggests, contain despair and terror. But in the end all lead to God: to *his thought in song*.

The second part, which deals in abstracts, also deals with *language* and *thought*. The *husky melody* of the blackbird is what that *presence beyond the silence* has *chosen*. To do what? *Convey* (which picks up the *distance* we mustn't *despair* at, because this *presence* communicates across it) *his thought in song*.

This idea draws on Christian phrases (the Word made Flesh) and paradox. *The austerity of his thought* is conveyed through *feathered creatures*. *Feathered* suggests angels but also (perhaps) feathered beds and nests, the opposite of austere. To us who depend on our senses to receive the world, God does not *convey his thought* naked, but softened, covered. This will give it to us, apparently, *with peculiar clarity*.

Back to the first part, the glitter in darkness. His *language is not our language*. We can only perceive *austerity* in concrete images, in *gold amid shadows*. These are what we take for *clarity*.

In Thomas Hardy's famous poem 'The Darkling Thrush', another feathered creature conveys God's thought to man. Hardy wrote it in December 1900; its speaker sees the millennial winter twilight as *spectre-gray, shrunken*, full of *dregs*:

> *Every spirit upon earth*
> *seemed fervourless as I.*

But an *aged thrush* begins to *fling his soul / Upon the growing gloom, in a full-hearted evensong / Of joy*. This *frail* and *gaunt* bird seems to have as little going for him as the world. In the *terrestrial things around*, the speaker sees *little cause* for *such ecstatic sound*, but is the bird receiving some message from further away?

> *I could think there trembled through*
> *His happy good-night air*

> *Some blessed Hope, whereof he knew*
> *And I was unaware.*

Thomas must be thinking with that poem. His own poem too finds beauty and comfort in *listening*, a word which echoes the unspoken message of the first half: *glistening*. *Listening* helps you move from visual to aural, from hope of God to knowledge of Him. Music is the bridge between visual and aural, concrete and abstract, human and God. So the poem's own music is vital.

Musically, this poem turns on the relationship between soft S (*Its, its, its, Sirius, husky, suppressed, despair, stars' distance, listening, space, silence, Pascal, presence, austerity*) and the strong Z of the affirmative word which the poem is about: *is* five times (underlined by *amid* and *bridge*), plus *glitters, goes, tears, quarries, shadows, music, chasms, chosen* and *his*. But the S we are finally left with is the soft one of *song*, the word the poem leads up to. Like the Beethoven quartet in Aldous Huxley's *Point Counter Point*, this *song* is music that proves God's existence. His *austerity* comes to us softly. The music with S at its heart (like *despair*), *bridges* the *chasms*, lets us *know* that this *presence*, though its *language* may be bleak (like *the dark pool*), comes over to us through a *feathered* creature, softly.

Prayer

What of   the quicksand.
My desperate eye   looking too hard.

Or of the eye   of the world
looking too   hard

for me. Or, if you prefer, *cause*,

looking to take in
what could be sufficient –

Then the sun goes down   and the sentence

goes out. Recklessly towards the end. Beyond
the ridge. Wearing us as if lost in

thought with no way
out, no eye at all to slip through,

none of the hurry or the between-
hurry thinkings to liquefy,

until it can be laid on a tongue

– oh quickness – like a drop. Swallow.
Rouse says the dark.

Graham, a Pulitzer prizewinner and one of the leading voices in
American poetry today, was born in New York in 1950, grew up in
Italy speaking French, Italian and English, went to the Sorbonne,
studied film-making with Scorsese in New York, taught at the Iowa
Writing Programme from 1983, and in 1998 succeeded Heaney as
Professor of Rhetoric and Oratory at Harvard.

Her poems are both highly conceptual and lushly sensual. They
ask big philosophical questions in language of the senses. She has a
gift for landscape, the shifting shadings of sky, light, wind, leaves;

will bring in history, art or medieval philosophy, then find metaphysical insight in a spider's web or a schoolgirl's Science Project. When her poems began appearing in the early 1980s, many American reviewers praised their originality and ambition, but it was the rhythm that particularly struck the critic Helen Vendler, who helped make her poetry known.[3]

There are several bilingual poets in this book,[4] but Graham grew up trilingual. Her language and rhythms are simultaneously hesitant and penetrating, always aware of being not enough, always asking, 'how deep can you see?' The poems resist finishing any explanation as if questions, and the process of thinking, matter more than knowing. They weave and unweave, go for mystery. They seem to want us to listen to them intuitively and physically as if they were music, but they also want to be precise about seeing, feeling and thinking. A good poem, she says in her introduction to *The Best American Poetry 1990*, tries 'to clean the language of its current lies, make it capable of connecting us to the world'.

She has published many collections, and at one point shifted from short poems with short lines to long poems with more explicitly abstract thought in them, and very long lines. Her work became a philosophic tidal wave, splashing over the page.

She has written several poems called *Prayer*: two in the 2002 collection *Never* (which is about the nature of time); two (including this one) in the 2000 collection *Swarm*, which she said tackled 'history, destiny and God'. This poem belongs to a sequence which asks whom you address, if you want to address God. What do people still feel *subject to*? Not only God, perhaps, but sex, love, law and rules of physics, like gravity. The same collection has a lot of poems called 'Underneath' (*painful to look up*, one of these begins). *Quicksand*, with which this poem opens, is a vital image in the whole sequence. Something you sink into; something uncertain and shivery which looks solid but behaves like liquid, looks safe and is not. The poem contrasts *hard* (in two senses, including 'difficult') with liquid (see *hard, hard, liquefy, drop, swallow*). *Quicksand* is a perfect Graham image for everything shifting, labile, dangerous; which seems other than it is and to which hesitation is the right response.

Several poems in this book also use white spaces in the line. This device was developed by the Black Mountain Poets in the Fifties, especially Charles Olson, to notate the poet's individual voice and mark a way to breathe the line and the words. It separates units of breath, phrases and words without punctuation (as a line-end can) while still holding them in relation. (Critics might say it has its break and eats it too; or that you should be able to get the same effect with words alone.)

In this poem, spaces have peculiar point. Prayer reaches out across a gap. Across *chasms of space-time*, as R. S. Thomas puts it. *Space-time* is exactly what these white gaps mark in Graham's line.

Prayer is a reaching out, and there is reaching out everywhere here. Across those spaces in the line (until *the sun goes down*) and also between the material and verbal world (*the sun goes down, the sentence goes out*), between the *eye* (which rhymes with *my* and implies an 'I') and the *world*. And between that same *eye* (or I) and the object of the title word prayer: whatever one prays to. Maybe God.

The poem starts with danger (*quicksand*) and urgency (*desperate*), and moves toward something *laid on a tongue* like a Communion wafer in ecstatic unity (*oh quickness*). But *quickness* picks up *quicksand*. By trying to unite you might fall in: into gaps across which you are reaching; into the *quicksand*. Most of the couplets turn on phrases suggesting what *quicksand* does to you or you might do in it (*take in, goes down, recklessly, lost in, no way out, slip through, liquefy, swallow*). The last verb tries to get you out of there (*Rouse*).

The poem begins with speed and urgency (*quicksand, desperate*, followed by *recklessly, oh quickness*), and ends with two urgent imperatives (*Swallow, Rouse*). But the stages of thinking pull against urgency. They are slow and broken up. They want *none of the hurry*. They do not even want *between-hurry thinkings*.

So these gaps, part of how the poem lies physically on the page, contribute to the sense; they are part of the slowing down, the hesitancy. There are only four of them. They stop *when the sun goes down*, after *the sentence goes out*. They also, in this first phase of the poem, mark pauses in thinking. *Looking to take in / what could be sufficient*, trying to understand the world adequately, the poem makes *looking* its image of trying to understand. Understanding, perhaps, is what this *prayer* is praying for.

The one action is *the sun goes down*, though the poem ends with the hope of more (*the dark* says *Rouse*). The key thing is light, which lets an *eye* contemplate *the quicksand*, but which *goes out* halfway through the poem. Light is the chief image of knowledge and reason in the Western philosophical tradition. It pervades Greek poetry as well as philosophy; and also the later theologies which use Greek philosophy. You need light to see; you need God and reason to understand. In the light, before *the sun goes down*, the poem (*desperate* to understand this *quicksand* of a world) pauses to think about its own *looking* and asks the question (*what of*), then pauses again. It mentions the looking *eye*, then pauses again, self-conscious. Being *desperate*, it is *looking too hard*. Too hard for comfort. Too hard to get it right. The poem starts considering alternatives (*or, or*), and other ways of looking at *looking*. Maybe looking flows both ways. *The eye* (pause) *of the world* may be *looking* back. But this *eye* may also be *looking too* (pause) *hard*. A big pause now, of line break and stanza break. *Too hard* for what? *For me*, which suggests *too hard for me* in another sense: too difficult for me.

Plato's theory of vision (which has fed medieval philosophy and philosophical language ever since) drew on Greek poets' imagery of light and looking (it had to: this was the language and imagery Plato was thinking in) to suggest vision was a two-way flow. Rays flowed from the looked-at object as well as from eye into object. To perceive something meant you interacted with what you were perceiving.

This poem suggests that understanding is also a two-way thing. Understanding is a *quicksand*. You have to enter it. It will receive you. You have to *take in* enough of it (*what could be sufficient*), but have to get out of it too. You mingle, then have to step back. You cannot understand without stepping back. You must be part, but also not part, of what you understand. And when you step back you have to understand how it came to be as it is. *Cause* explains. Hence the second *or*: the other way of seeing is causal explanation. *Or, if you prefer, cause.*

These first five lines stage a way of grappling with understanding the world in three ways: in terms of *my* own *looking*; in terms of *the world* looking back; and in terms of *cause* (how the world came to be; and how I came to be, looking at the world).

The poem stops this line of thought with an alternative way of breaking up words. Not a space, but something in the space. A dash, followed by *then* (which brings us into specific time, jumping us out of timeless reflection) and the poem's one action.

There is no full stop, but the new line has a capital letter as if it began a new sentence. The thought of the last seven lines, and the sentence begun in the fifth, stop dead with that dash.

The eighth line gives images for what has just happened. *The sun goes down* and *the sentence goes out*, like a light.

The central line (ninth of the seventeen) is the beginning of smooth linguistic flow. No more white spaces. The only break in the flow comes from two more dashes. This poem that hesitated and paused before *the quicksand* is going on *towards the end*.

But there are no more proper sentences for a while either, no grammatical subject or main verb in the next three utterances, which ignore the rules of language, syntax, our best medium for *hard looking* in trying to understand. Who or what is *wearing* us? The *sentence*?

We are in the dark now, no longer in charge, nor able to pause. The source of light has gone *down*, grammar and syntax have gone *out*. Yet this is when we are taken, with no more hesitation gaps, *beyond / the ridge*.

God is light, but you tend to find Him, paradoxically, in the dark night of the soul. When you stop struggling to make rational sense of this *quicksand*, give up grammar and *hurry* or *between- / hurry thinkings*. When you get *lost in / thought with no way / out*. As if thinking has no window to outer reality, is only a labyrinth with *no eye at all*.

Gerard Manley Hopkins, a priest-poet who knew the dark night of the soul intimately, compares a rural landscape to the eye (*this sleek and seeing ball*). If we damage it irrevocably, he says, we make of it *no eye at all*. These words, backlit by Hopkins' powerful sense of God inherent in nature, echo through Graham's poem. It is when you are in that dark night that you listen to the voice of *the dark* and accept its imperatives (*Swallow, Rouse*).[5]

The Greek image which nourished Plato's language of vision and understanding, which underlies all Western thinking about insight (and had enormous resonance in twentieth-century psychological writing), is that illumination only comes (to the seer, the mad, the melancholy, any mind in uncertainty and sorrow) through and in *the dark*.

George Herbert (another poet-priest) wrote a poem called 'Prayer'. It is a series of urgent images for prayer, among them *the soul in paraphrase* and *heart in pilgrimage*. It ends with *something understood*. Graham's poem 'Prayer' also suggests a heart on pilgrimage and soul in paraphrase (*oh quickness*) in its quest for understanding.

In image terms, that quest is a journey through loss of light towards an image of swallowing (liquid threatened to engulf you but now is *like a drop*), which ends in a *dark* that 'rouses' you.

Understanding is never complete. Not of the world, nor of a 'resistant' poem. If everything goes two ways, your uncertainties are part of the world's own uncertainties. Uncertainty is what we exist in. But being in *the dark* makes you get up and go on trying to understand.

25   Helen Farish

*Mesoplodon Pacificus**

I have shown myself to you
only as drift and you have presumed
to deduce me from this.

I routinely descend
into abysmal depths,
am far from land, secretive.

But what do you know of my breach,
how the lightless world
bursts off me –

how I can feed on this
for thousands of miles,
the routine weight of air crushing

the sea's surface suddenly
gone, suddenly
an opening into which I pour.

* *Mesoplodon Pacificus*: A species of whale known to exist only because of '*drift*'
(stranded specimens). A 'breach' is when the whale clears the sea in a spectacular
jump.

Farish, born in Cumbria in 1962, worked at Oxford University
Press and now teaches writing at Sheffield Hallam University. She
won the 2005 Forward Prize for Best First Collection with a book
of poems about love, desire, childhood and grief. She wants to stress
the 'distance' between poet and poem but her influences are
confessional poets (Sharon Olds, Anne Sexton) and her mode is
confessional. This poem is not only in the voice of a rare type of
whale, telling human beings how little they know of it (since they
only see stranded specimens), but a female persona telling *you*
(presumably a man) about her unknowability.

The first word is *I*, and the first line (if you say it naturally) seems to have two strong beats, on *shown* and *you*. Their long O and OO run through the poem. After *only*, the long O comes back in *what do you know* and in the last line's sudden *opening* when the whale breaks surface, getting away from the water's pressure (and all that stands for, emotionally) into air. The OO of *you* echoes through another *you* into *presumed*, *deduce*, *routinely*, *routine*, then slants into *gone* and ends in the last word *pour*.

Internal half-rhymes knit the first two deep-sea verses, which describe where and how the whale lives: below the surface, *far from land*. *Drift* is picked up by *this*, the second syllable of *abysmal* and *secretive*. The long nasal of *shown* is echoed in *presumed*, *from*, *descend*, *land*. *Routinely* echoes *only* in the same place in the line. This is a close pair of verses, describing a closely held privacy.

The strong vowels in the first line are I, O and U. These are reversed in the central stanza, where the whale turns fiercely (apparently) on *you* and begins to show itself, coming out from under, up from below. *What do you know of my breach?* We hear the beats as U, O and I (*you*, *know*, *my*). Then comes the surprise word *breach*, the leap out of the water, whose long EE changes the soundworld.

Breach is echoed first in *me*. We have had *me* before (*deduce me*) but now it is an end word, stressed. The poem is basically about how *you* fail to *know me*. The Latin title, the name of a creature known *only* through *drift*, makes its knowability, the possibility of knowing *me*, that much more remote. Then the long EE follows through in *feed*, *routine*, *sea's*, *suddenly*.

After the central verse (the *But* verse, the question) comes the whale's rise: its triumph is the self bursting out of the water. But everything in these verses is experienced inside out. Instead of the whale bursting out of the water, here is *the lightless world* (the dark deep-sea fathoms) bursting *off me*.

Escaping from her own privacy (those *abysmal depths*) is violent relief. She can *feed on this / for thousands of miles*. Not on food, but on the relief that *the routine weight* (echoing *routinely* from her descent in the hidden verses) has *gone*.

Even this comes over inside out. She does not feel deep-sea pressure as a *weight* of water crushing her, but as the *weight of air crushing / the sea's surface*. The words keep removing the speaker from her own experience (of feeling and action). Release comes from acts of *the lightless world* and *weight of air*. They have the active verbs (*bursts*, *gone*). Then, when the repeated *suddenly* has stressed sudden freedom, the escape route *opening* through the surface and up into the air, she can finally act and show herself in *I pour*.

So is this a confessional poem?

It is a very precise portrait of a feeling – of not being properly known, of being able to show yourself only in private, *far from land*, observed *only* when stranded and lost. But it keeps the distance Farish says she wants between poet and poem. This poem about being private keeps its privacy. In the last word, the whale escapes the water in a verb which makes it seem water itself: *pour*. The whale becomes the medium in which it swims as the poet's persona becomes the poem, unknowable even at the moment she 'shows herself' in a poem whose first line is *I have shown myself to you*.

Mahout

We trust each our own elephant
till our own elephant kills us.
The attendants holding the silk umbrellas,

the one who plies the fan
of peacock feathers, the man
with the flyswatter of yaktails.

You cannot cheat on the amount of oil
poured in the lamps, for an elephant
will always honour the pace of the ritual.

Nor is the elephant's love less manifest.
He will insert his trunk, like a hand,
inside your garments and caress your breast.

He will follow, with his mate,
the undulations in B minor of the *Iphigeneia in Tauris*
or, on solo bassoon, *Oh my Tender Musette*.

And the cow will stroke him with her long
and flexible member before bringing
it back upon herself, pressing its finger

first in her mouth, then in his ear
While over their transports, whistling fire,
the harmony of two human voices

falls like summer rain.
Meat that walks like a mountain
among giant flowers, huge nettles and lobelia.

Child, don't be afraid.
The circle of nine precious stones
is never absent from his forehead.

Khalvati, born in 1944 in Tehran, spent much of her childhood at school on the Isle of Wight, returned to Iran at seventeen and has lived in Britain since she was twenty-five. She has published seven collections of poetry and a children's book, edited anthologies, acted and directed in theatre, and is a much-loved tutor for the Poetry School. She resists being seen as a Persian poet but does feel, says one poem, *caught between / two alphabets*. Her relation to both Persian and British influence comes out in form as well as content: she often writes ghazals, an Arabic form, based on couplets in which the last phrase of the first two lines is repeated as a refrain.

This poem, however, is in tercets, three-line stanzas. In most of them, two lines (not always the same two) make a rhyming relation (*kills us / umbrellas; fan / man; oil / ritual, ear / fire; rain / mountain; afraid / forehead*). But in the sixth all three end-words chime in different ways. Its first two lines are both enjambed (i.e. they run on into the next line, as in *long / and flexible* and *bringing / it back*), and the three lines twine together reflecting what they describe: the female elephant taking *her long and flexible member*, her trunk (which also evokes the bull's *member*) *back upon herself*. The central line of this verse is the poem's only line to end on a verb (the most urgent enjambment, hurrying the reader on to hear the object of the verb). This verb, *bringing*, has a rhyme relation both with the first line-end (*long*) and the third (*finger*). An intertwining tercet, summing up *the elephant's love*.

The poem is in the mahout's voice, a man controlling something of his *own*, something honourable (*you cannot cheat, always honour*), loving, enormous (*mountain*), obedient to the tempo of *ritual* and music (*follow the undulations*), ultimately lethal (*kills us*) but made safe for the moment (even for a *child*) by a *circle of nine precious stones*. Symbolically, as well as literally, his *elephant* is his life.

The poem is a charm of *nine* stanzas rather than a *circle* of *nine stones*. A meet-the-elephant addressed: we find out at the end, to a *child*. The poem ends with the person to whom it is introducing the animal – or life. Life, the *elephant*, is standing still a moment so the *child* (beginning its own life) can see it whole.

In the first two verses, and verse eight, the speaker gestures without verbs (reinforcing the sense of stillness) to people attending the elephant (*attendants, the one who plies, the man with the flyswatter*) and the animal itself (*meat that walks*). The only things that move are the elephants' trunks (*insert, caress, stroke, bringing back, pressing*), whose sexual movements *follow* musical *undulations*. Music is the source of movement and also its image.

The poem's own music runs on L, the first syllable of the animal it is describing: *elephant, elephant, till, kills, holding, silk, umbrellas, plies, flyswatter, yaktails, oil, lamps, elephant, will, ritual, elephant's love, less, will, like, will follow, undulations, solo, will, long, flexible, herself, while, whistling, falls, like, flowers, nettles, lobelia, child, circle*.

But the stanzas are held together by vowel sounds (*trust, our, our, us, till, kills, silk; plies, flyswatter*). The music motif begins as the poem's own music becomes more insistent. The short E of *less, manifest, caress, breast* is picked up in *tender, Musette, flexible, pressing*. The short O of *follow* is followed up in *solo, Oh, stroke, over, lobelia, stones*, widening to *cow, mouth, flowers* and underpinned by the OR of *poured, nor, minor, or, before, transports, falls, walks, forehead*. The I of *child* is echoed in *nine*.

Emotionally, the climax of this poem whose music is movement is again music: the *harmony of two human voices*. For the dominant note is tenderness. We start with luxuriant softness (*fan of peacock feathers, silk umbrellas*) and the gentleness of help (*attendants*) moving on to the *elephant's love*. Love for people, expressed in response to *tender* music, and also for his mate, expressed in an image of entwinement and (as *harmony* falls over them) the kind of connection in which music specialises, between *mouth* and *ear*. And in the end, this tenderness is turned upon the child told not to *be afraid*, of the elephant or life. We began with the danger (*kills us*); we end with the magic which will (the poem implies) protect you from it.

A Martian Sends a Postcard Home

Caxtons are mechanical birds with many wings
and some are treasured for their markings –

they cause the eyes to melt
or the body to shriek without pain.

I have never seen one fly, but
sometimes they perch on the hand.

Mist is when the sky is tired of flight
and rests its soft machine on ground:

then the world is dim and bookish
like engravings under tissue paper.

Rain is when the earth is television.
It has the property of making colours darker.

Model T is a room with the lock inside –
a key is turned to free the world

for movement, so quick there is a film
to watch for anything missed.

But time is tied to the wrist
or kept in a box, ticking with impatience.

In homes, a haunted apparatus sleeps,
that snores when you pick it up.

If the ghost cries, they carry it
to their lips and soothe it to sleep

with sounds. And yet, they wake it up
deliberately, by tickling it with a finger.

Only the young are allowed to suffer
openly. Adults go to a punishment room

with water but nothing to eat.
They lock the door and suffer the noises

alone. No one is exempt
and everyone's pain has a different smell.

At night, when all the colours die,
they hide in pairs

and read about themselves –
in colour, with their eyelids shut.

Born in 1944, Raine read English at Oxford, taught there, edited magazines, was Faber's poetry editor in London, then returned to Oxford. He has published several collections, a *Collected* and two books of essays, and founded a literary magazine, *Arete*. His poems go for big issues (love, cruelty, suffering, history, war, death) in three main ways. By startling metaphors; by weaving funny, shockingly intimate personal comment into a background of cultural reference (art, travel, literature, European history, the Second World War, the holocaust); and also by physicality: earthing experience in the body.

He made his name with his second collection *A Martian Sends a Postcard Home* (1979) of which this was the title poem. James Fenton accordingly christened Raine's poetry Martianism. It wanted to see the world freshly, in surprising metaphor, as if an alien were watching. (A couple about to make love are called, 'One excited watering can, one peculiar rose'.)

This was Martianism's flagship poem. Describing life on earth, the Martian gives three couplets to books then turns to the outside world and gives two couplets to *mist*, one to *rain*, two to the car which end with *movement so quick there is a film / to watch for anything missed*. The central couplet on *time* (watches and clocks) is tied to the car idea (as the watch *is tied to the wrist*) by the bond of *missed* and *wrist*, and by the notion of speed. The car is quick, 'freed' *for movement*, but time is fettered. Then comes the home. Three couplets for the phone, three for lavatories, and two for bed (and dreaming), where human beings retreat *in pairs* (like the poem's own lines).

It all offers a vivid, apparently simplistic way of looking at our actions and world. A book perches *on the hand*, the phone is a *haunted apparatus*, turning on the ignition frees *the world for movement*, dreaming is reading about yourself *in colour with the eyes shut*. But it also hints that the world the Martian is coming from is not that different from the one he is in. His references start with technology: books are *mechanical birds*, mist is *sky's machine*, rain is *television*. He is innocent of cars, watches, phones, lavatories, yet his default concepts are very like ours: brand names, or the inventor's name (*Caxtons, Model T*) like Hoovers and Wellingtons. He knows about *engravings, tissue paper, film*; *rooms, punishment* from which *no one is exempt*, and *colour*. He homes in on emotion (the watch is *ticking with impatience*, the phone has to be *soothed*) but knows nothing of tears (verse two) or dreams.

So this is not really an innocent eye at all. The poem suggests the ways we manage our lives are oddly, sometimes cruelly, contingent. The locked privacy of the Western toilet may be as bizarre as Western inhibitions about *pain*, which 'allow' *only the young* to *suffer openly*. Shitting in private stands in for keeping your feelings private. *Everyone's pain has a different smell.*

The poem moves towards the possibility of a tenderer world. The Martian's horizon of ideas is kinder than ours, at least about need. He may think in terms of machines, but he sees these as animate. The sky's *machine* is *soft* and needs to rest when *tired*. Bird-books *perch on the hand*; the *haunted apparatus*, a *ghost* (that philosophical idea of the soul as 'ghost in the machine' of the body) that *cries*, needs comforting. *Everyone* suffers *pain* differently in solitude. Bed is where we *hide*.

This poem is illuminating, fresh and funny, but also highly literary. It turns on the relation of world and book. The tone is faux naïf (*mist is when* . . .) but the references are knowing. What they know, above all, is reading and books. *Mist* makes *the world dim and bookish*; dreaming is reading about yourself *with the eyes shut*. The poem opens and closes (like a book, or a bird's wings) with books and reading. *Caxtons* are *treasured*. They make *the body shriek without pain*. When you *hide* in sleep, you *read*. And the *Martian* apparently expects his *postcard* to be read.

Mantles

White as the sacrament, in my grandmother's house the mantles
Were taught to flower in the dusk. On their soft weighbridge
They balanced the light, on their milkmaid's yoke they carried it
Over mahogany mountains,
Till the room was breathing its secret to the ghost of the wind in
    the bay.

That radiant patience made a lake of the stern piano
Where she sang *The Isle of Capri*. Such
Beauty in the frail old voice, so long a river of widowhood
The light went running with through the banks of shadow . . .

It caught the little pointed breasts of brass
Nubian goddesses on the mantelpiece. It put in the shade
A mysterious cavern under the table
Where African butterflies, in the pinned tomb of their wooden
    boxes,
Spread their gorgeous wings that reeked of camphor.

In my grandmother's house there existed a borrowed shrimping
    net
And a maiden aunt, your best friend ever.
A peacock feather. An ostrich egg. A time
When the breathing of time was audible in gas mantles,
Conspiratorial and benign.

Wright, born in Kent in 1944, went to Oxford, taught in Canada, then returned to England. He has written over twenty-five collections, won many awards, and is beloved as children's poet and poetry teacher as well as a poet for adults. He has exuberant formal passion and virtuosity. *I like what vamped me / In my youth*, says one of his poems (about poetry): *Tune, argument, / Colour, truth*. His rhyming and formal brilliance can be comic or satiric; people compare him to Betjeman. But he is serious as well as funny, savage as well as tender. Whether he is being rumbustious (one collection was called *Bump-starting the Hearse*), ribald or benign, all through his work there is a dark thread of pity and despair.

This poem turns *my grandmother's house* into a fairytale image of gentle welcome and the safe mystery of old treasures from another time, seen by a child. The key ideas of *secret, soft, breathing its secret, breathing of time* hang on the image of the sacred with which the poem begins (*sacrament*) and are summed up in the objects the poem is about: *mantles*, covers of old-fashioned gas lights.

But that word also means shawls such as a grandmother might wear, and the feel of the whole poem is gentle covering: for the *frail* life she has lived alone so long in this *room* that speaks of exotic places but is also a confinement, like the butterflies' *pinned tomb*. The poem breathes out a lost past, lovingly remembered, and drops over the *house* (and implicitly over the child the speaker is projecting himself back into) its own gentle mantle of time. The *mantles*, and their *radiant patience*, characterise the *grandmother*, *so long* widowed, too.

The poem starts with *white* and you can track its journey visually by the *light* the *mantles* make in surrounding darkness (*dusk, shadow, shade, cavern, tomb*).

White irradiates the first stanza (*flower in the dusk, balanced the light*). The *light* that begins here, *carried* over furniture, reaches out to the wider world. The furniture becomes *mahogany mountains*, the *mantles* are a *milkmaid's yoke*, a *soft weighbridge*, are *white as the sacrament* and *taught to* blossom like flowers. The quick sequence of metaphor compactly collects church ritual, Edwardian pastoral (*yoke, weighbridge*), and a child's sense of learning (*taught*) into the *secret* of this *room* with its mysterious, half-understood associations. The *room* breathes all this out too. Not just to the *bay*, nor even the *wind*, but *the ghost of the wind*. The distant third-handness of this prepares for the grandmother's *frail old voice* and old-fashioned song in the next stanza.

In the next stanza, it is again light (*radiant*) that changes, creates, accompanies. It *made* the piano a *lake*, *went running with* her voice and *widowhood*. The first stanza's imagery suggested pastoral landscape: church, agriculture, mountains, flowers. This stanza, following on from *bay* (last word of the first), is all water imagery: *lake, Isle of Capri* (evoking sea in the Bay of Naples), *river of widowhood, banks of shadow*, which suggests the banks of Styx, the river which separates the living and the dead, and which the shades of the dead cross in Virgil's *Aeneid*. Dots mark where a line in the poem would otherwise stand. The other stanzas have five lines; this one only four, as if the river has run through the shadowed banks into the sand or underground. The poem, these dots suggest, is about time and death as well as gentleness.

But *the light* is in charge of this vision as well as the last, and in the third stanza it is the verbs' subject (*It caught, it put in the shade*), in active control (*caught, put*) of the room. It controls the high points, *pointed brass breasts* shining on a *mantelpiece* (named for the *mantles* that are this light's source), creates a *cavern* under *the table*, lets you see *gorgeous wings* of *butterflies* in their *tomb*.

Again the furniture is a landscape, the room a world, but now this world is a children's adventure world of mystery and glamour (*Nubian goddesses, mysterious cavern, African butterflies*) as evoked by the small boy *under the table*.

The poem is written from the perspective of child and adult at once, and elides both tones of voice. The child thinks *best friend ever* and sees a *mysterious cavern under the table*. The adult comments on the grandmother (*frail old voice, such beauty, river of widowhood*), using words like *audible* or *conspiratorial*. The difference between the tones implies the time lapse in which the *grandmother* has gone between those *banks of shadow*.

The poem gestures to death but the last stanza brings back from the first the sign of life: *breathing*. Then it transfers to the *mantles'* sound, the feelings the child had about the hushed scenery of *my grandmother's house* (repeated, like *breathing*, from the first stanza): this sound now is *conspiratorial* and *benign*. By the end, the play of *light* and *shadow*, life and death are summed up in the elements it closes with (which are also what poetry is made of): *time* and sound.

The rhythm is all-important. As *butterflies* spread *wings* in their *boxes*, so the word *grandmother* spreads its shape through the poem. A dactyl (long short short) repeated in single words: *sacrament, [ma]hogany, widowhood, goddesses, Nubian, mantelpiece, [mys]terious, African, butterflies, grandmother's* (again) and *audible*. The last line has a double dactyl, *conspiratorial*. Dactyls ripple through phrases that come to rest on a long accented vowel: *ghost of the wind in the bay, Isle of Capri, breathing of time*.

Dactyls and anapaests melt into each other. In a sequence, 'short short long' can be heard as 'long short short'. The last line of the first stanza, after the short line of *Over mahogany mountains*, is a pure anapaestic hexameter: six beats which evoke the past (and earlier anapaestic poems of the English tradition) rhythmically, just as the description evokes visual details of a lost world. All of this making *audible* the gentle anapaestic (or dactylic) bubble of the *gas mantles*.

Inside the rhythm, vowel sounds hold the stanzas together in a chain stitch flow-on. In the first stanza, it is short A (*sacrament, grandmothers, mantles, balanced, mahogany*), but the AY of *weighbridge* and *bay* prepares for the AY of *radiant, patience, made, lake, frail*).

The short A continues (*that, sang, banks*) but meanwhile the OH of *yoke, over* and *ghost* is picked up by *piano*; and by more sombre words: *old, so, widowhood, shadow*. The third picks up the OR of *taught* (*caught, gorgeous, camphor*) and hisses (like the *mantles*) with S (*breasts, brass, goddesses, mantelpiece, shade, mysterious, boxes, spread*).

The fourth stanza picks up the short E of *breasts* and *spread* in the third, in *existed, net, best, feather, egg*, but the final vowel is long I, echoing *white* where the poem began. Running gently through the poem in *light, Isle, light* and *butterflies* to end with *time*: *time* and the word which sums up the whole scene over which the *grandmother* presides: *benign*.

The Evening of Greuze

As a group we were somewhat vulnerable
and are so today. My brother-in-law has fixed
me a tower in the mill, from whose oriel
I can see the bluebottles who nag heaven
with their unimportance. But what are they expected to do?
Raise families? Become deacons? If so my calculations
collapse into bric-a-brac, my equations
are undone.

Across the road they are building a cement house.
It will seemingly have no windows. A columbarium
for cement pigeons. And ever as I talked to you
down the decades in my letters one thing was unsure:
your reply. Now we are again endangered,
like dead birds, and autumn's ruby spittle mounts
in the sky like a tornado. Try to keep
cold and empty in this bare room.
Examine mirrors in the studio.
The lizard's glint, the horse's velvet blanket
will surprise you into veiled hope one day.

Ashbery, born in 1927, son of a fruit grower in Rochester, New York, originally wanted to be a painter. He wrote poetry at Harvard, was looked up to there (for that, and for being 'funny and brilliant'), and in the Forties came together with the poets Frank O'Hara, Kenneth Koch and James Schuyler. They were later known as the New York School but had no idea, then, that a school was what they were. They were excited by avant garde painting (de Kooning, Jackson Pollock), knew John Cage, and wanted to do similar things in poetry.

Ashbery lived in France in the Fifties writing art criticism. His early poetry was barely reviewed. In 1976 three major awards shot him from the obscure avant garde into the forefront of American literary life. 'Our major poet since the death of Wallace Stevens,' said the critic Harold Bloom. He has published twenty-three collections, fiction, plays and critical essays on literature and art. He is Professor at Bard College, living in Manhattan.

His work is experimental. He keeps changing but the heart of his work is linguistic reverie and its principle is uncertainty. He works by weaving and unweaving, interested not in conclusion but in travelling through the poem through mutually incongruous registers of language. The subject of many poems is their own process of thought, not what they are looking at.

His most characteristic poems are long, restless, many-faceted. One called 'Just Walking Around' says *the longest way is the most efficient way.* They seethe with plural observations: a surreal string of non-sequiturs which braid high and low culture and different voices. They try to incorporate everything. *There ought to be room for more things,* says a poem 'For John Clare'.

Mark Haddon, whose novel *The Curious Incident of the Dog in the Night-time* is written in the voice of an autistic boy, says he finds John Ashbery's work very freeing. 'He offers you the chance to not make sense in the normal way.'[6] You can hear Ashbery's poems as an autistic impression of the plural hum from the endless meanings (or maybe no meaning) of suburban America. His long lines seem to offer an elusive promise that we do have a future, that there is meaning we can at least try to find. Walt Whitman said the modern American poet should be indirect, 'not direct or descriptive or epic'. Ashbery approaches anything as stable as meaning very indirectly indeed. His syntax is often slippery, his characters elusive, any story uncertain.

This poem comes from a recent collection called *Chinese Whispers* after the whisper game in which words, messages and ideas change as different mouths pass them on, different ears hear them. Nothing need ever finish. The message is continual change, continual new meaning.

'In my life poetry followed painting,' Ashbery has said, and he has always thought with painting.[7] But this poem draws not on the avant-garde painters who excited him by experimenting, but one of the least experimental painters ever, whose work glowingly confirmed clichéd popular morality in pre-Revolution France.

The French painter Jean-Baptiste Greuze was adored in the mid-eighteenth century for his 'morality paintings': sentimental melodramatic tableaux (*A Father Explaining the Bible to His Children*) with a brilliantly voluptuous surface. A patisserie realism. Diderot praised his work as 'morality in paint'. In private, Greuze was constantly in trouble, with a poisonous marriage and court proceedings involving the new legal institution of divorce. 'An excellent artist, but a very disagreeable character,' Diderot also said. When Neoclassicism came in, Greuze's work fell out of fashion. He lost his fortune in the Revolution and died poor and obscure in 1805. Modernism, which spotlit the medium not the message, obliterated his reputation, since his medium was high gloss cliché.

So what is he doing in Ashbery's work?

No book by Ashbery is ever quite like the one before. In many places *Chinese Whispers* is satirical and jokey. The poet pretends he is above it all, but despite his shimmery images, poise and jokes, the poems express enormous love and praise for the world's ephemeral, twilit beauty. They look for meaning in the molten tumble of modern life through poems like 'Theme Park Days' or 'I Asked Mr Dithers Whether It Was Time Yet He Said No To Wait'.

There are jokes in this poem, too. One way in is through the concept of space. 'What strikes us all immediately in painting is space, or rather the illusion of space,' Ashbery once wrote, comparing it to the space of a poem.[8] The space this poem develops is full of structures. Structures falling, structures remaining and one being built. From the *tower in the mill* to *bare room* and *studio*, the poem tells of a structure which the speaker (presumably Greuze) is left in, and one he looks out at from his *oriel* window: a *cement house with no windows*.

The Revolution has (presumably) happened. Known social structures have collapsed (see *collapse*, line seven). The speaker's *group* is *vulnerable* and *endangered*. He was once fêted. Now he is high in a *bare* room, in a *tower*. It is the *evening*, not only of his life but of the world he knew, where he was popular and rich. *Autumn* rises *in the sky like a tornado*. The *ruby spittle* of sunset and *autumn* hint at the Revolution's violence, blood-flecked political storms, maybe people who spit at you; the death of an era and the *group* he belongs to; maybe also of the safe, cliché-confirming art he represented. His *calculations* and *equations* may be *undone*, or *collapse into bric-a-brac*.

These images build up a collage, which you could call by the main Ashbery principle: uncertainty.

There are things to *examine* in this *empty* place, this *studio*. He studies reflection: *mirrors*. He is a painter so he looks through frames (*from whose oriel / I can see*), and pins his *hope* to texture: *glint* and *velvet*. Animal life is everywhere: there are no people in the space of this poem. The speaker identifies with part of this animal life: his *group* is *endangered, / like dead birds*.

Dead birds, you might think, are birds no longer in danger, but *Girl with Dead Bird* was a famous Greuze portrait which hints voluptuously (like his *Girl with Broken Pitcher*) at the loss of virginity. Aristocrats were killed in the Revolution, others were *endangered*. This is the endangerment of a species. The speaker identifies with *dead birds*, but what about those *bluebottles* who *nag heaven / with their unimportance*? Is he feeling his own *unimportance*, a painter who has had his day, a rococo painter in the Revolution? Or is he looking down and seeing blue-denimed workers, victors in the Revolution, *bluebottles*? Will their success make his *calculations collapse*?

All the images suggest the end of structures, the end of a way of seeing. But a *cement house* is being built, *across the road*: a new structure comes in place of the old, at the beginning of the new stanza. A new type of art, perhaps (as well as political system) which the artist who perfected gloss cannot see into or out of? A *columbarium for cement pigeons*. Animal life in the new order, as he sees it, is inanimate.

This poem is more traditional in form than many Ashbery poems and uses traditional musical techniques of echo and pick-up. In the first chunk, two main sounds are repeated: the EL of that key word *vulnerable* (in *mill, oriel, bluebottles*, and the centre of *calculations*) comes back in the second in *building* and *spittle*, and echoes in the last line's determined hope: *will, veiled*. The ON (or EN, or UN) of *heaven, unimportance* and *deacons* comes out strong in *undone* and is echoed in *columbarium, pigeons, unsure, endangered, autumn, room, examine*.

The first chunk's longest line ends in *do*, answered in the second chunk by the line which tells us this is a letter – to *you*. So who is this *you* he is reporting to from wherever he has landed up, in this 'evening' of his fashionable life? And why have the replies always been *unsure*?

The poem ends in imperatives which seem to be the painter's commands to himself: to try and give himself a future, hang on in this new world where his colourful sentimental painting is no longer appropriate. *Try to keep cold and empty, examine mirrors*.

So is the *you* of the last line himself: is he encouraging himself? Or is it the *you* of the *letters*, someone he *talked to down the decades*? Or are these people one and the same? Is the *you*, whose reply is always *unsure*, the self he sees in the *mirrors*?

Ashbery's playfulness involves the reader on what Walt Whitman called 'equal terms'. It is up to you, whoever *you* are in or out of the poem, to decide what he is really up to, this *endangered* painter in his *tower*, this poet who pretends to be above the world but constantly shows us he is not.

Moving House

I   *Middle Watch, Battersea*

Wash of traffic; the crush
of waves on a windowed shore;

the windows, worn to a shiver, let in rain.
The wind is posting litter through the door.

Behind the gas-fire in the hearth
a soot-fall clears the chimney's throat

and the wind sings wire-songs: the filament
blown like coal to a white gasp.

A scuffle in the skirting-board
as something frees itself from something else.

The bulb stirs and the room shifts
twice towards the cellar door.

II   *Defrosting*

The satisfying creak and give
of another white slab: ridged,
tectonic, holding the ice-box shape
in a curved mould; as if the polystyrene
once packed around the fridge
now packed inside, heavier and cold.
Small ice clatters in the salad drawer
as I hack at the top with a knife,
hands raw and hot in the sharp snow.
Bored, I take a warm beer through and write.
The fridge ticks with water, dripping;
the kitchen bobs towards me in the night.

Robertson, born in 1955, grew up in north-east Scotland. He has
written three collections, won awards in Britain and America, and

works as a publisher in London. His fierce eye homes in on landscape and sea, love, sex, and violence – and also on vision itself, as if the act of seeing paints itself on to its subject. This poem comes from his first collection *A Painted Field*, whose first poem begins with the verb *I see*. The collection ends by relating early photography to visions of contemporary Edinburgh. Its centrepiece is a poem about a painting of Apollo flaying the skin off Marsyas and Robertson uses language like a surgeon making an incision: tense, precise, unforgiving.

The 'movement' announced in the title of this poem is simultaneously external and internal. The *house* is both the verb's object and its subject. Someone is *moving house* but this *house* is *moving* too.

The setting seems to be the night before a house move. The first couplet picks up the *sea* of *Battersea*, turning the sound of *traffic* outside the window to the *wash* of *waves* on the *shore*. An image which the sound underlines by repeating the SH of *wash* (in *crush*, *shore*, *shiver*, and the sixth couplet's *shifts*) in movement that is heard but not seen.

These first two couplets set the scene indoors (*windows let in rain, wind posts litter through the door*), the next two move closer in (*hearth, gas-fire*). Again *wind* turns up in the second couplet of the two. Again the movement is unseen (*soot-fall*). But there is visible movement too now (*filament blown*). In the last two couplets, the unseen movement is *behind the skirting-board* and the visible movement (*bulb stirs*) may be due to that *wind* (through *windows* or *door*) or something worse. The *room shifts twice*, the whole house seems to be *moving* now. The word subsidence hovers in the background.

Appropriately for a poem about moving on, the form changes from the first to second poem. Both have twelve lines and could be laid out the same way. The first shows what there is to get away from. Each couplet gives a different reason to move: *traffic* noise; leaky windows *worn to a shiver* (suggesting both their thinness and the effect of thin windows on the speaker); draughty doors; *soot-fall* from a blocked *chimney*; fire nearly *blown* out; hidden mice (or is it part of the structure that *frees itself from something else?*); more draughts swinging *the bulb* (or else a seismic tilt, shifting *the room towards the cellar*). The room, maybe the whole house, is coming apart in the poem's hands.

The second poem moves towards undoing the clench of frost in the fridge: by, paradoxically, clenching itself into a *slab*. Again we focus on heard movement (*creak and give* of ice). Inside and outside turn inside out: the ice *inside* looks like the *polystyrene once around the fridge*. As everything melts, the ice gets smaller. No more *tectonic* plates, only *small ice*.

Now the speaker becomes part of the movement (*I hack, I take and write*). But movement goes on around him. Again first heard (*fridge ticks*), then seen (*kitchen bobs towards me*). The poem ends as it begins, with *water*. The whole thing moves from *wash* to *water*, *dripping*, and to a *kitchen* bobbing in a flow which the speaker has created linguistically (as well as by hacking at ice and *defrosting* a fridge).

The second poem is a slab compared to the first, but the flow of thought and music gets quicker. The twelve lines take up less space, aptly for a poem moving towards liquefaction.

And maybe *defrosting* suggests the unlocking not only of fridge-ice but the speaker's own life. He is no longer stuck where he was; he is about to move *house*, move on; and move on in writing. In the first poem, the fire's *filament* is *blown* to a *gasp*. Now *hot* and *warm* take over. *White* slabs loosen, *small ice clatters* free, just as in the first poem *something frees itself from something else* and soot *clears the chimney's throat*.

Vowel echoes hold each poem together but also relate the pair. The second picks up key vowels from the first. In the first, the short O of *watch* in the title goes on through *wash, on* and *songs*, and the title of the second (*Defrosting*). The first poem's long OH (*windowed, windows, blown, coal*) is repeated in the second poem's *holding, mould, cold, snow*. The first poem's OR (*shore, door, door*) is echoed in the second only by *drawer*, but its short I (*traffic, windowed, shiver, in, wind, windows, in, chimney's, sings, filament, in skirting, shifts*) is picked up by *give, ridged, tectonic* and *ticks*, while the IRE of *wire, fire* gives way to the second's long I (*white, ice-box, inside, ice, knife, I, write, night*).

The poem closes with *I, write* and *night*, gesturing to Coleridge's poem 'Frost at Midnight' whose speaker is alone at night while *frost* works its *secret ministry*.

In Coleridge, *frost* is outside the house not inside a fridge. The poet sits beside a sleeping child, watching a fire which has a ghostly *film*. His poem moves towards freedom, of place, life, imagination. In Robertson's pair of poems, the speaker is writing alone with a *gas-fire*. He is *defrosting* his fridge in the *middle watch*, darkest hour of *night*. But his poem, unlike Coleridge's, is subdivided. The first poem has no person, just a fire, its *filament blown* (like Coleridge's fire) to a strange *white gasp* accompanied by *a scuffle in the skirting*. Everything outside – *rain, wind, litter* – is trying to get in. For the first half of the second, the action seems again impersonal. The *white slab* (recalling *white gasp*) *gives*. But the subjective has come in. The sound is *satisfying*, not to the ice but the poet, who reveals himself in the second half. *I hack, I take and write.*

Like Coleridge's, this is a poem about freeing up. But where Coleridge's accepts the *frost* and its *ministry*, this one ends it. It is about unfreezing, and moves towards writing. The poet's *raw, hot* hands take a *knife* to *sharp snow*. Homing in on contemporary domestic details (*salad drawer*), with strong sudden verbs (*posting*) and a characteristic strangeness (*wire-songs*), Robertson turns his poem into a meditation on *moving*. Moving on your life, and your own writing, within a frostlit, firelit poetic tradition.

Sighting the Slave Ship

We came to unexpected latitudes –
sighted the slave ship
during divine service
on deck.

In earlier dog-days
we had made landfall
between forests of sandalwood,
taken on salt, falcons and sulphur.

What haunted us later
was not the cool dispensing
of sacrament
in the burnished doldrums

but something more exotic –
that sense
of a slight shift of cargo
while becalmed.

Stainer, born in Stoke-on-Trent in 1941, went to Oxford, lived a while in Orkney and now lives in Suffolk. She has won prizes in competitions, published many collections and recently a *New and Selected Poems* called *Lady and the Hare*. She writes at the edge of something sacred. Her language is precise, numinous, very pared. A sharp, bare, free verse, both violent and ethereal at once, addressing myth, science, metaphysics and the sea.

Her poems often start from art, music, science, or slightly way-out skills that need precision (skydiving, tiger-training, calligraphy), whose delicate techniques reflect her own spare lyricism. They often spotlight the person using the skill – a bell-ringer or wound-dresser; or they are in the voice of people whose title or function ('The Falconer's Bride', 'The Red King's Dream') have a peculiar role magic.

This is the title poem of her second collection. Its speaker (an anonymous crew member on a plundering commercial voyage) contrasts the horror of a *slave ship* with the surface smoothness of society as it overlooks its own inhumanity. The voice glides over the inner meaning of what is *sighted* just as *divine service* happens on a *deck* whose surface stands for the surface values of a culture dispensing *sacrament* in full view of accepted iniquity. Slave traffic is literally above board; society offers absolution like a pharmacist selling asprin, ignoring the sin it sanctions. *Sacrament* creates a state of grace, but this crew is *in the doldrums* – a word that works on two levels. A windless sea (evoking the one in Coleridge's 'The Ancient Mariner', with its albatross of guilt) and the state of spiritual nullity – *burnished*, as society polishes its rectitude in the *service* of God while really 'serving' commerce through plundered luxuries (*falcons*), things that promote its own consumption (*salt*), or violence (*sulphur*, connected to gunpowder, associated with hell). Pursuing its appetites, society takes *unexpected latitudes* (also working on two levels) with morality.

The immorality, the very existence of a slave ship, is announced in the title and reappears in the second line. But the voice seems to ignore it, following the sequence of ordinary procedure (including *divine service*), unconcerned at what the sailors have *taken on*. A sense of unease begins in the second half with *haunted*, but the words go on denying wrongness. *What haunted us was not* hypocrisy, only a *sense*. A sense only of *something* very *slight*, a *shift of cargo*.

The second stanza describes concrete things but the third moves into the abstract (*the dispensing, sacrament, doldrums*), qualifying its abstractions with physical adjectives (*cool, burnished*). By the last verse, where you are expecting specifics (what the *slave ship* looked like, what they saw on it, what it made them feel), the voice becomes even more abstract and vague. They are *haunted* by *something more exotic*: the *sense / of a slight shift*.

Treating human beings as *cargo*, calling any feeling about this *cargo exotic*, smoothes away guilt just as *cool* and *burnished* suggest the superficial care for communion during a sea-calm. *Exotic* literally means 'from outside': from Greek 'out of', 'away from'. The *falcons*, living creatures taken from their home, caught to be sold, hint at what that word *cargo* means on the other ship: human suffering, people taken 'out of' or 'away from' (*ex*, in Latin) their home.

The poem is about standing still: both at sea and morally. So its journey is towards vagueness and abstraction that smooth over guilt. The voice progressively distances itself from what it sees, in bitten-back lines and archaisms (*sighted, made landfall, becalmed*). Until, in the last word, the speaker's feelings are *becalmed* by denial: denying the horror of what is *sighted*.

The sounds turn on the two vowels of *slave ship*, beginning with the AY of *slave* (*came, slave, days, later*), sliding into the OR of *landfall, salt, falcons, haunted, more* and the ER of *sulphur*, and into the AH of *cargo* and *becalmed*. Short I (*ship, latitudes, service*), reappears in the third (*dispensing, burnished*), and finally in the last words glossing over guilt: *exotic, shift*.

This poem gets at the stilling of conscience through getting its ship *becalmed* in (and about) a system of greed and violence (*salt, sulphur*). A system which serves mammon while paying surface *service* to God. The vowels do the same thing. They make only *a slight shift*, stay in the same careful register and end in a slight AH-sigh of moral giving up.

The Lammas Hireling
(For Robert Walters)

After the fair, I'd still a light heart
And a heavy purse, he struck so cheap.
And cattle doted on him: in his time
Mine only dropped heifers, fat as cream.
Yields doubled. I grew fond of company
That knew when to shut up. Then one night,

Disturbed from dreams of my dear late wife,
I hunted down her torn voice to his pale form.
Stock-still in the light from the dark lantern,
Stark naked but for the fox-trap biting his ankle,
I knew him a warlock, a cow with leather horns.
To go into the hare gets you muckle sorrow,

The wisdom runs, muckle care. I levelled
And blew the small hour through his heart.
The moon came out. By its yellow witness
I saw him fur over like a stone mossing.
His lovely head thinned. His top lip gathered.
His eyes rose like bread. I carried him

In a sack that grew lighter at every step
And dropped him from a bridge. There was no
Splash. Now my herd's elf-shot. I don't dream
But spend my nights casting ball from half-crowns
And my days here. Bless me, Father, I have sinned.
It has been an hour since my last confession.

Duhig, born in 1954 in London to Catholic Irish parents, the
eighth of eleven children, left school at sixteen but eventually went
to Leeds University. He worked with homeless people for fifteen
years in London, Yorkshire and Northern Ireland, and now teaches

in the north of England. He has won the National Poetry Competition twice, the Forward Prize for Best Poem (with this poem), and many other awards in Canada, America and Britain.

He is one of the most original poets of his generation. His poems may go anywhere and do anything. They are learned, ironic, rude, elegant and funny. They mix delicate images, belly laughs and esoteric lore (about, for instance, English or Irish language, art, history, politics, folk art, fairytales, social history, children's games, local history) with compassion and wit, ignoring boundaries between high and low. The Venerable Bede sits easily beside the price of coal. Formally, the poems have wonderful control and variety. 'Compression', he says, 'is poetry's distinguishing feature. It allows words to have resonance and create a space around themselves.' His subjects veer from Apollinaire to Welsh ballads, Yorkshire pudding, sutras, string vests, or a Russian butcher in the *Wehrmacht* catering corps.

There is grim humour too. His poem 'Chocolate Soldier' addresses a folk music club in York where people sing about homelessness ('I am a jolly beggarman'), which refuses entry to anyone connected to the next-door hostel for the homeless. Another poem reveals that Lent used to end with a ceremony ridiculing herrings. 'There is No Rose of Such Virtue', a hymn to Our Lady of Atheists, is about Cumbria during the foot-and-mouth epidemic.

Despite the extraordinary learning, his poems give you all you need to know to understand them, whether what you have to understand is the Hiroshima setting of 'From the Plague Journal', or the ancient Irish hero Sweeney. There are a lot of monologues. You pick up clues to who is talking and what is happening as you go. No word is wasted; all are there for a purpose.

This poem, title poem of his fourth collection, turns on ancient British folk belief but is immediate and fresh. The speaker has hired someone at a *fair*. *Lammas* in the title tells us the era when it happens (pre-industrial revolution), and also something of the speaker. He is a farmer, able to hire people. Lammas, the 'loaf-mass' season, fell on 1 August, but more important than knowing that is picking up tone, context and feel. The subtly archaic language fills in the sense of a past rural era full of magical belief. *Light heart and heavy purse* sounds like a proverb. *Struck cheap* (as in strike a bargain) sounds like archaic colloquialism. *Doted* sounds antiquated.

Three lines in, and a lot has been established. The cowhand is hired, cows love him, the speaker is pleased with his bargain.

But then his success begins to seem uncanny. The speaker *grew fond of company*. You think this is because he is getting richer (*yields doubled*), but *company* is not what it seems. It comes at the end of its line and the next tells us what *company* he likes: people who know *when to shut up*.

Shut up about what? Sex he can now afford, women or boys who will keep quiet? Or is it the success itself, something uncannily achieved, like Faust's, which no *company* must question? Or does the new hand, the *hireling*, cause of the new wealth, stand out as somehow strange: is that why he was *cheap*, and what he wants them to *shut up* about? Or does their relationship suggest embarrassing closeness?

As in an M. R. James ghost story, or Henry James's *The Turn of the Screw*, unease seeps in gradually. *Company* and *shut up* begin it, but in the second verse unease becomes disaster. *Disturbed* describes the speaker but also this stanza's events. *Dreams of my dear late wife* (why did she die? Who or what killed her?) lead to violence (*torn voice, fox-trap biting*), a vision of sexuality (*stark naked*), and revelation of the cowhand's magical powers: *I knew him a warlock*, i.e. in league with the devil, a sorcerer or faith breaker.

Cow with leather horns sounds again like a proverb, suggesting horned head-dresses, witchcraft. It was also a phrase for the hare, the most magical hunted animal in British folklore. This verse is about transformation: *dreams* to *voice*, *light* from a *dark lantern*, the *naked* cowhand *a pale form* with a *fox-trap* on his *ankle*. *To go into the hare*, i.e. change into a hare, *gets you muckle sorrow, muckle care*. Christianity said man was made in the image of God, so the idea of shape-shifting was abhorrent.

Muckle means 'much'. The white space between these stanzas, splitting *muckle sorrow* from *muckle care*, is the poem's structural centre. Much *sorrow* on one side, much *care* on the other. The third stanza which contains the core violence is tamped to the third by this split proverb. What is going on: or rather, what does the speaker think is going on? Has the hireling been imitating the dead wife's *voice*? Has it been *torn* from her ghost, is that what disturbed the speaker's sleep? Or was he magically making love to the wife's ghost in a spectral orgy?

Whatever is happening, the hired hand is the focus of the speaker's sexual fantasy, and the third stanza stops it. *I levelled and blew the small hour through his heart.* The *small hour* is the darkest time of night, when dreams and fantasies most (to pick up that word describing the speaker) disturb. Is he shooting darkness into the hireling's heart? Or blowing a hole in him so that when *the moon* immediately comes *out*, it seems to be coming because of, even through, this shot?

All this is mysterious. That is the point. The speaker is mysterious to himself. How he describes his own acts is as uncertain as what he saw, or says he saw, in that *light from the dark lantern*.

By the moon's *witness*, he sees the body change. It furs *over*, the *head* hair thins, the *top lip* gathers like a hare's slit upper lip. In the fourth stanza, the sack he carries this body in grows *lighter*. Transformation is continuing: unseen, after death. The line that ends *no* makes you realise this poem has put you in a world where you really have no idea what might come next.

Splash follows *grew lighter*. The corpse may be so light by now it has blown away, dwindled to nothing. But *no splash* also follows up the suggestion that, as soon as the hireling was shot, the *moon* came *out* (growing *lighter* in another sense).

These images make us reinterpret everything. Was the good man the hireling not the speaker? Why that strange word *lovely*? Did the speaker love the hireling's beauty: was that why he liked *company* that *shut up*, why he reacted to the nakedness? Had he known him naked already? This young man, so close to nature the *cattle doted on him* and *dropped heifers*: has being close to this sensuality and in-tuneness with nature made the speaker feel this man had crossed a species barrier or a sexual boundary? Has this unhinged the speaker's version of Christianity? He ends in confession, but he has thought all along with pagan beliefs.

Pagan belief comes out strong in *elf-shot*. The *herd*, which had been *fat as cream*, is sickened by magic in revenge for what he did. Is this a force of evil or of justice? *Sinned* will bring into the open the possibility that he, not the shape-shifter, was the wicked one.

Elf-shot pronounces the word he does not use when he describes shooting the hireling: *shot*. Increasingly, the speaker's language (like *blew the small hour*, climax of the action) glosses over what actually happened. He went down at night and shot his labourer. The poem is about transformation: but whose? Was the speaker hallucinating when he *hunted*, and saw a *fox-trap*? Was his vision of the body furring over his guilty imagination? Is this about his own transformation into lunatic and murderer? Has the idea of magic (*warlock* and *hare*) seeped from contemporary rural lore (as *the wisdom runs*) into his head, rather than into reality? Did he perhaps do away with his wife before?

Unreliable narrators are part of the normal armoury for all twenty-first-century writers, and the poem whose speaker hints at but covers up his own violence or madness became increasingly important through the nineteenth century. The narrator in Browning's poem 'My Last Duchess' (1842), for instance, has had his wife murdered. Duhig's poem is a tale either of witchcraft and magic, or of a speaker who believes in all that and uses it to explain or justify a murder. The question is how unreliable he is. Each word of the world this poem creates builds an impression of a different truth behind the speaker's words. The poem reveals what the speaker's language covers.

We end with a narrator who 'spends' *nights* melting money for shot and his *days* compulsively confessing, turning to a priest or to God (*Father*) as if to a reader, acknowledging *I have sinned*. He reveals his own obsessiveness (as Tennyson thought the speaker of his poem 'Maud' did, in the first line)[9] by revealing that he confesses every *hour*. Like Salieri who murdered Mozart, in Peter Shaffer's *Amadeus*, this speaker is confessing. The poem is his confession.

What about the melting down? Is he destroying *half-crowns* earned in the *time* of the hireling, when *yields doubled*? Is this a penal task? 'Casting ball' meant the process of making shot. (Gamekeepers often made their own.) But why *half-crowns*: because of the symbol of the King, God's representative? He is preparing more violence, of exactly the kind he committed. Is it silver bullets he is after, to deal with more witches? Is he trying to commit the same crime over and over again? Catholics who confess without a 'firm purpose of amendment' are not absolved. They have to return, confess again, and mean it this time. But if he keeps making more shot, that is not going to happen.

Then this talk of 'spending' his *days*. His story ran on money. The *heavy purse* and *cheap* bargain has led to a heavy conscience. Is he the real *hireling*: did he hire out his own soul for gain?

And where is *here*, apart from being the place of the poem? A church? A prison? The lonely farm? Or the confessional: a place where the speaker compulsively returns with his story like the wedding-guest in Coleridge's 'The Ancient Mariner', who also killed a magical creature?

The point is not to answer these questions (you can answer them in many ways) but to follow how they arise, track the sequence of feeling and build-up of atmosphere. The poem's journey reveals a psyche *disturbed* by superstition and guilt. He was doing well, he became *disturbed*, killed the man who made him wealthy but also disturbed him. (Why did he say the man's head was *lovely*?) He got rid of the body. Retribution followed. He is now *here*, a place of guilt. It is a fable of superstition and violence told in a modern way, through an unreliable voice.

Why is it so powerful? Why do people call it a contemporary classic?

Its power comes from a combination of things. The tension between violent action and flowing rhythm, what is said and what is unsaid: the way most key sentences end midline (after first, second or third beat), suggesting what is important is hidden; above all its coherence: the way the words hang together, how sounds, syllables and images glide and gather through the whole.

The first stressed vowel sound, AIR, moves from *fair*, narrows in stanza two for *dear*, echoes through *pale* and carries on into the key word *hare* (Dürer's picture of a hare is on the collection's front cover), *care* in stanza three, and narrows again for *here*. The long I of *light* (a word which will go through various meanings in the poem) and the often-repeated *I*, is picked up in *time*, *mine* and *night*, widens in stanza two for *late*, echoes into *wife* and on into *light* (in a different sense) and *biting*, resonates in the third to *heart* (which picks up *light heart* in the first line) and *out*; re-emerges in *eyes*, and in the fourth stanza for *lighter* and *nights*.

The long EE of *cheap* sounds at the end of one of the few end-stopped lines. In the first three verses, the main action is advertised in the first two lines, which are all end-stopped. In these stanzas the speaker makes the action (at least) clear in the first two lines. But in the last stanza, the sentence ends on the third beat (*bridge*), before the end of the line. The speaker is losing his grip as we rapidly revise our view of him. So that first EE is important. It echoes on in *cream*, *yields*, *dreams* (stanza two), *dreams* again (stanza four), and the entreaty, *bless me*.

EE also chimes with its own thinner version IM, which begins at the end of the second sentence, *him*. This is another vital sound. Musically, you can hear the poem (and the story) as a murderous dance between the long I of *I* and the short I of *him*. After the first *him* comes *I knew him*, *I saw him*, and a new version of this sound, *thinned*. Then comes *him* in *I carried him*, *I dropped him*. It lengthens into *dream* before emerging again in the confession word, *sinned*.

Meanwhile the YEW of *grew, knew, knew, blew, grew* is increasingly associated with the growing sinisterness. The short U of *struck* echoes through the important words *doubled* and *shut up*, is muted until *muckle, runs, muckle* and echoes once more in that ambiguous word *lovely*. The ER of *purse* mutates to OR in *torn* and *form*, shifts back to *lantern*, on to *warlock* and *horns*, widens for *hour* and *out*, narrows to *fur*, widens in *crowns* and comes back in the last line to *hour*.

The consonants stress the sinister words, weaving through each stanza to make each stanza a discrete soundworld on its own, but relating the stanzas so different sounds create a coherent story through the whole. The P of *cheap* marks the first verse (*dropped, company, up*), lies dormant in the second (except for *pale*) until the startling word *fox-trap*. The K of that odd word *struck* is connected to apparently calm ideas afterwards in the first stanza (*cattle, cream, company*) but prominent in the violence and compound words of the second (*stock-still, stark-naked, fox-trap, ankle, warlock, cow, muckle, muckle*). It then sails on through the aftermath (*carried, sack, casting, crowns*), to end in the last word, *confession*.

I could go on. The power of this poem comes not only from the magic in the story but the way the complex patterning and relationships of sound and music bring out both the sense but also the mystery and finally the unknowability of what, exactly, happened. The poem gives you all you need to understand the basic emotional arc but also leaves things open for every reader to go deeper.

IV

Who Are You Beside Me?

And did you get what
you wanted from this life, even so?
I did.
And what did you want?
To call myself beloved, to feel myself
beloved on the earth.

Raymond Carver, 'Late Fragment'

The stranger and the enemy
we've seen him in the mirror.

George Seferis, Mythistorema

The traveller meets other people on the path.

From Homer's *Odyssey* to *Pilgrim's Progress, Canterbury Tales* or Byron's *Childe Harold*, a vital part of the journey is other people. The traveller walks into strange societies, meets welcome or hostility, and enters the *holy city* (J. H. Prynne's phrase) of love. Even Beckett's lone lame tramp in *Molloy* feels his soul 'leap out to him, at the end of its elastic' when he sees another traveller on the road.

We may not see these other people accurately. 'I saw him only darkly,' says Molloy, 'because of the dark and then because of the terrain, in the folds of which he disappeared from time to time, to re-emerge further on.' But who they appear to us to be – that is vital to our journey.

This section has more poems than the others because it is about the most uncertain thing of all, the thing we 'make strangest': relationships. These poems explore the complicated journey of being connected to other people. Falling in love and realising (with nothing said) the other person may feel something like that too (James Fenton); a relationship that may (or may not) be moving from *on* to *off* (Jamie McKendrick); realising you made a damaging choice (Rosemary Tonks); hurtling on through relationships thinking you'll find another (or will it be the same one?) *on the ledge* (Alan Jenkins); a moment shared on *the loved side of the temple* (J. H. Prynne); a wedding (Alice Oswald); living with someone, separate but in deep contact (Julia Darling); looking back to when you first met (Andrew Motion); eating the same food however revolting it looks (David Harsent) and walking the same road however sad its meaning (Eavan Boland); becoming a parent (Kate Clanchy); caring for toddlers on your own (Maurice Riordan); divorce (Carol Rumens).

But there are other relationships on the road as well. *When I count, there are only you and I together*, says the traveller of the section 'What the Thunder Said' in Eliot's *The Waste Land:*

> *But when I look ahead up the white road*
> *There is always another one walking beside you.*

Other travellers may misunderstand you, suspect you, take up a position as enemies. Fairytale heroes fall among thieves at the inn. In Homer's *Odyssey*, every island holds a different community. Whether it is the Lotus-eaters with their home-forgetting drug, or the man-eating Laestrygonians and Cyclops, these island societies directly threaten the hero, his companions, and their journey home. The soul's 'leap at the end of its elastic' may not be towards but against the other person. The white road throws at you not only friendship and love but malice, injustice, ambush – and war, which affects the whole landscape around us whether in prehistoric Troy (in Christopher Logue's poem) or twentieth-century Europe (in Caroline Forché's); threatening animals and nature as well as people. Judith Wright's poem compares animal relationships to those of human characters in the West's first war poem, Homer's *Iliad*. In a passage from the *Iliad* itself (in Christopher Logue's version), gods fight each other for the sake of warring human beings: the pro-Trojan river god is up against the pro-Greek fire god, who is scorching the plain before Troy and blackening the trees.

Murderousness (whether in Northern Ireland, Auschwitz, or Eastern Europe in and after the Second World War, all sparingly explored in the poems of Caroline Forché and Nick Laird) is the dark side of relationship. The mythic *katabasis*, descent to hell, is about human relationships and the self: you go into the dark to learn from another person.[1] But there is another sense in which going into the dark, or descending to hell, might be about relationships: it can mean the plunge into violence.

Moniza Alvi adds the twenty-first-century crisis of relationship. Alvi was born in Pakistan and brought up in Hertfordshire. Her poem is a tiny potent image for what 9/11 has done to relationships all over the world – above all where she grew up, modern Britain. At the end of her poem, after the moment of schism, the only thing left capable of going *from one side to the other* is a beetle, carrying *a luminous tear*.

Serious

Awake, alert,
Suddenly serious in love,
You're a surprise.
I've known you long enough –
Now I can hardly meet your eyes.

It's not that I'm
Embarrassed or ashamed.
You've changed the rules
The way I'd hoped they'd change
Before I thought: hopes are for fools.

Let me walk with you.
I've got the newspapers to fetch.
I think you know
I think you have the edge
But I feel cheerful even so.

That's why I laughed.
That's why I went and kicked that stone.
I'm serious!
That's why I cartwheeled home.
This should mean something. Yes, it does.

Fenton, born in Lincoln in 1949, sang in a church choir at prep
school, discovered Auden's poetry at Repton (where he met Auden
and became his friend – 'I think of Auden as the starting point,' he
said once) and at Oxford won the Newdigate Prize for a poem on
the nineteenth-century encounter between the West and Japan.

That poem (twenty-one sonnets and two haiku) foreshadowed
stylistically the musical mixing of disparate forms which Fenton later
perfected, and politically his sympathy with invaded cultures. After
Oxford he worked as a political and literary journalist. As a freelance

reporter in Vietnam and Cambodia, he watched the American withdrawal, and collapse of regimes. He has also been a foreign correspondent in Germany and South East Asia, a London theatre critic, Oxford Professor of Poetry and essayist for the *New York Review of Books*. He has published many pamphlets and four books, and there are milestone poems in all of them. Through them he forged a poet persona which is journalistically objective, full of irony and puns, but also a deeply engaged witness to history, powered by pity and anger. The core of 'A German Requiem', an elegy for victims and survivors of war, is the need to forget. 'Dead Soldiers' describes a surreally elegant battlefield lunch with a prince, Cambodia's military governor, and a drunk obsequious aide who turns out to be Pol Pot's brother. His poems are highly polished and combine a lot of disparate things. Virtuoso technical skills, traditional rhymed stanzas, deadpan free verse, political insight and anecdotal experience with reflection on history, trauma, economic misery; comedy, violence, slang, long stories and (in his nonsense verse) ironic play on serious themes. They are both artful and vulnerable.

This one is a falling-in-love poem. Like many of Fenton's poems it has a light touch for a serious theme. It advertises its seriousness in the title, then follows the second repeat of the title word with a playful explanation. *Why I cartwheeled home* has extra resonances of 'head over heels' and love as a coming *home*.

One way into the poem is through its formal mix of the traditional and playfully innovative. The rhyme scheme is *abab* introduced by a line without a rhyme: *Alert*, followed by *love/ enough, surprise/eyes*, *I'm* followed by *ashamed/change, rules/fools*. The pattern is hesitation that leads nowhere, then a confident and clear rhyme scheme.

Rhythmically, the two-beat line (*awake, alert*) is followed by a three-beat (*suddenly serious in love*), back to two (*you're a surprise*), with a last line of four (*now I can hardly meet your eyes*). The beat pattern suggests what the scenario describes: a speaker saying something short and shy, moving forward then dropping back (because *hopes are for fools*); then going on again and going further, into four beats. The variable line suggests different ways of feeling and seeing in a poem about suddenly seeing (*I can hardly meet your eyes*) and feeling about someone in a new way (*I've known you long enough; I think you know*).

More largely, both rhyme scheme and beat pattern balance the traditional with something independent and new. This is what the thought does too. It mixes traditional ways of going about things (rhyming, declaring love) with fresh revelation.

The first two lines make you think the opening adjectives, *awake, alert, serious*, will qualify the speaker. But they end up qualifying *you*, the first sentence's grammatical subject (*you're a surprise*). In the last verse, *serious* does finally and triumphantly qualify *I* (*I'm serious!*). The implied grammatical confusion between *you* and *I* in these first three lines foreshadows what the poem is about: feelings about *you* and *I* coming together.

Like an opera aria, the words are spoken to a *you* who does not hear them. It is a poem about expressing unspoken feeling, which moves towards expressing it in other ways than words (*that's why*).

The first half sets this up. The only physical action is *hardly* carried out (*meet your eyes*). The submerged *would* of the crucial subjunctive (the mood which describes what might happen, but has not yet) hides in an apostrophe (*they'd change* not *they would change*).

The verbs are interior ones: what *you* and *I* feel, think, know and hope about each other (*known you; not embarrassed, changed, hoped, thought, hopes*). Informal elisions between thinking, knowing and meeting are marked grammatically by the apostrophe that flicks back and forth between *you*, *I* and the situation: *You're, I've, It's, I'm, You've, I'd, they'd*. The whole thing (grammar, punctuation and action) is about admitting a disclosure, but uncertainly, hesitantly.

The central line at the beginning of the second half moves things on. *Let me walk with you*. A journey has begun, from privately admitted feeling to physical action. At one level, this line could be an invitation to long-term partnership. *I've got the newspapers to fetch* pitches it at a domestic everyday level which the title, *Serious*, playfully belies.

The new thing, physical action (*walk, fetch*), moves on, taking along with it the internal acts of the first two stanzas (*think, know, feel*). But now it is *you* knowing (not *I've known* but *I think you know*). The fourth stanza explains external actions which have already expressed the interior ones: from *I feel cheerful* to *I laughed, I went and kicked, I cartwheeled*.

The last line takes both physical action and interior feelings forward into meaning (*should mean*) and ends with the impersonal *it* – the situation holding both *I* and *you* – in an actively affirmative open verb: *it does*. Which carries the extra resonance of 'it will do' and 'this is it'.

The careful simplicity of this language increasingly takes on the tone of English children's literature. *Embarrassed*, coupled with *It's not that I'm*, could come out of a handbook of embarrassed English declaration. *Went and kicked*, *got the newspapers to fetch*, *cartwheeled home* and *this should mean something* (followed confidently by a full stop, then *Yes, it does*) all echo with the direct speech of *Now We Are Six* or the verse of Kipling's *Just So Stories*: a grown-up giving a child a voice.

The little tasks, the confidential tone and childlike actions suggest trusting someone who has more power than you (*you've changed the rules the way I'd hoped*; *you have the edge*) and being happy about it (*I feel cheerful even so*). This tone draws brilliantly on British children's literature of the first half of the twentieth century, as the world began to absorb Freud's insight that childhood is crucial to adult experience and that laughter signals something important (*that's why I laughed . . . I'm serious!*).

In the whole collection, this poem prefaces another, 'The Ideal', in which falling in love makes you reach back in yourself for everything you are and have been. The self is not a mask but fetched out for the other person:

> This is where I came from.
> I passed this way.
> This should not be shameful
> Or hard to say.
>
> A self is a self.
> It is not a screen.
> A person should respect
> What he has been.
>
> This is my past
> Which I shall not discard.
> This is the ideal.
> This is hard.

Serious is a preparation poem, therefore: both for a sequence of love poems and for love.

On/Off

>The switch stuck through the lampstand's neck
>like an arrow shaft of walrus ivory
>in a Welsh epic
>has lost its feathers and its head.
>Peacock feathers and a gold head.
>Its Fiat Lux
>with a length of flex,
>its shift, its crick has made me
>blink like a lemur at the lack
>of the moon or a star
>or a thing between. But it's good
>how someone takes off their earrings
>with the motion of shelling a pea.
>A tiny snap. Like the hasp-click
>of a calyx
>at the press of a picker's thumb.
>A sound like lifting an airtight lid
>or a pin dropping in a pyramid.
>Then the lobe's set free
>and breathes with delight
>to shed the slight weight
>of the earrings.
>Earrings that might be
>twin filaments, a pair of ball-bearings
>or a hammock-faced moon and a tarnished star.

McKendrick, born in Liverpool in 1955, has taught in Italy and now works in Oxford as writer, journalist, translator and freelance teacher. He has won the Forward Prize, published several collections and edited *The Faber Book of Twentieth-Century Italian Poems.* His delicately crafted poems, intricately interested in making and in made things, often take off from what is violent or overlooked (rusty mudguards, Frankenstein, volcanoes, the reptile house), but this one turns (as it were) on a light switch.

Physically, the poem is about turning on or off a light as a woman *takes off* her *earrings*. It seems to be set beside a bed – before, perhaps, making love. But, since the title is *On/Off* and the last words are *a tarnished star*, maybe not. More largely, it is about relating sound (especially the click of the light *switch* which flicks through the poem's first half in *neck, epic, lux, flex, crick, hasp-click, calyx, picker's*) to sight; sight made possible by that light. It is also about translating carefully untold emotion and lavishly intricate imagination into art.

On the surface, the poem's focus is on surface decoration, and the principle of layout is symmetry. O*n* and *off* are apparently evenly balanced and these twenty-five lines are balanced and centred. The first and last (the longest, with four beats) rest on the margin. Those inside vary between two, three and four beats: the lines in relation to the margin flick *on/off*.

In the collection from which it comes, this poem is followed by another ('Aphrodisiacs') in which *it was over between us and you couldn't / pretend*. So this poem, opening with *switch* and *stuck*, suggests the relationship too may be *stuck*, that this could be the moment it will *switch* from *on* to *off*.

This possibility is reinforced by loss and *lack*: these dominate the first ten lines despite the exotic artefacts they shimmer with. (Which are not, of course, really there. They are absences; images charged with that energy of 'making strange'.[2] But they also blind us and take our eye off the title's question: *on* or *off*?) The all-important *switch* starts out as a weapon from the Arctic, or from the ancient world (*arrow shaft, walrus ivory, Welsh epic*), which has *lost* its means of flight and attack (*feathers, head* – and is there an echo also of 'lost his head'?).

The poem makes good this loss, decoratively and luxuriously (*peacock feathers, gold head*). It also describes the power the *switch* has to make light, in Latin (*Fiat Lux*) whose ritual overtones evoke another burnished, ancient, public world quite different from the intimate world where *someone* might take off earrings.

The light switching on (or off) makes the speaker *blink like a lemur*. A nocturnal animal: perhaps these two people have been in the dark and the light has suddenly gone *on*?

But what he blinks at is *lack*. There is no light now, no *moon or a star / or a thing between*. Nothing to mediate between dark and light. So perhaps they were in the light, and the switch produced unrelieved dark, and this is what he blinks at?

Then we hear *But*, and *it's good*. Despite the confusion of light and dark, something is *good*, something is seen: *someone* taking off earrings *with the motion of shelling a pea*. He must be in light to see that.

These uncertainties we have, as readers, about which way the switch is going mirror the emotional and relationship uncertainties stitched into the poem.

The *shelling a pea* line, telling us we are in the light (for the moment), is the central line in the whole symmetrical pattern. Here the poem moves from sight to sound. Again it leaps straight from the real thing (*tiny snap*) to what it resembles. A hop *picker*, pressing a plant's *calyx*. And even this imagined sound is decorated further. The imagination that gave us *walrus ivory* and *peacock feathers* is decorating the words themselves. Not just a click, a *hasp-click*. Or *like lifting an airtight lid* – although the idea of plastic Tupperware is immediately wrenched away from the domestic world by the next comparison, *a pin dropping in a pyramid*. Both images call on the idea of airlessness. If the first half secretly suggested there is a *lack* in this relationship, the second suggests it is stifling.

The poem is, in fact, curiously impersonal. Whoever takes off the earrings is simply *someone*. Feeling is not felt directly by that person (*it's good*) and, after *set free*, the poem presents a small part of her (presumably her, but we don't even get that), as emotion moves on into something stronger (*delight*) which is still not felt by a person, rather 'breathed' by a *lobe*. The *delight* is in getting rid of something (*light weight*); in being *set free*.

More comparisons. For not the *switch* but the earrings *shed*, as if the earrings have become the image of the relationship. This (the images suggest) has been airless. Now the *earrings* are *off*. With the *weight* gone, the poem can see them as *twin filaments, a pair of ball-bearings*. Two similar things: twins: *a pair* – like the lovers when they felt together, perhaps. Then as two different things: a *moon* and *star* (like the *moon* and *star* felt to be lacking in line ten). That *moon* is *hammock-faced*: it looks comfortable but only on its *face*. And then the imagery journeys into *tarnished*.

The poem's imagery started out with *gold*, *ivory* and *peacocks*, like Walter de la Mare's 'Tartary', a rich template of romantic imagining, full of shining luxuries and compound words. *If I were*

Lord of Tartary, the speaker of that poem says, he would have an *ivory* bed, *gold* throne, *peacocks* in the courts. *Lamps* would shine at evening under *flashing stars* and *bird-delighting citron-trees*.

This poem summons the same de luxe images but makes sure we know they *are* images. The scene itself is not luxurious and maybe not romantic either. It is imag-ination, the making of images. The luxurious compounds depend on the speaker's way of seeing and the power of the light. But also on the switch. It is the switch that can let the poem say *Fiat Lux*, enable it to *switch* (via metaphor) from a domestic scene (possibly the end of an affair) to the court of Tartary, Welsh epic or the pyramids.

At one level, everything is small-scale, the opposite of *epic*. Like a lyric poem, all is miniaturised (*switch, shelling a pea, tiny, pin, ball-bearings, slight*). But at another level, this tiny *motion* of flicking a *switch* or taking off earrings evokes whole worlds of history, adventure, religion. Walruses and lemurs, ancient Wales or Egypt, hop-picking and high church ritual.

The images move outwards – the opposite of those in another poem about light and two lovers in a bedroom: Donne's 'The Sun Rising'. Donne's poem sees the whole world (*Indias*, spices) *contracted* to the bedroom and the bed (*This bed thy centre is, these walls thy sphere*). McKendrick's poem, however, rather plays down love. The *delight* it moves towards is in made things, and parallels delight in its own making; in the made words.

So what about these words? How is their pattern made?

Intricately, like the artefacts it mentions. Down to the end of the second stanza, the main consonants are SH, ST and K (*switch, stuck, lampstand, neck, shaft, Welsh epic, lost, peacock, lux, flex, shift, crick, blink, lack, star*). After the break before *but*, K becomes interwoven with the softer P (*takes, pea, tiny snap, like, hasp-click, calyx, press, picker's, lifting, pyramid*). *Lid* and *pyramid* ring back to *head*, echoed in *good*. The consonant sounds switch to T, winding back to the ST of the first line (from *delight, weight, might* and *twin filaments* to *tarnished star*).

The vowels' journey starts with short vowels and moves to long. In the first half, stressed vowels tend mainly to be short (short I, U, A, E). In the second half, long vowels take over. You can track the move of stressed long vowels through to the end: the long I of *tiny* is echoed in *like, airtight, delight* (plus *slight* and *might*); the AH of *hasp* is underlined by the repeated AH of *tarnished star* – the goal to which all lines, sounds and impulses are heading.

Am I reading too much of an ending into this affair? Well, the title is *On/Off*, not off/on, which suggests from the start which way the relationship (as well as the poem) is heading. On the other hand there is *delight* near the end. You have to decide for yourself. And if you can't, maybe the poem can't either. Maybe, in the end, that's what it is about: not knowing if things are *on* or *off*.

35 Rosemary Tonks

Badly-Chosen Lover

Criminal, you took a great piece of my life,
And you took it under false pretences,
That piece of time
– In the clear muscles of my brain
I have the lens and jug of it!
Books, thoughts, meals, days, and houses,
Half Europe, spent like a coarse banknote,
You took it – leaving mud and cabbage stumps.

And, Criminal, I damn you for it (very softly).
My spirit broke her fast on you. And, Turk,
You fed her with the breath of your neck
– In my brain's clear retina
I have the stolen love-behaviour.
Your heart, greedy and tepid, brothel-meat,
Gulped it, like a flunkey with erotica.
And very softly, Criminal, I *damn* you for it.

Tonks, born in London in 1932, emerged in the Sixties as an
excitingly original poet and novelist influenced by French symbolism
and surrealism. Few people know much about her now, however.
She seems to have converted to fundamentalist Christianity in the
early 1970s, stopped writing and disappeared from public view.[3]

This poem is often anthologised. Its humorous tone is
interestingly at variance with its subject, a farewell to a damaging
lover whom it addresses as *Turk* and, three times, as *Criminal*. Even
those capital letters seem to add to the fun. But the fun is all in the
voice; the content is violent and painful. The reproach is bitter, and
moves starkly from *you took* to *I damn you*.

The facts come in the outer edges of each verse. Inside (lines two
to seven in the first verse, two to seven in the second), the tone is
strangely Gothic, dominated by violently physical, increasingly

disgusted imagery. *Muscles of my brain, lens and jug, breath of your neck, brain's retina, brothel-meat, a flunkey with erotica.*

In writing the reproachful valedictory to a lover not worth suffering for (the genre goes way back beyond several brilliant Roman poets to Greek lyric), the most difficult thing is always tone. No one wants to know about shrill or preachy. Rage and disgust are one-dimensional. An interesting poem needs play, variety and quick shifts of perspective. Shakespeare's Sonnet 87, for instance, begins *Farewell, thou art too dear for my possessing*, and then shifts to bitter: *And like enough thou know'st thy estimate.* 'Greensleeves', the song supposedly by Henry VIII, moved from regret and praise to reproach (*Alas my love that you should own / A heart of wanton vanity*) and ends with a plea that things are not over (*Come once again and love me*).

Tonks's poem is about waste and resonates with some of the furious self-disgust of Shakespeare's Sonnet 129: *Th' expense of spirit in a waste of shame / Is lust in action.* But she gets at *waste* in several different ways which avoid any sameness of tone. She sets tone and content, outside and inside, against each other, mixing images (*clear muscles of my brain*), surreal detail (*lens and jug, cabbage stump*), disgust (*brothel-meat*) and humour (*Criminal, Turk*) with a hint of reluctance – some whiff of a suggestion that she, like Henry VIII, still feels tenderly towards the ex-lover (*very softly, very softly*).

Like Shakespeare (sometimes), she blames herself for investing so much in this love. *Very softly*, in the first and last lines of the last verse, qualifies her own act, not his (*I damn you*), and so does the only other adverb, the one in the title. He was not bad, but *badly-chosen*. Her fault.

The second stanza reflects the structure of the first. A first line addressing him (in the first stanza, an accusation; in the second, a condemnation), answered by the stanza's last line: again, accusation and condemnation.

The second and third lines of each stanza give what happened in more depth. They explain the accusation and move towards the condemnation (*you took it under false pretences, my spirit broke her fast on you*). Then comes a break marked by a dash. The speaker leaves a sentence in mid-air and switches to the effect on her mind now, of what happened then. The seventh line talks of waste (time and feeling consumed, *spent, gulped*) leading to the end-line's condemnation.

In each stanza the violence starts with the dash introducing the fourth line. Each of these lines says the same thing: *in . . . my brain / I have*. Each says *brain* and *clear*. Each mention of the *brain* sees it in terms of the eye: *muscles, lens, retina*.

This mix of brain, *clear* and eye suggests she is now seeing and thinking clearly (another Shakespearean echo, perhaps, from Sonnet 113, *Since I left you, my eye is in my mind*). A contrast to that *piece of time* when she was with him (involving *books, thoughts, meals, days, and houses*), when (she now implies) she was not thinking clearly at all.

Yet this fourth line (in the first verse) is also where the imagery begins to go mad. As if, in this symmetrical structure bounded by the beginnings and ends of each verse which make crystal *clear* what is happening (he *took*, she damns him *for it*), something is out of control inside.

In verse one, she has *the lens and jug* of what, exactly? That *piece of time*? Does this mean she can still see that *time* now; has a handle on it; holds it in her mind like a vessel she can pour?

And what does *coarse* mean in the seventh line? Moral condemnation, preparing for the second stanza's steadily increasing disgust, from *greedy* and *brothel-meat* to a climax (again in the seventh line) of *flunkey* and *erotica*? Or does *coarse*, evoking what went on between them before, also suggest rough-textured: a contrast to what she has now which, though she is looking at *mud and cabbage stumps* rather than all she had with him (*half Europe, books, houses*), is at least *clear*?

In the second stanza the way-out imagery begins even before the fourth line. The first stanza has eased us into it. *Spent like a banknote* reckoned the emotional cost of the relationship in money terms (as in Shakespeare's *too dear for my possessing* and *expense*). After *cabbage stumps*, the image of cost translates into one of mutual consumption (picking up *meals* in the first verse).

Her eating was a spiritual breaking of fast. His was a blow-out. His *heart* is not *clear*, like the organs inside her. It is *greedy* but *tepid*: an eating agent that resembles *tepid* stew. His attitude to love was both voracious and tacky. Like consumers of *brothel-meat* and *erotica*, he didn't care about the object eaten or loved.

But the eating imagery begins with the speaker and her *spirit*. This is what we have of her: internal things, *spirit* and the eye of her *brain*. Her *spirit* was hungry before, and fed on him.

She had him for breakfast, perhaps? Is the poem questioning her side of things? Who was the taker, who the giver? She calls him *Turk* (raising literary images of harems, enslavement, the historical era when the Ottoman Empire threatened *half Europe*). But for feeding her, not taking from her. What he fed her was *breath* of his *neck*.

What is this about? Does it gesture to *neck* as 'impudence' ('he had the neck to . . .')? This is the nearest the poem has got to evoking two bodies beside each other, the closeness summoned by *lover* in the title. Is her *spirit fed* by breathing in the smell of his *neck*?

This image seems unbearable – or is it unsustainably mysterious, total loss of word control at last? It is left in mid-air, as she looks at what lies behind it: *stolen love-behaviour.*

Which raises more questions. Is this *behaviour* his or hers, or both? Who or what was it *stolen* from? Did he lie to her? Was he (for example) married? Is that what *false pretences* meant? Is this why their *love-behaviour*, together, was *stolen*?

Or was the *love-behaviour* hers? The *lover* was *badly-chosen*, he seemed to be what he was not (*false pretences*), so she was stealing from herself, from her own good sense and *life*, in being with him: is that the story? Or was he simply unfaithful to her?

Whoever this *behaviour* belonged to – her alone, or him and her together – his *heart* ate it up. He *gulped it*, without the *love-behaviour* meaning much to him, *like a flunkey with erotica.*

Once we see his *greedy heart* gulping, we look back on *my spirit broke her fast on you* differently. His 'hearty' gulping replaces her spiritual eating. The first three words of her eating reverberate differently now: *my spirit broke*. Another echo of Shakespeare's *expense of spirit.*

Though she curses him *very softly*, she does it with a lot of hard Ks. They open and close the poem (*Criminal, Criminal*), running from *took, took, took, clear, books, coarse banknote, cabbage, Criminal, broke, Turk, neck, clear, flunkey* to *erotica.*

The long vowels are hers: *life, time, clear, brain, thoughts, meals, days, houses.* What he wields is *false* and *coarse*. Apart from these OR sounds, his vowels are short and brusque (*mud, stumps, fed, breath, neck; brothel, erotica*). She is replying to his short vowels by flourishing three-syllable words and images at him: *criminal, retina, behaviour, brothel-meat, erotica* (echoed in *for it* at the finale).

He may be a *criminal*, but the poem has caged him, and basks in its control. No more paying and eating: she is running rings round him, in words.

Portrait of a Lady

She's been in too deep and out too far, oh *man*,
her dark eyes spill nearly twenty years of bruises,
roll-ups and cider, and a battered Morris van
holds everything she ever wants or uses –
her Dylan tapes, her Steeleye Span and Fleetwood Mac
(he told her once she looked like Stevie Nicks,
and 'Go Your Own Way' still takes her back),
her daughter's scribbles, her I-Ching spill-sticks,
the bag of grass hand-picked from her veggie-patch,
some tattered old Viragos, Mervyn Peakes
and a book of newish poetry. There's a catch
in her voice as she half-sings, half-speaks
of the slow blues she wrote about him when he left,
that neither of you will remember by the morning
when you have to leave as well and she offers you a lift
through dripping lanes – but it draws you, yawning,
shivering, to huddle in the pile of blankets, quilts
while she clings close, and seems on the edge
of tears; your breath, the frost-blurred ghosts and guilts . . .
We're gonna meet, she tells you, *meet on the ledge*.

Jenkins, born in 1955 in Kingston, Surrey, grew up in the suburbs of
south-west London, went to Sussex University and since 1981 has
worked (sometimes also teaching at the American University in Paris)
at the *Times Literary Supplement*. He is its deputy editor; he has also
published five collections and won the Forward Prize. His most
recent collection is full of grief for dead parents and friends (especially
poets, including Brodsky, Gavin Ewart, George Macbeth, Ian
Hamilton) and lost love. The dominant note is regret. At things not
said or said wrong (*the chances missed, the friends betrayed / the love I
did not want or could not keep*). At failed relationships and *what I
know, what I must love, The loneliness that fits me like a glove.*

Under many of his poems is a sense of tide, of drifting up against the flotsam and jetsam of human lives, then drifting on. The words are honest and dissatisfied but the forms are smooth and classical, and often look back to French and Latin poets. Inside the regret and self-reproach is unspoken compassion for fellow travellers in the same boat. This poem (from 1994) is a portrait that could, titled another way, suggest a self-portrait for the poet's persona. *In too deep and out too far* echoes the boat imagery that under-runs much of Jenkins' work.

The scenario seems to be a joyless one-night stand. The first half describes the contents of the woman's *battered Morris van*, relics of her attachments through the voyage of her life. The man, the *daughter*, the songs, the books. The *roll-ups, cider* and marijuana grown in the *veggie patch*. Does she live in this van? No way of knowing; it does not matter. There is a patch of earth somewhere, that is all. Part of the poem's point is that the speaker does not want to know much about her. The epithets of her belongings sum her up too: *battered, tattered*, with *a book of newish poetry*. (Has he given it to her? Is she suggesting a *newish* poem?)

Halfway through the eleventh line, *There's a catch* turns things round; suggesting, at the end of a line, that what is coming is the *catch* to her life: to her enjoying *everything she ever wants or needs*.

The next line says it is a *catch* in the *voice* – but the larger impression stays, for this really is the *catch* to her life, its great sadness, prefigured through the first half. In *he told her once she looked like Stevie Nicks*. In the title of the song she highlights, 'Go Your Own Way', with its echo of 'go away' (foreshadowing *you have to leave as well*). In the catching-at-straws vulnerability of those *I-Ching spill-sticks* (echoing the *spill* of *bruises* from her eyes). And also in the Sixties buzzword *oh man*, which seems to be said by her, or in tune with her style. Her language is italicised in the first and last lines (*gonna, man*). But *Oh man* is also what her whole being (and all the detritus around her) is still saying.

This *catch* to her life is what *neither of you* (switching the *lady* from third-person to a plural *you* shared with the speaker, which then shrinks to mean the speaker alone) *will remember by the morning*. (Because of the *grass*? The *cider*?)

Yet at the poem's other switch and pause, this *catch* is what *draws you* to stay *close* to her, in the blankets, *while she clings*. Her pain holds him. She *seems on the edge / of tears*. Everything is a muddle, from the *battered van* and *tattered old Viragos* to the *pile of blankets*.

Your breath (meaning the speaker's) mingles with *ghosts* (for her) and *guilts* (perhaps for him). They have drawn together for the night but the *morning* is cold. He is *shivering*. The *lanes* are *dripping*.

As for the last line, with its note of defeated optimism: whom does she think she will meet? Her past lover, or the speaker again? Does it matter? Is *on the ledge* a prophetic image from the *I-Ching*? Is its vague hope all the future she has left (*gonna*), the only new thing (except for *newish poetry*)?

He knows he represents a chance for her: a *spill-stick*, a c*atch*, a *ledge*. But *ghosts* (plus, perhaps, his own identification with her lostness) are too strong for him to do anything but *leave* (*as well* as the man who left before), accepting the *lift*.

Except that, for a moment, drawn by the *catch* in *her voice*, and the feel rather than the words of her *slow blues* (a now unremembered elegy for a relationship that failed) he can *huddle with her in the pile of blankets*. A fleeting, third-best image of what *close* might be: for her, for him or for all human beings.

The end-rhymes alternate in groups of four, *ababcdcd* and on. The strong vowels laid out at first are short A (*van, battered, Span, Mac, back, bag, patch, tattered, catch*) and EE (*been, deep, Steeleye, Fleetwood, Stevie, Peakes, speaks, leave, seems*), climaxing in the defiantly repeated *meet* of the last line.

The second half's sequence of one-syllable end-words whose sounds blur into each other (*left, lift, quilts, edge, guilts, ledge*) is punctuated by *morning* and *yawning*. As if this poem were both echoing the *slow blues she wrote* (one of those blues, perhaps, which starts, 'Woke up one *morning*, found my love had gone') and suggesting that its listener (who will also *leave*) may be bored.

Without spelling anything out, the poem describes in bric-à-brac detail someone who has never moved on from a love that has gone. The speaker re-enacts that abandonment, leaving her on the shelf rather than *the ledge*. It could be read as cruel or guilty but the dots after *guilts* suggest a third element is actually the most important – compassion.

37   J. H. Prynne

The Holy City

Come up to it, as you stand there
that the wind is quite warm on the sides
of the face. That it is so, felt
    as a matter of practice, or
    not to agree. And the span,
to walk over the rough grass – all of this
is that we do, quite within acceptance
    and not to press
    the warm alarm
    but a light
    surface, a day
    lifted from high
    thick roots, upwards.
Where we go is a loved side of the temple,
a place for repose, a concrete path.
There's no mystic moment involved: just
    that we are
    is how, each
    severally, we're
    carried into
the wind which makes no decision and is
a tide, not taken. I saw it
    and love is
    when, how &
    because we
    do: you
could call it Ierusalem or feel it
as you walk, even quite jauntily, over the grass.

Prynne, born in 1936, grew up in Kent (his mother was a head-
mistress, his father an engineer), went to Cambridge, spent a year
on National Service, another at Harvard, and became a teaching

Fellow at a Cambridge college. He is Britain's leading Modernist poet, deeply influenced by philosophy, especially phenomenology.

No living British poet divides readers as much as Prynne. You would call him a late Modernist: he carries on extending and questioning where Pound's later poems (and the *Maximus* poems of Charles Olson) left off. Avant-garde writing is passionately interested in process; in the poem as a fluid thing forming as you read, breaking and re-forming like floating oil in psychedelic projections, and Prynne's shifting language challenges our sense of the world.

But please trust me, or rather trust his language, and I'll make my journey into it as clear as I can.

Prynne's first collection was in 1962. Bloodaxe published a selection in 1999 (revised 2005), drawing on eighteen volumes published mainly in small presses and private printings between 1968 and 1997. Its first poem begins, *The whole thing it is, the difficult / matter: to shrink the confines / down*. Throughout his work (as sometimes in Ashbery, Jorie Graham, Peter Reading, W. S. Graham) you feel very powerfully the great Modernist double of great hope yoked to great despair. Hope – of getting the whole 365 degrees of experience and world into a poem. Despair, because this is impossible. Shrinking *confines down* (what Duhig calls compression) is part of writing a poem.

It is as if, ninety years after the wonderful bubbling transformative energy of Modernism (and also since the *Quarterly Review* called Eliot and Pound 'drunken helots'), Modernism has become a form of elegy: a lament for the fact that words can never exactly match *things*. (*What kind of beast would turn its life into words?* asks a poem by Adrienne Rich. *What atonement is this all about?*) Or else it has become an intense form of yearning driven by two incompatible desires: to get everything in and say you can't. A poem may want to be all of life but has to use form and language. Form and language limit it, so the poem can never fulfil what it longs for. However much you go at things with intellect, paint them with glittering images, reflect them in form and sound, words can never completely represent the world.

Formal traditions make a virtue of this; they revel in it. Avant-garde work, like space travel, always wants to go for broke, go farther, strip away frontiers and boundaries.

One of Prynne's early poems talks of *The century roar* as *a desert carrying / too much away* so that *the plane skids off / with an easy hopeless departure*. That *too much* includes, I think, all the experience and perceptions which are you-in-relation-to-the-world. The *plane* (whatever it stands for, which might include a poem) is *carrying away* all you have seen, felt, been part of. Loss (of ourselves, of how and what we experience in our lives) is the touchstone for how we see. Or as he says in another poem, *nearly too much / is, well, nowhere near enough*.

So we may be dealing with poems which feel they can never do what they long for. There is sadness, sometimes anger, about the whole process of poetry as a netting of the world. *Write a letter, walk across the wet pavement*, says a poem called 'The Western Gate':

> the lines are taut with
> strain, maybe they'll
> snap soon. The explosion
> is for all of us and I dedicate the results
> to the fish of the sea and the purity of
> language: the truth is sadder but who
> would ask me to hope only for that?

You can't, says this poem, *hope only* for *the truth*. There are more *fish in the sea*, more flickers of meaning and possibility in the world, than just one truth. But we have to try to make sense of our experience. *The explosion* (of understanding, perhaps) *is for all of us*. And Prynne's poems also delight in the wonderful linguistic energy released by Modernist techniques. In an essay on Chinese poetry he compared language to a 'great aquarium' where 'the light refracts variously'.

His own language is extraordinarily refracted. Its surface shimmers like streams of iridescent fish. He has a wide range of different tones, vocabularies and kinds of speech, which suddenly interrupt each other. Lyric language like gold-dust blown and scattered by irony, puns, colloquialisms, slabs of current affairs, mountains of technical jargon about information processing systems, biochemistry, geology, computer language. Anything from the stock market to TV cookery. And many voices: severely impersonal, impatient-sardonic or personal and passionate, with jokes, inverted clichés, golden phrases but also asides like *stuff it* slithering between them all. No voice or line of reasoning lasts for long. He can switch from a lyrical description of a cheque to the financial reality behind it. (*These petals, crimson and pink, / are cheque stubs, spilling chalk in a mist / of soft azure. At the last we want / net costs plus VAT.*)

Or he can describe a feeling as if it were a chemical reaction (*a slight meniscus floats in the moral / pigment of these times*), and chase up the chemical experiment, not the feeling: *meniscus tilts the / water table, the stable end-product is dark / motion, glints of terror the final inert / residue.*

Prynne's poems fiercely reject the idea of the poem as a tidy enclosed space. No gardens (as for Marianne Moore).[4] No fences. All that is poetry over-tamed, *too kissed and fondled.* His poems are jungles rearing angrily against their own culture. *No / poetic gabble will survive which fails / to collide head on with the unwitty circus.*

Over the decades, his poems have become junglier, more densely textured and impenetrable. This one is from an early collection, *The White Stones* (1969), full of love, music, desert, geology and the image of the city. *The social cohesion / of towns is our newer ligature, / and the binding, you must see, is / the rule for connection.* This collection spotlit human connection: *That's / the human city, & we are / now at the edge of it.* So one key to any poem from it is the idea of human ties: what binds people (*ligature*) and *rules for connection.* The fluidity of these human ties is reflected in the fluidity of relationship between words, syllable and meaning in the poems themselves.

This poem is about making or strengthening such a *connection.* Its central movement is a walk over the *rough grass* of that geometric web of human relationships called a *city*: an image of human relationships which, like bodies in a dance or syllables in a stanza, are constantly changing. Its action is a walk to *a concrete path* and, in the central line, the *loved side of a temple.* All sorts of biblical phrases (holy of holies, temple of my body) about sanctity and love echo under the relation of the title to the central line. There is a *you* here, a *we*, and at one moment *I.* That central line connects love, *we* and a holy place at the city's (and poem's) heart; and love between people to love for a holy place (*loved side*).

At first you think the poem's structure, built around this holy place, is instantly visible from the layout on the page. But when you look closely, the structure keeps changing. Stress and line length are key to its fluid patterning. We start with three four-beat lines at the margin, then two three-beat lines indented. Then two longer lines (four or five beats) at the margin again, then six one- or two-beat lines indented.

This takes us to the centre, but the two halves are not symmetric. This is very different from the asymmetries of Donaghy's 'Machines' (Poem 1). That poem came out of formal lyric tradition, while this comes also from the Modernist tradition.

'Machines' plays with the sonnet form, that ideal form for love poetry. This poem does so too. It could be two shaken-up sonnets stuck together, as the poem is about a connection being made between two people. Fourteen lines up from the central line, fourteen lines down. But instead of playing *with* boundaries of form, it is playing *beyond* them, wriggling free. That central line starting *where we go* is a classic pentameter, beginning another three four- (or five-)beat lines to the margin. But then comes a run of two- or three-beat indented lines. Only three of them, not six (as in the first half), for they are interrupted by a single four-beat line about a *wind which makes no decision*.

Is this the *wind* from the first half, which was *quite warm* on the *face* in the second and third lines? Which also seemed to act as a *warm alarm*? A *wind* that was image for unspoken emotional ruffles on a *light surface*: for some *felt* but unspoken stir, through which this *day* is *lifted upwards*?

We (whoever *we* are) are separately (*severally*) *carried* into this *wind*: this movement which is outside the people themselves and is also *a tide, not taken*, echoes Shakespeare's *Julius Caesar*: that *tide in the affairs of men, which taken at the flood leads on to fortune*. So, in affairs of the men (or women) in this poem, is this *wind* (or *tide*) not going to do anything, even 'decide'?

But *we* are *carried* by it. We are suddenly not in charge of 'our' actions, pushed by that *wind* just as the run of indented lines has been pushed (from the pattern in which they appeared before) by the wind's line.

These *wind* and *tide* images could mean two opposite things: that something did not happen (a *decision* not made, *a tide not taken*) or that it did. The *wind* carried them, so what happened was like a decision (though they did not make it). It was a *tide*, and took them with it. Their decision was *not* actively *taken*.

This impasse of meaning is followed by another run of shorter lines. *I saw it*. The reader may not know what happened but the speaker has registered it, whether this was negative (something that failed to happen) or (more likely given the forward movement at the end) positive. Immediately the lines get shorter and more emotional. And just after *I* appears for the first time,

Love (much stronger than the passive participle *loved*) comes in.

These lines use an ampersand (instead of the normal *and* used elsewhere) to bind more closely (in a collection spotlighting *ligature* and *rules of connections*) *when, how, because*, the causal and temporal 'connections'. Answer words, which explain some shift of feeling that has happened through the poem – possibly between the *you* and the *I*.

But there may be an extra spin on this too. *We* and *you* sound personal but could also suggest the French '*on*': they could be a generic, universalising *you* and *we*, saying, 'This is how human beings behave, how *we* all are (how *you* are) as *we* go (or *you* go) through life, walking over *grass*, visiting places *we* feel are holy.'

After these short intense inner lines, the poem returns to the margin with two longer lines ending in a pentameter, which echoes the calm classic pentameter at the centre. *Ierusalem*, too, suggests someone has got where they longed to be. That way of spelling the name underlines its relationship to Greek *hieros*, 'holy'. The last line almost smiles, sounding a faint note of private achievement.

Another way into this poem is by tracing through it three inter-linking journeys. In Part One, I suggested there are many sorts of journey in a poem; that all tell you something about what it is doing, what it might mean.

One journey, here is – follow the verbs. They begin active (*Come up, walks, we go*). Verbs and movement stop at the centre, *a place for repose*. The next verb is passive (*carried*). Then acts are done (or not) not by *we* but by other things, *wind* and *tide*. After *Ierusalem*, movement starts again, but now it is not *we* who *walk* but *you*, the pronoun which began the poem stationary (*you stand*), as if the poem's achievement is to get *you* going. Something has moved forward. We got to some centre, rested, then went on.

A second journey might be – follow what happens to *we*. This begins at *we do*; then comes *we go*. After *repose* comes *we are*, then *we're carried* into the *wind* and *tide* of no decision. The climax of this journey is what *love is*: *when, how & / because we / do*. This journey is edging *we* closer to *love*.

A third journey – track what happens to the physical; to bodies, warmth, *wind, grass*. The poem opens with an imperative: *Come up to it*, i.e. (perhaps) 'face it'. Face the fact *that the wind is quite warm on the sides / of the face*. Are we talking attraction, a blush, sensual feeling between *you* and the speaker, facing the fact *that it is so*; that this feeling is *felt / as a matter of practice*? Someone is 'practised' in reading signs of attraction; but what about *not to agree*? Maybe the other is unpractised; maybe it still feels open whether attraction is 'agreed' to exist. Either way, there are bodies as well as minds involved. Hence *walk* is what *we do*. This is *within acceptance*. (*Within* one or other person's *acceptance*? Or social *acceptance*?)

The outward signs of whatever is *felt*, therefore, are socially unremarkable; but things may be wilder and warmer inside. On the *light surface*, all is casual and gentle. But underneath is momentous, sensual; it is *thick roots* and lifting *upwards*.

On this journey, the poem's first half increasingly suggests sensual assent. Then comes *where we go*. As in *holy* of the title, the syllable at the poem's heart is long O (*go, repose, no, moment*), like a gasp of delight, as *we* are at rest on *a loved side of the temple*. Embracing, perhaps?

This is where *love* comes in. And *Ierusalem*, holiest of all *holy* cities.

The poem began with one imperative (*Come*) followed by *as you stand*. It closes with another (*feel*) followed by *as you walk*. Relationships and connections have happened under the reader's nose. Bodies have registered each other, moved together. Warmth and *love* have occurred. Now *you* walk on again: jaunty. The bodily journey suggests a movement not only forward but towards and into each other: the way the poem's own margins move.

The point of this poem is not knowing precisely what happened. It is keeping everything open-ended, all possibilities in play.

But if you put the physical journey together with the other two (of the verbs, of *we*) you get a lightly brushed erotic journey: two bodies and sensibilities moving together, staying still a moment in a sacred central place (*love*), then moving on again in the outside world. It is a dance which discloses, but never completely; a journey happening within *the holy city* of human relationships, feeling and connections – but also in that other *holy city* of connections and relationships, a poem.

Wedding

From time to time our love is like a sail
and when the sail begins to alternate
from tack to tack, it's like a swallowtail
and when the swallow flies it's like a coat;
and if the coat is yours, it has a tear
like a wide mouth and when the mouth begins
to draw the wind, it's like a trumpeter
and when the trumpet blows, it blows like millions . . .
and this, my love, when millions come and go
beyond the need of us, is like a trick;
and when the trick begins, it's like a toe
tiptoeing on a rope, which is like luck;
and when the luck begins, it's like a wedding,
which is like love, which is like everything.

Oswald, born in 1966, studied Classics, worked as a gardener and now lives in Devon. She has published three collections: the first won the Forward Prize for Best First Collection, the second (which followed the River Dart, telling its story in different voices in verse and prose) won the 2002 T. S. Eliot Prize.

She is best known for nature poetry (inspired partly by Ted Hughes, who also lived in Devon). But all good poets have a variety of voices, forms and interests and this, from her first collection, is a playful love sonnet (in English or Shakespearean form), with a turn between the eighth and ninth lines where dots announce a change of tack. And changes of tack, in a procession of images for love, and love's progress as the partners journey on, is what this poem is all about.

It begins with the words *from time to time*. These words do exactly what the poem is talking about: they move from one thing to another; but the two things are also the same thing, same word (*time to time*: *tack to tack*). This is the key to the succession of images presented in a pattern of repeated words which sums up the wedding message: that *love* too may be a voyage forward which tacks from side to side but ends up in the same place.

The starting image, the *sail*, as it moves *tack to tack*, also tacks the images away from *love*; *love* comes back in the last line. The journey of images passes through *swallowtail* in the third line (which could conjure a butterfly or bird's tail, but *swallow* and *coat* in the fourth picks up two different images out of that: the bird, the *coat*) to a *tear* in a *coat*, a *mouth* for *wind*, a *trumpet* which *blows*: both *wind* and *blows* gesture back to the tacking *sail*. After the turn, *love* comes in again, now elided with the *you* assumed in *our* (line one) and *your* (line five).

The new images travel on to the *trick* of love (shutting out *millions* of other people who have no *need of us*), a *toe* on a tightrope (evoking the riskiness of love, how you need to keep on your toes), *luck*, *wedding* and back to *love*. Which, in the last words, *is like everything*. If you have the *trick* of it or *luck* to be in it, the whole world becomes an image for love.

When the repeated *and when* appears (in a context of *and if, and this*) *it* keeps ushering in new changes (lines two, six, eleven, thirteen) and that hopeful word *begins*. Three times out of four, it comes at the same place in the line: *the sail begins, the trick begins* and finally *the luck begins*, which introduces the title word, *wedding*, and brings us back to *love*.

The sound of repetition is everywhere. Sometimes in the same line, sometimes in the next: *sail/sail, swallowtail/swallow, coat/ coat, mouth/mouth, trumpeter/trumpet, millions/millions, trick/ trick, toe/toe*. Above all in the key word *like*, which dominates from the start, quickening its appearances at the end like a foot tapping faster (*time, time, like, like, flies*, then nine *likes*). You could also hear the poem as a journey from the long I of *time*, echoed by this powerful word comparing love to the world outside, to the short I of the last syllable, which describes what this world is: *everything*.

These repeats in the box of the sonnet, the tacking from one word to the same word, get across playfully how *love* works: through same moves that are always different or different moves that are all, in the end, the same.

Two Lighthouses

I would like us to live like two lighthouses
at the mouth of a river, each with her own lamp.

We could see each other across the water,
which would be dangerous, and uncrossable.

I could watch your shape, your warm shadow,
moving in the upper rooms. We would have jokes.

Jokes that were only ours, signs and secrets,
flares on birthdays, a rocket at Christmas.

Clouds would be cities, we would look for omens,
and learn the impossible language of birds.

We would meet, of course, in cinemas, cafés,
but then, we would return to our towers,

knowing the other was the light on the water,
a beam of alignment. It would never be broken.

Darling (1956–2005) was a poet, playwright and novelist. Born in Winchester, she went to Falmouth School of Art and worked in community arts before turning to writing full-time in 1987. Her first novel was longlisted for the 1988 Orange Prize, her second longlisted for the Man Booker Prize and shortlisted for the Encore Award. She lived in Newcastle, loved north-east England and in 2003 was given the Northern Rock Foundation award, the largest annual literary award in England. She had two daughters.

At thirty-eight she was diagnosed with cancer. It went into remission but returned five years later. Her 1998 play, based on this experience, was nominated for three awards. She co-edited a remarkable anthology (*The Poetry Cure*) of poems about being ill, going into hospital, the pain and humiliation of illness and its treatment, and bereavement. From 2002 on, her online diary charted the progress of her illness alongside details of her daily life. Readers fell in love with its charm, optimism, honesty and moving generosity. In her last entry, she counted 'blessings': 'No pain unless I try to dance the hokey cokey'; 'Cornflakes and milk'; the fact that 'you only have to do death once'. Just before she died she got up to watch the first night of her new play.

Her two last collections explored living with cancer. 'Poetry gave me a voice to express the comedy and tragedy of my illness,' she said, and the poems combined her pragmatic approach to it with romance, lyricism, her surreal anarchic imagination, her laughing spirit and art. *Be late. Be sordid. Eat six pies.* Because, *Beneath your feet / worms aren't worrying.*

This poem is from her 2004 collection, *Apology for Absence.* It is about living with someone you love but doing so in the unspoken-of shadow of mortality, so that both the living and the love are incalculably precious and intense.

It is dominated by soft liquid consonants, the L of the unspoken word *love*, the W of *we* and of the auxiliary *would* that denotes the subjunctive mood, the mood of wishing. W runs through *would, with, we, water, which would, watch, warm, shadow, we would, were, would, we would, we would, we would, towers, knowing, was,* to *water* and back to *would.* L (gesturing to the title word *lighthouses*) from *like* to *live like, lighthouses, lamp, uncrossable, flares, clouds, look, learn, impossible language, light,* to the word where the whole long fantasy comes to rest and which sums it up: *alignment.*

The other consonant in 'love', V, flicks in at the beginning in *river*, resurfaces in *moving* and comes back at the end in *never.* Another important word through the poem, which sets going the *lighthouses* fantasy, is *like.* The K in it skims from *like* to *like, like, could* (another wishing word), *uncrossable, could, jokes, jokes, secrets, rocket, Christmas, clouds, look, course, cafés,* and ends in *broken.*

This too is a love sonnet, but very differently laid out from Oswald's (Poem 38). Partly I think, because its image of love is so different. Two separate *lighthouses*, either side of a *river*, are joined by their lights, by remote communication and *signs.* The lines fly apart on the page. There is no rhyme scheme: the two lines of each couplet stay together because they want to, because they have things in common. What marks each couplet out from the others is what each line has in common with its partner. Musically, the first couplet has the IV of *live* and *river*, the images of *lighthouses* and *lamp.* The second has the water, and the OR echo between *water* and *uncrossable*, which is also picked up in *watch* and *warm* in the third. The third is separated off by its image of the *shape* in the *rooms*, the hint of physicality and flesh after the *uncrossable* remoteness that has gone before. After this tactile suggestiveness, the fourth and central couplet (knitted to the third by the repeated *jokes*) has the intimacy of things *that were only ours*. This is marked out musically by the chime of *ours* and *flares*, the K of *jokes*, *secrets*, *rocket* and *Christmas*, the long O of jokes and *only*, and the almost-rhyme of *secrets* and *Christmas*.

The last six lines look outside and up. The fifth couplet looks to the sky (*clouds, birds*) with a half-chime between *cities* and *language*, and the accompanying mental picture of a whole public world outside the two towers. The sixth couplet lets the pair *meet* in that public world.

These two lines are marked from others by pauses in rhythm. Instead of the easy flow (like *water* flow, or a beam of *light*) of previous lines, there is a comma after the first beat (*meet, but then*) and in the first line also after the second beat (*of course*). This breaks things up, suggests hesitation, as if these two people operate most easily – or perhaps the love flows easiest – when they are separate but (as we see in the last couplet) secure in *knowing* what *the other* is to them.

The last couplet evokes what exactly they are to each *other* by picking up images from earlier couplets. *Light* from the first. *Water* from the second. Rhythmically, *never* picks up *other*. Musically, the long I ties *light* and *alignment* together, while conceptually the *light* is, itself, a form of *alignment*: it draws the line between the two buildings, the two people who are each other's *alignment*. So the alignment of the lines becomes an image of the relationship: these are partner lines in separate couplets.

The final *never be broken* is of course poignant in a collection charting the swift progress of cancer. But the poignancy is unwistful, pragmatic and restrained; and it echoes (from the centre of the poem and all possible *signs* and *secrets* of intimacy) the one repeated noun: *jokes*.

On the Table

I would like to make it clear that I have bought
this tablecloth with its simple repeating pattern
of dark purple blooms not named by any botanist
because it reminds me of that printed dress you had
the summer we met – a dress you have always said
I never told you I liked. Well I did, you know, I did.
I liked it a lot, whether you were inside it or not.

How did it slip so quietly out of our life?
I hate – I really hate – to think of some other bum
swinging those heavy flower-heads left to right.
I hate even more to think of it mouldering on a tip
or torn to shreds – a piece here wiping a dipstick,
a piece there tied round a crack in a lead pipe.

It's all a long time ago now, darling, a long time,
but tonight just like our first night here I am
with my head light in my hands and my glass full,
staring at the big drowsy petals until they start to swim,
loving them but wishing to lift them aside, unbutton them,
tear them, even, if that's what it takes to get through
to the beautiful, moon-white, wanting skin of you.

Motion, born in London in 1952, won the Newdigate Prize at Oxford like James Fenton, taught English at Hull University (where he met Larkin), edited *Poetry Review*, worked in publishing, taught Creative Writing at the University of East Anglia (he currently teaches it at Royal Holloway College) and became Poet Laureate in 1999. Since then he has been a wonderful champion for poetry. He has published eight books of poems, a study of Edward Thomas, a novel, several biographies (including those of Larkin and Keats) and a memoir.

  Through many different forms – romantic lyric, prose poems,

narratives in different voices – his poems have a tactful, elegiac, watercolour restraint. They are explanatory and empirical, fusing beauty with loss. His biographies set other poets' sense of loss scrupulously in the contexts of family, love, society, history, politics; his poems do the same for their subjects. In 'The Letter', a girl in the Second World War describes scrambling off to the hills to read a love letter, seeing a German pilot crash to death, *legs / splayed wide in a candid unshameable V*. The gently transferred sexuality, the interweaving of pastoral and violent death, the half-aware, half-wondering voice work like a period film to disclose a past world. He pans out from individual vulnerability to wide-angle shots of the human and historical landscape.

They are reticent poems, but the lives they reveal are often cut short or cut up. The tragedy of his mother (who fell on her head in a riding accident and lived ten years in coma before she died) shadows many poems, above all 'Serenade', about the horse she was riding that day. Others focus on people whose lives were curtailed by accident or war (Anne Frank, Princess Diana and a friend in the *Marchioness* disaster). Many ask if we can find meaning in the random events of life: *Are we just waiting for something important to happen, only nothing ever did, / beyond the next day and the next?*

But this is a love poem and finds meaning in three things, one for each stanza. First a tablecloth, then a dress which the tablecloth's pattern reminds the speaker of, and finally (declaring need, putting its cards *on the table* of the title), the beloved: *you*. Its journey is from *I* to *you*. From polite wish expressed by *I* to *wanting* felt by *you*.

It is a declaration which changes as it goes the sort of declaring it does. It begins with a tone you could hear as self-mockingly pompous like an after-dinner speech. Or anxious. Or defensive, perhaps in an argument, perhaps correcting a false impression (*I would like to make it clear*). It calls the flowers (in the *repeating flower-pattern*) *blooms*, and explains the reason for buying them in a smooth run until *we met*, where a dash introduces a bit of back history and a verbal tangle of *I* and *you*, illustrating *we met* with a plethora of mixed feelings and communications from both *I* and *you*. (*You have said, I never told you I liked; I did, you know, I did; I liked, you were.*)

In the second stanza those *blooms* are now *heavy flower-heads* and already lost, maybe covering *some other bum*, maybe *torn to shreds*. In the third, they are *big drowsy petals*. The speaker wants to *lift them aside, unbutton them, tear them* (picking up *torn* in the second verse). The original flowers disappeared but the speaker wants to repeat their disappearance, tear the new pattern (which *reminds me of that printed dress*) *if that's what it takes to get through* to what really brings meaning: *the beautiful moon-white skin* for which those flowers were both a covering and an image.

The poem suggests that love, too, is a *repeating pattern*. It has gone on repeating itself from *the summer we met* right up to *tonight*. They met *a long time ago now, darling, a long time*, another repeated phrase with an appeal to the beloved in the middle (like *I did you know, I did*). As with *we met*, the relations between the words themselves illustrate what is said. They too are *repeating pattern*.

The central stanza widens the focus to society (dresses given to Oxfam, a municipal *tip*, a garage, plumbing) but also moves towards sexual intimacy. This stanza, one line shorter than the outer stanzas, is the centre of the flower, a woman's waist. The poem moved from patterned cloth to the idea of her not being *in* the dress at the end of the first stanza. Now *slip* suggests the dress slipping off, looking forward to the third stanza's images, lifting it *aside*, unbuttoning, getting to *wanting skin*.

So despite the wider focus, the second stanza also ups the sexual symbolism. After *bum* comes *heavy flower-heads* (with the suggestive familiarity of *swinging*), *tip, dipstick, crack, torn to shreds* (anticipating *tear them*). The vowel harmonies (*life, I, right, wiping, tied, pipe*, and *slip, tip, dipstick*; also *heads, shreds*), the Ps and Ks (*tip, dipstick, pipe, piece, crack*), hang together to make this stanza a different aural world from the others, full of words that in themselves sound sexually intimate but on the surface conjure the outer world of other people.

The suggested sexuality moves into open sensuality in the third stanza. The *pattern* goes on *repeating*. Lose or *tear* it, it turns up again. Internal rhymes add to the background sense of lulling, affectionate repeats. In the first stanza, the last line rhymes its second beat, *lot*, with its fifth, *not*. So does the last line of the second (*tied, pipe*). And the last line of the third rhymes its third as well as its second beat (*beautiful, moon*) with the fifth (*you*).

In the final stanza, the poem declares itself in a different way. The amusement in the voice comes over in *here I am*. The *head* of *My head light in my hands* gestures back to those *heavy flower-heads* over the *bum* in the second stanza. But desire takes over as the flowers which began by *swinging* now *start to swim*, and the poem drives on (through images of 'unbuttoning' and 'tearing' the very dress the poem says it is about) to get to what is more *beautiful*, what is underneath: *the moon-white, wanting skin of you.*

Poem XVI from *Marriage*

I perch on a 'Bauhaus'-style chrome and raffia
stool as you drop your knife and pause to consider
this fish and its fistula,

this fish with its deep deformity, its head like a cosh,
its raw flank and blood-brown eyes,
its lips of lopsided blubber,

this fish we are having for supper.
You laid out cold cash
to have them deliver this fish, close-packed in ice,

a glacier coelacanth preserved against all the odds,
as if some throw of the dice, some coin
turning a thousand years to come down heads,

had brought to the marble slab in our kitchen
of all kitchens this fish, sporting
its jowly truncheon-lump of sorbo rubber

and the great wet ulcer opening beneath its backbone.
As you start again, flensing good from bad, you let spill
a viscous flub of gut that slips

from your wrist to the marble, where it spells
out the hierogram most often linked
with the once in a lifetime, miraculous

descent of the goddess, her gills
crisp enough to cut as you trade kiss for kiss.
Flesh of her flesh. I'll eat it if you will.

Harsent, born in Devon in 1942, has published nine collections,
won the Forward Prize, written a TV opera; he has written one
opera libretto (and song cycle) with Harrison Birtwistle and is

working on another; he also writes crime fiction under the name David Lawrence.

His poems are cerebral and physical, lyrical and vernacular, full of muscular energy conveyed with a very precise musical ear. They address war, love, history and art with humour and startling imagery. This one, from a sequence called *Marriage*, explores the risks involved in being one *flesh* by focusing humorously, mock-shocked, on an expensive fish (*you laid out cold cash*), specially delivered (*close-packed in ice*) but internally deformed.

The poem starts with the speaker's disengagement (*I perch*). He (we assume) stays on a dry high modern *stool* of *chrome and raffia*, well away from the wet fish with which *you* deal. *This fish*, the poem says five times (as if the speaker's increasingly appalled at what *we are having for supper*), is a lot of disgusting adjectives and nouns (*raw, blood-brown, blubber, rubber*) with a *great wet ulcer*; and *viscous flub of gut* which spills and *slips*. The speaker keeps reminding *you* that this costly ugly thing is her (presumably) responsibility. *You pause and consider* it. *You* bought it. *You start again. You* cut *good from bad*. You *let spill* part of its innards *from your wrist*.

This weaponlike fish (*head like a cosh, jowly truncheon-lump*) is a danger. But the speaker, though appalled, moves towards sharing it with *you* when the *goddess* (Love, perhaps) descends; or rather flips on to *the marble*; and *you trade kiss for kiss*. The speaker ends, daringly, *I'll eat it if you will*. Marriage is taking risks together.

There are religious as well as fleshly implications here. For persecuted Christians, a fish was the symbol of Christ drawn on cave walls. Greek *ichthus*, fish, was a secret acronym for *Iesus Christos Theou Uios Sôter*: 'Jesus Christ Son of God Saviour'. This poem lightly suggests a dangerous communion atmosphere: *flesh of her flesh* for 'Eat of my flesh'. *We are having* a (possibly last) *supper*. This all plays on the idea of union (man and wife as one flesh) in something spiritual, not only in partly bad fish. *Marriage*, the title noun, is not just flesh but a sacrament.

But the religion invoked is pagan too. Instead of the Holy Ghost descending, we get a *miraculous descent of the goddess* whose *hierogram* ('holy writing') lies on *the marble*. Gut has flopped into a shape that could be a symbol or letter in exotic script, which might stand for Love as the fish stood for Christianity.

I asked the poet if I was missing something here. Was there a real hierogram and real goddess I did not know about?

No, he said. He made it up. The gut falls into the configuration of the hierogram, whatever that might be. No prior knowledge needed. Readers must imagine the shape, and the goddess, for themselves. The modern world is pinned down by *Bauhaus*. The ancient pagan one is left to the reader to fill in.

The power of the poem comes from the violent language in tension with what the poem is talking about underneath: affectionate union. The language is both technical (*flensing, fistula, coelacanth, hierogram*), and comically ugly (*viscous flub, jowly truncheon-lump, lopsided blubber*). But despite the rebarbative words, the rhymes and vowel harmonies create a sense of union and belonging. End-words echo from one stanza to the next. The first stanza chimes the last syllable of all three end-words with the poem's first stressed sound, the ER of *perch* (*raffia, consider, fistula*). This rhyme carries through in the second, third and fifth stanzas (*blubber, supper, rubber*). The second stanza's *cosh* and *eyes* are echoed by the third's *cash* and *ice*; the fifth's *kitchen* by the sixth's *backbone*; the sixth's *spill* by the seventh's *spells* and eighth's *gills* and *will*.

In all this, the poem gives the impression of chain-rhyme. The most famous kind of chain-rhyme is Italian *terza rima* used by Dante, which also has three-line stanzas. The middle line of the first gives the rhyme for the two outer lines of the next, and so on: *aba*, then *bcb, cdc*. etc. Enough of the lines here do the same (in stanza four, for instance, *odds* and *heads* could be the two outer lines of a *terza rima* stanza) to make the reader feel the effect of chain-rhyme.

The point of this formal procedure for the message is the impression of union, backing the idea that *marriage* means uniting, even over *this fish*. Everything is linked. Partnerings of words may be random and shift around, but everything is *close-packed*: fish-flesh, lovers' flesh, words.

That the Science of Cartography Is Limited

– and not simply by the fact that this shading of
forest cannot show the fragrance of balsam,
the gloom of cypresses
is what I wish to prove.

When you and I were first in love we drove
to the borders of Connacht
and entered a wood there.

Look down you said: this was once a famine road.

I looked down at ivy and the scutch grass
rough-cast stone had
disappeared into as you told me
in the second winter of their ordeal, in

1847, when the crop had failed twice,
Relief Committees gave
the starving Irish such roads to build.

Where they died, there the road ended

and ends still and when I take down
the map of this island, it is never so
I can say here is
the masterful, the apt rendering of

the spherical as flat, nor
an ingenious design which persuades a curve
into a plane,
but to tell myself again that

the line which says woodland and cries hunger
and gives out among sweet pine and cypress,
and finds no horizon

will not be there.

Boland, born in Dublin in 1944, published her first book in 1967 and has published many since. She teaches at Stanford in California but keeps a presence in Ireland and reviews regularly for the *Irish Times*. Her influential essay collection *Object Lessons* describes how a woman poet of her generation had to find her voice both within and against male tradition. Her poems set domestic life, and the fabric of women's lives, in a context of myth, love, history and Irish landscape. In this one she sets up the title as if on the blackboard of a lecture hall, as a proposition which the poem wishes (it says at the end of the first verse) to *prove*. It wastes no time about it – the title becomes part of the poem, so the beginning of the poem is a continuance, a dash.

No proper beginning, then, for this poem about a road that does not end. Or rather, it ends without meaning, having got nowhere. It ended *where* its makers *died*. Endings and beginnings are unclear.

The poem has several different strands and tones of voice. It begins with the intellectual proposition, then moves sensually into a *forest* full of soft F (*fact, forest, fragrance*) and S (*simply, shading, forest, fragrance, balsam, wish*). Then it turns to love, for this is the beginning of a relationship too (*you and I first in love*). The lovers enter more forest (*wood*). At the end, the poem will return to that *wood* (*woodland*), bringing back the swish of S (*says, cries, gives, sweet, cypress, finds, horizon*). But it will end on a negative, *not be there*.

Its stanzas are of three or four lines, except for three single lines which follow the road's fate from the lovers' first glance at it, to its end and disappearance. The first chunk, four lines followed by three, ends firmly *there*, with a full stop. *There* being a *wood* on *the borders of Connacht*.

Then comes a single line, the lover's words and *the famine road*. Which could have been the title of the poem, except that the poet is interested in the abstract idea, the argument, as well as the concrete thing.

Another chunk follows, again of four lines followed by three, ending in a full stop after *build*. Now the imagination follows the people building this road through three four-line stanzas with no full stops until the single last line. The only end, the only full stop, will come at *not be there*.

Increasingly, as the poem gets angrier and more hurt about this pointless road, the lines end in words which you would expect to have some other word follow them in the line: connective words, prepositions, auxiliary verbs, comparisons (*of*, *had*, *in*, *down*, *so*, *of*, *nor*, *that*). When the speaker sees the road for herself, in the stanza where *stone disappears* into *grass*, punctuation too disappears and even the grammar is less clear.

In prose, the structure of this would be: 'I looked at ivy and grass, into *which* the stone had disappeared, as you told me *that* in the second winter, in 1947 when the crop failed twice, Committees gave them road to build.' But the words I've italicised are missing. So are the commas which would make the sense clear, though there are perfectly good commas elsewhere. The run-ons and confusion suggest the speaker's incredulous realisation about what this disappearing means. It is a disappearing not only of *stone* but of people. The next line will be *where they died*.

The more intellectual strand of this poem is a meditation on *cartography* as power. Brian Friel's play *Translations*, about the British military mapping of Ireland, shows how mapping 'translates' not only local names but reality. And, by translating, changes that reality. Mapping (or translating) is like road building, a way of exerting control: 'giving' *the starving Irish such roads as this to build*.

A map is *masterful* as well as clever. The lecturing, intellectual voice describes how clever: *apt rendering of / the spherical as flat; ingenious design which persuades a curve / into a plane*.

The speaker's voice has come a long way since the lover told her *Look down*, showing her the road. She can now expound and point to things herself. But she has not lost the feeling. *You and I*, and *first in love*, are the starting point and impetus for the poem, even for its intellectual explaining. Midline, she moves from the end of the *road* to its effect on her. *There the road ended / and ends still and when I* . . .

The *not* of the last line shows what is lacking. Another line, not of poetry but a *line* on the map, which would represent this road which *gives out*, ironically, in the midst of softness (*among sweet pine and cypress*). A *line* that would represent experience properly. Would say *woodland*, cry *hunger*. Mapping and control, says the poem, are about imposing limits, but their power *is limited*. Maps cannot show feeling, *hunger*, *ordeal*. The poem itself is its own only record of suffering *not there* on the map.

This is where being *in love* has led: to sharing this thought with *you*. Sharing not just the experience of that *wood* but these shifts of register from the sensuous swish of *forest* to intellectual proof. Love, suggests the poem, is not just gazing into each other's eyes but looking in the same direction, at the same things and in the same way.

When You Cried

I sat and mourned, let you
thrash on my lap like a choking fish.
The way your soft spine
chain-linked, grew strong!

It was as if you were a salmon
and our arms were nets, as if
you were searching upstream,
upstream, for the dark pool

you came from, for your
proper ground. I thought
you'd seen through us, that
you knew this wasn't home.

Born in Glasgow in 1965, Clanchy was educated in Edinburgh and Oxford, worked as a teacher in the East End, and is now a teacher, journalist and freelance writer. She has published three collections marked by witty skilful reveries that take a situation out of the day-to-day into realms of history and surreality. They can move swiftly from domestic love to colonial exploitation to sex with an angel, for instance. Her first collection won the Forward Prize for Best First Collection and a Somerset Maugham Award.

This one, from her third collection, gets the baffled helplessness of a new mother, the feel that this is all wrong somehow until the bond between mother and new baby has grown (as the baby's *soft spine* is growing) *strong*. The speaker explains to the baby how she felt at first when it cried.

Mourned starts things off. An extreme verb, suggesting crying is dying, invoking all possibilities of maternal grief including the saddest of all mother images, Mary mourning Christ. The helpless *sat* is echoed by *let*, *thrash*, *lap*: the sharp repeated little mono-syllables suggest shock at the way she did nothing but sit there and *let* the child lie in that *lap* (which ought to be the place of help) *like a choking fish*. The second two verses will explain that shock.

Chain-linked follows up the idea of this baby as a *fish* out of water, something whose right place is another medium. *Grew strong* suggests (gratefully, perhaps) it is surreptitiously growing more human despite being *let* to cry and *thrash*. But the second verse develops the idea that it belongs somewhere else and is repeatedly, in all this crying (suggested in the repeated *upstream*), *searching* for this mysterious elsewhere; for a *dark pool* whose AR replaces the offered AR of *our arms* (all set to hold *you*). *Searching* also echoes the repeated *were* of the subjunctive, the tense for what may not be true.

The speaker knows this is all fantasy. Her baby is not a *fish*, not *searching* for where it came from. She is putting this fantasy forward to explain why she did nothing *when you cried*, just *sat* and *mourned*.

The last verse makes it more explicit. She felt the baby had a *proper ground*, knew that living with its human parents was not *home*. That the baby *knew* more than she did; had *seen through us* as parents.

Which reflects, perhaps, a still-unanchored feeling that her *lap* is not the *proper ground* for a crying baby. That for the mother, too, it does not yet feel like *home* to hold in her *arms* something so different, a *fish* from an unknown *pool*, a creature from other *ground*.

The long, dragging, chiming syllables of the last two lines (*you'd seen through, you knew*) slow everything down saying yes, listen, this is where the poem has been heading, the central fear. The poem's journey is not forward so much as inward. A journey of helpless explanation into the fear, which parallels the fantasy journey of the *fish* (or baby) back in again, *upstream* (urgently repeated, like *salmon* that have to keep trying to leap *upstream*) where it has *come* from. A journey of unrolling or developing the fantasy that the baby *came from* somewhere else. A journey of using the *fish* and *pool* fantasy as an explanation for why, in the first line, as a very new mother, she simply *sat* and *mourned*.

But behind these three four-line stanzas is also the traditional lullaby, the song telling a baby not to cry, cajoling it but also (in old songs) threatening it. ('Stop that crying or the bogeyman will take you away.')

The internal echoes that run though the whole thing give a

lullaby feel, a singing rhyming effect without a rhyme scheme. *Mourned* is echoed in *ground*, *strong* by *home*, the end-word *you* (picking up *you* in the title) flickers through the poem (*you, you* in the second stanza, *you, you'd* in the third) ending up in the last line as *you knew*. The slightly shocking word *let* in the first stanza is echoed by *nets* in the second, and widens into *thought* in the third. The poem's key image, the *fish* of the first stanza, is picked up in *as if, as if* in the second.

The lullaby is also, perhaps, designed to have a calming effect on the mother, who felt her crying, thrashing baby was an alien and holding it was not yet *home* for her, but is now in tune with it enough to explain, and say, 'That was then, not now.'

From a Conversation During Divorce

It's cold, you say, the house.
Yes, of course I'll go back one day,
Visit, that is. But the house

Will be cold, just as you say.
Two people have left home,
One of them me, and one

Our youngest child. So of course
It's cold, just as you say,
And big, too, bigger at least

Than it was with everyone there.
Don't think I don't think about you
Being cold in a house that size,

A house that gets bigger, too,
And colder each time I dare
Think about you and the house.

It used to be warm in the days
Before I decided to go,
And it didn't seem big at all,

In fact, it was rather small,
Which is partly the reason I . . .
Don't keep on asking me why

And telling me how it is
In the house. I don't want to know.
How can I go back, how can I

Even visit a house that size,
And getting bigger every minute
With all the cold rooms in it?

Rumens was born in 1944 in south London, and studied philosophy. She has been writer in residence in Kent, Belfast, Cork and Stockholm; and taught creative writing in Belfast, Bangor and Hull. Her first collection came out in 1973. Many have followed, and a *Selected*. She has written a novel and plays, and collaborated on translations from Russian. Her subjects range from the personal and domestic to the historical and political, in a wide range of international settings from Belfast to Russia and the holocaust. She has a very direct voice, very watchful of people's lives (especially women's) and how they are affected by the places where they live.

This one's journey seems a circle from *it's* (first word) to *it*, the last, reflecting the way any *conversation during divorce* (and this is only part of it, says the title's *from*) goes in circles: of emotion, reproach, ideas, defence. It is a monologue that seems part of a dialogue, like a phone conversation of which you only hear one side. The speaker responds to what *you say*: two words repeated through the first three stanzas and echoed in *one day*. A sense of defensive response comes through *yes of course, just as you say, don't keep asking why, don't think I don't think about you*. Other repeated words (like *bigger*, three times, or *that size, of course* and *visit*) and vowels underline the feel that both poem and house are structures of constantly returning echoes, explaining that claustrophobia which is the only reason given (but it was only *partly*) for leaving. *In fact, it was rather small*. Vowel partnerings reverberate in the echoey sound structure as through an empty *house*.

Cold, the first stressed sound (highlighting the cooling of love and marriage), runs right through. In the first stanza it is echoed in *go*, then *cold* in the second and third stanzas (backed up by *so*). The fourth stanza echoes its long O in *don't* and another *cold*; the fifth makes it *colder*. The sixth, remembering how *it used to be*, replaces long O temporarily with the OR of *warm* (backed up by *before, all* and the seventh's *small*). But long O resurfaces in *Don't* and the eighth's *don't know* and *go*. And *cold* reappears decisively in the last line, as in the first.

House, another key word (image of family, safety, the home of the self), is the end-word of the outer lines of the first verse, as if this is going to be *terza rima* (see Poem 41). It is echoed in *of course* (first and third); reappears in the fourth stanza and twice in the fifth, where it emerges as an end-word. Like *cold*, *house* is absent from stanzas six and seven but comes back in the eighth (which repeats its vowel in a repeated *how, how, how*) and ninth.

The seventh stanza's middle line trails off into the unsayable, *the reason that I . . .* This final sound, the moment where the speaker breaks off, adds its echoes to the rest of the poem in *why* and *I*, and comes to rest in *size*. Retrospectively, you realise this sound has been there from the beginning, not only in the first *size* but *I'll* and the emotive word *child*.

This is between *I* and *you*, long I and OO. The first line's *you* returns in *you* and *two*, then *you* and *too*, then *you, too, you*. Again this stops for the sixth stanza. But this vowel, unlike that of *cold* and *house*, never comes back. *I* does not really *want to know* about *you*. Instead, the last stanza picks up the sound of *visit* from the first (where it is a careful gloss on the way she will *go back*: it will only be a *visit* not a return to *the days / Before I decided to go*) and repeats it (*visit, minute, in it*). But this is a step forward, not a circle. The speaker is now not sure she can even *visit*, since the house *gets bigger and colder* whenever she *dare think about you*.

So though the journey seems a circle, the thought moves firmly forward. From *I'll go back one day* to *How can I go back?*.

Time Out
('*Such is modern life*' – Stephen Dobyns)

The two young ones fed, bathèd, zippered, read to and
    sung to. Asleep.
Time now to stretch on the sofa. Time for a cigarette.
When he realises he's out. Clean out of smokes.
He grabs a fistful of coins, hesitates to listen before
Pulling the door softly to. Then sprints for the cornershop.

When he trips on a shoelace, head first into the path of a
    U-turning cab.
The screech of brakes is coterminous with his scream.
The Somalian shopkeeper, who summons the ambulance, knows
    the face,
But the name or address? No – just someone he remembers
Popping in, always with kids (this he doesn't say).

Casualty is at full stretch and the white thirtyish male,
Unshaven, with broken runners, is going nowhere. Is cleanly
    dead.
Around midnight an orderly rummages his pockets: £2.50 in
    change,
A latchkey, two chestnuts, one mitten, scraps of paper,
Some written on, but no wallet, cards, licence, or address book.

Around 2 a.m. he's put on ice, with a numbered tag.
Around 3 a.m. a child wakes, cries, then wails for attention.
But after ten minutes, unusually, goes back to sleep.
Unusually his twin sleeps on undisturbed till six o'clock,
When they both wake together, kicking, calling out *dada*,
    dada

Happily: well slept, still dry, crooning and pretend-reading in the
    half-light.
Then one slides to the floor, toddles to the master bedroom
And, seeing the empty (unmade) bed, toddles towards the stairs,

Now followed by the other, less stable, who stumbles halfway
   down
And both roll the last five steps to the bottom, screaming.

To be distracted by the post plopping onto the mat: all junk,
Therefore bulky, colourful, glossy, illicit. Time slips.
Nine o'clock: hungry, soiled, sensing oddness and absence,
Edgy together and whimpering now, when they discover the TV
Still on, its 17-channel console alive to their touch.

The Italian Parliament, sumo wrestling, the Austrian Grand Prix,
Opera, the Parcel Force ad, see them through to half past nine
When distress takes hold and the solid stereophonic screaming
   begins,
Relentless and shrill enough to penetrate the attention
Of the retired French pharmacist next door

Who at, say ten o'clock, pokes a broomstick through her rear
   window
To rattle theirs: magical silencing effect, lasting just so long
As it takes for the elderly woman to draw up her shopping list,
To retrieve two tenners from the ice-compartment, deadlock her
   front doors,
Shake her head at the sunning milk, and make it to the bus.

Let us jump then to 10 p.m., to the nightmare dénouement . . .
No, let us duck right now out of this story, for such it is:
An idle, day-bed, Hitchcockian fantasy (though prompted by a
   news item,
A clockwork scenario: it was five days before that three-year-old
Was discovered beside the corpse of his Irish dad in Northolt).

Let us get *this* dad in and out of the shop, safely across the street,
Safely indoors again, less a couple of quid, plus the listings mags
And ten Silk Cut, back on board the sofa: reprieved, released,
   relaxed,
Thinking it's time for new sneakers, for a beard trim, for an overall
Rethink in the hair department. Time maybe to move on from the
   fags.

Born in 1953 in Co. Cork, Riordan lived in Canada and Spain before settling in south London. He teaches at Imperial College and Goldsmiths, has published two collections and edited two anthologies: one of poems about science, another to mark the fortieth anniversary of Rachel Carson's *Silent Spring*. In his own quiet poems, the light play on the surface overlays beautifully cadenced structures within. They run on intellectual curiosity about the outside world and explore technical intricacies of science, history or anthropology to illuminate human stories, especially of loss.

This tour de force, the first poem in his first book, is the single parent's *Dangerous Corner* nightmare, signalled by that *U-turning cab*, about looking after toddlers on your own. It has ten stanzas of five lines each. It opens with an eight-beat line, tells us we are in for an epic: an epic of 'modern life' as announced in the epigraph. But it is a fast-moving narrative and most lines have five or six beats (with a few of seven).

One big issue here is *time* (a title word). After the first line's string of five passive participles and one adjective (all describing the children, from *fed* to *asleep*), the second line introduces this key word. The father has achieved a lot. *Time now* for a rest; *time for a cigarette*.

The poem will journey towards more 'times' (*for new sneakers; to move on from the fags*) through a trail of time-words: *when* (first stanza), *when* (beginning the second), *around midnight* (third), *around 2 a.m.; around 3 a.m.; when* (fourth); *now* (fifth); *nine o'clock; when* (sixth); *when* (seventh); *ten o'clock* (eighth); *10 p.m.* (ninth); and *five days before* added as a bonus. After the first *time* comes *now*. The first thing he realises (having got past that effort-filled first line) is a word that chimes with *now: out*, the title's other word; one with many more meanings.

That word starts the problems. He is *out*. Stop. *Clean out* of smokes.

The pause, the tip into the man's own voice from the poem's voice, invests a lot in one small word. He goes 'out' (*pulling the door to*). This is where he is laid 'out'. Knocked down; then *put on ice*.

Then the children get out too: out of bed. Eventually the only neighbour, the only possible help, also goes out. But the ninth verse pulls us *out of* the nightmare and the tenth gets him *in and out of the shop* and *safely indoors again*. The poem itself has been a little foray *out*. Out of real life into *Hitchcockian fantasy*. Into (says the ninth verse) *a story, for such it is*, which nevertheless reflects the 'modern life' advertised in the epigraph.

'Modern life' means *casualty at full stretch*. Means a *17-channel console* which does not console. Offers *The Italian Parliament, sumo wrestling, the Austrian Grand Prix, / Opera, the Parcel Force ad*, but cannot avert tragedy in the home. Means a barrier between you or your family and the few people you have contact with. A *Somalian shopkeeper* who *doesn't say* he *always* sees the dead man *with kids*. An *orderly* who finds disorder: evidence of children (*two chestnuts, one mitten*) but no clue to them. An elderly *French* neighbour who keeps her money in *the ice compartment*, disapproves of *sunning milk* but does not wonder why it is there, *pokes* her broom through the *rear window* (echoing Hitchcock perhaps) to make the children shut up, then *deadlocks* her doors. A *dead* locking which suggests where the children might be heading as a result.

One journey is the journey of the voice. The poem starts out with the economical voice of the man's thoughts (*Clean out of smokes*), but has its own more objective eye view and vocabulary (*coterminous with his scream*) as well. When it kills him off, it cannot do his words any more. Instead it sees him from outside through the eyes of the overstretched medical staff (*white thirty-ish male; going nowhere; name and address*). He is *cleanly dead* (which ironically picks up his own thought, *clean out*). The *scraps of paper, / Some written on* suggests how outsiders might view the contents of a dead poet's pocket.

For describing what the children get up to, the poem has a drily sympathetic (*unusually, unusually*) tone which suggests it knows exactly (as the father did) what toddlers need and do: from *crooning and pretend-reading* to *distracted, sensing oddness, distress takes hold, stereophonic screaming* and *magical silencing effect*.

But even halfway through the children's story, the voice is beginning to change again, signalling that this story may be in its own control rather than following a set of real-life facts. *At, say ten o'clock* seems to wink at the reader, suggesting this account is not entirely accurate. The poem has seemed omniscient up to now (*happily; still dry; distracted by the post plopping onto the mat; they discover the TV*). But in the next verse the poem takes the reader with it (*let us jump*) then cancels that (*No, let us duck right now*), comes clean (*for such it is*), points (to justify having led us up a garden path) to a slice of real 'real life' (*a news item*), and gets the reader to co-operate with it interactively, in getting *this dad safely indoors again*.

275

Here it can revert to his thoughts (*an overall / rethink in the hair department*), since he is really alive, *reprieved* from the *U-turning cab* and *ice* of the morgue, and can *stretch* (as in line two) *back on board the sofa.*

The poem is a loop of time and a loop of tone. Back where it began, *safely across the street*. But its *time out* has made us aware of the abyss: how life is always unexpected and precarious – even, or maybe especially, in a modern city. And in his *time out* from childcare, his venture in the city, what he was going to get (apart from *ten Silk Cut*) was what sums it all up: *the listings mags*, London's entertainment guide, *Time Out.*

Trapped Dingo

So here, twisted in steel, and spoiled with red
your sunlight hide, smelling of death and fear,
they crushed out of your throat the terrible song
you sang in the dark ranges. With what crying
you mourned him! – the drinker of blood, the swift death-
    bringer
who ran with you many a night; and the night was long.
I heard you, desperate poet. Did you hear
my silent voice take up the cry? – replying:
Achilles is overcome, and Hector dead,
and clay stops many a warrior's mouth, wild singer.
Voice from the hills and the river drunken with rain,
for your lament the long night was too brief.
Hurling your woes at the moon, that old cleaned bone,
till the white shorn mobs of stars on the hill of the sky
huddled and trembled, you tolled him, the rebel one.
Insane Andromache, pacing your towers alone,
death ends the verse you chanted; here you lie.
The lover, the maker of elegies is slain,
and veiled with blood her body's stealthy sun.

Wright (1915–2000) was born in New South Wales. From 1946
she published many collections in Australia of lyrical, meditative
poems. (Her British Selected is called *The Human Pattern*, for a line
in a 1985 poem: 'Human eyes impose a human pattern'.) She was
awarded the Queen's Gold Medal for poetry in 1992 and was the
only living poet nominated by Australia's *Herald Sun* as 'Australian
of the Century'. She was a passionate conservationist; her great
theme was the Australian land: its flora, fauna and *tribal story, lost in
an alien tale.* Recalling her grandfather's encounter with the ghost
of an aboriginal warrior, she presents herself as the white latecomer,
a stranger *unloved by all my eyes delight in;* unlike *the blue crane in*

Cooloolah's twilight who belongs, who has fished here *longer than our centuries.*

But she takes that environmental issue much wider, and turns white Australian guilt (at being an invader culture, at wasting land conserved by the culture it despoiled) into a universal theme: alienation. This early poem (1946) reads animal pain through the human filter of ancient epic, identifying a female dingo (Australia's wild dog) with Andromache, wife of Hector, champion of Troy.

In Homer's *Iliad* the Greek champion Achilles kills Hector, Troy's defender, on the plain before Troy while Hector's wife Andromache is preparing a bath in the city for her husband's return. In this poem, the speaker sees a dead dingo, who has been howling for her mate: the mate she *ran with*, who was presumably killed before her. He was *the drinker of blood, swift death-bringer, rebel one.* She *mourned* him in howls that reverberate through the poem.

The speaker identifies with the howling (and now dead) dingo. She too is making a poem; and her poem becomes the dingo's elegy, beginning *so here* and ending *here you lie* as if carved on a tombstone.

She addresses the dingo as a colleague: *Desperate poet, maker of elegies.* What the dingo *chanted* was a *verse*, a *terrible song*; the poem stresses throughout the common syllable between *dingo* and *singer* (*you sang, wild singer, voice from the hills, lament, chanted, elegies*). The poem is the speaker's reply to the dingo's song: *did you hear / my silent voice take up the cry?* Its heart is the central line, *Achilles is overcome and Hector slain*, followed by the universalising *clay stops many a warrior's mouth.*

Achilles does not die in the *Iliad* itself. The epic ends with Hector's father ransoming Hector's body from Achilles, and with Hector's funeral games. It is only afterwards, out of the *Iliad*'s frame (though foretold within it), that Achilles too will die. The speaker is telling the dingo that every *warrior*, even a victor, dies too – and then women mourn. The focus is the female dingo and her howl, *crushed out of* her *throat. Death ends the verse* she *chanted.*

But, says the poem, *clay stops the mouth* of the *warrior*, too. Running, fighting, death-bringing, elegy-making: *death ends* them all. *Replying* to the dingo's *lament*, the speaker turns her *voice* to elegy in *lament* for the lot of them. Animal and human are alike in suffering and loss.

The poem identifies with the animal but it is presented in what Wright called a *human pattern*. A poetry pattern – nineteen lines,

278

mainly of five beats; though the fifth, imitating Homer's formulaic compounds in *drinker of blood* and *death-bringer*, has six beats like a Homeric hexameter. Other phrases sound archaic as if translated from Homeric epic (*with what crying you mourned him; and the night was long; many a mouth; maker of elegies; rebel one; slain*). They even invert normal word order (*for your lament the night was too brief; veiled with blood her body's sun*).

All this sets an archaic and epic tone, evoking in its names and language the West's first war poem, which Simone Weil called *The Poem of Force*. A tragic narrative which shows sympathy for both sides, just as this poem mourns the pain of both human and animal. The dingo and her mate are Andromache and Hector, but stars and moon are described in terms of things which interest dingos: *white shorn mobs* of sheep, a *cleaned bone*.

The rhyme scheme begins with ten lines in *abcdecbdae* pattern: each line has a partner somewhere. The second half is nine lines. The end-words here begin with *rain* (which will find a partner in *slain*), but the second is *brief* which will, like the dingo when her mate is dead, go unpartnered. Counting *brief* as X (the unrhymed end-word), the run is *aXbcdbcad*. And yet this half is more cohesive: most end-words are very close in sound: *rain/slain, bone/alone, one/sun*. As if the *terrible song* were still going on, even when the dingo is dead.

This poem about a spoiled body starts with spoiled grammar. If this really were Greek (or Latin), you could hive off the two first lines from the grammar of the main sentence with the neat construction in which both those highly inflected languages excelled, and which grammarians call 'Absolute'. You take some noun (say, *hide*), add on a passive participle (say, *spoiled*), and put both in the ablative or genitive, 'this hide having been spoiled,' i.e. 'After the dingo's hide had been spoiled'. Then you go on to a completely new grammar: new subject, new main verb (say *they* and *crushed*). English is not inflected and cannot do that. It has different sorts of flexibility. To translate the 'absolute' construction it has to use extra words like 'with' and 'after'; or else, clumsily, say something like, 'your hide having been spoiled, they crushed'.

Wright plays on this difference between the languages; the compact and inflected Greek which she lightly invokes and English with its spelling-it-out quality.

The first verb is a passive participle, *twisted*. It ought, by English rules, to describe the subject of the main verb. But no – the main verb is *crushed*, the subject of that verb is *they*, and *twisted* and *spoiled* describe the *hide* of 'their' victim. *Twisted* and *spoiled* make you think the grammatical subject will be the dingo, but she turns out to be the owner of a damaged object, her *hide*.

As English, then, the grammar is all wrong. The poem is announcing its theme of damaging interconnectedness between people and animals by starting with damaged syntax which harks back to the more complex archaic syntax of a dead language.

At first, the poet addresses the dingo as *you*; after *here you lie* the vocatives stop. In the last two lines (like lines on a grave) the dingo is third-person, the *lover* who has been *slain*. She *mourned* and *tolled* her mate. Her *lament* was *too long* for the night. Now she is no longer a singer but the object of song, being mourned. Her *hide* is *twisted*, *spoiled*, her brightness *veiled* like mourners in *blood* – like cloud covering *sun*: an image which echoes the one which began the poem, her *sunlight hide spoiled with red*.

At the heart of the poem, of course, is listening to the *voice* of pain. Those words *desperate poet* are folded between *heard* and *hear*. *Cry* echoes *I* and is echoed in *replying* (which partners *crying*). The *I* is a human I, thinking of Homer's human deaths (wives going mad with grief, women's laments for Hector which end the *Iliad*), but it echoes the howl of animal loss. The archaic word *warrior* suggests not only Homeric heroes but the group of people to whom Wright consistently turned in her work, whose *song* was also *crushed*: Australia's aboriginal warriors, like the ghost in the poem called 'At Cooloolah' whose ancient songlines echoed through these same *dark ranges*.

From Book XXI of Homer's *Iliad*

And the Fire God
From a carroty fuse no bigger than his thumb,
Raised a burning fan as wide as Troy
And brushed the plain with it until
Scamander's gleaming width was parched
And smoke stopped sunlight.

Then the garnet-coloured bricks
Coped with whitestone parapets that were Troy's wall,
Loomed in smoky light, like a dark wicket bounding
The fire's destruction.
Troy's plain was charred and all in cinders
The dead Trojans and their gear. Yet Heaven's Queen
Did not call her son, and the Cripple
Turned on the beaten river.

Flame ate the elms,
Sad-willow, clover, tamarisk and galingale – the lot.
Rushes and the green, green lotus beds crinkled – wet dust,
the eels and the pike began to broil.
Last of all, Scamander's back writhed like a burning poultice,
Then, reared up, into a face on fire:
'How can I fight you, Cripple? Flames in my throat,
My waters griddled by hot lacquer! Quit – and I'll quit.
As for Troy and Trojans – let 'em burn. Are not we gods
Above the quarrels of mere humans?'

You must imagine how the water
For boiling down the fat of a juicy pig
After the women pour it into a cauldron,
Seethes and lifts as the kindling takes
And the iron sits in a flamy nest.
Likewise Hephaestus fixed Scamander.

Logue, born in 1926 near Portsmouth, served in the Black Watch; in 1945 he was posted to Palestine and began writing poems. In the Fifties he went to Paris (where he knew Beckett and Henry Miller) and published his first books. He was a founder member of CND; in Sixties London he wrote for the Royal Court. For many years he edited Pseud's Corner in *Private Eye*; he played Cardinal Richelieu in Russell's film *The Devils*, has written a pornographic novel (in the Forties), an autobiography and two screenplays. But for over forty-five years he has also been reworking Homer's *Iliad* into a unique, blazingly original, pop-Modernist version. Not a translation (he does not know Greek) but all the more potent for that, on fire with new barbaric glitter.

The first bit, published in 1962, was a revelation. Logue was collaging Homer, intercutting images and names from other worlds like Africa. The savage lyricism and anachronistic mix of vernacular and archaism roared through the sober horizons of classical translation. A later part of the project was shortlisted for the International Griffin Poetry Prize and won the Bernard F. O'Connor Award from *The Paris Review*. The fifth instalment, the penultimate, won the Whitbread Prize.

Its language is a wonderful meeting of different textures. Logue invents new scenes, cuts Homer about, weaves ancient images with modern (an arrow makes 'a tunnel the width of a lipstick' through a soldier's neck). His take is cinematic, full of flashbacks and Tarantino-style jumps, now tracking the action from a distance, now zooming in on a single, horribly physical, close combat. The whole thing is rather like Logue's own view of the gods: very brutal but also very beautiful. He has been called England's best war poet and yet is a pacifist. 'The *Iliad* tells the truth about something very important,' he says. 'The propensity to violence in human males.'

This passage shows gods entering the human battle. The god of Troy's river (*Scamander*) supports Troy and has been trying to drown the Greek champion Achilles. So *Heaven's Queen* (Hera, Zeus's wife, an ardent Greek supporter) sends in her son *Hephaestus*, the *Fire God*.

Greek gods embody the thing they are god of. Aphrodite is sex, Ares is war. This is a fight between fire and water. *Hephaestus* is a god in human form, and lame (hence *Cripple*). His *flame* starts small (a *fuse no bigger than his thumb*), grows into a *burning fan as wide as Troy*, and turns everything to *cinders*. On the *charred plain*, only Troy's walls hem in *fire's destruction* (this comes late in the *Iliad*; the city itself is nearing *destruction*).

Scamander is now a *beaten* warrior. *Flames* in his *throat, face on fire* and as a river he is *parched, griddled, burning* like a *poultice*.

This *poultice* is Logue's own; it is not in the original. Homer himself makes the river god ask the fire god to stop, and then brings in the magic of simile.

Similes are the *Iliad's* windows. In its architecture of a world at war, the similes look out on a world of peace, nature, domesticity. A tree falling on a hill, flies round milking pails, a woman staining ivory. For Homer's original listeners, this was (we latercomers assume) the real world. But juxtaposed with the doomed protagonists, these vignettes conjure an impossibly remote peace glimpsed from a building under siege. In Homer, the river yells 'pax' to his opponent while eels are frying and the waters are seething 'as a cauldron boils'. So begins the long vivid image of women melting the lard of a fatted hog (*boiling down the fat of a juicy pig*, says Logue). The similes are about life going on, while on the battlefield life is in jeopardy.

Homer himself also puts a simile after the moment which Logue marks by *parched* (the fifth line here): comparing the drying river to an orchard withered by wind. Logue cuts that: he is paring Homer, while upping the savagery and glitter. (The *garnet-coloured bricks, dark wicket* and *whitestone parapets* are all his, not Homer's.) Also, I guess, he did not want more nature here, which might cancel the effect he has created already in *elms, willow, tamarisk, lotus, galingale*.

For the first two stanzas Logue keeps a rough pentameter, sometimes cutting a line to signal a change of attention, sometimes dropping to four, three or two beats. The musical presence haunting them is Tennyson, the great English master of epic flow, whose Lotus-Eaters live in meadows *set with slender galingale*.

Each chunk is governed by one image, as if each image is a single unit of breath. The *burning fan, dark wicket*, broiling fish, *burning poultice, boiling cauldron*. The different thoughts and images hang together musically in the vowels: the AH of *garnet, dark, charred*, ET of *garnet, parapet, wicket* (sounding against *bricks*), ALL of *wall, all, call*; then *ate* and *wet*, the A of *sad-willow, tamarisk, galingale*.

For the fire's assault on the river bank and river, Logue lengthens the line until, as climax, he has a dragging, delaying, seven-beat line

(*Last* to *poultice*) for the river's pain and call for pax. At the simile, Logue drops back to four beats. He works up to a pentameter again, but now in simpler, quicker language. *Flamy* (picking up *carroty* at the beginning), has a quirky, intimate tone which is all Logue's. Homer says simply, 'dry sticks lie under'.

This chunk is held together by more vowel echoes (*water, for, pour, imagine, pig, lifts, kindling, sits, fixed*). Starting with direct address (*You must imagine*) the language now suggests this domestic scene matches us, our voice, our vernacular life. It is a moment of relief. We have left, for a moment, the frenzied brilliance, the battle of fire and water. But he brings this back in *likewise*. You are not out of the maelstrom. There is much much more to come.

Poems XV and XXVI from *The Notebook of Uprisings*

XV

The past is not where you left it, Svetko.
It is a ruined city, spackled with grief.
    The house, still yellow stucco with pear trees.
Empty swallow nests hang in the eaves
    woven with bits of collar and sleeve.
There is a diary open to the words *cannot remain here.*

XXVI

Storm light, bare orchards, the heavens briefly open.
My heart flew to his roof.

We returned here after the war whose life the war took.

Last summer a wind from Byelorussia brought us blue roses.

Something was wrong with the milk.
Yellow brooks of waste lit the hayfields.

Forché, born in 1950 in Detroit, Michigan, teaches poetry at George Mason University in Virginia. In 1998 she was given a Peace and Culture award in Stockholm for her human rights work. She has published four collections, several translations and an anthology (*Against Forgetting: Twentieth Century Poetry of Witness*) and worked as human rights advocate in El Salvador.

Her poems tackle war, suffering and moral responsibility. In 1982 her second book, *The Country Between Us*, about the reign of terror in El Salvador by the US-backed military regime, sold over 70,000 copies. These two come from a sequence ('The Notebook of Uprisings') in her third collection *The Angel of History*, which is a fragmented reflection on lives lost and ruined in wars: in the Second World War in Eastern Europe, especially in Theresienstadt (she conjures members of her own family from Brno in Moravia); in Hiroshima; and also in the Russian invasion of Czechoslovakia. *Svetko* is a poet who left Czechoslovakia in 1969 to settle in the US. But these poems also turn on nuclear fallout: this *wind from Byelorussia* blows from Chernobyl.

The title of the whole collection came from Paul Valéry's vision of a 'book of history', which contained all you wanted to know but was written in an unknown language. All translations differed and eventually the book melted until it became indistinguishable from the world.

Forché's book is about the 'fallout' of history: the continuing contamination of violence over the landscape of memory. *The past* becomes *a ruined city spackled with grief*. Basic nourishment turns bad. *Milk* goes *wrong*. *Hayfields* are *lit* (an image that could be beautiful) by something horrible: nuclear glare, *yellow brooks of waste*.

Both poems use tiny images to represent loss and exile on a global scale. In XV, *empty swallow nests* mirror the empty human *house*. The *bits of collar and sleeve* embedded in them suggest clothing discarded in the death camps. The focus is on the outside of things, shells from which life has fled: *stucco*, *pear trees* in the garden, the *woven* mud wall of *nests*. The one inner thing is the *diary*, which is *open* (as if life, like a *swallow*, has fled from it too) at the decision to leave.

The *yellow*, the departed birds and the placing of *ruined* in the first beat of a line resonate with Shakespeare's Sonnet 73, which also speaks of time, of a poet feeling he is in the autumn of life. In Shakespeare, *Yellow leaves, or none, or few*, hang on trees whose *boughs* are *Bare ruined choirs where late the sweet birds sang*. But here past time is a past place: a ruined *city*, an abandoned *house*. The only person is *you* – who *left*.

Each poem is six lines, but differently laid out. In XV, the lines hang closely together (the four inner lines end in the same sound, *grief*, *trees*, *eaves*, *sleeve*) making a single picture. An abandoned *city*. In it, an abandoned *house*. In that, an abandoned *diary*. Vowels echo as in an empty house. The short E of *left*, *Svetko*, *yellow*, *empty*, *nests*. The long EE of *grief*, *trees*, *eaves*, *sleeves* widens into the EAR of *pear* (picking up *where*) and the climax, *here*. Consonants cement it all. Soft F (*left*, *grief*) bonds with V (*eaves*, *sleeve*) which picks up *Svetko*. T and K (*past*, *Svetko*, *spackled*, *stucco*, *nests*) are contained within the two negatives: *not*, *cannot*. The verb at the end, *remain* (the thing that *cannot* be done), looks back and sums up all these external tokens: these 'remains', what were *left*.

Poem XXVI is more disjointed. The lines have spaces between. It moves from a need for shelter (*my heart flew to his roof*), through dispersal caused by *war* (imaged on the page by dispersed lines), to images of sustenance that goes *wrong*. Internal echoes, holding the lines together, start with the OR of *storm* (followed by *orchard*, *war*, *war*, *Byelorussia*), the hard *K* of the monosyllables *took*, *milk*, *brooks*, and the soft F of *briefly*, *flew*, *roof*, *life*, *hayfields*, which evokes the insidious softness of falling contamination. There is return after dispersal. But the return is spoilt.

The focus is on the land's vulnerability – to sky (*heavens*), air (*wind from Byelorussia*), and light (*storm light*, *yellow*, *lit*). Things that are normally good have become contaminating, dangerous.

The one image of protection is the *roof*, to which the speaker's *heart* flies. But this roof's past owner is anonymous and lost, while everything still growing is spoilt. *Orchards* are *bare*, *milk*, *brooks* and *hayfields* polluted; *roses* are *blue*.

The complex construction, *We returned . . . whose lives the war took*, imitates the word order of an inflected language like Latin. (The relative pronoun *whose* picks up the verb's subject, *we*.) It suggests a harsh paradox, caused by that repeated word *war*, which separates *we* from *whose*, people from their *life*: *We returned*, but our lives were already 'taken'. When we came back we were already, in some sense, dead. To underscore that death, our land ran with *brooks of waste*.

Oświęcim

Someone has disturbed a hive.
What swell and gut the air and have
a million different fragments, are bees,

which we mistake for wind and seeds,
at first, but stride out of the jittered storm
thrilled and breathlessly unharmed.

So somewhere honey might be moving,
lazily, its amber tongue,
among leaf litter, acned bark,

bugs glossy-backed and clockwork
which it tastes and then displays
as proofs of end-stopped histories.

Not hard to conjugate the faces,
shorn and watchful in the hallways,
to anger or lovemaking, freckles,

stutters, drunkenness, book-learning,
to couples sleeping back to back, arriving
laden at a country station in the bleach of dawn.

Help me open up these cases
and place in them some spectacles,
a steel prosthetic foot, a fist of auburn hair,

an empty tin of Dutch shoe polish
and a chipped enamel patterned jug,
a yellow appleblossom-patterned jug,

and set each in a locker at the terminals
of all the major capitals, alongside stolen goods,
and photographs in envelopes, and bombs.

Laird, born in 1975 in Co. Tyrone, Northern Ireland, grew up in the Troubles, has worked in law, studied in Cambridge, lived in Warsaw and Boston, and now lives in London. He brought out his first collection the same year as his first novel. Like Ciaran Carson (Poem 22), Laird interrogates the experience of growing up in the Troubles. 'You don't understand how odd your childhood was until you get away,' he has said. 'Then you realise it's not normal to be stopped every day by soldiers with guns who look in your schoolbag. It's not normal to not be able to get to school because masked men have closed the roads and kicked the windows in at your dad's office.'

He was deeply influenced by Northern Irish poets before him, especially Heaney. '*Death of a Naturalist* changed everything around for me,' Laird says. 'Heaney makes internal music. The words all fit together with vowel sounds and consonant sounds.'

The main terrain of his first book (from which this comes) is post-conflict Northern Ireland. Killing has mainly stopped but the divisions are still there. The collection's title *To A Fault* gestures to fault-lines there (Catholic and Protestant) but also elsewhere. In 'A Guide to Modern Warsaw', Warsaw's first skyscraper, built *on the site of the Great Synagogue*, is plastered in graffiti, the Sony logo, prostitutes' cards and *nine pleas for missing dogs*.

This poem is set near another Polish town in a place now surrounded by wooded farmland, heavy in summer with lush grass, trees, ponds, lilies, flowering reeds. The Germans called it Auschwitz.

The Frankfurt philosopher and critic Theodor Adorno said there could be no poetry after Auschwitz. What happened there, he said, betrayed the norms on which civilisation and therefore poetry depends.[5] There had to be poetry afterwards, and was. But how does a poem describe the place itself?

W. H. Auden's poem 'The Fall of Rome' was written during the Second World War. In that context, Rome's fall was an image for the threat against Europe and all those occupied and (as Auden's poem puts it) *flu-infected* cities. Auden ends with a beautiful image from the natural world: creatures apparently unconnected to the fall of any city, ancient or modern.

> *Altogether elsewhere, vast*
> *Herds of reindeer move across*
> *Miles and miles of golden moss,*
> *Silently and very fast.*

Auden conjures the hordes (rather than herds) of Gauls who would sweep into Rome from the north. Laird, from his home context of Northern Ireland, approaches his terrifying subject through another apparently unconnected image: *bees* and their *honey* which must *somewhere* (like Auden's *elsewhere*) be *moving* (like Auden's reindeer), sucking into their flow small insects, *proofs of end-stopped histories*.

This is the point to which the first four stanzas are *moving*, and also what every reader who has deduced that this is a poem about Auschwitz will be expecting: *proofs* and *fragments* of *end-stopped* lives.

These things do emerge. *Spectacles, a steel prosthetic foot, auburn hair, shoe polish* and *a chipped jug* are some of the *million different fragments* we were expecting at the beginning but which there turned out to be *bees*. By the time we get to them (the seventh stanza), the poem has conjured up *faces* to whom they belonged. People with *freckles* and *stutters*, behaving like us (*anger, love-making, drunkenness, book-learning*). It has also asked the reader's co-operation to *open up* their *cases* (echoing the *faces* which these *cases* belonged to).

The poem is in three movements like a sonata. The first, the longest, is introduced by an anonymous act that must have happened somewhere else (*someone has disturbed a hive*). It stresses that unknown people disturbing things in other places affect people like us (now, here). But it is utterly indirect. On Auden's gold reindeer principle, this first half concentrates on *bees* and *bugs*. It does introduce a personal *we*. But a *we unharmed* by any *jittered storm*. It is other creatures that *might* be harmed, indirectly, by what happened.

The syntax of the first stanza needs a bit of effort. When you first read *What swell and gut the air*, you think this may be a question or exclamation. Only on rereading do you realise it means, 'What these things are, which are swelling the air, are bees.' The words slow down the realisation of their grammar, just as the realisation of what these *fragments* are is slow to come. *We mistake* them at first for other things – *wind and seeds*.

Shoah, the preferred Jewish name for the holocaust (which is a Greek word meaning 'burnt sacrifice'), is Hebrew for 'a great terrible wind'. When you look back (as the syntax keeps forcing you to do), every innocent-seeming word and thing in this poem and its landscape has deadly implications. But they are not spelt out. *Wind*?

At first (like journeys to the death camps) these words and things seem, or pretend to seem, innocent.

The sonata's second movement begins at *Not hard*. It keeps the personal *we* out of it (for now). Tone is crucial. The emotion is still at arm's length, the language impersonal. Again the syntax needs effort. Only rereading do you see it means, 'It is not hard to match up (*conjugate*) the imagined *faces* to imagined human behaviour like *lovemaking*.' These two verses are upping the emotion, but only behind the scenes. It all sounds (or could sound) like ordinary life. Even *couples sleeping back to back* (picking up *conjugate*). Even *arriving at a country station* could seem innocent; except for the ominous *laden*.

The third part, the last three verses, turns to the reader. *Help me*, says the poem, or the single speaker implicit in that original *we*.

The poem has worked and moved carefully, through impersonality and tough syntax, to earn the directness with which it now faces the reader. The imagery has moved from *bees* to their *honey*, the *honey* to stuck insects, from insects to *faces* and people. Now comes the request for *help* to *open these cases*.

Cases has a triple meaning. A police meaning: files on crime. Suitcases. And display cases (see *displays*, stanza four) at Auschwitz museum labelled Material Evidence of Crime, holding hair, shoes, wire glasses.

The poem focuses first on things that once were on bodies, or parts of bodies (*spectacles, prosthetic foot, hair*). Then on things that once put a surface sparkle into lives: *shoe polish, patterned jug*. It repeats the idea of surface, relating it back to the countryside round Oświęcim by zooming in on pattern: *yellow* (picking up *amber*) and *appleblossom* (picking up the country innocence of *bees, leaf litter, bark, glossy-backed* insects). People who turned up *laden* at this *country station* had lives very like the lives lived here now.

But the poem does not take these *fragments* out of *cases*. Instead it wants the reader's *help* in putting them back: in taking them (by rail again) to countries they came from (as the *shoe polish* came from Holland), putting them in lockers *at the terminals / of all the major capitals*.

So there is another journey too, through the poem's three movements. The poem starts in the place where the camp was. In the second movement (sixth and seventh verses), it follows the victims from their ordinary lives by rail to the camp. In the third (the last three verses), it asks the reader for help in doing something about this, sending them back. Or if not them, then these *proofs* of their lives, the *million different fragments* (as the speaker of Eliot's *Waste Land* has shored 'fragments against my ruins') from the waste land of a *million* lives lost at Oświciȩm.

The *goods* these people had left were *stolen* from them as their lives were stolen. When we help the poem stow them *in lockers*, we stack them *alongside* the *photographs*, yes, but why the last word *bombs*, a word more familiar as background for poems set in Northern Ireland?

Back to the *wind and seeds* which *we*, in the first verse, mistook the *bees* for. *Wind* gestured to the Shoah. But what about *seeds*? It is hard, seeing *bombs* at the end of a poem written by a poet from Northern Ireland, not to see them as *seeds* of new violence. The *cases* are going back to *terminals*, but the violence of the Shoah did not 'terminate' at Oświciȩm. It has been broadcast back, as *seeds* are blown by *wind*, to where the victims came from: *all the major capitals*. In 2005, this means not just capitals of Europe but of the Middle East. In Northern Ireland where Laird grew up, Protestants identified with Israel, Catholics with Palestinians.[6]

The poem's journey is from an apparently unimportant rural act (disturbing *a hive*) towards *bombs* in waiting. Bombs in lockers *of all the major capitals*. This 'poetry after Auschwitz' is seeing historically; seeing both past and future; suggesting, in *seeds*, that the violence of the Shoah may beget further violence. Unlike the victims' lives, violence is not *end-stopped*: that central word in a poem deeply aware of its own technique.

The poem's power comes partly from its indirectness, partly from the movement of imagery and tone. But neither would work effectively without the internal music, which comes from what Laird originally fell for in Heaney: the way 'the words all fit together with vowel sounds and consonant sounds'.

How the World Split in Two

Was it widthways or lengthways,
a quarrel with the equator?
Did the rawness of the inside sparkle?

Only this is true:
there was an arm on one side
and a hand on the other,
a thought on one side
and a hush on the other.

And a luminous tear
carried on the back of a beetle
went backwards and forwards
from one side to the other.

Alvi, born in 1954 in Lahore, Pakistan, came to England when she was a few months old, grew up in Hertfordshire, went to university in York and London, taught in secondary school and now teaches for the Open College of the Arts. She was one of the Poetry Society's New Generation Poets and joint winner of the 1991 Poetry Business Prize.

She has written five collections and been shortlisted for the T. S. Eliot and Whitbread Prizes. She has a metaphysical wit, both very economical and very wild; the power to create extraordinarily concrete images with a lot of space around them; and an imagination so surreal that surreal is where we start. We only gradually realise that she is using the surreal as a lens through which her poems marvel at so-called real life. It is all presented so fluidly and naturally, with a smile and subtle humour, that you accept it instantly. You start off, as it were, the other side of the rainbow and never worry you're not in Kansas any more. But from where her poems place you, you suddenly realise you're seeing Kansas as you never saw it before.

This poem opens a collection called *How the Stone Found its*

Voice. It begins a twelve-poem sequence inspired by creation myths, rather like Kipling's *Just So Stories*. As you read, you realise the sequence is speaking to the effects of 9/11, especially in Britain. One of the poems, 'How A Long Way Off Rolled Itself Up', finds a new, unjudgemental image for the way what had long been happening and had been felt in remote countries, which few people in the West thought about, suddenly affected everyone in America and Britain. *Once, there was a place called A Long Way Off – / it was too far away to contemplate . . . So people were unprepared / when A Long Way Off rolled itself up / and edged a little nearer . . . / People laughed uneasily. A Long Way Off / was close enough to singe their hair.*

Another poem, 'How the Children Were Born', asks about the origins and snowballing effects of violence. *Doctors and midwives were aghast. / There, embedded in each infant palm / was the barrel of a tiny gun . . . Enmity was handed down like an heirloom. / The guns grew with the babies, poking like bone through the soft skin.*

A second sequence, later in the same book, puts this first sequence in a more personal context. It shows the poet (who also came to England from 'a long way off') wondering as she grows up what it means to be *half-and-half*. One half of her (her father) comes from *a country that wasn't whole*, West and East Pakistan. When they visit Oxford, *a man spits at us, / and hurries on, revealing / my mother and father to me, / stripped of their protective glass, / their two colours like those double / erasers we used then, for ink and pencil.* After 9/11, in rural Norfolk, she watches a man walk down his own village street creating suspicious ripples wherever he goes because of his Muslim name and face. *The still ponds, the darting rabbits, / cow parsley by the field gates – / all are re-imagining themselves / because Tariq walks in his own village, / part of the scene, yet conspicuous / as if he is walking a tiger.*

In her London neighbourhood, the poet welcomes an imaginary camel, *shy from early persecution*, 'its *hump full of unfamiliar words / and disturbing customs*. It walks down the street. *These are heated times*, says its poem. *A number of residents / have not wished for / a black or brown person / as a neighbour. / And now they have a camel / suggesting itself as a means of transport.* 9/11 has made her neighbours see her, and her family, as intruders.

So this small poem, here, introduces an enormous and complex subject. The racism experienced by first- and second-generation immigrants, and childhood speculation about the country of origin (one of Alvi's earlier collections was called *The Country At My Shoulder*). How have these been transformed by 9/11?

The poem starts with the event, like the big bang theory of the beginning of the universe. The title is an important part of the poem, and its violent word *split* evokes both the moment of divide and the violence of the event itself.

The first chunk imagines the *world* as a freshly *split* stone like granite whose *inside* might *sparkle*. The voice and image suggest the child's literal wondering (*widthways or lengthways?*) which Kipling addresses in the *Just So Stories*, but with a deep echo chamber behind of adult sophistication and knowledge. The three lines question how the split happened, as later poems in the sequence will show a child questioning her own origins in a Pakistan split *because powerful people / had carved up the world like the Sunday joint*; and also the child watching (after the Oxford spitting incident) *my mother's furious face / my father's seeming absentmindedness*.

The second chunk strips the event of rhetoric, comment and explanation by looking at it simply in image terms. *Only this is true.* *Only* places the images that follow in a kind of vacuum, like the empty space of a de Chirico painting. This is all the image you need. Take away the rest. *Only* this is what we are left with.

First a body image. *An arm on one side / and a hand on the other.* Then a more abstract image, linking the idea and the appalled reaction: *a thought on one side / and a hush on the other.* Then a sense of the whole tragedy (*luminous tear*) shared by both 'sides': *backwards and forwards / from one side to the other.*

This image, like the *Just So Stories*, allows for both adult and child. It weaves a little creation myth for the beginning of the world after 9/11. As creation myths often do, it gives a small, insignificant, even comical animal the heroic task of shouldering alone the burden of mourning (*carried on the back*) and uniting the now separate sides of the once single *world* (as in the title) by putting them in touch with each other's grief.

An extraordinarily ambitious thing for twelve short lines to do. It is the compact internal music that makes the poem work. Each chunk has its own inner echoes and aural key. The first line's repeated AY (*widthways, lengthways*) leads up to that of *equator*, and keeps repeating the W in that key word of the title (*World was, widthways, lengthways*): a sound the second line repeats in *quarrel* and (again) *equator*. In the third line, *sparkle* picks up *quarrel*, the

OR of *rawness* picks up the stressed *was* at the beginning; *Did* echoes *widthways* and *with*.

They seem insignificant words, *was*, *did*, *with*. But at this level of concentration every syllable matters desperately. We are seeing poetry's power of concentration and distillation in an extreme form. These urgent questions (*Was? Did?*) about a sudden event are talking about something enormous, world-changing. This is an art of giving significance to the smallest detail, as the poem and its myth allow to the *beetle* at the end. Who this *quarrel* was *with* is the most important question of all.

The second chunk ends with a rhyme to the title (*two/true*), knitting it in, showing how important the new *two* is. Then begin the mirrorings internal to this chunk: repeats of *on one side, on one side; on the other, on the other*. *Hush* adds to the short U of *one, one, other, other*.

But these syllables also begin to announce their relationships to the first chunk by back-echoes. *Arm* reflects the AR of *sparkle*; *side* and *side* pick up *inside*; *other* and *other* echo *equator*; the OR of *thought* picks up *rawness*.

The third chunk harmonises *luminous* with *true*, while *tear* suggests a soft relation with the last syllable of *equator, other, other*. *Beetle* echoes *quarrel* and *sparkle*; the Ws of *went backwards, forwards* (repeated in the last line's *one*) remember the Ws of the first two lines (and those of *one, one* in the second chunk). *One side to the other* echoes the repeated pattern in end-words of the second chunk (*one side/other/one side/other*). The OR of *forwards* picks up both *thought* and *rawness* but the one echo internal to this verse alone (*backwards/back*) adds to the grief imaged by that *tear*.

The *world* has been *split* now into *one side* and the *other*. It can never go *back*. Music, said Ravel once, is the silence between the notes. In this poem, that 'silence between' is also the sorrow.

V

The Sun-warmed Earth:

Loss and Survival

But now he knows these hills, that is to say he knows them better, and if ever again he sees them from afar it will be I think with other eyes, and not only that but the within, all that inner space one never sees, the brain and heart and other caverns where thought and feeling dance their sabbath, all that too quite differently disposed.

Samuel Beckett, *Molloy*

The traveller loses a loved companion. Bunyan's pilgrim sees Faithful go down to the river ahead of him. Odysseus sees his men drown and dog-headed Scylla devour them. 'The saddest thing I saw', he says, 'on all my journey.'

You could say – some poets have said – that all poetry is about loss: about being, at the same time, in one place and another you can't get to, or get back to. The words come after the thing and, in a way, replace it. In the Preface to his *Lyrical Ballads*, Wordsworth says poetry is emotion recollected in tranquillity. His word 're-collected' suggests you are going back to a place or feeling you once had but now have no longer.

In most of these last poems, the traveller has lost someone he or she cannot go back for except in a poem. Losing what we love, or most long for, is part of the journey: miscarriage, signs of childless-ness (Simon Armitage, Jane Duran); hospital and cremation (Roger McGough, Tony Harrison). Everyone mourns – it is part of being human. *Look, a new anguish*, says Elizabeth Jennings in front of Rembrandt's self-portraits which show, one by one, how he aged. There is also a dying parent's helpless humiliation (Bernard O'Donoghue); trying on your dead husband's waistcoat (Tess Gallagher); choosing clothes to bury your child in (Paula Meehan).

Nothing can take the pain away. But even under the worst brutalities of Stalin there was what the Polish poet Czeslaw Milosz called 'the witness of poetry'.[1] As Wilfred Owen's poems witnessed to horror in the trenches.

All great art can make this witness. *About suffering, they were never wrong, the old masters*, says Auden, pointing to the *Fall of Icarus* by Pieter Breughel. In his day, Breughel was nicknamed 'Pieter the funny one', because he painted children's games and wedding dances. Yet he also painted scenes of brutality: *Massacre of the Innocents*, *Procession to Calvary*. His *Triumph of Death* shows the aftermath of a viciously suppressed rising against Spanish rule. Rebels die, tied on wheels on top of poles, the sky black with smoke from burning cities. A dog nibbles the face of a dead child. We have to stare at what is unbearable and live.

Poetry does this in the medium in which we all express pain: words. It *makes nothing happen*, says Auden's *Elegy for W. B. Yeats*, but it does survive *in the valley of its making*. Poetry is *a way of happening, a mouth*. When this mouth speaks of loss it also speaks of survival. Poems make sense and pattern out of pain. The head of the first poet, Orpheus, went on singing even when torn off and tossed in the river.[2]

The poems in this section are not about grief but about witnessing to it; about making sense and shape from it from what is lost as we, in Kathleen Jamie's words, *press on*. They enter loss and survive it and bring their own imagination to making something from it. They are energy, not elegy.

The last, by Milosz, is also the last poem in his own last book. Two years before he died, having lived through national and political agony, he had to test his belief in the saving power of poetry all over again when his wife died. In this poem, Milosz is Orpheus, the poet who has been to hell, come back, and goes on making words *against death*. He is still alive. His cheek is *on the sun-warmed earth*. Even in despair, it is possible to share words: to find ourselves, like Milton's downcast angels, *not lost / In loss itself*.[3]

Entering and taking part in a poem's musical organisation, finding out what the poem has made of its journey, what someone else has made of their experience of the world, illumines your own journey. You hear a voice say, in the words of Peter Reading (Poem 10), '*we were once here.*' As, in his poem 'The King of Asine', the Greek poet George Seferis traces the stones of an acropolis ruled by an ancient anonymous king, whom Homer remembered in half a line. Reaching back through Homer's dead language, the living poet seems to touch on the stones the touch of that lost king's fingers:

> *We've been searching this acropolis*
> *so carefully, sometimes touching with our fingers*
> *his touch on the stones.*

Part of what you find in poems is knowledge – which includes self-knowledge. This is what Adrienne Rich dives for, *into the wreck*.[4] *Your brush's care / Runs with self-knowledge*, says Jennings here to Rembrandt. Some of this knowledge is sad to have to know. But our journey has been to know it. I've said already that poetry is not a feel-good movie. But its physical presence and patterned words help us learn the landscape and be part of it for a while. Poetry fortifies our inwardness. The point is to feel more truly, make what we can of our feeling, while we are here.

51　Kathleen Jamie

Frogs

But for her green
palpitating throat, they lay
inert as a stone, the male
fastened like a package
to her back. They became,

as you looked, almost
beautiful, her back
mottled to leafy brown,
his marked with two stripes,
pale as over-wintered grass.

When he bucked, once,
neither so much as blinked;
their oval, gold-lined eyes
held to some bog-dull
imperative. The car

that would smear them
into one – belly
to belly, tongue thrust
utterly into soft brain –
approached and pressed on

Oh how we press on –
the car and passengers, the slow
creatures of this earth,
the woman by the verge
with her hands cupped.

Jamie, born in 1962 in Renfrewshire, Scotland, studied philosophy
at Edinburgh and used an Eric Gregory Award (given when she was
nineteen) to travel, especially in the Himalayas. She has published
eight collections, won two Geoffrey Faber Memorial Prizes, two

Forward Prizes and written two prose books, about travel in the Himalayas and nature on the Scottish coast. She teaches Creative Writing at St Andrews.

Her profound, meditative lyric voice gathers up philosophical reflections lightly in small true symbols. Scottishness and woman's experience were important themes in her earlier work. Scots language and rhythms run (sometimes satirically) through the poems. She can switch from English to Scots in a single poem. Scots is the language in which grannies cut you down to size, or mother hushes her child. More recently (especially in *The Tree House* from which this poem comes), she has emerged as a powerful nature poet using an increasingly formal technique, to question our relationship with the world surrounding us.

In 1838 the speaker of Tennyson's poem 'Locksley Hall' speculated on the future in lines that seem now to foretell aeroplanes, aerial warfare, world war, the United Nations, and equated that future, *and* our increasingly swift travel across the globe, with Progress. *Let the great world spin for ever down the ringing grooves of change*, he wrote after taking the first train from Liverpool to Manchester in 1830. (It was night. He thought the wheels ran in a groove.) A hundred and seventy years later few poets think the way we travel is a sign of progress. Like *the car* that comes out of nowhere at the end of its central stanza, this poem moves swiftly towards the phrase repeated both sides of the last stanza break: *and pressed on / Oh how we press on* The lack of a full stop after *pressed on* suggests one thought piling on top of another, and is the climax of the poem's reaction to the sudden annihilation of two mating frogs, made *one* in not sex but death.

In the last line of Bishop's poem (Poem 10), men *ripped away into the hanging fabric* and *Nature* was *always retreating behind it*. But that poem was written in the Sixties, when there was still a sense that Nature, though vulnerable, was infinite. Today we see *Nature* simply flattened – by *how we press on*.

After *press on*, the poem conjures a human figure feeling all this for the reader: a *woman by the verge*, as if on the bottom margin of a page, *with her hands cupped* – trying, perhaps, to contain (as this poem called *Frogs* contains the real frogs) all the fragile things we damage without noticing.

Each stanza is knitted together by the syllables it repeats, often in threes. The first has three short words ending in T (*but, throat, inert*); three short As (the first A of *palpitating, package, back*), four

AYs (*palpitating, lay, male, became*). It is bound to the second: first by the AH of *fastened* (which reappears in the same beat in the same line of the next stanza, *marked*), and second by repeating *back*. But the second stanza is also stamped with its own sound, three OOs (*you, looked, two*).

The third stanza picks up a consonant: the repeated L of the second (*looked, almost, beautiful, mottled, leafy, pale*) in its three central lines (*blinked, oval, gold-lined, held, dull*), and is distinguished also by the short U of *bucked, once, much, some, dull*. Its last sound, *car*, picks up the AH of *fastened* and *marked*, linking the frogs' *marked* and *fastened* backs with the object that grinds them into each other.

The fourth stanza's first lines move on rapidly to *one*, echoed in three short Us in succession (*tongue thrust utterly*), which narrows to *on* (repeated at the end of the first line of the last stanza). While *utterly* picks up *belly, belly*. In the last, the high point of the emotion, *Oh* is echoed in *slow*.

The world affects us, surprises, bereaves, delights and wounds us. But we (as Poem 10 reminds us) affect it too. In this poem *we* are the *car* and its *passengers* (whose first two syllables echo *pressed on, press on*): the hurtling vehicle of (to use Tennyson's word) change. But the loss this hurtling brings to the outside world is our own loss too. The *woman by the verge* redeems us. She sounds like a mourner. The last word *cupped* (echoing both *bucked*, that one tiny movement that should be life-engendering, and the short Us of the third and fourth stanzas) suggests eggs and nurturing. *Cupped hands* is how you hold something precious and vulnerable. Water, or a baby bird.

It is as if the poem, made of woven words and harmonies, is also a cup holding something small, frail but still alive, that might fall or spill. Life and nature, the poem suggests, are in human *hands*.

The Orange Tree in Córdoba

The gradual branches
just made out, grains, smudges,
the orange tree, its energy
behind a wall where children
gather, its sticky, searing juices,
its dust coming from nowhere
like a moment of sadness,
its branches laid softly
against women, like menstruation.

A girl comes down the steps.
There are summers still in her,
there is oil and bead on her.
She holds her child's hand.
Lavenders wash the streets
with their browns in the early
mornings in Córdoba.

To the cry of the childless
the orange tree answers with fruit,
to the suppressed cry of the childless
the mementoes of its armfuls,
to the red and white striped arches
of the womb, the sky hurrying past
the lilies of the womb, it answers
'There is nothing more to be done.

The long robes of air
drag the earth like bloodstains
like the caked hoofs of horses,
the blacksmiths harrying the horse-shoes,
the Moors leaving Córdoba endlessly.

Nine month, nine-month lanterns
never so extinct as now.
Go into the Mosque.
Feel the power of space inside you,
the insatiable leaf-turning hand.'

Born in Cuba in 1944, half-Spanish half American, Jane Duran
grew up in the USA and Chile, has lived in Spain, Greece and
Bangladesh, worked in third world development, and now lives in
England. She won the 1995 Forward Prize for Best First Collection
and has published two since. Her poetry combines tender domes-
ticity with an authoritative international experience. One sequence
recalls her father who fought with Spain's Republican army, and his
silence about the civil war (*He lays down his arms. / He raises his arms
over his head. / He will not tell*). *Coastal*, a Poetry Book Society
Recommendation, remembers childhood in New England, adoles-
cence in Chile, and speaks intimately of Algeria today.

Her richly textured poems build fluidly through images which
look unstructured but are very much not. The first section here
begins in half-light. *Branches* are *just made out*, belonging
apparently to the *orange tree* of the title, which is *behind a wall
where children / gather*. The line ends at *children*, a word-root that
will move on to *child* in the second section and go to ground in the
repeated *childless* of the third.

The light changes gradually (we deduce from *gradual*), but is
this morning or evening? We don't yet know. The poem moves
from sight to feel: the half-seen *orange tree* has *sticky, searing juices*
(which suggest fertility) but also *dust*, which feels *like a moment of
sadness* and suggests age. Its *branches* appear again, now *laid softly
against women*. The softness picks up *grains* and *smudges*. This tree
is softly seen, softly *laid*. *Like menstruation* looks back to *sticky
juices*, the tree's *energy* and the place *where children gather*.

Why are these *branches laid against women*? Is this visual
description or fertility ritual? You cannot know, but you remember
like menstruation when you see what *like* introduces in the third
stanza: *bloodstains*, something *caked* on *hoofs*. Blood again: these are
horses, vehicle of medieval war in a conquered city. And *blacksmiths*,
who in European folklore marry lovers, work in iron that keeps away
baby-stealing fairies, and make horseshoes which are a worldwide
symbol of good luck.

So far, the images suggesting women's fertility have concentrated on the *tree*. Running through this section is a sequence of final syllables with a short I sound: IZ (*branches, smudges, juices*: a sound which also softens into *sadness*), EN (*children, women*), and Y (*energy, sticky, softly, orange tree*).

The second section introduces a particular character. Not any old *children* or *women* but a specific *girl* with *her child*. This section is dominated by liquid images (*oil*), washed colours and a liquid consonant: the L of *girl* (*still, oil, holds, child's, lavender, early*), suggesting perhaps not just the notion of fertility like the first section but the sound of the word fertile. *Brown* in the last line echoes *down* in the first, *streets* echoes *bead*, *lavender* echoes *hand*, and the two endings *in her* and *on her* prepare for that of the last line, *Córdoba*, whose first syllable also echoes the OR of *wash* and *morning*.

So the half-light was not evening but *morning*, and the girl with *summers still in her* (gesturing back to *menstruation* in the first section) reflects it. There was *dust*, associated with *sadness*. Now *lavenders wash the streets*.

The third section makes explicit what the images have already told us: this is about fertility and the orange tree is centre of it. The *girl* with a *child* and *summers still in her*, and the *orange tree* symbolising marriage perhaps, with its *sticky juices* (and now also *fruit*), are a contrast to what comes now: *the childless*. That *moment of sadness* looked forward to *the suppressed cry of the childless*.

This section is built from incantatory repetitions like a prayer or ritual lament (*to the, to the, to the; answers, answers, arches of the womb, lilies of the womb*). The AH (suggesting grief, perhaps) of *answers* is repeated at the end of lines in *armfuls* (which is ambiguous: it could mean blossom or babies), *arches, past, answers*. The soft SS of *suppressed* thickens the effect of *childless, childless; fruit* anticipates *womb, womb; sky* echoes *cry, cry* (and the long I resonates in *childless, childless* and *striped*).

The poem has moved from grainy smudgy light, through *browns* of *early morning* to *sky*. But *sky* is *hurrying past / the lilies of the womb*. Time is moving on fast. *Lilies* suggest madonna lilies, annunciation, conception. Yet *There is nothing more to be done*.

In this last line, the orange tree takes over and finishes the poem. *More*, at the end of the third stanza, leads on to the OR in the abandoned city's name: *horses, horse-shoes, Moors, Córdoba*. The tree begins the fourth section by speaking of *air*, which seems to pick up from *sky* in the third, but then dashes any idea of lightness and *sky* (and also, apparently, hope) to the ground. We are back on the *earth*, with *bloodstains*. Before, there were *sticky juices, menstruation, red arches of the womb*. Now there are only *stains*, old blood, *caked hoofs of horses*.

This is where the larger context impinges. We have had a lot about the *orange tree* of the title but the resonances of the city's name, though they have been important musically, have stayed unexplored. Córdoba's abandonment by its Moorish population in 1236 was the subject of many famous laments. Here it is abandoned *endlessly*, like *the red and white striped arches of* a *womb* constantly losing its own population, *children. 'There is nothing more to be done'* for the abandoned city; or for the *womb*.

This is about loss, of blood, luck, and hope. About something *leaving* you. Even the colour with which *lavenders wash the streets* suggests dried blood. So do those *nine-month lanterns*. The fruit of an *orange tree* (which flowers and fruits at the same time) looks like glowing lanterns in dark glossy leaves. But these *lanterns* are not for celebration. They are saying that again, this month, too, you will not have a child.

At first, the visual description comes like a slowly developing photograph (*gradual, from nowhere*). Then the poem moves to thought and feeling, picking up the *sadness* which appears at first only in an image. To the poem's plants (*orange tree, lavenders*) the third stanza adds *lilies of the womb*, suggesting miraculous birth. But *robes* (more hints of Annunciation) brings us down (*drag*) to *earth* (where blood flows away) and endless *leaving*.

But the *orange tree*'s advice is, accept it. When everything is going out, go in. *Into the Mosque* (which will be empty of worshippers, since the Muslims have left and Catholic Spain has taken over). Everything is leading up to the words *inside you*.

What is happening in there: this is what the poem and images have been about. The movement downwards (from *sky* and *air* to *earth*) led to despair, the *cry of the childless: never so extinct as now*. At that *cry* the *orange tree* shows its true colours, girds up its *energy*. From behind its *wall* (which by now, retrospectively, also suggests walls of the *womb*) *where children gather*, it uses imperatives.

Go, it says, and *feel*. *Feel* what is outside (the sacred *space* of the dome) but feel it as *inside you*. *Feel* it as *power*. *Feel* whatever comes into you from outside like a *leaf-turning* (well, this is an *orange tree* talking) *hand*.

307

Childlessness, like history and the fall of cities, is governed by a divine *hand*. It 'turns' the *leaves* – of the body, of life, *branches*, a sacred book or creativity. Accepting it is accepting inner emptiness as power. The *power of* this place of worship that has, unlike a church, no human images: just pattern and *space*.

Birthday

Bed. Sheets without sleep, and the first birds.
Dawn at the pace of a yacht.

The first bus, empty, carries its cargo of light
from the depot, like a block of ice.

Dawn when the mind looks out of its nest,
dawn with gold in its teeth.

In the street, a milk-float moves
by throw of a dice,

the mast to the east raises itself
to its full height. Elsewhere

someone's husband touches someone's wife.
One day older the planet weeps.

This is the room
where I found you one night,

bent double, poring over
the *Universal Home Doctor*,

that bible of death, atlas of ill-health:
hand-drawn, colour-coded diagrams of pain,

chromosomal abnormalities explained,
progesterone secretion,

cervical incompetence . . .
Susan, for God's sake.

I had to edge towards it,
close the cover with my bare foot.

Dawn when the mind looks out of its nest.
Dawn with gold in its teeth.

From the window I watch
Anubis, upright in black gloves

making a sweep of the earth
under the nameless tree,

pushing through shrubs,
checking the bin for bones or meat

then leaving with a backward glance, in his own time,
crossing the lawn and closing the gate.

Armitage, born in 1963 in Huddersfield, grew up in Yorkshire, studied geography and psychology at Portsmouth and Manchester, and became a probation officer. Then poetry took charge. His first collection (1989) established him as a leading poet of his generation. He has published ten books of poems since, taught at the Universities of Leeds, Iowa and now Manchester Metropolitan. He has written two novels, a memoir, television films, stage plays. His many awards include an award for song lyrics in a BAFTA-winning Channel 4 film.

His early probation work gave his poems not just a rich seam of unexplored material but a particular social perspective which struck a note with many audiences, especially young urban readers. He has a wonderful ear for spoken language and timing. That part of his voice which is seemingly casual and off-the-cuff (with rhythms that appear to come naturally from the speaking voice – whoever is supposed to be speaking) disguises deeply sophisticated craft. His poems, often on the National Curriculum, are a rare mix of the genuinely popular and seriously literary.

This title poem in a collection called *The Universal Home Doctor*, is a quiet approach to a highly emotive subject, which discloses itself as you go. Through seventeen couplets it moves from a *bed* indoors to *closing the gate* outside, a last act watched *from the window*. The first six scene-setting couplets, with no people in them, look *out* from *bed* to the outside world. Six more present a central drama between *I* and *you* in the bedroom. The last five echo the first section, but now the speaker looks out to see an intruder: the Egyptian god of the dead *in black gloves* like an undertaker.

The first movement builds a picture of earliness and beginnings (*first*, *first*, *dawn*, *dawn*, *dawn*) that is somehow *without* (the poem's third word) promise. The words in these descriptions feel chilly, silent, negative. *Empty*. A *cargo of light* (which could sound lovely but actually, when you think about it, reinforces emptiness), *block of ice*. *Dawn with gold in its teeth* could also be lovely but sounds menacing too.

The first couplet has no verbs. When verbs do begin, inanimate subjects act almost eerily on their own. A bus *carries*, milk-float *moves*, mast *raises itself*. And *to its full height*, like someone intending to assert or dominate. Which strengthens the slight sinisterness behind the other images, as if *full* realisation (of something causing pain or fear) is coming back to the *mind*. Whose, we do not yet know. But it *looks out of its nest* as the poem looks out from the *bed* to the wider world.

When we get a person, he is *elsewhere*. This act, *someone's husband* touching *someones wife*, is a betrayal that is nothing to do with this room. It is the climax of the world starting up, unfolding into a new day; which at this point means *the planet* being *one day older*. Routine wrongness, how the world goes. So *the planet weeps*: climax of all these objects acting on their own. It puts on the table the despair behind this section's images.

Vowel sounds bind together these first six couplets. *Bed's* short E is echoed in *empty* and *nest*. The EE of *sheets* moves on through *sleep*, *teeth*, *street* and *east* to culminate in *weeps*. The IR of *first* echoes on through *birds* and *first*; its final ST is echoed in *mast* and *east*. The long I of *light* flickers through *like*, *mind*, *dice*, *height*, *wife*. The long O of *gold* picks up *depot* and is echoed in *older*.

After scene-setting, the drama. People: *you* and *I*. This *is* the same room, but the verbs now look back to how it was in the past (*found*; *I had to edge*; *[I had to] close*.) The central couplet describes a medical reference book in unusually emotive terms. *Bible of death* expands on *weeps*. We are talking about mourning. The poem is sad not only for the *planet*, but for loss inside *this room*.

Then another work of reference that every *home* needs, which brings in the geographical as well the sacred world. Not the family *bible*, but a map of this weeping *planet*: an *atlas*, which maps *ill-health* in a nice new modern way (*colour-coded*). This reference work is about not the outside world or sacred history like a real bible or atlas, but the inside of the human body, this thing through which we hurt and which lets us down (as *incompetence*). Its title in the central couplet contains the word which ties the *planet* and all objects in it to what is happening in *this room* (now and in the past) and to every *mind* looking *out of* any *nest*. It is *universal*, whose sound effect is prepared for by *double* in the line before. And its language of explanation for *pain* is the climax of the autonomous impersonality with which the poem began. It is technical, but in a human context the phrase *cervical incompetence* sounds unbearably reproachful. So the poem brings in real spoken language (*Susan, for God's sake*) to shut it up, for the name *Universal Home Doctor* is ironic. This is a *home*. But no book (or not one like this) can *doctor* what happened, cure the *pain*.

The drama is three slight actions. The speaker *found you*, edged *towards*, then closed this chapter of *pain* with a *bare foot*. Simple, personal *bare* words rise up and throw out the technical language which is supposed to map what happens inside you. They *close* down the impersonality.

These tiny acts move the poem forward to the final section. Some of the vowel sounds here pick up those of the first section. (*Night* echoes the long monosyllabic I; *bible* and *cervical* place the *I* in a new rhythmic context. *Bent* echoes *bed* and *empty*, and is followed up in *death*, *health* and *edge*. *Poring* echoes the OR of those two *dawns* and is repeated in *abnormalities*.)

But others create a new soundworld. The OO of *room* is echoed in *you*, *universal*, *Susan*, *towards* and *foot*. The U of *double* is echoed in *colour* and *cover*, its L in the frightening language around the central book: *universal* (the central line), *chromosomal*, *cervical*. The long O of *over* and *Home* (again in the central line, half-echoing *room*) reappears in *coded*, *chromosomal*, *progesterone* and *close*. The emotional AIN (*pain* and *explained*) mutates to *sake*.

With the drama past, the present tense returns. In the reprise of the third couplet, *teeth* seems even more sinister after *bent double*, *death* and *pain*. Action passes from the *I* who closed the book to what *I* sees. Not only inanimate objects now but a figure. We have had the *bible of death*, but this figure comes not from the Bible but an even more ancient sacred world. The poem describes the Egyptian guide to the topography of *death* in a string of present participles: *making, pushing, checking, leaving, crossing* and (bringing back the closing book) *closing*.

Meanwhile the OR of *dawn* returns twice, and again in the last line (*lawn*). The long I of *mind* now looks forward to *I, upright* and *time*; the EE of *teeth* to *sweep*, *tree*, *leaving* and *meat* (which widens into the last word *gate*); the long O of *gold* to *window*, *bones*, *own* and *closing*. *Shrubs* picks up *gloves*, *crossing* echoes the short O of *watch*.

I have read this poem with many groups. When I ask what they think it is about, most people say 'death' at first but one always says 'miscarriage' and eventually convinces the others by pointing to clues. *Cervical incompetence* reveals what kind of *ill-health* and *pain* is involved and reflects back on early images of emptiness and lack; on *without sleep* and *bent double*. It gives a human, biological dimension to the closing images of book and *gate*; and also (with muted horror) to *bones and meat*. This is not only a fox or dog nosing rubbish. There are undertaker-like *black gloves*.

Retrospectively, the *throw of a dice* associated with a *milk-float* suggests the biological lottery of miscarriage and lost maternity. And the poem's sad title is *Birthday*.

Anubis, jackal-headed god of the dead, is a surprise in this urban-sounding garden with its *street*, *shrubs* and *bin*. He mythologises the private, domestic sadness. The *nameless tree* could be a private reference (a tree in their garden whose name the couple do not know) but also sounds ancient and mythical as if familiar from some journey of the dead. And, significant, as if something were buried under it.

In his own time may reflect the calculatedly unhurried movements of any urban fox, but does it in the pseudo-comforting language used when someone in authority asks you to do something difficult. (In hospital, perhaps.) It sums up the silently autonomous way all objects in this poem have acted. It also says in a different register what the medical book explained through its *diagrams*: what happens in the body (as well as out of it) happens in its *own time*. There is nothing you can do but close the book, as *Anubis* closes the *gate*. Book of the body, gate of the body. The gate between living and dead.

A book of technical language, whose ambitious title can never be fulfilled, cannot *doctor* private suffering. But there are disciplines that do put suffering into bearable *universal* perspectives: myth, philosophy, religion; and poetry. *There was a time when only wise books were read*, says Milosz's poem 'Ars Poetica?', *helping us bear our pain and misery. / This is not quite the same / as leafing through a thousand works from psychiatric clinics*.

Anubis stands for myth and religion. If you lose a baby, it is *universal* to torment yourself trying to explain why. But also *universal* to try and comfort someone you love in pain, try and find 'closure' for her or both of you. To close the *cover*.

This is about *universal* grief. But it is the particulars, the specific details and sounds that give it universal power.

Child Burial

Your coffin looked unreal,
fancy as a wedding cake.

I chose your grave clothes with care,
your favourite stripey shirt,

your blue cotton trousers.
They smelt of woodsmoke, of October,

your own smell was there too.
I chose a gansy of handspun wool,

warm and fleecy for you. It is
so cold down in the dark.

No light can reach you and teach you
the paths of the wild birds,

the names of the flowers,
the fishes, the creatures.

Ignorant you must remain
of the sun and its work,

my lamb, my calf, my eaglet,
my cub, my kid, my nestling,

my suckling, my colt. I would spin
time back, take you again

within my womb, your amniotic lair,
and further spin you back

through nine waxing months
to the split seeding moment

you chose to be made flesh
word within me.

I'd cancel the love feast
the hot night of your making.

I would travel alone
to a quiet mossy place,

you would spill from me into the earth
drop by bright red drop.

Born in 1955, Meehan grew up in working-class Dublin, went to Trinity College and Eastern Washington University, has published many collections, won many prizes, run writing workshops in inner-city communities, prisons and universities, and written plays. Her work has been translated into ten languages, including Japanese, and adapted for stage, radio, television and film.

This poem's shocking title controls the words that follow, giving them a distancing archaeological perspective (especially powerful in Ireland, where ancient burial chambers, gesturing to older deaths, are a strong presence), which helps steady the details to come. This is going to be a painful journey. No false consolation or senti-mentality. It is very precise and takes in wider perspectives of life and the natural world as it goes.

It is possible to hear its journey in two stages, as two groups of seven couplets: the first ending in *creatures*, the second beginning with that archaic address, *ignorant you must remain*, with a final coda of two couplets. But I prefer to hear it as three movements: five couplets each, followed by the two-couplet coda. Because then the series of wishes (beginning *I would spin*) is a separate third movement which leads to the end, offering the dead child (with the cumulative weight of the poem's tenderness) the ultimate impossible gift: the wish that he had not lived.

The journey's goal is a self-sacrificial act of imagining and wishing. Imagining not having borne *you*, that you had not lived at all.

On this hearing, the first five couplets end with *cold down there in the dark*, which leads on to the next (starting with *no light*). The next describes what the dead child will never know, and ends with a list of young animals which the mother addresses him as (an image supported by *amniotic lair*). Coupled with *my*, this list is the apex of the mourning, the heartbreak point. It also continues the thought of the many natural things the child will be *ignorant* of: the natural world, all its variety and difference. Not just *flowers* and *fishes* but young animals like eaglets and cubs.

The third movement begins after another five couplets. The new thought starts midline, in the first line of the tenth couplet: *I would spin. Spin* (repeated in the eleventh couplet) has a complex echo chamber. It suggests fate spinning our life, the spinning wheels of Irish mythology and song, a world of craft and careful making (supported by *handspun* in the fourth couplet), and the spinning of tales. The speaker is going to *spin* a story backwards, to unmake (as she wishes she could physically do) the child.

The new thought introduces a sequence of subjunctives, beginning the impossible, the *would* (another common word and motif in folksong). A wish to unspool the child's life back through pregnancy, and *cancel* the moment of conception.

After these three stages and fifteen couplets, the coda. The woman is *alone* now, not yet a mother, and not (in this story) going to be. The *would* is still running: wishing the egg (that in being fertilised engendered this child) to spill out into the *earth*. Which is no longer *cold*, *down* and *dark*, but *a quiet mossy place*. The drops of lifeblood falling in it also stand for private tears.

The journey of the thought is controlled by the journey of its sounds. Each passage has its own nexus of sounds, which make the words belong to each other. This is a highly emotional subject. To convince, the words have to feel absolutely right together.

The first five stanzas start the different sounds off on their journeys through the poem, to make connections as they go between different words and their ideas. The first noun, *coffin* (which puts the grief up front), is echoed in *cotton*, and its last syllable ironically in *wedding*, a celebration whose joy is the opposite of what is happening here. Its short O reappears in the last line, in the repeated *drop*, which is the poem's last word.

The OO of *looked* is followed up in *blue*, *woodsmoke*, *too*, *wool* and *you*: a word which comes over and over. After the negative *unreal*, *fancy* brings in feeling, a world of response and judgement. Its music is echoed in *gansy* and its short A immediately after in *handspun*, which evokes the opposite of *fancy*: something made personally, with love; not sugary and custom-made.

The AY of *cake* reappears, again ironically, in *grave*. The sounds are making relationships between opposites, joy and grief, union and death. And then in *favourite*. We have moved from *your coffin* to *your favourite*: reminding us, even facing the *coffin*, of the live child's choices and affections. After that come *names, remain, again, made, making*. The AIN of *again/remain* narrows to *alone*, which is also the culmination of a series of long Os, like 'Oh' echoing repeatedly through the poem. This begins in *chose*, is echoed in *clothes, woodsmoke, October, own, so cold, no* and *colt* (the climax and closure of this list of grieving images), then moves on to *moment, chose* and *alone*. Through this sound the poem moves from *I chose* to *you chose*, and lands the speaker up *alone*. Not just without her child, but without ever having had him.

The short E of *smelt* is repeated in *smell* (in a line whose emotion is pitched that much higher by being unsaid) and later in *flesh*. The OR of *warm* picks up *your* from the four preceding couplets. *Fleecy* picks up the EE in *unreal*, and paves the way for a concentrated series of EEs: *reach, teach, creatures*; then *eaglet, seeding* and *feast*. *Dark*, at the end of its line, harks back to *cake*, another end-word, and prepares for (more end-words) *work, back* and finally (adding to the sound) *making*. The ER of *birds* echoes back to *care, shirt*, the last syllable of *October*, then moves on into *flowers, work*, widens out in *lair*, and comes to rest, along with the spilt blood, in *earth*. The short U of *sun* echoes *handspun* and the stressed word *must*, in a series of words that increasingly spotlight affection: *cub, suckling* and *love*.

The baby animals are mainly short, one-syllable words, all of different vowels: short A, AH, short U, short I, ending with long O. But these are interspersed with two-syllable words which stress EE, short E, short U. As if the poem is ringing all the changes not just of baby animals but of vowel sounds to conjure a whole world of animal youth in its relation to motherhood (underlined by *my, my, my*).

Nestling and *suckling*, nouns in the form of a present participle, conjure the child still *nestling* in her lap, still *suckling*. This image leads on to physical mothering in *womb, waxing months*, the *moment* of first *split* and separation – which turned out to foreshadow this other *moment* of separation, burial. But the moment of birth is now seen as the child's initiative: *You chose to be made flesh/word within me*.

This language recalls the divine Word made Flesh, and 'In the beginning was the Word'. Behind the *love feast* where the child was conceived is the shadow of sacrament and a *feast* of the Church. Which, in a poem from a Catholic culture, prepares for other religious shadows in the coda of this poem about *burial*, which does

317

not mention religion or a funeral service. Both the archetypal mother grieving for her child, *mater dolorosa*, virgin mother of God (who never had a *hot night of making*, as this mother wishes not to have had); and the sacramental cup in which *bright red* drops of Christ's *blood* become wine.

And maybe also, in this string of *would*s, the cup which Christ prayed might pass from him, as everyone reading this poem might pray that they themselves never have to face its particular grief.

The Wrong Beds
(*After Baudelaire*)

Life is a hospital ward, and the beds we are put in
are the ones we don't want to be in.
We'd get better sooner if put over by the window.
Or by the radiator, one could suffer easier there.

At night, the impatient soul dreams of faraway places.
The Aegean: all marble and light. Where, upon a beach
as flat as a map, you could bask in the sun like a lizard.

The Pole: where, bathing in darkness, you could watch
the sparks from Hell reflected in a sky of ice.
The soul could be happier anywhere than where it happens to be.

Anywhere but here. We take our medicine daily,
nod politely, and grumble occasionally.
But it is out of our hands. Always the wrong place.
We didn't make our beds, but we lie in them.

McGough, born in 1937 in Liverpool, is one of Britain's best-loved
poets: a warm, brilliant performer and poetry broadcaster, who has
written plays, an autobiography and many prizewinning collections
of children's poems. He went to Hull University, taught at a
comprehensive school and Liverpool College of Art, made his name
as one of the Liverpool Poets, was a leading figure in its Sixties scene
and part of a chart-topping pop group, The Scaffold. His live
performances and funny, direct, generous writing helped to give
poetry a massive new audience then and are still as popular today.
His 2003 *Collected Poems* brought together forty years of poems.
He was awarded an OBE in 1997, the Freedom of the City of
Liverpool in 2003 and a CBE for services to poetry in 2005.

The humour, inventiveness and playfulness of his poems often
mask their intelligence and generosity. He can tackle any form,
from elastic informal-looking children's poems to haiku.

This poem started out as a commission, a poem about a hospital, to put up in a hospital. It follows Baudelaire's poem 'Anywhere Out of This World', which opens *Cette vie est un hôpital:* life is a hospital. But it instantly changes that famous opening by adding *ward*, making it (subtly comically) more down to earth, more now.

In Baudelaire, every patient longs to change beds. *One would prefer to suffer by the stove, another that he'd get well by the window.* The speaker would always be happier in a different place from where he happens to be. He suggests to his soul they might move out to Lisbon, *built of marble* by the sea, where he'd *bask like a lizard* in a landscape of *light and minerals with water to reflect them.* What about other places? His soul is silent. Is it dead? Should he go to a land that looks like Death? Say the Pole, where sunlight is oblique, where he can bathe in darkness and watch Aurora Borealis like fireworks from hell. *Anywhere*, his soul says at last, *as long as it's out of here!*

McGough follows Baudelaire's movement and images, and many of his words, but condenses everything down to a sonnet split into two outer quatrains with six inner lines for the alternative worlds, the *faraway places* (*the Aegean*, instead of Lisbon, in the first triplet; *the Pole* for the second). The outer quatrains, above all the first and last lines, focus on the real world, the *beds* of the title.

McGough opens with a run of perfect dactyls in a pentameter which makes you feel everything will be jolly and straightforward. But this poem is about expectations that are not met, and metrical expectations are not met either. The second line is only half a pentameter. The third line gives up on the tripping dactyls, slows and lengthens everything with two-syllable trochees (words stressing their longer first syllable – *better*, *sooner*, *over*) which continue in the next line (*suffer*, *easier*); and this line moves from the personal *we* to the impersonal universal *one*. From this point we get pentameters where dactyls come and go but rhythm seems to follow the natural rhythms of the words.

One could suffer easier there sums up the poem's premise and point. In this *hospital ward* called *life*, suffering is what we're going to do. But it is universal to believe that where we do it may affect how.

Baudelaire's options were stove and window. McGough changes stove to *radiator*. The *window* moves us out to the triplets' other worlds. The *radiator* looks forward to the *sun* and warmth of the *Aegean*.

The two inner stanzas hang together with their own internal echoes. *Night* (echoing the poem's first word *Life*) is picked up by *light*, then by *sky* and *ice*. *Soul*, which in Baudelaire is the important interlocutor whose answer the speaker waits for, is now the *impatient* one, the dreamer. Its sound is matched in the second triplet by *Pole* and another *soul*. But also by *Hell*. *Dreams* is reinforced by *Aegean* and *beach*, *marble* by *bask*, and later by *darkness* and *sparks*. The short A of *flat* and *map* returns in *happier*, *happens*. Several lines repeat a vowel within one line (*flat/map*, *sky/ice*, *happier/happens*), and most of them pause after the first foot (after *night*, *Aegean* and *Pole*) or second foot (after *map*), as if taking a breath, having made the effort to get to an imaginary new place.

At the end of the triplets, McGough brings in Baudelaire's line *always happier in a different place from where I happen to be*, but gives it to the *soul*: which will cover the globe, meet light and *darkness*, *Hell* and *ice*, the feel of *sun*, the sight of *sparks*. But it does all this *at night*. Even as you dream, you are still in your *hospital ward*, in the bed *you are put in*, the one you *don't want to be in*.

The *ward* is what you cannot get out of. But in dreams (rather *than where it happens to be*) your *soul* is *happier*. These dreams (sounding like ads for modern holidays) are your *anywhere* away from normal life. The fourth stanza repeats that *anywhere* while returning to the *here*, the *ward*.

Here is where we really are: our lives, our clichés (like 'take your medicine', 'out of my hands', 'make your bed and lie in it'). Our conventions, manners, politeness and *grumble*s are how we deal with feeling always in *the wrong place*, in lives and *beds* we *don't want to be in*. Which we *didn't make*, just as we didn't make our bodies (which hospital wards are all about).

McGough is dealing with the issue of human suffering by playing skilfully with a famous French poem, ending with a wry smile at inverted clichés and a riddle. From the first noun, *life*, we move to a word which is nearly the same: *lie*. But this has two meanings. These *beds* are, as the title says, *wrong*. Do we *lie* down in them or tell falsehoods from them? Or both?

He also suggests poetry can be an important presence in the real world of *hospital*. We all have to be 'patients'. That unspoken word, the opposite of what the *soul* is (*impatient*), comes from the Latin verb *patior*, I suffer: a passive voice verb. When you become a patient you are forced to be passive, have things done to you, *lie* where you are *put*. *Hospital* sums up the human condition as one of forced submission to authority and fate. You can only get away from it inside the poem (the two inner stanzas) and also by something inside you. The *soul*, which refuses to be patient, which *dreams* – and turns to poetry.

'Dogs, Would You Live For Ever?'
(Frederick the Great)

She's bent at stool, as the saying is,
Next to her deathbed. Her arched back
Is like white fish
That has been too long in the fridge,
Greyed at the spine-bones.

Crying, she says 'this is the worst now.'
I say, 'Of course it's not.
You did as much for children
Often enough.'

But of course it was: the scene
Comes back, untriggered, more
Rather than less often,
Oddly enough.

I'd prefer you to wait outside.

O'Donoghue, born in 1945 in north Cork, a scholar and Whitbread Prizewinning poet, grew up first in Cork (where his father was a farmer) then, after his father died, in Manchester. He went to Oxford and returned there to do postgraduate research in Medieval English, which he now teaches. He writes what he calls 'miscellaneous medieval things' (books and papers on medieval poetry, including the courtly love tradition and Chaucer), is editing the *Cambridge Companion to Seamus Heaney*, has published many collections and a book about Seamus Heaney.

His voice is low, wry and scrupulous with a characteristically quiet, courtly approach to the reader. Philip Larkin was an early influence. Larkin's 'doleful self-mockery', he says, 'is very hard to escape once you get the feel of it'. Another constant is medieval poetry, which inspires his poems both indirectly and directly. He incorporates fragments of translation from Dante, Chaucer, *Piers Plowman* or *The Seafarer*.

Some poems are reflections on ageing, on how he may already have bought his last mackintosh, on how he has lived so long away from his homeland he no longer belongs there. Some focus on physical oddity no one else has noticed. How, for instance, the slow flow of glass down a window, which gradually swells the base of the pane, is like the body thickening with age. Other poems use Irish myth; many conjure memories of childhood in rural Cork, bringing people, farmland and community to a life so palpable you can hear and taste it, but also letting us glimpse submerged tragedies through everyday detail.

The past, he has said, is a way of talking about the present. 'Poems about sensitive or private subjects are just as revealing and embarrassing when set in the past.' People sometimes ask poets how they can bear to read or publish a poem that seems to spring from personal and revealing things. One answer is, you trust the poem (once made) as an artefact, separate from the experience that sparked it.

But this poem goes right into embarrassment itself (*'this is the worst now'* . . . *of course it was*). And then, at the end, gestures the reader to *wait outside*. It highlights the oddity (brought to the surface in *oddly enough*) and risk involved in putting any private thing into that very public artefact, a poem. *In the very essence of poetry there is something indecent*, says Milosz in his poem '*Ars Poetica?*'. In a poem, *something is brought forth which we didn't know we had in us, / so we blink our eyes, as if a tiger has sprung out / and stood in the light, lashing its tail.*[5]

The shape of this poem is a mashed-up sonnet (with a classic 'turn' of thought at *But . . . it was*), in three stanzas (two outer ones of five lines, an inner one of four). The last line is separated from its stanza, calling attention to a need, at this point, to separate things. *I'd prefer you to wait outside* refers both to the very private subject – a man helping a dying woman, presumably his mother, to shit – and the poet's relation to his readers. Who can't *wait outside*, because the poem has already taken them in – shown them her *greyed spine-bones* (so much more intimate than grey hair), and opened the door to her *crying*.

It would be unbearable, if O'Donoghue were not a master of voice, tact and tone. He distances and frames the scene, shifts the tenses, and implies much more than he describes. Using two quotations from other people (one a king, in the title, the other a *saying*) the title and first line gently give the indignity of this particular body, and its need to die, a historical universality.

The first stanza starts in the present tense. The first two lines tell the scene with intense economy. (The last three are all image.) The short E of *bent* is echoed three times in *next* and *deathbed*. *Fridge* chimes with *fish* and *is*. *Too* picks up the shocking euphemism *stool*. *Greyed* echoes the AY of *saying*.

The central stanza is again present-tense. The scene has been set; now comes the reaction. *Crying* (whose long I reminds us of her nakedness by echoing *spine*). *She says* (for in all this privacy, 'saying' is personal now, not quotation from long-ago kings or popular sayings). And *I say*. The attempt at comfort invokes the past (*you did*): how she wiped *children* (presumably him, among others), as he is now caring for her.

The past tense continues into the third stanza, but now that original scene is itself the past. The first two stanzas were happening *next to her deathbed*. In the white gap between the second and third stanzas, she has died; the speaker, looking back, admits what he said to her was a lie. *Of course it was* is a cry against what happens to the body, reverberating against the title's savage question.

Little echoes vein the stanza, holding it together: *as much* and *enough*; *this* and *did* (which cover with an uninteresting-looking word the humiliation of what's happening); *come* and *untriggered*, whose last syllable is reinforced by the stressed syllable of *prefer*.

In the first line of the third stanza, the stress is on *was*. This pivotal little word begins the aftermath of death, revises the truth (what was said) and points out that the present is now the past. Its importance is accentuated by its chime with *Dogs* in the title and *not* (the end-word in the second stanza) plus repeated *of*s and *often*. It will be reinforced by another *often* and *oddly*.

This little sentence is the emotional highlight, the most private moment of the poem, where the speaker admits his own feeling. We have moved from her pain and humiliation to his grief about it. Yes that really *was*, as she said, *the worst*.

After this the voice becomes more private. The first stanza disclosed upsetting physical details, the second the spoken intimacy around them. Now there is a retreat to impersonality, as if it is easier to reveal the physical facts than the pain of remembering them. The poem does not say, 'I think of what happened.' Instead it objectifies what happened as *the scene* – which *comes back* unexpectedly (*untriggered*) and surprises the speaker.

The poem seems to end there, with his intellectualising surprise at his own reaction: *oddly enough*. But after a pause he turns to the reader again with a polite subjunctive. *I'd prefer* finally distances the reader. It ends both the poem and the relationship between reader and poem, with a retreating silence which echoes with the unsaid pain of what reader and speaker have gone through together.

Timer

Gold survives the fire that's hot enough
to make you ashes in a standard urn.
An envelope of coarse official buff
contains your wedding ring which wouldn't burn.

Dad told me I'd to tell them at St James's
that the ring should go in the incinerator.
That 'eternity' inscribed with both their names is
his surety that they'd be together, 'later'.

I signed for the parcelled clothing as the son,
the cardy, apron, pants, bra, dress –

the clerk phoned down: 6-8-8-3-1?
Has she still her ring on? (Slight pause) *Yes!*

It's on my warm palm now, your burnished ring!

I feel your ashes, head, arms, breasts, womb, legs,
sift through its circle slowly, like that thing
you used to let me watch to time the eggs.

Born in Leeds in 1937, Harrison studied Classics and has published
many prizewinning collections since. He writes television and film
poetry and is a wonderful translator, dramatist and librettist,
especially from Greek tragedy, Racine and medieval Mystery plays.
His Alzheimers film *Black Daisies for the Bride* won the Prix Italia;
his film *Prometheus* involved driving a thirty-foot statue from
northern England to Greece through Germany and Eastern
Europe, and linked the mythic Greek hero to Yorkshire coal mines,
heavy industry in Eastern Europe, Auschwitz and the bombing of
Dresden.

His poetry is often deeply political. Much of it has sprung from
tension between his working-class childhood and his élitist-seeming

classical education. In 1987 the tabloids and a group of Conservative MPs failed to stop Channel 4 screening a filmed version of Harrison's long poem *V.*, written during the miners' strike. They said it contained 'torrents of obscene language', 'streams of four-letter filth'. (*V.*, not of course in favour of filth, described Harrison's parents' grave *littered with beer cans and vandalised by obscene graffiti*.) An Early Day Motion on 'Television Obscenity' was successfully opposed by a lone MP who argued they had not read or understood the poem properly.

Harrison is deeply and very thoughtfully knowledgeable about the Classics, and has wonderful metrical and rhyming energy. His poems are passionately compassionate; they combine brilliant rhyming with equally powerful colloquial speech. His version of the *York Mystery Plays* evoked a rhythmic and sacred world that existed before the King James Bible, or the iambic pentameter, entered the language. He also brings into his poems language from every source, from ancient Greek to Yorkshire dialect, inarticulate grunts, rhyming couplets, puns.

This poem is a run of four quatrains of simple *abab* rhymes, but the third is split in half and the fourth's first line is severed from the rest: the poem only picks up smoothly again in the last three lines. So even to the eye, the shape suggests a design gone wrong. Even before you enter the poem's world you expect a jolt at the beginning of the second half.

The poem moves from a universal truth (*gold survives fire*) and impersonal regulation objects (*standard*, *official*), towards concrete attachment in the fourth stanza (when the ring that *wouldn't burn* in the first meets the poet's *warm palm*) and a personal childhood memory in the last line, where *that thing* evokes a child who does not yet know the word egg timer, and *let* conjures the mother's power over that *son* who has now, as adult, *signed* for her clothes in the crematorium.

You, in the second line, is ambiguous. Is it part of the universal observation, does it allude to a personal event, or does it mark a slide from universal to particular? *To make you ashes* could mean 'make you into ashes' or 'make ashes for you, for anyone'. Only the fourth line (*your wedding ring*) resolves this, by revealing how personal this *you* is.

After this glide to the personal, the drama picks up pace. Stanza one: here is your *ring which wouldn't burn*, in an *official envelope*. Stanza two: *Dad told me* (a very personal tone now) to make sure it went into the crematorium fire, hoping this would mean *they'd be together, 'later'*. Stanza three: I signed for the clothes, but – and here comes a dash and the first split – where is the ring? *The clerk* checked. *Yes:* the ring is still on her finger in the coffin. Another gap, a stanza break, and the ring turns up again. *On my warm palm* now, instead of her cold finger. And *burnished* – because, presumably, it has been through the fire.

Another split. The father's hope has not worked: the '*eternity*' incised on the ring did not go up in smoke with her so he cannot base his *surety* of rejoining her on that. In the last three-quarters of stanza four we finally get the speaker's own sensation: *I feel*. This poem about a ring uses 'ring-composition'. Its end goes back to its beginning.[6]

Now we see the point of the initial generalisation. The *fire* that *burnished* this ring has burnt his mother's corpse to *ashes*. Gesturing back to those *ashes*, the poem imagines them sifting through the ring as through the waist of an egg timer.

Or, in the old name, an hourglass, that evocative ancient image of passing time and human life. Burns's 'My Love Is Like a Red Red Rose' promises *I shall love thee still, while the sands of life shall run*. Gerard Manley Hopkins' 'The Wreck of the *Deutschland*' has *I am soft sift in an hour-glass*. Even in *The Wizard of Oz*, the Wicked Witch puts a large egg timer in front of Dorothy to show time running out before she dies.

This poem's last lines put other symbols beside the evocative hourglass, domesticised as a *timer*. The *circle* of eternity (reflecting the father's hope in the second verse). *Eggs*, image of maternity, of where the *son* has come from (as in *womb*). Image of beginnings and rebirth. Instead of the funeral service's 'ashes to ashes', this poem describes a different journey: *gold* to *eggs*.

The vowel sounds are softly sifted themselves. The initial long O of *gold* runs through the first two stanzas (*envelope, told, go, both*) then stops – to be suggested, perhaps, in the ring's *circle* at the end. The poem's second sound, the ER of *survives*, runs through for longer (appropriate to *survives*), in *urn, burn, incinerator, eternity, later* and *parcelled*, up to the word that tells us the ring did 'survive' the fire: *burnished*.

The whole thing is wonderfully harmonised. You could draw a hundred lines of relationship (like *eternity/surety*, or *palm/arms*) between the words which all add up to a taut cat's cradle of sonic echoes. It is full of what Heaney's Nobel lecture called the 'buoyancy generated by cadence and tone and rhyme and stanza'.[7]

But in all the rhymes and inner echoes that hold the stanzas closely together, it is especially over the fragmented lines that the vowel sounds reach out to make you feel the lines belong. The sequence of stressed vowels after the first split, for instance, is AH, long O, OW (*clerk phoned down*). This is replayed by the lone line (which introduces *warm*, the first word that could refer openly to emotional as well as physical feeling) as OR, AH, OW (*warm palm now*).

The fragmentation starts after the list of *clothing* (which is matched by the list of body parts at the end). *Cardy, apron, pants, bra, dress* is a pentameter whose monosyllables slow you down as you stress each one. *Cardy* sounds like what she would have said herself, but in this poem it is political too. Another of Harrison's poems was called 'Them and [uz]'. (*Uz* pronounced OO, as in 'hood'.) It began in Greek letters, with the Greek tragic lament, *aiai*, used the square brackets which signify words that have got lost or 'fallen out' of ancient texts, recalled a schoolteacher who ridiculed Harrison at school for reciting Keats in a Yorkshire accent and attacked anyone who thought poetry should only be spoken in Standard English. It claimed for all dialects and accents the right to make poetry (*So right, yer buggers, then! We'll occupy / your lousy leasehold Poetry*). It also said *My first mention in the Times / automatically made Tony Anthony!*

As 'Tony' stayed Tony throughout his fame and honours, *cardy* in this poem stays *cardy* despite *official* envelopes. *Gold survives the fire*; poetry survives patronising exclusivity; and personal feeling, memory and relationships survive impersonalising treatment from officialdom.

Black Silk

She was cleaning – there is always
that to do – when she found,
at the top of the closet, his old
silk vest. She called me
to look at it, unrolling it carefully
like something live
might fall out. Then we spread it
on the kitchen table and smoothed
the wrinkles down, making our hands
heavy until its shape against formica
came back and the little tips
that would have pointed to his pockets
lay flat. The buttons were all there.
I held my arms out and she
looped the wide armholes over
them. 'That's one thing I never
wanted to be,' she said, 'a man.'
I went into the bathroom to see
how I looked in the sheen and
sadness. Wind chimes
off-key in the alcove. Then her
crying so I stood back in the sink-light
where the porcelain had been staring. Time
to go to her, I thought, with that
other mind, and stood still.

Gallagher, born in 1943 where she now lives (Port Angeles, Washington, on America's north-west coast below Canada), studied under the charismatic and influential American poet Theodore Roethke, has taught in many universities, received many awards and published many collections. For eleven years she was the companion and (for two months) wife of the poet and master short-story writer Raymond Carver, who died in 1988. Her introductions to his *Collected Poems* and last book, *A New Path to the Waterfall*, are moving essays from a lover who was also an essential collaborator.

She met Carver after he'd stopped the alcoholism that dominated twenty-five years of his life. She helped him start writing again. His later short stories and poems were made possible by her support. 'Tess, Tess, Tess, Tess' runs the dedication to *A New Path to the Waterfall*. 'Late Fragment' (which introduces Section IV), the last poem he wrote, was written to her.

The central line of these twenty-five lines (those *buttons* that *were all there*) divides this poem and its action into two parts. The first half's three sentences end midline. First, at *silk vest* (American for 'waistcoat'). Then at *fall out*; thirdly at *lay flat*. Then comes the end-stopped central line, followed by more midline stops until the last line's *stood still*. The one exception is the moment of direct speech, where a line ends with what is absent from the poem and the scene: the person who wore this *vest*. A *man*.

The poem is about mourning, as the title implies. The *black silk* is not mourning cloth, though, but the dead man's dress waistcoat. The poem does not describe him or the grief. He, and their grief, are internal. Grief happens on the inside of the words, just as the sentence ends, and pauses for breath, happen on the inside of the lines.

She found, she called me, we spread it out is the sequence of verbs. Now the speaker takes the initiative. *I held my arms out*. She is dressed in his *old* waistcoat (much too big for her, says *wide armholes*) like a bride. But this is dressing a widow.

I went into the bathroom to see / how I looked. The feeling that has hovered around the whole thing is now spelt out by what she is dressed *in*. Not just the *sheen* (of the *silk*) but the *sadness*. Of *black*, like a widow's new weeds. Of his absence.

After this one abstract noun *sadness*, key to the whole poem, the poem brings in sound. *Off-key in the alcove* suggests the tolling of church bells, a sound that says all the poem is not saying.

Now *we* are in separate rooms, the other person starts *crying*. They have been strong for each other (perhaps) but seeing *black* has set her off.

So I stood back – to give her time and privacy to cry. The speaker is now *in the sink-light / where the porcelain* was *staring*. This is the longest, most surreal line, and climax of the grief. *Porcelain* implies

331

white, but there is no colour in this poem except in the title. White (implied) is *staring* at black (implied) while *she* cries.

The speaker feels she should *go to her*, but feels it with *that other mind*: the mind of duty, perhaps, which thinks it should comfort this other person, her co-mourner. But her real mind is occupied (though still not saying so) with the man and his death.

Stood still. The speaker was *called* into the poem in line four. She responded, but has now *stood back*, *stood still*. As time stands still. After someone dies, *there is always* cleaning *to do* but underneath, you feel, there is nothing *to do*. At this point (you feel the poem's real *mind* thinking) no 'doing' has the slightest point. The speaker ends as she began, inactive.

Rhythmically, the poem is built round the heaviest of metrical units, the spondee (two long stressed syllables). The title itself is a spondee and there are many others: (*silk vest*, *called me*, *fall out*, *came back*, *lay flat*, *armholes*, *sadness*, *wind-chimes*, *off-key*, *alcove*, *sink-light*, *staring* and the last, *stood still*). This is a poem about the ending of a marriage by death and most of the important line breaks end on a spondee, often after the first foot (*silk vest*, *fall out*, *lay flat*, *sadness*, *other mind*). The emotional climax comes in a pair of spondees (*sadness. Wind chimes*) with a break between.

By contrast the short A of *black* ricochets throughout the poem: *that* (the stressed first word of the second line), *back*, *flat* and again *that* (last word of the second-last line). But the long EE of *cleaning* echoes alongside it: *me* (the stressed last word of the fourth line), *we*, *she* (the stressed last word of the fourteenth line), *be* (stressed by the following comma in the seventeenth), *see* (stressed by its end position), *sheen*, *off-key*. Long O is picked up like a moan from *old* (stressed by its end position) into *unrolling*, *armholes*, *over*, *alcove*, *go*. The knell of *chimes* is repeated in the stressed end-word *time* and *mind*. And the last word *still* echoes the title word, the suddenly found lost object that sparked the poem's quiet drama of grief at loss: *silk*.

Rembrandt's Late Self-Portraits

You are confronted with yourself. Each year
The pouches fill, the skin is uglier.
You give it all unflinchingly. You stare
Into yourself, beyond. Your brush's care
Runs with self-knowledge. Here

Is a humility at one with craft.
There is no arrogance. Pride is apart
From this self-scrutiny. You make light drift
The way you want. Your face is bruised and hurt
But there is still love left.

Love of the art and others. To the last
Experiment went on. You stared beyond
Your age, the times. You also plucked the past
And tempered it. Self-portraits understand,
And old age can divest,

With truthful changes, us of fear and death.
Look, a new anguish. There, the bloated nose,
The sadness and the joy. To paint's to breathe,
And all the darknesses are dared. You chose
What each must reckon with.

Elizabeth Jennings (1926–2001) was born in Lincolnshire, but aged six moved to Oxford where she lived for the rest of her life. She studied at St Anne's, worked in advertising, at the City Library and in publishing, before becoming a full-time writer. The Somerset Maugham Award for her second book (1955) allowed her to travel to Rome. She was a Catholic anyway but Rome, she said, 'brought my religion alive'. She received the W. H. Smith Literary Award and a CBE, and published over twenty books. At first she was grouped with 'Movement' poets (along with Kingsley Amis and Larkin), but instead of irony and wit she stood for scrupulous technical craft. Her work is direct but restrained and unobtrusive; full of grace; informed by devotion in the tradition of English religious poetry. 'You cannot fake anything', she said once, 'if you are trying to write serious poetry.'

The poem here is from a 1975 collection *Growing Points*. The first two lines could be the poet talking at her own mirror. They make clear that for everything the poem says here about a particular artist and his *craft*, there is also another resonance: this poet's relation to poetry.

The third line, though, makes the *you* specific and picks *Rembrandt* out of the title. All the sentences are short and simple, but the poem uses them to braid together four different journeys of thought.

The first journey, mapped by a change of tense in the verbs, moves from the painter's still living art to his own relation to it. The poem's first half is present-tense. Art is timeless: *you* are still here in these portraits. In the first stanza, *you are confronted, you give it all, you stare*; in the second, *you make light drift*. Then the tense changes: the poem no longer addresses Rembrandt as a face in pictures but as the person he was, in relation to the art that made them. He is not here; but his paintings are the result of what he did. *You stared, you plucked . . . and tempered; you chose.*

Within this journey is another which follows changes in Rembrandt's face and feelings. From *pouches fill, skin is uglier* to *your face is bruised and hurt*, the fact that *love* is *still left:* then the *bloated nose, the sadness and the joy*.

A third journey is made up of observations on Rembrandt's art, from *self-knowledge* (on the brush like paint) to *humility*, the power to make *light* do what he wants, the *experiment* that continued *to the last*.

This mixes with a fourth journey whose path of thought is towards general observations on art and making art. It begins at *pride is apart / from this self-scrutiny*, continues with *self-portraits understand*, and the idea that *old age* can create *truthful changes* in us and cancel *fear*. It culminates in *to paint's to breathe*; and – the climax of what Rembrandt and any serious artist has to do – *all the darknesses are dared*.

The only adjectives are those that give necessary information: *uglier, bruised* and *hurt, old* (for *age*), *truthful* (for one of the key words, *changes*), *new* (for *anguish*), *bloated*. There are no relative clauses, which would deflect attention away from each point made. This is about art made and facts faced *unflinchingly*. There is no ambiguity until the last line, which does bring in a relative clause. *What* is a contraction of '*that* (thing) *which*', a relative clause in disguise. But what exactly does *what* mean? What is this thing that *everyone must reckon with*? What did Rembrandt choose in his self-portraits?

The poem is not only talking about the sequence of self-portraits, in which each *new anguish* (his wife's death, bankruptcy, his son's death) made Rembrandt's face *uglier*. Nor about the generosity with which he records this (*you give it all*) or the love (*of the art and others*) which shines out from his paintings, transcends time, and demanded *experiment to the last*, driving him both into *the past* and *beyond the times*. It is also addressing the relation of the artist to both his life and his work.

The only words we know Rembrandt said about what he wanted to do in his work were to make 'the greatest and most natural movement'. No one knows what this means. 'Movement' in the painting, of body and line? Or of feeling, in the observer's response? Or maybe both? Rembrandt's great theme was the world and the bodies we really live and feel in. He concentrated on making beauty out of what was ordinary and potentially ugly. He flouted the creed of his day by rejecting Italian Renaissance smoothness. (Contemporary critics said he did not understand 'our rules of art, such as anatomy and the proportions of the human body', because he 'always associated with the lower orders, whereby he was hampered in his work'.) He did not go in much for classical themes, but when he did, in *The Rape of Ganymede*, he painted the boy (who was reputedly so beautiful that the king of gods desired him) peeing and scrunching his face in terror as the eagle snatches him up. He painted the bare soles of an angel's feet; painted plebeian bodies and ugly, ageing, wrinkled faces, including his own.

All this is behind the poem's last line. Rembrandt *chose*, in his art, to face himself, what had happened to him and what he saw round him, including ageing and death. He did it *unflinchingly*. We all have to face things in our bodies, lives and work. Every artist and poet *must reckon with* facing it as truthfully as possible.

But the poem is also about the way Rembrandt's art makes feeling *one with craft*. Jennings' rhyming structure embodies this theme. The pattern is *ababa* for each stanza, but in the first verse the *a*s and *b*s melt into each other, and the rhyming vowels change through the verse and bleed into the next. *Year* is partnered by *stare* and *here*, *uglier* by *care*, but you only realise these partnerings by checking the pattern in the following stanzas, because when you meet them here the *a* and *b* rhymes (*stare*, *care*) themselves rhyme.

In the second verse, the *a* rhyme drifts from *craft* to *drift* to *left*, while the *b* rhyme *apart* is partnered by *hurt* but has the same long AR as the *a* rhyme *craft*, which is repeated in the next verse's *a* rhyme: *last*, *past*. This mutates into *divest* – whose own short E is repeated in the next verse's *a* rhyme *death*, which itself mutates into *breathe* and *with*.

The vowel changes make the poem's point, that superficial changes overlie and blur existing structure: Rembrandt's facial structure. The *pouches* and texture of *skin* change. The face gets *bruised and hurt*, the *nose* is *bloated*. *Anguish*, *sadness* and *joy* put new marks on the surface. But these *changes* are *truthful*. They tell us about an inner, permanent truth of self: an underlying rhyme scheme, as it were, of personality, there from the beginning but more apparent at the end. Just as, in the last verse, that initial *stare/here* sound (which fused the *a* and *b* rhymes in the first) comes back (prefigured by *stared* in the third verse) in *fear*, *there* and (the climax word) *dared*, which makes explicit the bravery of looking at yourself *unflinchingly*.

Staring into yourself, self-scrutiny without *pride* or *arrogance*, is *staring beyond*, *daring the darkness*. To stare is to dare. Elizabeth Jennings once talked about Gerard Manley Hopkins' line (from 'As Kingfishers Catch Fire') *What I do is me, for that I came*. She applied it to herself writing poems. 'My poetry is me,' she said. 'It justifies my existence.' Here she projects this on to Rembrandt and painting: *To paint's to breathe*.

Rembrandt, the great artist of self, often set his portraits (of himself and others) against an uncompromising darkness, an image for the lonely gallantry with which each self inhabits the world. Just as, from its first word *you*, the poem makes Rembrandt stand for all of us.

Painting self is choosing *what each must reckon with*. The *self-knowledge* with which Rembrandt's *brush runs* means working with the *light* and *darkness* of everything we meet: *anguish*, *joy*, *fear*, *death*. Until the thing you have made, rather than you yourself, becomes the vehicle of insight.

Self-portraits understand. Painting *truthful changes* means, in the end, a loss of self (*humility at one with craft*) which *can divest* you of *fear* when confronting (the poem's first verb) that other loss of self which is death.

Orpheus and Eurydice
(*translated by the author and Robert Hass*)

Standing on flagstones of the sidewalk at the entrance to Hades
Orpheus hunched in a gust of wind
That tore at his coat, rolled past in waves of fog,
Tossed the leaves of the trees. The headlights of cars
Flared and dimmed in each succeeding wave.

He stopped at the glass-panelled door, uncertain
Whether he was strong enough for that ultimate trial.

He remembered her words: 'You are a good man.'
He did not quite believe it. Lyric poets
Usually have – as he knew – cold hearts.
It is like a medical condition. Perfection in art
Is given in exchange for such an affliction.

Only her love warmed him, humanized him.
When he was with her, he thought differently about himself.
He could not fail her now, when she was dead.

He pushed open the door and found himself walking in a
    labyrinth,
Corridors, elevators. The livid light was not light but the dark of
    the earth.
Electronic dogs passed him noiselessly.
He descended many floors, a hundred, three hundred, down.

He was cold, aware that he was Nowhere.
Under thousands of frozen centuries,
On an ashy trace where generations had mouldered,
In a kingdom that seemed to have no bottom and no end.

Thronging shadows surrounded him.
He recognized some of the faces.
He felt the rhythm of his blood.

He felt strongly his life with its guilt
And he was afraid to meet those to whom he had done harm.
But they had lost the ability to remember
And gave him only a glance, indifferent to all that.

For his defence he had a nine-stringed lyre.
He carried in it the music of the earth, against the abyss
That buries all of sound in silence.
He submitted to the music, yielded
To the dictation of a song, listening with rapt attention,
Became, like his lyre, its instrument.

Thus he arrived at the palace of the rulers of that land.
Persephone, in her garden of withered pear and apple trees,
Black, with naked branches and verrucose twigs,
Listened from the funereal amethyst of her throne.

He sang the brightness of mornings and green rivers,
He sang of smoking water in the rose-coloured daybreaks
Of colours: cinnabar, carmine, burnt sienna, blue,
Of the delight of swimming in the sea under marble cliffs,
Of feasting on a terrace above the tumult of a fishing port,
Of the tastes of wine, olive oil, almonds, mustard, salt.
Of the flight of the swallow, the falcon,
Of a dignified flock of pelicans above a bay,
Of the scent of an armful of lilacs in summer rain,
Of his having composed his words always against death
And of having made no rhyme in praise of nothingness.

I don't know – said the goddess – whether you loved her or not.
Yet you have come here to rescue her.
She will be returned to you. But there are conditions:
You are not permitted to speak to her, or on the journey back
To turn your head, even once, to assure yourself that she is behind
    you.

And so Hermes brought forth Eurydice.
Her face no longer hers, utterly gray,
Her eyelids lowered beneath the shade of her lashes.
She stepped rigidly, directed by the hand
Of her guide. Orpheus wanted so much
To call her name, to wake her from that sleep.
But he refrained, for he had accepted the conditions.

And so they set out. He first, and then, not right away,
The slap of the god's sandals and the light patter
Of her feet fettered by her robe, as if by a shroud.
A steep climbing path phosphorized
Out of darkness like the walls of a tunnel.
He would stop and listen. But then
They stopped, too, and the echo faded.
And when he began to walk the double tapping commenced
   again.
Sometimes it seemed closer, sometimes more distant.
Under his faith a doubt sprang up
And entwined him like cold bindweed.
Unable to weep, he wept at the loss
Of the human hope for the resurrection of the dead,
Because he was, now, like every other mortal.
His lyre was silent, yet he dreamed, defenceless.
He knew he must have faith and he could not have faith,
And so he would persist for a very long time,
Counting his steps in a half-wakeful torpor.

Day was breaking. Shapes of rock loomed up
Under the luminous eye of the exit from underground.

It happened as he expected. He turned his head
And behind him on the path was no one.

Sun. And sky. And in the sky white clouds.
Only now everything cried to him, Eurydice!
How will I live without you, my consoling one!
But there was a fragrant scent of herbs, the low humming of bees,
And he fell asleep with his cheek on the sun-warmed earth.

Czeslaw Milosz (1911–2004) was one of the greatest poets of the
twentieth century. He was born in Lithuania (son of a civil
engineer), studied in Wilno (then in Poland), worked for Polish
Radio and in the war for underground presses and the Resistance.
After 1945 he worked for the Polish diplomatic service in Paris,
defected to France in 1951, moved in 1960 to Berkeley, California
and was given the Nobel in 1980. In his last years he lived in
Kraków where his second wife, thirty years younger, died (from
sudden cancer) two years before he did.

He published many collections after his first in the 1930s; and also influential essays. Unsentimental and like Rembrandt unflinching, his work is very human, immensely learned, very humble; and also political. It had to be. Poetry, he felt, was about life and for life. Some things (he says in '1945') cannot be learned *from Apollinaire,/Or Cubist manifestos.* He lived through Marxist betrayals and massacres as well as the occupation of Poland, the creation and razing of the Warsaw ghetto. His poems address everything – theology, philosophy, eroticism. He wrote dramatic monologue, metaphysical reflection, elegy, epigram and lyric, and the wisdom and knowledge in all this was won first-hand at great cost. He fiercely believed poetry had a holy force. He called it 'the passionate pursuit of the Real', philosophy's 'ally in the service of the good', news 'brought to the mountains by a unicorn and an echo'. Poetry is what we have, what we can do, to fight with against death and nothingness: it is the tireless messenger, says his poem 'Meaning', *who runs and runs/Through interstellar fields, through revolving galaxies,/And calls out, protests, screams.*

This final poem is the only one in this book written in another language: Polish. But Milosz collaborated closely with its translator and in its English words (even though there are Polish words behind them) you hear truly lived and felt experience, and an understanding that sees everything as real both ways round: symbolic as well as tangible. 'I love Milosz', said Heaney in memorial, 'because there is such a guarantee in his tone.'

At sixty, Milosz began learning Greek. In this last poem of his last book he turned to the mythical Greek figure of the first poet. As befits a journey to the dead, there are the ghosts here not only of other languages but of other poems and poets; above all Rilke, whose *Sonnets to Orpheus* suggest the poet belongs to the living and the dead: you have to have *tuned your lyre* in both worlds.[8]

In this poem, you can feel this underworld journey in two halves, the there and the back. One way into it is following the verbs. In the first half, Orpheus is active. He hesitates at the beginning (*Standing*, he *hunched*; *he stopped*, *he remembered*), but makes his decision (*he could not fail her*) and acts (*pushed open*, *descended*), never mind what he feels (*he was cold*).

Next comes the music. Here Orpheus becomes more passive, for music has the power, not him. It is *his defence.*

Milosz believed in 'the passivity of a poet, who receives every poem from his *daimonion*. He should be humble enough not to ascribe what he receives to his own virtues.'

As Orpheus goes down, his relation to his music is a giving in. (*He submitted*. Soon he will have to submit to other things too.) But when he reaches the heart of hell (*he arrived*) he makes his music actively (*he sang*). Milosz believed that a 'poet's mind and will should be alert', and 'the effort to capture as much reality as possible is the health of poetry'. As Donne said, we ourselves are in the plot: you cannot just be passive and let poetry come to you; you need to be taut, ready to make the effort.[9]

This is what Orpheus is doing. Making that effort, appealing to what is real. It is the climax of his verbs and of his journey, the one way he can get Eurydice back. His song is a bid for life and for where we live it: the locale in which we find ourselves, the nature which we have been given to live our lives in. Our bodies, our landscapes, the world. Milosz felt a poet should 'glorify things just because they are'. So Orpheus's song is about earth. As his music (says the eighth section) is *music of the earth*.

After his song, hell takes the initiative and starts acting on him. He must accept its *conditions*: react, submit. The verbs have other subjects (*said the goddess*; *Hermes brought*). Orpheus co-operates (*they set out*), but is now the recipient of verbs, not their subject (*It seemed closer*; *doubt entwined him*). His acts are not active but expressive (*he wept*; *he dreamed*). Even when he gets outside, the action is not his (*day was breaking*; *shapes loomed*; *it happened*).

He finally does one thing, the thing he was told not to do: *turned his head*. The world reacts by presenting him with nothing: *On the path was no one*. After this, for a while, there are no verbs, only nouns. (*Sun. Sky. White clouds.*) Then the world speaks for him (*Everything cried*). It offers back to him what he sang about: the beauty of earth (*there was a scent of herbs*). His last act is to trust and rest on that (*fell asleep . . . on earth*).

This image comes out of long-held belief. *I am a faithful son of the black earth, shall return to the black earth*, Milosz wrote in a 1930s poem ('Hymn'). And, *To exist on the earth is beyond any power to name* ('Report'). His faith in poetry was part of his faith in the beauty of things that grow in earth, live on it, are part of it. *Out of reluctant matter / What can be gathered?* he asked ('No More'). *Nothing, beauty at best. / And so, cherry blossoms must suffice for us / And chrysanthemums and the full moon.*

For Orpheus is not only the archetypal poet, and poet of

archetypal loss; he also links music and poetry with all nature, animate and inanimate. Rilke's poem 'Orpheus. Eurydice. Hermes' says a *whole world of lament arose* out of Orpheus's lyre: *forest and valley, field and stream and animal.* Orpheus stands, above all, for coherence and harmony (from *harmottein,* to fit together): the harmony of us-in-the-world – which is poetry.[10] Poetry draws together our joy, in life and in each other, our grief, and also *the slow / creatures of this earth* (as Poem 51 calls them). Creatures as vulnerable as us, whose own music (says Poem 23) can *bridge chasms* for us, speak to us of a presence *whose language / is not our language.*

At the beginning of this book I mentioned the stargazing love scene at the end of *The Merchant of Venice.* While musicians play to *draw* their mistress *home with music,* Lorenzo explains to Jessica that Orpheus drew close to him all animals, and even *trees, stones and floods,* to hear his music. Because there is *nought so stockish, hard, and full of rage, / But music for the time doth change his nature.* He ends by simply saying what Milosz and all the poets in this book would say, with Shakespeare: *Mark the music.*[11]

Notes

Part One – pages 1 to 56

1 Patsy Rodenburg, *Speaking Shakespeare*, Methuen, 2002, pp. 72, 108, 111–15.

2 Virginia Woolf, *To the Lighthouse* (1927), Penguin, 1992, p. 131; Shakespeare, Sonnet 98.

3 Walter Benjamin, *Das Passagen-Werk*, N. I. 1, see George Steiner, *Antigones*, Clarendon Presss, 1984, p. i.

4 Quoted by J. P. Collier, who wrote a report on lectures Coleridge gave at Cambridge in 1811–12. See *Coleridge's Writings on Shakespeare*, ed. T. Hawkes, Capricorn Books, 1959, p. 35.

5 T. S. Eliot, *The Use of Poetry and the Use of Criticism*, Faber & Faber, 1933, p. 19.

6 W. H. Auden, *The Dyer's Hand and Other Essays*, Faber & Faber, 1963, p. 6.

7 Keats started studying poems furiously at fifteen, in 1810, and regularly read *The Examiner*, which printed a lot of poetry. Leigh Hunt published 'On First Looking into Chapman's Homer' in it on 1 December 1816, and introduced Keats, in an essay he called 'The Young Poets', as one of three 'young aspirants . . . who promise to help the new school revive Nature and put a new spirit of youth into every thing'.

8 Eliot, *The Use of Poetry*, pp. 18–19; and also 36, where he goes on, 'Anyone whose taste in poetry does not bear the stamp of their personality, so there are differences in what he likes from what we like, as well as resemblances, and differences in the way of liking the same things, is apt to be a very uninteresting person with whom to discuss poetry.' See also Wordsworth, 'Advertisement to *Lyrical Ballads*' (1798).

9 Aristophanes, *Birds*, 785–90.

10 Aristophanes, *Frogs*, 832–1471.

11 See p. 215.

12 George Steiner, *Grammars of Creation*, Faber & Faber, 2001, p. 14.

13 See Poems 9, 11, 13, 24, 29, 37.

14 Eavan Boland in W.H. Herbert and M. Hollis, *Strong Words*, Bloodaxe Books, 2000, p. 217; Ezra Pound, 'Homage to Sextus Propertius' XII, *Personae: Collected Shorter Poems*, Faber & Faber, 2001, p. 224; T.S. Eliot, 'Introduction to Ezra Pound', *Literary Essays* (1954), Faber & Faber, 1960.

15 C. K. Stead, *The New Poetic* (1964) Continuum Impacts, 2005, pp. 3, 33–45.

16 Ezra Pound, reviewing *Prufrock and Other Observations* in *Poetry*, 1917.

17 Robert Frost, Letter to John Bartlett (1913), see John Hartley Williams and Matthew Sweeney, *Writing Poetry and Getting Published*, Hodder & Stoughton, 1997, pp. 117–120, 28.

18 Arthur Waugh, 'The New Poetry', *Quarterly Review*, October 1916, p. 226

343

(see Eliot, *The Use of Poetry*, p. 71); J. C. Squire, *London Mercury*, III (10), October 1923. For fuller coverage of Eliot's early reception, and its context, see Stead, *The New Poetic*, pp. 97–103.

19 Michael Schmidt, Lecture at 'Stanza' Festival 2006, printed in *Poetry Review*, Spring 2006.

20 Herbert and Hollis, *Strong Words*, p. 217.

21 Wordsworth mentioned something like this in 1804 when he said in his Preface to his *Lyrical Ballads* that people expected a poet to 'make a formal engagement' with the reader, and 'gratify certain known habits of association'. He thought some people might feel he had ignored the terms of this contract, but *he* felt he was fulfilling it in a new way.

22 George Steiner, *On Difficulty and Other Essays*, Oxford University Press, 1978, pp. 19–47.

23 V. S. Naipaul, *Literary Occasions*, Picador, 2004, p. 52.

24 Eliot, *The Use of Poetry*, pp. 30–2.

25 Christa Wolf, *Cassandra*, Virago, 1984, pp. 71, 106, 14.

26 John Ashbery, *Selected Prose*, Carcanet Press, 2004, pp. 250–1.

27 Geoffrey Hill, *Speech! Speech!*, Penguin, 2002.

28 In 1937 Picasso went in the opposite direction, to make a parallel statement of outrage. Cubism had shattered the idea of a readable picture. Then he shattered the (painfully acquired) new idea, that art was abstract and opaque, by *Guernica*. He was using his new language, Cubism, to say art should be capable of clear moral witness. But his statement would not have had the authority it did if he had not, like Celan, formed his own language first, against the realist idiom.

29 N. H. Reeve and R. Kerridge, *Nearly Too Much*, Liverpool University Press, 1995; see also Philip Gross's review, *Poetry Review* (Summer 1996), p. 20.

30 Geoffrey Hill, *Lords of Limit*, André Deutsch, 1984, p. 146. Donne felt the poet must take responsibility and control too, of course: 'Ourselves are in the plot. Wee are not onely passive but active too,' *Devotions Upon Emergent Occasions*, Cambridge University Press, 1923, pp. 68–9.

31 J. H. Prynne, 'Resistance and Difficulty', Prospect, Winter, 1961.

32 Keats, Letter to J. H. Reynolds, 3 February 1818.

33 Mark Haddon, *Guardian*, Review, 24 September 2005, p. 11.

34 Geoffrey Hill, *Paris Review* 90/91, pp. 276–7; Mourid Barghouti, *I Saw Ramallah*, Bloomsbury, 2004, p. 160.

35 Eliot, *The Use of Poetry*, p. 17.

36 U. A. Fanthorpe, 'Patience Strong', *Collected Poems*, Peterloo Press, 1986, p. 16.

37 *The Times*, Weekend Review, interviews by Michael Pilgrim, 2004.

38 Barghouti, *I Saw Ramallah*, p. 160.

39 Dryden was against borrowing from abroad, which the Elizabethans did when, not only Greek and Latin, but Italian models were the new thing. See T. S. Eliot, *Use of Poetry*, p. 24; Barghouti, *I Saw Ramallah*, p. 132.

40 Wordsworth, 'Advertisement to *Lyrical Ballads*', 1798.

41 Seamus Heaney, *Preoccupations*, Faber & Faber, 1980, p. 62.

42 Daniel Barenboim, BBC Reith Lectures 2006, Lecture 3.

43 In 1886 Hallam, Tennyson's son, asked Tennyson (aged seventy-seven) to

write a poem based on a Homeric hymn. According to Hallam, Tennyson said OK he would but 'when I write an antique like this I must put it in a frame – something modern about it. No good giving just a réchauffé of old legends.' Fifty-six years before, in 1830, he upset himself badly for ten years by provoking critics with his innovations. From start to finish, he tried to 'get beyond the tradition'. See R. Pattison, *Tennyson and Tradition*, Harvard University Press, 1979, p. 412.

44 Plato, *Republic*, Book 7, 514–17.

45 Ezra Pound, *Literary Essays*, p. 25; Charles Olson, 'Projective Verse', *Poetry New York*, no. 3, 1950.

46 Barenboim, BBC Reith Lectures 2006, Lecture 1.

47 Thomas Campion, *Observations in the Art of English Poesie*, 1602, Ch. 2.

48 Eliot, *The Use of Poetry*, pp. 37–40; *On Poetry and Poets*, Faber & Faber, 1957, p. 55.

49 Stephen Dunn, *Walking Light*, Boa Editions, 2001, p. 125; see also Hartley Williams and Sweeney, *Writing Poetry*, pp. 119, 126.

50 Josef Brodsky, 'How to Read a Book' in *On Grief and Reason*, Hamish Hamilton, 1996, p. 101. Thanks for this to Ian Duhig, great nomad of the mind.

51 Homer, *Odyssey* 8, 479–81; 22, 347. The Homeric *Hymn to Hermes*, 451–2, says Muses are keen on 'dancing and the glorious path of song'.

52 Pindar, *Pythian Odes* 11, 38–40. He then shifts the image cheekily to a sea voyage. 'Did some gale blow me off-course?' The Muses' chariot appears throughout his poems (*Pythian Odes* 10, 61–4; 2, 1–2, *Olympian Odes* 9, 86–7, *Isthmian Odes* 8, 59–62), and in his contemporary Bacchylides (*Odes* 19, 1–14; 5, 176).

53 Aristophanes, *Frogs*, 1323.

54 Olson, 'Projective Verse'.

55 *Satire* 3, 79–81. 'If the poem has no obvious destination', Paul Muldoon once said, 'there's a chance we'll all be setting off on an interesting ride.'

56 Rodenburg, *Speaking Shakespeare*, p. 111. Thanks to Michael Crawford, in Herbert and Hollis, *Strong Words*, p. 262, for the image behind *versus*. He adds, 'On its little journey, each verse line leads silence into sound, sound into silence.'

57 To show the patterns, I have set these all out as two quatrains for the octave, and two three-liners for the sestet, but many sonnets make no break at all; or break at the turn; or elsewhere, like Poems 12, 39 and 56.

58 See P. Levine, *Penguin Book of the Sonnet*, Penguin, 2001, p. xlvii; Don Paterson (ed.), *101 Sonnets from Shakespeare to Heaney*, Faber & Faber, 1999, p. xxi.

59 George Herbert, 'Jordan' (I).

60 Donaghy, 'By Any Memes Necessary', *Poetry News*, October 2004.

61 Wallace Stevens 'Notes Towards a Supreme Fiction': 'It Must be Abstract', VII, *Selected Poems*, Faber & Faber, 1953, p. 105.

62 Hesiod, *Theogony*, 22–8.

63 Dunn, *Walking Light*, pp. 108–9; Heaney, *Preoccupations*, p. 34.

64 Harold Pinter, 'Art, Truth and Politics', Nobel Acceptance Speech, reproduced in the *Guardian*, 8 December 2005.

65 Kathleen Jamie in Herbert and Hollis, *Strong Words*, p. 281; Jorie Graham, see Helen Vendler, *Music of What Happens*, Harvard University Press, 1995, p. 455; Donaghy, 'By Any Memes Necessary'.

66 'Making Strange' came from *Station Island*, Faber & Faber, 1984, p. 32 and appears in *New Selected Poems 1966–1987*, Faber & Faber, 1990, p. 154.

67 From an essay on the Romantic poet Hölderlin by M. Heidegger, *Poetry, Language and Thought*, Harper & Row, 1971, p. 226.

68 Heaney, *Preoccupations*, p. 18.

69 I. A. Richards, *The Philosophy of Rhetoric*, Oxford University Press, 1936, p. 96, called one of the two ideas in a metaphor the 'tenor', the other the 'vehicle'. See Aristotle, *Poetics*, 1457B, who also says you can use a "foreign" word while refusing it one of its "home" attributes', i.e. call a shield not just the 'cup of Ares' (implying that the shield is to Ares the war god as the wine cup is to Bacchus the wine god), but (skipping Ares entirely) 'the wineless cup'.

70 Aristotle used that word 'a carrying across', *epiphora*, abstractly. It meant 'application'. 'Carrying across' is its original, physical meaning, made of the same verb as metaphor itself: *pherein*, to carry.

71 Brian Friel's play *Translations* uses the fact that *metaphora* and *translatio* describe the same movement: the forced reversioning of place names is a metaphor for the British mapping and takeover of Ireland (see Poem 42).

72 Aristotle also says (*Rhetoric*, 1410B36) that it is from metaphor that we 'best get hold of something fresh'. Foreign and home, the metaphor by which the West's first great literary critic talked of metaphor, points to that word alien or foreign, used by Keats and Heidegger; 'to the way poetry makes the familiar strange', in Seamus Heaney's words – or, as the American Stephen Dunn describes it (*Walking Light*, pp. 17–34) 'brings the strange home'.

73 Samuel Beckett, *Texts for Nothing* (1954), John Calder, 1999, p. 62.

74 J. H. Prynne, *Poems*, Bloodaxe, 1999, p. 319 (from *The Oval Window*, 1983).

75 Prynne, *Poems*, p. 319; George Eliot, *The Mill on the Floss* (1860), Book Second, Ch. 1: 'Tom's First Half'.

76 Stevens, 'Notes Towards a Supreme Fiction': 'It Must Be Abstract', IV.

77 George Seferis, *Mythistorema* (1935), 8, *Poemiata*, Ikaros, 1972, p. 53.

78 Plato, *Republic*, Book I, 328DE; Richard Holmes, *Footsteps* (1985), Harper Perennial, 2005, p. 66; Theodore Roethke, 'Journey into the Interior', *Collected Poems*, Faber & Faber, 1968.

79 Salman Rushdie, 'On Adventure', *Imaginary Homelands*, Granta Books, 1991, p. 225.

80 See M. F. Burnyeat, 'Long Walk to Wisdom', *Times Literary Supplement*, 24 February 2006, p. 9.

81 Homer, *Odyssey* 12, 166–200; Gregory, *Moralia* 8, 54; Psalm xxviii, 13; First Epistle of St Peter, ii. 11; Hebrews, xi.13; Ladner, 'Homo Viator', pp. 233–9.

82 Plutarch, *De Exilio*, 17, 607D.

83 Tennyson, 'Ulysses' (1842), 57, 19–21; T. S. Eliot, 'East Coker' V, *Four Quartets*, Faber & Faber, 1944.

84 See *Gilgamesh*, translated by Stephen Mitchell, Profile Books, 2005, Book 4, Book 9ff; and Prologue, p. 69.

85 Plutarch, *Moralia* 8, 92; Ruth Barnes and Crispin Branfoot, *Pilgrimage*, Ashmolean Museum, 2006, p. 38.

86 Farid Ud-Din Attar, Introduction, *Conference of the Birds*, Frances Lincoln, 2002, p. 10.

87 See Steiner, *Grammars of Creation*, Faber & Faber, 2001, p. 14.

88 Rushdie, 'On Adventure', *Imaginary Homelands*, p. 225.

89 John Bunyan, *Pilgrim's Progress*, Part 2 (the Eighth Stage); he is quoting I Corinthians 15.55.

90 Margaret Atwood, *Negotiating with the Dead*, Virago Press, 2003, p. 159.

91 Seamus Heaney, 'The Golden Bough', *Seeing Things*, Faber & Faber, 1991.

92 Virgil, *Aeneid* 6, 265; 5, 725–38; 6, 10, 98, 107, 124–9; 260, 298ff.

93 Dante, *Inferno*, Canto 1; Canto 12, 87.

94 Rilke, *Sonnets to Orpheus*, Part 1, Sonnets 6 and 9 in *The Selected Poetry of Rainer Maria Rilke*, edited and translated by Stephen Mitchell, Vintage International Editions, 1989; Atwood, *Negotiating with the Dead*, p. 140. Kathleen Raine argued that to make a good poem the poet has to go into the unconscious, into the past, and interrogate both the self and the dead, *Inner Journey of the Poet*, Allen and Unwin, 1982, pp. 25–39.

95 Atwood, *Negotiating with the Dead*, pp. 159–9; Adrienne Rich, 'Diving into the Wreck', in *Diving into the Wreck*, Norton, 1973.

96 Atwood, *Negotiating with the Dead*, pp. 139–40.

97 Heaney, 'Station Island', II, *Station Island*.

98 Ibid., XII.

99 Quoted by Hugh Ruttledge in *Everest 1933*, Hodder & Stoughton, 1934; Stephen Venables, *Everest Kangshung Face*, Hodder & Stoughton, 1989.

100 Czeslaw Milosz, *The Witness of Poetry*, Harvard University Press, 1983, pp. 4, 97. The Palestinian poet Mourid Barghouti, returning to the occupied West Bank after thirty years, family and friends scattered round the world, wanted 'to sew the times together, attach one moment to another'. He felt, lying awake at night in his former home, that in his poems as in his life, 'something wants to be completed', *I Saw Ramallah*, p. 163.

101 Rilke, *Sonnets to Orpheus*, Part 1, Sonnet 1, with Stephen Mitchell's translation p. 227; see also Robert Hass's Introduction, pp. xv–xvi.

102 Joan Didion, *The Year of Magical Thinking*, HarperCollins, 2005.

103 Seamus Heaney, *Crediting Poetry*, Gallery Books, 1995.

104 Marianne Moore, 'Poetry', *Complete Poems*, Penguin, 1982, p. 36.

Part Two Section I – pages 57 to 128

1 Gwyneth Lewis in Herbert and Hollis, *Strong Words*, p. 265.

2 George Steiner, *Extraterritorial*, Faber & Faber, 1972, pp. 10, 14–21.

3 John Burnside in Herbert and Hollis, *Strong Words*, p. 260.

4 'Binsey Poplars', 'Spring and Fall', 'Wreck of the *Deutschland*'.

5 Elizabeth Bishop, *One Art: Selected Letters*, Chatto & Windus, 1994.

6 See Elizabeth Bishop (ed.), *Exchanging Hats: Paintings*, Carcanet Press, 1997.

7 Thomas Traherne, *Centuries of Meditations, Poetical Works*, Bertram Dobell, 1906, pp. xix–xxi. See pp. 109, 177.

8 Robert Lowell, 'For Elizabeth Bishop 4'.

9 Robert Graves, 'The Cool Web', *Collected Poems*, Cassell, 1975, p. 37.

10 See p. 32.

11 See pp. 45–6, 48. 'Strand at Lough Beg' (*Field Work*, 1979), a poem for his murdered cousin, carried an epigraph from *Purgatorio*.

12 *Nightwaves*, BBC Radio 3, 31 March 2006.

Part Two Section II – pages 129 to 174

1 Hugo Williams in Herbert and Hollis, *Strong Words*, p. 232.

2 Kathleen Jamie in Herbert and Hollis, *Strong Words*, pp. 280–1.

3 Selima Hill in Herbert and Hollis, *Strong Words*, p. 247.

4 Heaney, *Preoccupations*, pp. 58–9; or *Finders Keepers*, Faber & Faber, 2002, pp. 23–5.

5 Louise Glück, *Proofs and Theories*, Ecco Press, 1994, pp. 125–6.

6 See Ruth Padel, *52 Ways of Looking at a Poem*, Chatto & Windus, 2002, p. 69.

Part Two Section III – pages 175 to 221

1 Thanks to Selima Hill for this (Herbert and Hollis, *Strong Words*, p. 247).

2 *Agenda*, vol. 36, no. 2, 1998, p. 7.

3 Vendler, *The Music of What Happens*, pp. 455–8; *The Breaking of Style*, Harvard University Press, 1995, pp. 71–95; *The Given and the Made*, Faber & Faber, 1995, pp. 89–130.

4 Lewis, Bhatt, Carson and Herbert. 'Binta' Breeze and Jamie write in dialect as well as Standard English. Milosz helped translate his own poems into English.

5 G. M. Hopkins, 'Binsey Poplars'. For the darkness, see 'I Wake and Feel the Fell of Dark, Not Day'; also the journey from line 6 of 'My Own Heart Let Me Have More Pity On', (*blind / Eyes in their dark*) to line 11 (*let joy size*) and the last words, *lights a lovely mile*.

6 *Guardian*, Review, 24 September 2005, p. 11.

7 Ashbery, *Selected Prose*, pp. 215, 246.

8 Ibid., p. 212.

9 See p. 8–9.

Part Two Section IV – pages 223 to 296

1 See pp. 45–8, 124, 127.

2 See pp. 34–5.

3 If you want to track it down, look for *Notes on Cafés and Bedrooms* (1963), *Opium Fogs* (1963), *Iliad of Broken Sentences* (1967); *Businessmen as Lovers* (1969) and her last known published work *The Halt during the Chase* (1972). She also reviewed Adrienne Rich's *Diving into the Wreck* (above, pp. 47 and 88–92) in the *New York Review of Books*, 4 October 1973.

4 See p. 53.

5 See George Steiner, *Language and Silence*, Penguin, 1969, p. 75, and above on Celan, pp. 14–15. Adorno, born in 1903 in Frankfurt, son of a German Jewish wine merchant and a Catholic from Corsica, took his mother's surname in the late 1930s. He was a key member of the Institute for Social Research in Frankfurt (others included Walter Benjamin and Herbert Marcuse), which developed crucial concepts in critical theory.

6 See p. 124.

Part Two Section V – pages 297 to 342

1 Milosz, *The Witness of Poetry*, pp. 11–12 *et passim*.

2 Ovid, *Metamorphoses*, 11. 39.

3 Milton, *Paradise Lost* (1667), Book 1, 526.

4 See pp. 47, 88–9, 92

5 Milosz, 'Ars Poetica?' (1968), *New and Collected Poems (1931–2001)*, HarperCollins, 2001.

6 See p. 32.

7 Heaney, *Crediting Poetry*, p. 28.

8 See p. 46.

9 Czeslaw Milosz, *New and Collected Poems* (1931–2001), HarperCollins, 2001, Introduction, p. 1. See p. 15

10 See pp. 26, 33, 54.

11 See p. 67–8; Shakespeare, *Merchant of Venice*, V. 1. 80–8.

Further Reading

Ashbery, John, *Selected Prose,* ed. E. Richie, Carcanet Press, 2004

Attar, Farid Ud-Din, *Conference of the Birds*, translated and introduced by Raficq Abdulla, Frances Lincoln, 2002

Atwood, Margaret, *Negotiating with the Dead: A Writer on Writing*, Virago Press, 2003

Barghouti, Mourid, *I Saw Ramallah*, Bloomsbury, 2004

Barnes, Ruth and Crispin Branfoot, *Pilgrimage: The Sacred Journey*, Ashmolean Museum, 2006

Beckett, Samuel, *Texts for Nothing* (1954), John Calder, 1999

Bishop, Elizabeth, ed., *Exchanging Hats: Paintings*, Carcanet, Press, 1997

Bishop, Elizabeth, *One Art: Selected Letters*, ed. R. Giroux, Chatto & Windus, 1994

Brodsky, Josef, *On Grief and Reason: Essays*, Hamish Hamilton, 1996

Campion, Thomas, *Observations in the Art of English Poesie*, 1602

Coleridge's Writings on Shakespeare, ed. T. Hawkes, Capricorn Books, 1959

Daniel, Samuel, *A Defence of Ryme, Against a Pamphlet entituled Observations in the Art of English Poesie*, 1603

Donaghy, Michael, 'By Any Memes Necessary', *Poetry News*, October 2004

Donne, John, *Devotions Upon Emergent Occasions*, ed. John Sparrow, Cambridge University Press, 1923

Dunn, Stephen, *Walking Light*, Boa Editions, 2001

Eliot, T. S., *The Use of Poetry and the Use of Criticism*, Faber & Faber, 1933

—— *On Poetry and Poets*, Faber & Faber, 1957

Glück, Louise, *Proofs and Theories: Essays on Poetry*, Ecco Press, 1994

Hartley Williams, John and Matthew Sweeney, *Writing Poetry and Getting Published*, Hodder & Stoughton, 1997

Heaney, Seamus, *Preoccupations*, Faber & Faber, 1980

—— *Crediting Poetry*, The Nobel Lecture, Gallery Books, 1995

—— *Finders Keepers*, Faber & Faber, 2002

Heidegger, M., *Poetry, Language and Thought*, trans. Hofstadter, Harper & Row, 1971

Herbert, W. H. and M. Hollis, *Strong Words: Modern Poets on Modern Poetry*, Bloodaxe Books, 2000

Hill, Geoffrey, *The Lords of Limit: Essays on Literature and Ideas*, André Deutsch, 1984

Holmes, Richard, *Footsteps* (1985), Harper Perennial, 2005

Ladner, G., 'Homo Viator', *Speculum: A Journal of Medieval Studies*, vol. xlii, no. 2, April 1967

Levine, P., ed., *The Penguin Book of the Sonnet*, Penguin, 2001

Milosz, C., *The Witness of Poetry*, Harvard University Press, 1983

Naipaul, V. S., *Literary Occasions: Essays*, Picador, 2004

O'Brien, Sean, *The Deregulated Muse: Essays on Contemporary British and Irish Poetry*, Bloodaxe Books, 1998

Olson, Charles, 'Projective Verse', *Poetry New York*, no. 3, 1950

Padel, Ruth, *52 Ways of Looking at a Poem*, Chatto & Windus, 2002

Paterson, Don, ed., *101 Sonnets from Shakespeare to Heaney*, Faber & Faber, 1999

Pattison, R., *Tennyson and Tradition*, Harvard University Press, 1979

Pinter, Harold, 'Art, Truth and Politics', Nobel Acceptance Speech, reproduced in the *Guardian*, 8 December 2005

Pound, Ezra, *Literary Essays*, ed. T. S. Eliot (1954), Faber & Faber, 1960

Prynne, J. H., 'Resistance and Difficulty', *Prospect*, Winter 1961, pp. 26–30

Raine, Kathleen, *The Inner Journey of the Poet and Other Papers*, George Allen and Unwin, 1982

Reeve, N. H. and R. Kerridge, *Nearly Too Much: The Poetry of J. H. Prynne*, Liverpool University Press, 1995

Richards, I. A., *The Philosophy of Rhetoric*, Oxford University Press, 1936

Rilke, Rainer Maria, *The Selected Poetry of Rainer Maria Rilke*, edited and translated by Stephen Mitchell, Vintage International Editions, 1989

Rodenburg, Patsy, *Speaking Shakespeare*, Methuen, 2002

Rushdie, Salman, *Imaginary Homelands: Essays and Criticism 1981–1991*, Granta Books, 1991

Stead, C. K., *The New Poetic* (1964), Continuum Impacts, 2005

Steiner, George, *Language and Silence*, Penguin, 1969

—— *Extraterritorial*, Faber & Faber, 1972

—— *On Difficulty and Other Essays*, Oxford University Press, 1978

—— *Antigones*, Clarendon Press, 1984

—— *Grammars of Creation*, Faber & Faber, 2001

Trotter, David, *The Making of the Reader*, St Martin's Press, 1984

Vendler, Helen, *The Music of What Happens*, Harvard University Press, 1988

—— *The Given and the Made*, Faber & Faber, 1995

—— *The Breaking of Style*, Harvard University Press, 1995

Permissions

For permission to reprint copyright material the publishers gratefully acknowledge the following:

MONIZA ALVI 'How the World Split in Two' from *How the Stone Found It's Voice* (Bloodaxe Books, 2005), reprinted by permission of the publisher; **SIMON ARMITAGE** 'Birthday' from *The Universal Home Doctor* (Faber & Faber, 2002), reprinted by permission of the publisher; **JOHN ASHBERY** 'The Evening of Greuze' from *Chinese Whispers* (Carcanet Press, 2002), reprinted by permission of the publisher; **SUJATA BHATT** 'Swami Anand' from *Point No Point: Selected Poems* (Carcanet Press, 1997), reprinted by permission of the publisher; **ELIZABETH BISHOP** 'Brazil, January 1, 1502' from *The Complete Poems 1927–1979* (Farrar, Straus & Giroux, 1983), © 1979, 1983 by Alice Helen Methfessel, reprinted by permission of the publisher; **EAVAN BOLAND** 'That the Science of Cartography is Limited' from *Collected Poems* (Carcanet Press, 1995), reprinted by permission of the publisher; **JEAN 'BINTA' BREEZE** 'Baptism' from *The Arrival of Brighteye & Other Poems* (Bloodaxe Books, 2000), reprinted by permission of the publisher; **JOHN BURNSIDE** 'The Old Gods' from *Swimming in the Flood* (Jonathan Cape, 1995), reprinted by permission of the Random House Group Ltd; **CIARAN CARSON** 'O' from *Opera Et Cetera* (Gallery Press, 1996), reprinted by permission of the author and the Gallery Press; **KATE CLANCHY** 'When You Cried' from *Newborn: Poems on Motherhood* (Picador, 2004), reprinted by permission of Macmillan Publishers, London; **JULIA DARLING** 'Two Lighthouses' from *Apology for Absence* (Arc Publications, 2004), reprinted by permission of the publisher; **MICHAEL DONAGHY** 'Machines' from *Dances Learned Last Night, Poems 1975–1995* (Picador, 2000), reprinted by permission of Macmillan Publishers, London; **MARK DOTY** 'No' from *My Alexandria* (Jonathan Cape, 1995), reprinted by permission of the Random House Group Ltd; **IAN DUHIG** 'The Lammas Hireling' from *The Lammas Hireling* (Picador, 2003), reprinted by permission of Macmillan Publishers, London; **JANE DURAN** 'The Orange

Tree in Córdoba' from *Breathe Now, Breathe* (Enitharmon Press, 1995), reprinted by permission of the publisher; **HELEN FARISH** 'Mesoplodon Pacificus' from *Intimates* (Jonathan Cape, 2005), reprinted by permission of the Random House Group Ltd; **JAMES FENTON** 'Serious' from *Out of Danger* (Penguin Books, 1993), reprinted by permission of PFD on behalf of the author; **CAROLYN FORCHÉ** Poems XV and XXVI from the 'Notebook of Uprisings' from *Angel of History* (Bloodaxe Books, 1994), reprinted by permission of the publisher; **TESS GALLAGHER** 'Black Silk' from *My Black Horse: New & Selected Poems* (Bloodaxe Books, 1997), reprinted by permission of Rogers, Coleridge & White Ltd, on behalf of the author; **LOUISE GLÜCK** 'Vita Nova' from *Vita Nova* (Carcanet Press, 2000), reprinted by permission of the publisher; **JORIE GRAHAM** 'Prayer' from *Swarm* (Carcanet Press, 2000), reprinted by permission of the publisher; **W. S. GRAHAM** from 'What Is the Language Using Us For?' from *New Collected Poems* (Faber & Faber, 2004), © The Estate of W. S. Graham, 2004, reprinted by permission of Margaret and Michael Snow; **TONY HARRISON** 'Timer' from *Tony Harrison: Selected Poems* (Penguin Books, 1987), reprinted by permission of the author; **DAVID HARSENT** 'Poem XVI' from *Marriage* (Faber & Faber, 2002), reprinted by permission of the publisher; **SEAMUS HEANEY** 'District and Circle' from *District and Circle* (Faber & Faber, 2006) and 'Station Island' from *Station Island* (Faber & Faber, 2001), reprinted by permission of the publisher; **W. N. HERBERT** 'Breakfrost' from *The Laurelude* (Bloodaxe Books, 1998), reprinted by permission of the publisher; **GEOFFREY HILL** 'Mercian Hymns VI' from *Collected Poems* (Penguin Books, 1985), reprinted by permission of the publisher; **KATHLEEN JAMIE** 'Frogs' from *The Tree House* (Picador, 2004), reprinted by permission of Macmillan Publishers; **ALAN JENKINS** 'Portrait of a Lady' from *Harm* (Chatto & Windus, 1994), reprinted by permission of the Random House Group Ltd; **ELIZABETH JENNINGS** 'Rembrandt's Late Self-Portraits' from *New Collected Poems* (Carcanet Press, 2002), reprinted by permission of David Higham Associates; **MIMI KHALVATI** 'Mahout' from *The Chine* (Carcanet Press, 2002), reprinted by permission of the publisher; **NICK LAIRD** 'Oświcięm' from *To a Fault* (Faber & Faber, 2005), reprinted by permission of the publisher; **GWYNETH LEWIS** 'The Flaggy Shore' from *Chaotic Angels* (Bloodaxe Books, 2005), reprinted by permission of the publisher; **CHRISTOPHER LOGUE** 'From Book XXI of Homer's *Iliad*' from *Selected Poems* (Faber & Faber, 1996), reprinted by permission of the publisher; **ROGER McGOUGH** 'The Wrong Beds' from *Last Words: New Poetry for the New Century*, edited by Don Paterson and Jo Shapcott (Picador, 1999), reprinted by permission of PFD on behalf of the author; **JAMIE McKENDRICK** 'On/Off' from *Sky Nails: Poems 1979–1997* (Faber & Faber, 2000), reprinted by permission of the publisher; **PAULA MEEHAN** 'Child Burial' from *The Man who was Marked by Winter* (Gallery Press, 1991), reprinted by kind permission of the author and Gallery Press; **CHRISTOPHER MIDDLETON** 'Disturbing the Tarantula' from *111 Poems* (Carcanet Press, 1983), reprinted by permission of the publisher; **CZESLAW MILOSZ** 'Orpheus and Eurydice' from *Second Space: New Poems*, translated by Robert Hass and Czeslaw Milosz (HarperCollins Publishers, 2004), reprinted by permission of the publisher; **ANDREW MOTION** 'On the Table' from *Andrew Motion: Selected Poems 1976–1997* (Faber & Faber, 2002), reprinted by permission of PFD on behalf of the author; **BERNARD O'DONOGHUE** 'Dogs, Would You Live For Ever?' from *Here Nor There* (Chatto & Windus, 1999), reprinted by permission of the Random House Group Ltd; **ALICE OSWALD** 'Wedding' from *The Thing in the Gap-Stone Stile* (Oxford University Press, 1996), reprinted by permission of PFD on behalf of the author; **KATHERINE PIERPOINT** 'Swim Right Up to Me' from *Truffle Beds* (Faber & Faber, 1995), reprinted by permission of the publisher; **JACOB POLLEY** 'Smoke' from *The Brink* (Picador, 2003), reprinted by permission of Macmillan Publishers; **J. H. PRYNNE** 'The Holy City' from *The White Stones* (Grosseteste, 1969), available in *Poems* (Fremantle Arts Centre Press and Bloodaxe Books, 2005), reprinted by permission of the author; **CRAIG RAINE** 'A Martian Sends a Postcard Home' from *A Martian Sends a Postcard Home* (Oxford University Press, 1979), reprinted by permission of David Godmin Associates on behalf of the author; **PETER READING** 'Salopian' from *Collected Poems 3: Poems 1997–2003* (Bloodaxe Books, 2003), reprinted by permission of the publisher; **ADRIENNE RICH** 'Midnight Salvage: Poem 6' from *Midnight Salvage: Poems 1995–1998* (W. W. Norton, 1999), reprinted by permission of the publisher; **MAURICE RIORDAN** 'Time Out' from *A Word from the Loki* (Faber & Faber, 1995), reprinted by permission of the publisher;

ROBIN ROBERTSON 'Moving House' from *A Painted Field* (Picador, 1997), reprinted by permission of Macmillan Publishers; **CAROL RUMENS** 'From a Conversation During Divorce' from *Best China Sky* (Bloodaxe Books, 1995), reprinted by permission of the publisher; **CAROLE SATYAMURTI** 'Broken Moon (for Emma)' from *Stitching the Dark: New & Selected Poems* (Bloodaxe Books, 2005), reprinted by permission of the publisher; **PENELOPE SHUTTLE** 'Taxing the Rain' from *Taxing the Rain* (Oxford University Press, 1992), reprinted by permission of David Higham Associates; **PAULINE STAINER** 'Sighting the Slave Ship' from *Poems* (Bloodaxe Books, 2003), reprinted by permission of the publisher; **ANNE STEVENSON** 'Granny Scarecrow' from *Poems 1955–2005* (Bloodaxe Books, 2005), reprinted by permission of the publisher; **TOM STOPPARD** *Rosencrantz and Guildenstern Are Dead* (Faber & Faber, 1973), reprinted by permission of the publisher; **R. S. THOMAS** 'Blackbird' from *Agenda*, vol. 36, no. 2 (1998), reprinted by permission of Gwydion Thomas; **ROSEMARY TONKS** 'Badly-Chosen Lover' from *Iliad of Broken Sentences* (The Bodley Head, 1967), © Rosemary Tonks, 1967, reprinted by permission of Sheil Land Associates on behalf of the author; **HUGO WILLIAMS** 'Making Friends with Ties' from *Collected Poems* (Faber & Faber, 2002), reprinted by permission of the publisher; **JUDITH WRIGHT** 'Trapped Dingo' from *A Human Pattern: Selected Poems* (Carcanet Press, 1992), reprinted by permission of ETT Imprint; **KIT WRIGHT** 'Mantles' from *Hoping It Might Be So: Poems 1974–2000* (Leviathan, 2000), reprinted by permission of the author.

Every effort has been made to trace copyright holders of the poems published in this book. The editor and publisher apologise for any material included without permission or without the appropriate acknowledgement, and would be grateful to be notified of any omissions or corrections that should be incorporated in the next edition or reprint of this volume.

Index and Glossary

New York School 203
9/11 51, 124, 226, 295

octave, octet = eight-line section of sonnet
O'Donoghue, Bernard 299, 322–5
Odysseus (Roman name Ulysses) 5, 37, 39, 41–3, 45, 61, 299
O'Hara, Frank 33
Olson, Charles 24–5, 29, 32, 185, 244, 345n. 54
Orpheus 32, 46, 49–50, 123, 125, 300, 339–42
Oswald, Alice 225, 250–1

Parmenides 38
Pasternak, Boris Leonid 71
Paz, Octavio 82
pentameter = line of five beats or five feet
Petrarch 29
Picasso 10, 33, 344n. 28
Pierpoint, Katherine 131, 149–5
pilgrimage 40–44, 61
Pindar 28, 345n.52
Pinter, Harold 57, 116, 345n.64
Plato 7, 23, 37, 187–8, 345n. 44, 346n. 78
Polley, Jacob 131, 138–41
popular poetry 8, 10–11, 17–23
   as 'democratic' 8
Pound, Ezra 9, 11–12, 20–24, 32, 244, 343n.16, 345n. 45
privacy, of poet 191, 323–5
Prynne, J. H. 15, 32, 36, 71, 225, 243–9, 344n. 31, 346nn. 74, 75
pushing readers away 15

quatrain = stanza of four lines 327

Raine, Craig 177, 196–8
Raleigh, Walter 43, 61
Ravel, Maurice 296
Reading, Peter 100–4, 244, 300
Rembrandt 299–300, 330–6
rhyming wars, of 17th century 27–8, 30, 55
Rich, Adrienne 47, 244, 300, 346n. 95, 348n. 3
Rilke, Rainer Maria 46, 50, 340, 342, 347n. 94, 347n. 101

www.vintage-books.co.uk